To Lynda on
Carl

Bound to the Soil

Bound to the Soil

A SOCIAL HISTORY OF DORSET 1750-1918

BARBARA KERR

Illustrated by Ann F. Wilson and I. H. C. Highet
Photographs by John N. Wilson

DORSET BOOKS

First published in 1968 by John Baker Publishers Limited
Republished in 1975 by EP Publishing Limited
Republished in 1993 by Dorset Books

British Library Cataloguing in Publication Data
CIP Catalogue Record for this book
is available from the British Library

ISBN 1 871164 18 4

DORSET BOOKS

Official Publisher to Dorset County Council

1 Chinon Court
Lower Moor Way
TIVERTON EX16 6SS

Tel: 0884 243242
Fax: 0884 243325

Printed and bound in Great Britain by Bookcraft, Midsomer Norton

CONTENTS

v

ILLUSTRATIONS

Preface

TO GLANCE through an uncurtained window into a lighted room
is to have a momentary and vivid insight into the way of life in the
house. In the same way to hear the accounts of the living is to have
a sudden insight into the past. Among Marc Bloch's great legacies
to historians was his teaching that history 'requires us to join the
study of the dead and of the living'. More than anything else the
memories of old people enable us to do this; and in Dorset these
memories can transport us back into the eighteenth century. Until
the 1960s Dorset has been a slow-moving agricultural county so that
many farming changes, which in more progressive districts took
place in the early nineteenth century, were here delayed until the
eve of the First World War. Mr. Fox of Holwell remembers at the
end of the last century planting beans by hand then drawing earth
over the rows with bramble cuttings, a practice that was considered
backward in early nineteenth-century Croatia. The numbers of
people who can recall life at the end of the last century are constantly dwindling; the landmarks they remember are being fast
obliterated by motor traffic and by urban expansion. This book is
an attempt to record by photograph, sketch and text the landmarks
and the memories of Dorset before 1914. The fact that all human
memories must have a strong subjective bias in no way lessens their
value. In the great events of history as well as in small daily hap-
penings, emotion is a stronger driving force than reason, and only
by some understanding of human emotions do events become com-
prehensible. Where it has been possible to check recollections of
persons or incidents by reference to written records, the memories
of old people have been found to be outstandingly accurate.

Soils and landscape change more slowly than customs, buildings
and field patterns; but they cannot escape the effects of intensive
cultivation, modernisation and road building. Man is battling to
master his environment which once moulded his whole way of life.
To understand the way men lived and farmed it is necessary to
consider the soils to which so many families were bound. This
interplay of soils and human destinies began to interest me while
soil sampling in Dorset for the National Agricultural Advisory
Service during the years 1949-1952. It only did so as my attention
had been drawn to the close relationship of man and countryside
by Canon H. P. Thompson, rector of Hayes, Kent, 1919-1933.

The acknowledgments at the end of each chapter are but an inadequate expression of the heartfelt thanks due to those whose recollections, photographs and family papers are the whole substance of this book.

The spoken word has been supplemented by local and other records. Searching through records means making constant demands on their custodians. For all the trouble they have taken most grateful thanks are due to Miss Margaret Holmes and her assistants at the Dorset Record Office, and also to the officials at the Public Record Office, the Tithe Redemption Commission and the British Museum Newspaper Library at Colindale.

No acknowledgments have been made to my family as, from first to last, this book has been a family affair.

Grants Farm,
Longthorns, Wool.

NOTES ON SOURCES USED THROUGHOUT THE BOOK

The plan has been followed of giving here an outline of the main written sources used throughout the book. Those used for special activities appear at the end of the relevant chapters, as do the names of those who have supplied verbal or unpublished information.

Contrary to custom a start has been made with published sources, as all Dorset studies depend on three main authorities without whose guidance the understanding of unpublished sources is likely to be incomplete.

PUBLISHED SOURCES

J. Hutchins, *The History and Antiquities of Dorset.*
The first edition appeared in 1774, the second between 1796 and 1815 and the third, which has been used throughout this work, between 1861 and 1870. Hutchins threw his net back as far as prehistoric times but his outlook and comments are essentially those of an enlightened eighteenth-century parson. Pedigrees, royal proclamations and peregrinations and antiquities were Hutchins' main interests but luckily few facts were too trivial for him to overlook. Where he knew a parish personally, as for instance Arne, Hutchins could make apposite comments on agriculture. All writers on Dorset owe this antiquarian a very great debt for undertaking so much spadework. They should also be grateful to the subscribers, including Thomas Hyde of Arne, who made possible the publication of Hutchins' massive volumes.

J. Claridge, *General View of Agriculture of the County of Dorset*, 1793.
W. Stevenson, *General View of Agriculture of the County of Dorset*, 1812.

Claridge writes concisely and with an authority that is sometimes lacking in Stevenson's more diffuse account of Dorset activities, manufacturing and mining as well as agricultural. Both authors knew the county well but drew heavily from information given by prominent farmers and the agents of large landowners. But agents, such as David Park on the Shaftesbury estates, and well-to-do farmers tended to take an over-hopeful view of agricultural and social conditions.

Among the less monumental surveys perhaps the most informative and interesting account of Dorset farming appears in William Marshall's *The Rural Economy of England including Devonshire and Parts of Somerset, Dorset and Cornwall*, 1796, Vol. I. Marshall had a more profound understanding of farming than either Claridge or Stevenson but unfortunately he only cast a brief, and contemptuous, glance at farming in West Dorset.

The two most thorough-going travellers through the British Isles in the eighteenth century were John Wesley and Arthur Young, but both travelled with preconceived ideas as to what they hoped to find rather than observing actual conditions. In his *The Farmer's Tour through East England*, 1771, Vol. III, Arthur Young could never get over the fact that farming in Dorset was not carried out on the same principles as in East Anglia. He, therefore, considered Dorset practices, in some respects, 'barbarous'. John Wesley, who had Dorset forbears, would have concurred with Young's opinion. In the parishes he visited, such as Motcombe and Shaftesbury, Wesley found groups of ardent supporters who made the barbarity of the heedless appear unrelievedly black. In his *Journals* Wesley dwelt on the few who had seen the light rather than the many in outer darkness. In this respect he was unlike Young who took pleasure in describing the agricultural enormities of Dorset.

William Cobbett understood farming on chalkland better than Young and many of his comments on Wiltshire and Hampshire downland farms apply equally to Dorset, which he hardly visited on his rides through England. The Everyman edition of *Rural Rides*, which covered the years 1821-1832, has been used.

On general agricultural questions great use has been made of *The Complete English Farmer*, 1771, attributed to David Henry, who was more factual and less contentious than many of his contemporary agriculturalists; and Lord Ernle's *English Farming Past and Present*. This sympathetic study first appeared in 1912; the 1936 edition has been used.

For the geology, climate and soils of Dorset great use has been made of R. Good, *A Geographical Handbook of Dorset Flora*, 1944. Professor Good's botanical areas have been used as a basis for differentiating between different farming patterns. Information concerning soils has been drawn from Chapter 2, on Dorset soils, in *A Dorset Flora* by Dr. K. L. Robinson, and also from my own observations.

For geology frequent recourse has been made to the following memoirs published by the Geological Survey:

W. J. Arkell, *The Geology of the Country around Weymouth, Swanage, Corfe and Lulworth*, 1947.

H. J. Osborne White, *Geology of the Country South and West of Shaftesbury*, 1923.

V. Wilson, F. Welch, J. Robbie and G. Green, *Geology of the Country around Bridport and Yeovil*, 1958.

Accounts of weather and of harvest yields have been taken from:

T. S. Ashton, *Economic Fluctuations in England 1700-1800*, 1959. This indispensable handbook on economic conditions has chapters on 'The Elements' and 'The Influence of the Harvests'.

T. H. Baker, *Records of the Seasons, Prices of Agricultural Produce and Phenomena Observed in the British Isles*, undated, last entry 1883. This fascinating collection of facts and observations has been summarised and edited with comments on economic factors by:

E. L. Jones, *Seasons and Prices*, 1964.

Footnotes have been given for information concerning climate conditions from sources other than the three quoted above.

Information from recognised authorities has been supplemented wherever possible, by references to novelists and periodicals. Nineteenth-century novelists were nearly all committed people so their outlook is interesting as illustrating the view of a particular section of society. For the propagation of their ideas the wiser authors used settings in which they were completely at home, and so transmit to us the minutae of daily living which brings an age alive. Surtees was anxious that foxhunting should maintain the high standards laid down by Peter Beckford, a Dorset man, but not a foible of the sportsmen or a cranny of the country houses he knew so well escaped his attention. Similarly Charlotte M. Yonge used the daily events in middle-class country homes to disseminate her moderate Tractarian views. Charles Kingsley is less thoroughly at ease in his settings than Surtees or Charlotte M. Yonge because of the multiplicity of the ideas he was anxious to put across to the public and also because his ideas were sometimes confused and conflicting. Other Victorian novelists well worthy of consideration for information on mid-Victorian life in the country and small towns are Mrs.

Gaskell, M. Oliphant and Cuthbert Bede, whose best-known novel is *Verdant Green*.

The great writers of the eighteenth and nineteenth centuries naturally throw much light on contemporary country life, but absorption in the narrative and in the character delineations prevents us being so conscious of the settings of their narratives. Thomas Hardy is an exception, but he presents his country settings with such accuracy and passion that they are as much part of his plots as the living characters.

Jokes indicate the values of an age more clearly than the pronouncements of preacher or politician; *Punch* reveals shades of public opinion not easily discerned from other sources. In particular, numbers for the 1880s show the conflicting attitude towards farming. The public had a nostalgic affection for the sturdy and independent figure remembered, probably inaccurately, from the 1850s; but growing public boredom with agricultural depression showed itself in tart references to the alleged cause of the trouble, the spendthrift ways of the contemporary farmer. Grateful acknowledgments are due to the directors of *Punch* for permission to use quotations and to reproduce the illustrations on p. 204, p. 205, p. 232 and p. 233.

UNPUBLISHED SOURCES

The scaffolding on which to reconstruct rural life in any parish in the late eighteenth and early nineteenth centuries is provided by:
The Land Tax Assessments
Census Returns
Enclosure Awards
Tithe Apportionment and Maps

DORSET RECORD OFFICE, DORCHESTER, after referred to as D.R.O.

Land Tax Assessments

For most parishes these assessments cover the years 1780-1832. In the case of a few parishes some years are missing or the entries are illegible from age. All returns give owners, among whom lifeholders are often included, the occupiers and the tax for which they were assessed, and the names of the assessors. Many returns give the names of the land holdings; in others the description 'land' was used by assessors to lighten their burden. Only a very rough estimate of the size of the holdings can be gained from the tax assessments which took into account the value of the land as well as its extent. The owner generally paid the land tax, but in times of exceptional prosperity the tenant was made responsible. In 1796 Gregory Syndercombe's account shows that his substantial tenants, William Hussey and Charles Chick, were paying land tax.

The returns are invaluable for showing the changes in ownership and occupation, which were unexpectedly frequent at the end of the eighteenth century, and for indicating the engrossment of holdings. This gradual amalgamation is particularly marked in the returns for Bere Regis and for Arne.

Enclosure Awards

A list of the parliamentary enclosure awards for Dorset appears in the *Index to the Dorset County Records*, 1938. The earliest of these awards was made for West Stafford in 1736, but the majority of the awards date from the first decades of the nineteenth century. The surveys made for enclosures were not so comprehensive as those for tithe apportionments because enclosure awards so often concerned a specific area, such as Tenantry Down in Fontmell Magna or Worgret Heath in Arne, rather than a whole parish which was only covered in the case of Winterborne Monkton. The enclosure maps and awards are chiefly interesting as they generally indicate the course of new roads, the building of which often accompanied enclosure. Also for parishes not paying tithe, such as Broadmayne and Charlton Marshall, the enclosure awards give the only picture available of their field patterns at the turn of the nineteenth century.

Tithe Apportionments and Maps

The complicated provisions of the Tithe Commutation Act of 1836 (see page 182) necessitated maps being drawn to show the parish boundaries and those of the fields, the area on which tithe payments were computed. No survey was necessary if the question of tithes had been settled at the time of parliamentary enclosure but in Dorset most tithe-paying parishes are covered by maps and apportionments in accordance with the 1836 Act, as enclosure awards for the county were concerned with specific areas rather than whole parishes.

Maps indicating the field boundaries were accompanied by an apportionment giving the owners and occupiers of every field and the value of the apportioned tithe charge. Field names and cultivations are also shown, and fields can be identified on the map by numbers. Some of the maps, like those for Fontmell Magna and Nether Compton, are works of art giving a visual image of the mid-nineteenth century parish. Most of the Dorset tithe surveys were drawn up between 1839 and 1845; as the dates of the maps and apportionments do not always tally, all references to surveys are indicated by the date of the apportionment which was generally completed a year after the map.

PUBLIC RECORD OFFICE, after referred to as P.R.O.

Census Returns

The census returns of 1841 were the first to give names, ages, relationships within a household, occupations and, with varying degrees of precision, street or district addresses within the parish. In 1851 the birth-place was added and, in the case of land occupiers, the acreages cultivated and the numbers of labourers employed. This information and the fact that nearly all the returns were made in ink rather than scrawled in pencil, as often was done in 1841, give the 1851 returns a distinct advantage over those made a decade earlier. Enumerators were instructed to use a standard list of occupations but, luckily for us, their mother wit and interest in their neighbours' affairs, caused many to deviate from this rule. So entries such as 'flower-grinder' for 'miller' appear, and also the surprising information that in 1851 Isabella Kidd, 'Regius Professor of Medecine from Oxford', was staying at Holwell Rectory.

The census returns make compulsive reading and more than any other source of written information help us to feel at home in a village of the mid-nineteenth century.

N

SHERBORNE

R. YEO

THORNFORD

B L

PUL

MIDDLEMARSH

BUCKLAND
NEWTON

STOKE
ABBOTT

BEAMINSTER

CERNE ABBAS

NETHERBURY

R. BRIT.

R. CHAR.

WHITECHURCH
CANONICORUM

LODERS

R. FROME

CHARMOUTH

BRIDPORT

DORCHESTER

BURTON
BRADSTOCK

WINTERBORNE
ST. MARTIN

SKETCH MAP OF DORSET
SHOWING
VILLAGES AND TOWNS UNDER DISCUSSION

WEYMOUTH

0 1 2 3 4 5 6 7 8
MILES

PORTLAND
ISLE

CHAPTER I

Dorset: The Inexhaustible Resources

Interplay of soil and human activities – kinship of Romantics and early soil scientists – soils and vegetation of Dorset – all classes of rural society bound to the soil – no standard classification possible for the three basic groups, land-owners, farmers and agricultural labourers – man's mastery of the soil too late to stop drift from the villages.

Bradpole

'The soil offers inexhaustible resources, which, when properly appreciated and employed, must increase our wealth, our population, and our physical strength . . . The true objects of the agriculturist are likewise those of the patriot.'

> Sir Humphrey Davy, *Agricultural Chemistry*, 1814.

ON FIRST setting foot upon English soil travellers were not impressed. Ralph Waldo Emerson complained that 'the fields have been combed and rolled till they appear to have been finished with a pencil instead of a plough'; while Hippolyte Taine's Gallic sensibilities recoiled from the 'foliage of turnips . . . green shot with purple, a harsh colour'. Whether they came from west or east, visitors all disliked the 'ash-coloured sky' and the constant rain. Nevertheless Emerson allowed that 'in variety of surface, Britain is a miniature of Europe, having plain, forest, marsh, river, sea-shore'; the rocks which helped to mould this topography also produced a great variety of soils. Until the present day topography and soil determined methods of farming and so shaped the pattern of living throughout the countryside. The soil held in bondage not only farmers and labourers, but the whole rural community. Tithe-seeking parsons, rent-collecting landlords, wheelwrights, brewers and attorneys, with their fees in mind, all watched with equal interest the fields of ripening corn.

A survey of the interplay of the soil and human activities on a national scale would be a monumental undertaking so great is the variety of soils in this island. To take the county as a field for study makes the task possible, but to work within the limits of a parish boundary gives a better understanding of the men and the soils. As understanding comes from familiarity and from affection, it is best to choose a county that is known and loved; here each one must make his own decision. Dorset has been chosen for this survey and a selection has been made of parishes where some of the main soil types are represented, and for which records are available to trace the fortunes of those who lived on the land. Even with such limits the choice is so wide that the field has further been narrowed by personal inclination.

Millions of years before man appeared, parent rocks, climate and vegetation played their part in slowly building up the layers of soil which may be seen in the face of any trench cutting (see Figure 1). These layers, or horizons, make up the profile by which soils can be identified. Of the horizons making up the profile the cultivator is mainly concerned with those most enriched by organic matter. It would be a foolish farmer, however, who neglected the lower horizons, or subsoil, made up of parent rocks, such as Chalk or Kimmeridge Clay and, in some cases, of substances washed from other parts of the profile. In areas of East Dorset some of these illuvial horizons form a hard pan which long daunted the plough-man. As man has been turning the soil in Great Britain for about five thousand years, some limitation must be set in time as well as space to a study which deals primarily with the use man has made of the developed or mature soils. The interplay of soil and human activities is interesting in any period, but during the long ages when man was inexorably governed by his environment documentary evidence is lacking or scarce. From the earliest days of cultivation man realised that though he had to accept steep hillsides, rock and flood, he could achieve partial mastery over the soil, particularly when the areas cultivated were small and individually owned. With the development of the common-field system the cultivator's interest in improving his soil languished. Improvement of the open fields as a whole was out of the question, as the area, often covering hundreds of acres, was too large. Furthermore the management of the whole unit, whether arable or grassland, was the concern of no single person. The fact that every farmer held a number of strips in each open field militated against individual initiative. Most cultivators hoped that the produce of their more fertile strips would counterbalance inferior yields from holdings lying in steep, stony, or poorly drained areas. Attempts by the conscientious to improve their less fertile strips were impeded by difficulties in carting manure through the

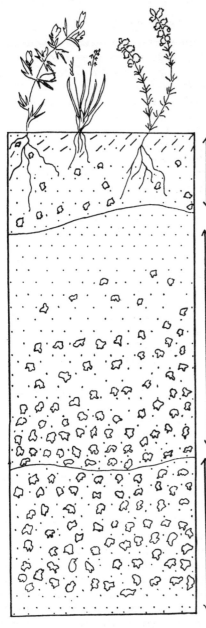

raw humus

A HORIZON
eluvial horizon
sand with flints

B HORIZON
illuvial horizon
sandy loam on
grey sand with flints

C HORIZON
parent material
flints in coarse sand
on yellow-brown sand

PROFILE DIAGRAM OF PLATEAU
GRAVEL PODSOL ~ NORTH FACE OF
LADIES LOOK OUT QUARRY ~ EAST STOKE   FIGURE 1

patchwork of holdings, and by the unwillingness of neighbours to bestir themselves by clearing ditches or pulling weeds. This unwillingness was due not so much to laziness as to the great loss of time in trudging from strip to strip and also to the fact that the greatest efforts of tenants could be set at naught by straying cattle or the lord's flock which, according to Tusser, did 'yearly the winter corn wrong'.

When the Saxon settlers cleared the forest for cultivation, their survival depended on all members of the community receiving enough land to provide for their families and stock. As this struggle to survive became less stark, enterprising cultivators considered the possibility of their land providing profit as well as sustenance. Enclosures in the open fields did not originate with the greed of profit-seeking landlords in the sixteenth and the eighteenth centuries. The eyes of the Norman manorial lords were well open to the main chance, and their open-field strips were not negligible in either quality or quantity. The Plantagenets set the pattern, so often to be copied by English monarchs, of protecting the lesser man, providing he was free and likely to thrive, against the greater. Security and the opening of the King's Court to under-vassals gave the smallest freeholders increased self-confidence. Small closes appeared in waste land, and wattle fences were set around temporary, or inhoc, enclosures in the open arable fields. This practice accounts for the many fields in Dorset which in the early nineteenth century still had names such as *Inhooks* and *Innox*. The boom in the wool trade gave an impetus to both enclosing and the reclamation of waste in the fifteenth century. By the middle of the next century it became increasingly difficult to find markets and landlords had to seek profits from their ploughs rather than sheepfolds. Systematic efforts to improve the soil of arable and meadow closes started. The sum of these efforts amounted to keeping the dung carts moving, to careful crop rotations in which pulses played an important part, and to clearing weeds.

These remained the basic principles of soil management until the eighteenth century when men awoke to a new realisation of themselves and their surroundings. Plants, clouds, rivers and clods of earth were regarded by Romantics and scientist alike with newly opened eyes. The complexity and mystery of plant life impressed both Shelley and Linnaeus; the poetry of one and the systematic classification of the other helped the world to share their vision. Wordsworth and Sir Humphrey Davy both found in the soil 'a secret and mysterious soul'. Until technical complexities separated them the poet and the scientist were akin, both drawing inspiration from the natural world around them. In this world the soil was one

of man's first concerns, and the systematic study of geological formations and of soils started in the mid-eighteenth century. Not only
were men more conscious of the earth beneath their feet but, as new
areas for cultivation were limited, they became increasingly anxious
to render fertile the soil of the land already reclaimed. Love of their
land and of the bustling supervision of improvements induced many
landowners to experiment with little tried crops, new rotations and
more effective implements. The new imaginative vision illuminated
both manures and weeds. 'Muck's your man' was no longer the
infallible rule for increasing soil fertility. Fields became the depositories for every possible item of waste; decaying fish, 'taylor's
shreds', horn and hoof shavings and 'coney clippings' were thrown
upon the pastures some of which responded to this treatment, but
weeds continued to flourish often as a result of under grazing.
Agriculturalists tried to frighten farmers out of their tame acceptance of weeds as inevitable burdens by reviving old beliefs; for
those unwise enough to nibble crowfoot leaves death was a 'certain
consequence, and they die laughing'[1]. Though looking askance at
many popular beliefs, the scientists favoured rather than discouraged
the new enthusiasms. Robert Bakewell, the geologist, offered for a
moderate sum to instruct country gentlemen in the 'useful and
pleasing science' of agricultural chemistry; while Sir Humphrey
Davy assured landowners that 'a small closet is sufficient for containing all the materials' required for experiments on their soil.[2]
The glow of enthusiasm which suffuses accounts of these early experiments makes the mid-eighteenth century both a fitting and enthrall-
ing time to start a survey of man's relations with the soil. It is not
so easy to find a clearly defined stopping point. The end of the First
World War has been chosen as the time when the cultivator ceased
to feel responsible for his soil and handed over his problems to the
chemist and the contractor.

The pioneers in soil science and in farming improvements were
lucky in having a wide reading public who had much leisure, some
education and limited opportunities of entertainment. The literate
public not only read, but wrote; the stream of pamphlets in the
seventeenth century became a torrent in the eighteenth. A glance
through the communications to the Board of Agriculture will show
that no farming activity was too humble to arouse discussion, but
the nature and improvement of soils were foremost in men's minds.

[1] T. Hale, *A Compleat Body of Husbandry*, 1756, p. 717. In quotations from eighteenth and early nineteenth century works the capitals often used for common
nouns have been replaced by lower-case initials.

[2] R. Bakewell, *An Introduction to Geology*, 1812, p. 302 and Sir Humphrey Davy,
Agricultural Chemistry, 1814, pp. 28-29.

Attempts were made to classify soils, notably by Thomas Hale whose collected writings appeared in 1756 under the title of *A Compleat Body of Husbandry*. In his pioneering enthusiasm Hale thought all soils capable of improvement; and some moved him to lyricism, ' . . . pure mould is tender and pliant; short and ready to crumble and moulder to pieces from which it has its name; it is also called the Heart of the Land, and Live Earth in some places'. Both Hale and Bakewell attempted to describe the formation of soils. These accounts differ mainly in style, Hale's being marked by his usual expansiveness: 'most probably the rich mould, when the earth was first made, was spread everywhere in purity over the several other beds; but at Noah's Flood they were in part mixed together, and hence the land is less fruitful than it was at first'. Bakewell struck a more lofty note by referring to the disintegration of rock whereby 'new and productive soils are formed to renovate the surface of the globe, and prepare it for the support of animal life: this appears to be the final cause for which the world was created, and to which all terrestrial changes ultimately refer.' The enthusiasm for soils was shared by many not professionally connected with geology or with farming. Once Napoleon was on St. Helena the pent-up longing for travel found an outlet. English travellers, well acclimatised during the war years to the study of crops and soil, did not neglect to make careful observations. Wyburn was delighted by 'the almost incredible richness of the soil of Wallachia, which resembles the black mould of an English artificial melon-bed'; but, mindful of English needs during the war, he observed that this 'pure couch' did not produce the 'nobler grain' but weeds and grasses 'of such extraordinary vigour, that in passing through meadows near Widdin on horseback, the grass touched my elbows, and the thistles left their film upon the crown of my hat'.[1] Englishmen travelling took with them their own world, in which one of their first delights was in an outdoor life. Arthur Young attributed this taste to the English habit of dressing only for dinner, not at noon according to the French custom. Young pertinently demanded, 'what is a man good for after his silk breeches and stocking are on, his hat under his arm, and his head *bien poudré* – Can he botanise in a water meadow? – Can he clamber rocks to mineralise? – Can he farm with the peasant and the ploughman?'[2] Emerson considered it was not so much taste as the Englishman's 'passion for utility' which drove him 'to agriculture, to drainage, to resisting

---

[1] *Contrasts in Emerging Societies*, Readings in the Social and Economic History of South-Eastern Europe in the Nineteenth Century, 1965, ed. Doreen Warriner, p. 142. Extract from – Wyburn, *Report on Wallachia*, c. 1820.

[2] A. Young, *Travels in France and Italy 1787-1789*, Everyman ed., p. 34.

encroachment of sea, wind, travelling sands, cold and wet subsoil'.[1]

Taste as well as necessity made Englishmen pioneers in the study of soils. The classifications used by Thomas Hale in the mid-eighteenth century have been changed, but by his descriptions in *Soils of Europe* Professor Walter Kubiëna has shown that the passage of two centuries has not blunted the sensibilities of the soil scientist. The cultivator alone knows intimately not only the feel of the soil, but the sound it makes when worked, so many folk names have been rightly retained in modern soil nomenclature. Rendsina describes a soil formation which is characterised by a shallow and often stony surface horizon, high in lime content. The term is said to be derived from the Polish word, *rzezic*, indicating the sound of the plough grinding through stony soils, which were described by Hale with the somewhat similar word, 'creachy'. The ominous crunch as the plough turned over the stony rendsinas on the limestone uplands of north-west Dorset almost broke the hearts of the occupiers of the 'outpost' farms around Gillingham (Chapter VIII). Besides the rendsinas, three other global soil groups are represented in Dorset: the gley, podsol and brown earth formations. Gley is the Russian folk name for those waterlogged soils for which neither soil scientists nor farmers can find a good word. Hale exactly described such soils as 'cold, wet, spewy and sower'; but warned 'hasty youths' from trying in desperation to convert their furrows to grass without considering the consequences. These were, as many a farmer in the Marshwood Vale well knew, rushy meadows overrun with creeping bent, Yorkshire fog and fleabane. The Russian word, *sola*, for ash, from which the term podsol is derived, has hardly more hopeful associations. In these soils excessive leaching from an acid, black, humus-packed surface horizon produces an ashy grey lower horizon and often, at about three feet, an iron pan. Even the optimistic Hale could find little to recommend in these desolate soils save the fact that 'worms and other insects . . . love a moist earth where they can burrow and lie at ease: they are burnt up in these soils', a statement which Professor Kubiëna endorses in more measured terms.[2] The activity of worms in the mild humus of brown earths partly accounts for the fertility of these soils, in which the soft crumb structure of the upper horizons helps to ensure good water permeability and aeration. Luckily in Dorset pockets of desirable brown earths often occur in districts where less favourable gleys, rendsinas and podsols predominate.

[1] R. W. Emerson, *English Traits and other Essays*, first published 1856, Everyman ed., p. 42.

[2] W. Kubiëna, *Soils of Europe*, 1953, p. 272 and p. 266 and T. Hale, op. cit., p. 5, p. 445 and p. 19.

The spine of Dorset, covering nearly half the surface of the county, is the chalk belt. The grey rendsinas derived from Chalk were marked according to Hale, by their 'starved appearance, [and] by the scarcity and lowness of weeds'. Though Hale was prone to exaggerate the poisonous properties of plants like dog's mercury, water crowfoot and lousewort, he accurately observed how the soil types determined the distribution of natural vegetation. Few modern ecologists would quarrel with Hale's statements that the yellow flag indicated peat and wild garlic land of a 'clayey nature'. They might shake their heads at his observation that the shade of knapweed flowers varied from pale blue on 'chalkey soils' to a deeper shade on 'light, loose soils'; but where brown earths and rendsinas mingle on the Edmondsham–Wimborne St. Giles road knapweeds with flowers of markedly different shades are growing. Long before Hale told them, farmers on the chalk upland knew that on their thin, freely drained soils no dressing was 'so good as that which is given by folding sheep upon them'. Besides feeding his sheep on the rounded summits of the downs, a farmer could grow barley on the lower slopes and provide an early bite for his ewes and lambs in the pastures which flourished on the alluvial soils often bordering the valley streams. This terrain, providing Cobbett's favourite sequence of 'water meadows at the bottom, corn growing up the hills, those hills being downland', was particularly suited to common-field farming which continued in these areas well into the nineteenth century and even, in the parish of Stratton, three and a half miles north-west of Dorchester, into the twentieth. Leazes, or rights to graze sheep on the open downland, were generally stinted in proportion to the amount of arable land held by a tenant. By the end of the eighteenth century these rights were often taken over by a single farmer whose lease prohibited the ploughing of downland. The steeper slopes where the terrain, and often patches of clay with flint, made cultivation difficult were longest left open; while, except for a few tenaciously held common pastures, the fertile valley soils and areas of brown earth on the uplands were early enclosed. The pattern of chalkland farming has been followed at Bere Regis (Chapter VI), a small town where, before 1815, many inhabitants oscillated between farming and trade. Bere, like other towns on the chalk downlands, was not a cheerful place in the mid-nineteenth century. Increases in the population made it difficult for the listless, undernourished inhabitants to find livelihoods in either the small-town trades, many of which were already overcrowded, or on the large farms of the chalk downland, where machinery was early introduced. It was the poverty of downland villages which, in the heat of the Corn Law debates, caused Dorset to be cited as the

TWO ASPECTS OF CHALK. **1.** Bere Regis (*above*). View from Woodbury Hill across the once open East Field enclosed into large fields with sparse, treeless hedgerows. **2.** Turnworth (*below*). Areas of brown earth in many chalkland coombs support natural woodland or, as at Turnworth, parkland timber.

'*The value of the houses in Britain is equal to the value of the soil.*' R. W. Emerson.
3. Kingston (*above*). Local quarries and a community of well-paid craftsmen account for this row of substantial stone cottages. **4.** Beer Hackett (*above right*). Standing at the junction of Forest Marble and Oxford Clay, Lower Knighton Farm was built of limestone and clay. **5.** Martinstown (*below right*). Buildings of stone from the Upwey quarry gave the village an appearance of prosperity most unusual in the mid-nineteenth century.

THE WESTERN AND EASTERN VALES. **6.** Stoke Abbott (*above*). Rounded hilltops and small irregular fields with thick hedgerows are typical of the gleys and brown earths of West Dorset. **7.** Kingston (*below*). Stone Walls, gorse and grass heath are the chief features of the many Purbeck bottoms running to the sea.

THE DORSET COAST. **8.** Kimmeridge (*above*). Free trade ruined the prospects of both corn-growing farmers and smugglers whose activities along the indented Purbeck coast had long been more profitable than fishing. **9.** Lulworth Cove (*below*). As fishing villages become holiday resorts the fisherman's gear is fast disappearing from the beaches.

THE NEW STYLE FARMING INTEREST. '*The old style farmer, solid and substantial . . . was a crusty curmudgeon where silk and satin, kid gloves and so forth were concerned.*' Other ideas were held by the farming families of the 1860s. **10.** Thomas Scutt (*above*). **11.** Frances Homer (*below left*). **12.** Charles Hawkins (*below right*).

THE WOODED APPEARANCE OF THE COUNTRYSIDE BEFORE 1914.
13. Sydling St. Nicholas (*inset*). Double hedgerow with trees planted at the gate as guides to foxhunters. **14.** Frampton (*below*). The trees and grass verges lining the Maiden Newton and Sydling roads were general throughout the county.

15. The Stour. Riparian fields and water power helped many Gillingham copyholding families, such as the Hannams and Matthews, to rise to affluence.

terrible shape of things to come for the whole country if Protection remained.

To the east the Chalk dips to the Poole Basin where the Bagshot Sands often give rise to podsols. When Young surveyed the featureless landscape of the East Dorset heathland broken only by clumps of birch he exclaimed 'what fortunes are here to be made by spirited improvers!'[1] Quick profits from the clay pits rather than hardly earned ones from the slow reclamation of 'dreary deserts' tempted the improvers at Arne (Chapter II). Nevertheless few with capital in the eighteenth century could withstand the temptation of trying to become improving farmers however unpromising the field of their labours. Proximity to the land-hungry merchants of Poole ensured improvers at Arne, but reclaimed podsols are often best improved by the constant and diligent attention of the small cultivator. Once the typical heath vegetation of ling and purple bell-heather is disturbed, bracken invades the reclaimed area and can only be repelled by ceaseless vigilance and hard work. Also, as podsols often appear in exposed areas, crops here thrive in small fields well protected by hedgerows. By 1750 the copyholds of Arne manor had passed to men of substance, but most of the holdings remained under 100 acres until the mid-nineteenth century when they were amalgamated to form three farms. Had the small holdings remained, fields of rye, potato and artificial grasses might have flourished, whereas on the larger holdings fields were soon invaded by bracken and furze as well as the weeds flourishing on sour soils, fat hen, corn marigold and spurrey. Arne is one of the Dorset parishes where the population increase in the early nineteenth century might have been supported had intensive small-scale farming been encouraged, and the planting of birch and osiers been extended. Birch wood was in great demand for smoking hams and herrings, while osier baskets would have found a market in Poole. Expenditure on these plantations would have cost the ratepayers less than the building and maintenance of the Poor House.

North, west and south of the chalk uplands wind William Stevenson's 'recluse vallies'. Here heavy, waterlogged loams, or gleys, in the valley bottoms favoured rush; but large areas of light, freely drained loams, locally called foxmoulds, on the hillsides of the Western Vales, encouraged the growing of hemp, flax and corn. The chief characteristic of the 'new men' of the eighteenth century was their ability to utilise for their own profit the soil, the vegetation and the climate of their environment. The water power and the brown earths of the Western Vales, where flax and hemp had been grown and spun since the Middle Ages, were not likely to be overlooked

[1] A. Young, *The Farmer's Tour Through East England*, 1771, Vol. III, p. 274.

by men like Richard Roberts of Burton Bradstock (Chapter IV).
Roberts' management of his mill and his wayward relations
help us to realise the buccaneering spirit with which early industrialists often embarked on their undertakings. Roberts needed flax
and hemp so he had come to terms with the 'croaking' farmers.
Instead of negotiating with the slow-moving men of the soil, he
would have greatly preferred, as he once planned, to obtain ship-
loads of hemp from a nephew who, having married a chief's daughter, was taking his ease in Tahiti.

The mild climate and light loams of the Western Vales were noted
for 'throwing out full crops of wheat, beans, flax and hemp'; and the
'most broken and *troubled* surface'[1] of the little valleys was generally
believed to cradle the yeomanry of Dorset. A survey of one valley,
that of the Char (Chapter III), shows that, though holdings of
under a 100 acres were usual because of the nature of the country,
few by the mid-nineteenth century were worked by their owners.

In the Northern Vales heavy loams and rendsinas, derived from
the clays and limestone of the area, predominate. Both types of soil
are found in the parish of Thornford (Chapter VII) which stands
at the western extremity of the heavily wooded area lying in the
triangle Thornford-Holwell-Middlemarsh. The woods consisted
mainly of hazel, ash and chestnut coppice, cut regularly for making
hurdles and cribs, and of some oak, ash and chestnut grown for
timber. Despite demands from shipyards and exhortations from
agriculturalists, who assured proprietors that 'Nature does the whole
business' in plantations, the woodlands of Dorset were by the early
nineteenth century 'continually diminishing'.[2] The love of sport
succeeded where appeals to patriotism and to self-interest failed; by
the mid-nineteenth century there was a minor reafforestation of
Dorset by the planting of coverts for game. Copse with its mixture
of timber and underwood provided excellent cover, so the woodlands preserved for game were sometimes profitable to the woodman.
By renting a few acres of copse a man might increase his small savings by cutting for firewood or by woodwork, as did Charles Gould
of Thornford. The history of the Goulds is typical of the age. The
Napoleonic Wars built their fortunes as tenant farmers and small
proprietors, and the peace broke them. Every individual family gives
a slight twist to a common story. Their determination and hopefulness and the fact that they lived near Honeycomb Wood enabled
the Goulds to rise again so that by the 1890s they were tenant farmers and people of responsibility in the parish.

[1] W. Marshall, *The Rural Economy of the West of England*, 1796, Vol. II, p. 129 and
p. 127.
[2] W. Stevenson, *General View of the Agriculture of the County of Dorset*, 1812, p. 325.

No such happy turns awaited even the most industrious and sanguine labourers in the Blackmoor Vale (Chapter V). The water-logged loams of the Vale fall into Hale's classification of 'clayey soils' as being 'tough, wet and cold'; but these soils, rich in plant nutrients, supported grasslands which were nor far behind those admired by Wyburn in Wallachia. Claridge noted that one and a quarter acres of Blackmoor pasture would feed an ox during the whole summer, but labourers could not earn a living once hay-making and harvest were over. The life of the agricultural labourer was no harder in November 1830 than in any winter since 1816, but long brooding in the Vale, isolated from the outside world, caused the labourers to rise here with greater determination and more effective leadership than elsewhere in Dorset. The very fertility of the Vale made human poverty seem more desperate; men languished but oxen, grasses and wild flowers, especially garlic and violets, flourished as nowhere else in the county.

Pedologists can quarrel with the grouping of soils within a county, but the classification of men is open to criticism from every quarter. An attempt must be made else we are at the mercy of terms like landlord, peasantry and yeoman which all have strong emotional implications.

In this survey the term agricultural labourer is used to describe all those physically working on the land. This description, therefore, includes owners and tenants working under thirty acres, labourers hired by the day, as well as craftsmen and tradesmen working on the land in their spare time. In the fluid village society before 1800 a man could belong to all these groups, but as the nineteenth century rolled on economic pressure and public opinion put, and kept, men firmly in clearly defined places. Agricultural labourers are generally considered as a homogeneous group; but the accounts of any old skilled agricultural labourer in Dorset will dispel this idea. The carter who recalls his working days with pride is not so much think-ing of the extra shilling a week which separated from him the ordi-nary labourer, but of the fact that he drove by cracking a leather whip, lent by his employer for long journeys, while the other man straightened his back from cleaning a roadside ditch to watch the wagon pass. The archtype of the poorly paid agricultural labourer was Thomas Hardy's Joseph Poorgrass in *Far From the Madding Crowd*. Whatever his working capabilities, Joseph's diffidence, 'a' awkward gift for a man', put him low in the estimation of his fellows and employers. Just such a man was William Miller of Sutton Poyntz who for twenty years earned 5s. a week and knew his only respite from toil when, for failing to pay 1s. 6d. a week for the main-tenance of his illegitimate child, he spent three months in Dorchester gaol. To-day its inmates acknowledge this prison to be 'a snug little jug', but this was far from the case in the early nineteenth century. Nevertheless Miller benefited from his respite from home rigours. On his return his sister observed that he appeared 'very well and looked very nice in his face and said he was never better'.[1] The army of sub-labourers helped to keep wages low in Dorset villages as effectively as the Irish labourers did in industrial areas. Despite the fact that by the early nineteenth century the voice of the labourer, whether skilled or not, was only officially heard when he asked for relief, his influence was not altogether negligible on the farms. Marshall believed that 'farmers in all countries being more or less warped by the opinion of their workmen' were held back from trying new farming methods.[2] By the middle of the nineteenth century these new ways widely prevailed despite the reluctant co-operation of the labourers. In Surtees' opinion, however, the fashionable model farms gave the worker a chance to get his own back by swindling the often ignorant owner. The Duke of Donkeyton in *Hillingdon Hall* was at the mercy of his labourers; among these were John Tolpiddle, the Dorsetshire dairyman, and his wife. They tended cows 'in a sky-lit byre, littered like Newmarket racers', and the 'loss upon this branch of the establishment was something under two hundred a year' as the cheese-making activities of the Tolpiddles were carried on with considerable financial benefit to themselves.

Until the mid-nineteenth century agricultural labourers, in the widest sense of the term, were often small craftsmen and traders. Any village with a population over 500 was a self-contained community whose members expected to have their boots, carts, tools and leather trousers made or repaired on their doorsteps. A mid-eighteenth century survey of the manor of Bere Regis shows that thirteen of the twenty-six tenants holding under thirty acres were engaged in trade. This combination of shop or craft with land holding was only possible if activities in both spheres were unambitiously keyed to meeting the constant and well-established demands of home and district. Uncertainty and fluctuating prices after 1815 ruined many small tradesmen, but fathers desperately continued to seek apprenticeships for their sons to save them from the treadmill life of a whole-time labourer. By the 1840s Bere had a surfeit of cobblers, carpenters and dressmakers so that only the most skilful

---

[1] *Poole and Dorsetshire Herald*, 7 January 1847. As William and his father died from starvation their lives attracted public attention which was not accorded hundreds of other similarly poorly paid workers who died less dramatically.

[2] N. Riches, *The Agricultural Revolution in Norfolk*, 1937, p. 87, quoting from W. Marshall, *The Rural Economy of Norfolk*, 1795.

and determined survived the grinding competition. Those who managed to hold on enjoyed the short Indian summer of village industries in the last decades of the century. During this period those concerned directly with agriculture had no respite from anxiety. Tenant farmers and landlords both agreed that:

'The old business of Ceres seems going to smash . . .
Free Trade and the Yankees have finished her clean.
From furrow and sheaf there seems little to glean . . .'[1]

As they turned this way and that in their search for profits, many farmers hoped that machines, particularly steam ploughs, would salvage their arable profits. Steam threshing, ploughing and haulage all provided openings for contractors whose profits depended not only on the land but also on their ability to work the machines and keep their books. With the contractor and his men, working most frequently on the large farms of the chalk belt, a new element appeared in Dorset villages. These men had money to spend freely and the mechanical knowledge which made them masters of the squire, parson and farmer. Before the rise of the contractor Loudon had rightly named surveyors, engineers and valuers 'agricultural counsellors, artists or professors'. They were the intellectuals urging on labourers and farmers from the touch-lines; equipped with their specialised knowledge and some capital the contractors entered the field itself. Radicals preached reform, but it was these men, who had often taught themselves the skills which enabled them to dominate the rural community, who changed the social structure of the village and helped to emancipate the agricultural labourer (Chapter X).

If agricultural labourers were a class in which skills and social standing varied greatly, the farmers were an even more complex group. The class-conscious sixteenth century had already made a clear distinction between the ambitious farmer, or Ben Jonson's 'boisterous whale swallowing the poor', and the yeoman who was 'taught by nature to be contented with little; his own fold yields him both food and raiment'. Farming, more than any other activity, is judged by moral as well as economic standards, and the two are often at variance. From Jonson's time to Cobbett's the efficient farmer who prospered was dubbed a rogue, while the small cultivator was considered a compound of all manly virtues. To understand the judgement that moral worth declined as acreages increased, some understanding of land tenures in Dorset is essential. Superficially these seem simple enough, but freehold, lifehold, leasehold and copyhold were not only more complex than they appear, but one farmer could hold his land by all four tenures.

[1] *Punch*, 20 October 1888, A Bucolic Ballad . . . dedicated to the British Dairy Farmers' Association.

A copyholder was a manorial tenant who in Dorset generally held his land for three lives by an agreement inscribed in the manor court rolls. A copy of this agreement or other 'evidences' of property were the most important contents of these chests, guarded with miserly vigilance, which play so large a part in Elizabethan come-dies. Copyholdings were generally, though not necessarily, in the open fields and were held by men who, according to H. J. Massing-ham, belonged to 'the old open fields community of co-operative self help destroyed by the Enclosures'.[1] The effects of enclosure varied greatly from county to county, but in Dorset the self-help that preceded enclosures was mainly on the part of substantial copyholders seeking to increase their holdings. Nearly all the copy-holdings of Arne were by the mid-eighteenth century in the hands of a few well-established tenants (Chapter II). This was not an isolated example for by the 1750s common fields throughout Dorset were collecting grounds for the well-to-do rather than spheres for self-help and co-operation among those cultivating under thirty acres. Taylor's map of the open fields of Bere Regis might also serve as a guide to the soils of the area (see Figure 2). The small strips lie on the thin, flinty loams of steep slopes; while the larger ones, whether bounded by balks or enclosed, mark the pockets of fertile brown earths. Had an equitable apportionment of common-field holdings been maintained it is unlikely that these could have supported the larger families of the early nineteenth century whose needs could only have been met by an excessive fragmentation of holdings. This problem faced peasant communities in Europe, where the poverty of many small holders equalled that of landless labourers in England. In Northern Slovenia arable holdings were estimated at two-fifths of an acre per head and the common pastures were heavily over-grazed.[2] In parts of Europe fragmentation was due to the division of land among all the heirs, but the population increase would have made the pressure on the land equally great in England where theoretically copyholdings remained intact when they passed from life to life. The success of open-field farming depends on effec-tive manorial authority, a slow rate of increase among the tenants and land being available for the extension of arable fields or com-mon pastures. None of these factors prevailed in England after 1750, but the open-field system remained for a number of reasons. Chief among these were the unwillingness of manorial lords to relinquish a system whereby nominal rents could be offset by in-creasingly large fines for 're-living', or the insertion of new lives in

[1] F. Thompson, *Lark Rise to Candleford*, World's Classics, 1954, p. XIII, introduc-tion by H. J. Massingham.

[2] *Contrasts in Emerging Societies*, pp. 356-357.

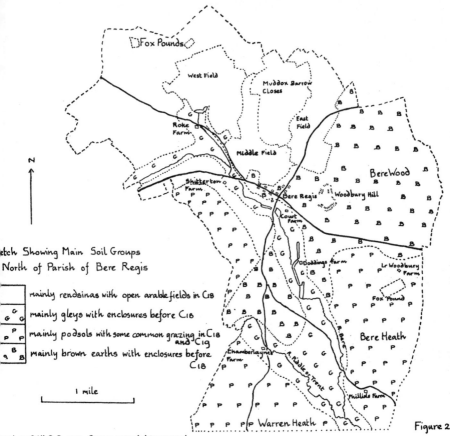

Figure 2

Based on 2½" O.S. map. Crown copyright reserved.

an agreement, and the anxiety of men with capital to acquire land, on any terms, at a time when large and small landowners were reluctant to sell any part of their property. The fact that after 1750 manorial copyholds were generally in the hands of substantial men did not mean that the land was immediately lost to the small men, for sub-letting was general on the part of the many absentee copyholders. The absentees tried to let their holdings to tenants likely to pay their rent regularly; these in turn often sub-let a few acres to cottagers. The small man was only gradually ousted from the open field where even enclosure, or the consolidation and fencing of strips, did not immediately exclude him from land holding as a sub-tenant. To be profitable small holdings, whether in open fields or not, needed to be supplemented by grazing rights. Even if commons and waste had not been enclosed, England lacked the reserves of land, like the 'vast ranges of the fjelds' which in Norway enabled small holding to prosper without producing 'that infinitesimal parcelling out of the soil, with its consequences in a wretched cultivation . . . and general pauperism'.[1]

The leasing of land for lives, generally three, had some attractions for the great landowners of Dorset, whether old-established families, chapters or collegiate bodies. These were slow to relinquish time-sanctioned copy and lifeholds since they felt comfortably sure that their possession of the land would last long into the future. Owners of small estates were not so ready to wait patiently for half a century or more to raise large renewal fines on fallen-in copyholds. These were the landlords who, anxious to lay hands on immediate cash, consolidated their copyholds when they fell in and leased out their land during the golden years of the Napoleonic wars. Landlords realised that even Bonoparte could not hold the field for ever and were reluctant to grant the leases for seven or fourteen years on which go-ahead farmers had pinned their hopes even before the struggle with France reached its closing stages. This ardour for long leases cooled when peace released all the sorrows of Pandora's box on the agricultural world. Many Dorset farmers found that falling prices of 'stock, crop, fine wool etc.,' left them 'without a shilling' and their chief anxiety was to sell out rather than secure long leases.[2] In the general panic smaller landlords might have granted these had they not feared being bound by the emergency rent reductions that they had been forced to allow. Rents of even chalk-land farms, where tenants had hopes of profits from the maltster if not the woolstapler, fell by almost a quarter. Forebodings that worse might yet befall them made landlord and tenant chary of long leases and yearly tenancies were accepted until 'the alteration of the times'. The times, however, never quite altered as men hoped, so that yearly tenancies remained general in Dorset until the mid-nineteenth century.[3] Many tenants, like the holder of Waterson Farm near Puddletown who complained before the 1848 Select Committee on Agricultural Customs, illogically nursed a grievance. The feeling that short leases militated against profitable intensive farming and that they were over-pressed for tithes did nothing to

[1] T. Forester, *Norway in 1848 and 1849*, 1850, p. 79 and p. 81.
[2] *The Agricultural State of the Kingdom, Feb.–March 1816*, being the substance of replies of many of the most opulent and intelligent holders to a circular letter sent by the Board of Agriculture . . . , Dorset replies pp. 74-77.
[3] *Select Committee on Agriculture, 1833*, p. 111, evidence from a Wiltshire witness but conditions were similar in Dorset, and J. Caird, *English Agriculture in 1850-1851*, p. 58.

improve the farmers' relations with the landowner, the parson or the labourers who felt the backwash of the tenants' resentment. After a short sunset glow in the 1860s and early 1870s the dusk of depression spread over the farming world. All hopes of an 'alteration of the times' went so, knowing the worst, tenants felt that only long leases would help them to adjust their methods to changed conditions. It was then that 'all the agricultural world agreed that a lease was the best thing possible – the clubs discussed it, the papers preached it'.[1] This clamour was unavailing in Dorset, where the assistant commissioner, reporting in 1894 on the agricultural depression, noted that 'the universal practice is to let farms on a yearly tenancy'.

'Am I not a man and a brother?' was the phrase appearing under a chained negro on anti-slavery prints, plates and handkerchiefs. Farmers in the eighteenth and nineteenth centuries might have asked the same question as their press was almost uniformly unfriendly. Cromwell's honest patriots in russet coats had become Cobbett's 'monsters'; or the man 'in a black hat and a black frock coat' with 'a cold and thoughtful expression' whom Taine observed in the 1860s. Little distinction was made between tenant farmers; the small man struggling to make a profit on his 30-100 acres and to pay tithes, rates and rent, the moderate tenant holding 100-500 acres and the farmer with over 500 acres all incurred public disapproval. Compared with some of the great shire farms, these acreages for small, moderate and large holdings seem low; but it must be remembered that though many farms in Dorset were in the hands of landowners the practice of throwing them together was not general. New farms created from amalgamated open-field strips were usually under 500 acres as landlords feared to put all their eggs in one basket.

The ambitious and efficient farmer who generally had a large holding was perhaps singled out for special attack. If he attempted to adorn his farmhouse Cobbett accused him of behaving 'just in the true stock-broker style'; while if he left it bare he was Halévy's 'businessman with his fortune to make . . . He would not hear of any useless luxury'. Every note of a farmhouse piano was a discordant one to the public. George Eliot sourly commented on the 'bad piano' to be found in 'the least imposing farmhouse'. Even the gentle poet, William Barnes, told a moral tale of the sad end of a piano-playing, farming family. An old-style farmer heard his nieces pass by to their music lesson during milking time and remarked 'moosic and it be milken toime! Zummat will come o' that,' and it

---

[1] R. Jefferies, *Hodge and His Masters*, first published 1880, ed. C. H. Warren 1949, p. 27.

did; the father of the musical girls had to sell up his farm.[1] The whole popular attitude towards farmers who tried to enlarge their families' interests is summed up in the jingle:

> Man with his tally-ho
> Wife's squalling pian-o
> Girl with her satin-oh!
> Boy with his latin-oh!
> Is splash, dash and must end in ruin-oh![2]

The Victorians readily preached the doctrine of self-advancement but they were singularly hard towards those who practised it.

The tenant farmer pleased nobody: the freeholding farmer, or yeoman, seldom put a foot wrong. This was probably because farmers owning under 500 acres were, from the eighteenth century onwards, a diminishing race and therefore aroused an antiquarian affection. Like a butterfly, a yeoman loses half his charm when pinned down for closer examination. The description varied from county to county, but in Dorset, a county of small farms, a yeoman was a man who owned and occupied himself with a holding of between 30 and 500 acres. It is immediately obvious that men owning about 500 acres merged with the gentry while those with 30 acres were perilously near becoming agricultural labourers. Throughout the country there were only two static classes in agricultural society, the labourers and the great proprietors with over 10,000 acres. In the groups between the peer and the peasant were constant rises and falls particularly among the yeoman whose ownership of land could prove to be a burden crushing them down as well as a stepping stone to gentry status. The boundary between the yeomanry and the gentry is almost imperceptible.

The gentry can be defined as armigerous families owning land between 1,000 and 10,000 acres, in which case this class in the 1870s owned 35 per cent of the total area of Dorset.[3] It was the gentry who exerted most influence over the day-to-day life of the county. Families like the Sheridans and Framptons had a far greater local importance than the aristocratic families who arrived periodically with all that clatter and bustle which Trollope described so well when relating the comings and goings of the Barsetshire Plantagenets. The squire aroused as much emotion as the yeoman or the tenant farmer, but his reception by the public was more mixed. He was the man who received anonymous messages

---

[1] Interview of William Barnes at Winterborne Came, from unnamed and undated newspaper cutting in Gillingham Museum, Book 144, Box 56-170.

[2] *Colfox Family Papers*, ed. E.M.C.H. and C.A.H., p. 148, D.R.O.

[3] F. M. L. Thompson, *English Landed Society in the Nineteenth Century*, 1963, pp. 114-115.

during the 1830 agricultural risings, one of which ran 'Banks and your sett ought to be sent to hell'.[1] He was also the man whose dignified memorial declared 'He graced a gentleman's fortune with a gentleman's deportment. He was a friend to all, especially the poor: in private by the charity of his hands; in publick, by his judgement and munificence towards the support of those institutions intended for their relief. He left two sons . . . may they imitate their father's virtues.' This was an epitaph to Thomas Gollop of Lillington, but similar memorials worded with varying degrees of fervour appear in nearly every Dorset parish church. It was not only their sorrowing relatives who thought highly of the deceased; they had been equally important in the eyes of the state, for wise governments cherish the goose that lays the golden eggs. Until the end of the eighteenth century Parliaments well understood that much of the country's wealth came from the large landowners. The pill of the Land Tax was coated with the sugar of office. As payments of the Land Tax increased so did the opportunities for places as justices of the peace, as sheriffs and as members of Parliament. Yeomen and labourers were constantly reminded of the blessings of a free constitution, but the government's solicitude for their welfare was proportionate to their financial contributions which were small. Only in times of national crises did a few crumbs, like the flax and hemp bounties, fall to the small man. Concern for the taxpayer was common to all wise governments of the time and explains the benevolence of despotic rule in many Continental countries. The provident Hapsburgs were farsighted in cherishing their taxpayers. The great landowners of their Empire had a decorative rather than a financial value; the country lived not only by the labour of the peasants on the great estates but also from the taxes which they paid. The good housewife, Maria Theresa, cut her coat according to her cloth; and by her decree, or urbarium, of 1767 protected the rights of the tax-paying peasantry. Only the prodigal Bourbons imagined they could safely disregard the interests of those who bore the cost of running the state.

In England possession of land had for so long conferred political and social distinction that the landowners forgot that their consequence depended on their financial utility to the state. This fact could be overlooked even at the end of the eighteenth century as those who made fortunes from trade and manufacture cleansed their tainted wealth by sinking it in the land. In the series of agricultural crises after 1815, however, even the hopes of social consequence

[1] *Proceedings of the Dorset Natural History and Archaeological Society* (after referred to as *Proc*), LII, pp. 75-99, W. H. Parry Okeden, 'Agricultural Riots in Dorset 1830,' quotation from letter sent to Mr. Castleman of Wimborne.

could not always tempt men of business to make doubtful invest-ments. The landowners had to face the fact that as the traders and manufacturers contributed more to the national income their in-terests would be paramount. The repeal of the Corn Laws in 1846 which set the seal on this state of affairs was an emotional rather than economic shock to the landowners who realised that not so much their incomes as their whole way of life was assailed. No Marxist could have hated the industrial capitalists more than the mid-nineteenth century landlords; and no desperate peasantry could have attacked the great landowners, or 'gothic clods', more violently than the respectable manufacturers of Manchester and Birmingham. As holders of political influence the great proprietors were singled out for the most concentrated attack; the lesser gentry and squires were contemptuously left to plod along in their old 'clay-brained' way. Once the dust of battle subsided after the Repeal the great landowners were almost aggrieved, in view of all their prognostications of doom, to find their lands intact. By the end of the nineteenth century the estates of the great Dorset landowners, those holding over 10,000 acres, covered 36 per cent of the county.[1]

In Dorset, as in the rest of England, the fortunes of many great landowning families, like the Ashley Coopers, Digbys and Fox-Strangways, were founded in the sixteenth century. Ambitious families who failed to rise in this century often had to wait until industrialism brought a second wave of opportunities two centuries later. Tractarianism, romanticism and laissez-faire principles caused a great revulsion in the mid-nineteenth century against Tudor methods of government and church reform. Yet the peers whom Disraeli envisaged as playing leading parts in his neofeudal society nearly all sprang from families who owed their rise to the dissolution of the monasteries and to the Tudor habit of searching county by-ways for efficient servants. Dorset provided her share of such men: Cardinal Morton, the Russells, the ill-fated Pitts who garnered manors, including Arne and Burton Bradstock, and peer-ages, yet lacked the cornerstone of male heirs to consolidate their honours, and the Ashley Coopers. Before these families came to the notice of the Tudors they had made good use of the opportunities offered by a county with thriving ports and extensive sheep pastures. Provided that a nice balance was maintained between Parliamen-tary and Royalist interests, families, who were well up the ladder in the sixteenth century, mounted still higher in succeeding centuries. The later Stuarts and Hanoverians, however much Bolingbroke might have liked to have moulded their views, had no inclination to shake their thrones by attempting to re-arrange the established

[1] F. M. L. Thompson, op. cit., p. 32.

orders. So under these monarchs the families of many homespun, hardworking Tudor servants emerged with all the glitter of peerages, mansions and great estates. Some found their honours more than they could manage and in the press of political and social affairs the management of estates had to be left to stewards. This was no innovation; but until the end of the eighteenth century much of the steward's work was undertaken in the manor courts over which he often presided. Though their numbers and powers had dwindled the jurors could still ensure adherence to traditional forms and keep an eye, however sleepy, on the steward's activities. The chief trouble was that stewards, like parish overseers and constables, found themselves having to undertake work of a magnitude and complexity which was far beyond their powers. Stewards wearily drew up lists of presentments of misdemeanours (there were 68 in the Gillingham manor court of 1798) but had no power to enforce payments of quit rents, or to prevent encroachments on commons or even to stop 'John Gough butcher of Bourton from letting the blood etc., run from his killing house into the turnpike road, being very offensive to travellers'. If stewards 'presented all things well' it was from despair at being unable to record the numbers of infringements of manorial custom. Although many courts continued to meet well into the nineteenth century the sessions were purely formal, and were held from an antiquarian reverence for the old days which were fast slipping out of memory. The real business of the estate was carried out by the steward, with the help of a clerk or two, in his estate office. Since the mid-eighteenth century activities of the manor courts had been marked by a drowsy ineffectiveness, but the surrenders of land, the admissions of new tenants and the infringements of manorial custom could be heard by tenants with time and patience to attend the meetings. In estate offices business was conducted behind closed doors, and in this way troubles started. A surprising diversity of great landlords, Coke of Holkham, the Duke of Wellington, Lord Palmerston, and Lord Shaftesbury, were swindled of thousands of pounds by their stewards. The activities of Robert Waters, agent to the seventh Earl of Shaftesbury, have been chosen for investigation (Chapter IX) as they show the surprising scope for, in Shaftesbury's words, 'Mis-management, peculation, trickery and direct fraud, . . . yearly and occasional plunder' available to a steward working for a landowner who disarmingly confessed, 'mere warmth of heart is a very deceptive guide in the details of life.'[1] Too much temptation was put in the way of men who needed no special qualifications for their work beyond audacious

[1] E. Hodder, *The Life and Work of the Seventh Earl of Shaftesbury*, 1886, Vol. III, p. 149 and p. 203.

self-confidence. Surtees well understood this when he described in *Hillingdon Hall* the rascally Sneakington gazing at lumps of soil and murmuring, 'silicious sand – clay – calcareous sand – carbonate of lime – humus' to the astonishment of simple tenants and the fury of a knowing one who shouted that he would 'as soon think of sending my 'ard sow to survey an estate'. Outwardly, estate affairs seemed to be conducted with Anglo-Saxon decorum, for there was none of the almost joyous Slav abandonment to chaos which Turgenev described in his sketch 'The Estate Office'; but the chaos was there nevertheless. The great landowners, whose visits to their estates were often gala occasions rather than opportunities to discuss rents and dilapidations, were the last to realise this. Onlookers were more clear-sighted and in 1882 Professor Buckman, speaking at Blandford, asserted 'he knew of nothing the landlords knew less about than farming except it might be as a general rule jurisprudence'.[1]

As well as their interest in the land, labourers, farmers and landowners had one other feeling in common, resentment towards the clergy. It was widely held that payment of tithes in kind helped country parsons to share the interests of their parishioners. This was true, but these shared interests set vicars at variance with the tithe owners, with the farmers who paid the tithes and with the labourers who believed that the parson's share was partly met from their wages. Consequently between ill-feeling on the part of their parishioners and their own pride many vicars found themselves in the isolated position of John Fisher of Gillingham concerning whom Constable wrote, 'Fisher is here lonely, and in a melancholy place – there is not a creature near him who does not look on him as a robber come for the milk, butter, etc., etc. – but that is always the case'; and again 'there is not a single person in the village that the Fishers will visit – though the inhabitants are over *four thousand*, all poor or farmers, and cattle dealers etc.'. In fairness it must be added that Fisher visited 'insufferable' cottages where he did 'wonders in cures'.[2] Before the benefits of state-assisted medical schemes were felt the clergy often did the work of doctors. Many elderly people remember with gratitude Charles Edmund Duff, vicar of Sydling St. Nicholas, who eased their hacking coughs or healed suppurating cuts.

[1] *Dorset County Chronicle*, 14 April 1882. As a lecturer at the Cheltenham and Birmingham Literary Institutes and at the Cirencester Agricultural College, Thomas Buckman, F.G.S., F.L.S., F.S.A. (1814-1884), helped to popularise scientific discoveries. His successful farm at Bradford Abbas, Dorset, demonstrated the effectiveness of these discoveries when applied to agriculture.

[2] *John Constable's Correspondence*, ed. R. B. Beckett, 1964, Vol. II, p. 283, p. 285 and p. 286.

The notable herds which grazed on the rich grasslands east of Gillingham partly accounted for the ferocity of the tithe war in that parish as vicars could not bear to see the profitable milk tithes evaded. As their profits depended on their pastures, the dairy farmers and cattle dealers, whom Fisher could not bring himself to visit, paid more attention to their grasslands than was usual in the early nineteenth century. Gillingham farmers with moderate means were willing to experiment with temporary grasslands and to grow artificial grasses; practices which, in the previous century, had been the hobbies of the well-to-do. A local smallholder and corn dealer, Shadrach Dunn, started to supply the wide demand for reliable seeds. The drive which enabled Dunn, the founder of the existing firm of seedsmen, to exploit his knowledge of grasses in the local markets made his fortune. He invested in the land but here he was less successful than his contemporary Henry Deane, vicar of Gillingham. Though their spheres were widely separate, the parson and the seed merchant had much in common, particularly the ability to understand the needs of their time (Chapter VIII).

Shadrach Dunn, Richard Roberts, flax manufacturer of Burton Bradstock, and clay-dealing Thomas Hyde of Arne, were all men who showed the world that not only the plough wrested profits from the soil. Seeds, fibres and clay all contributed wealth to men who, Emerson considered, had 'the taste for toil, a distaste for pleasure or repose, and the telescopic appreciation of distant gains'. The drive of such men and the way they worried fortunes from the countryside around them must command respect, but the great interest in their histories is that they show us self-help in action. To the timid three ps, punctuality, prudence and perseverance, advocated in copybooks, these men added a fierce determination and the advantage of some capital at the onset of their careers. It was no comfort to the labourer to know with what small savings he might have started upwards, since such small sums were as far beyond his reach as great ones. Nothing can lighten the darkness in which labourers struggled, but to see rural society as a whole the lives of those striving to advance – of the Goulds, the Dunns and the Hydes – must be kept in view as well as those of the men who never lifted themselves above unskilled agricultural work.

During the Napoleonic Wars governments endeavoured to reconcile the agricultural labourer to his hard lot by comparing his free state with that of his enslaved fellows on the Continent. Even during the heat of the struggle observers were not wanting to question this assertion. Stevenson, with unusual perspicacity, wondered if the building of tied cottages deprived the labourers 'of the power of choosing their own masters . . . an unpleasant idea, and forcibly brings to mind the ancient feudal tenures of England, and the modern ones of other countries, where ignorance, vice and poverty, go hand in hand.' When Englishmen travelled again even the time-honoured belief that wooden shoes and rye bread were the lot of all European peasants was undermined. Wyburn was struck by the gorging Wallachian peasants who, because of low prices, found 'difficulty in eating a farthing's worth of bread a day'. They ate 'regularly four times a day and no prince in Christendom fares more luxuriously' at a time when an English labourer, under the provisions of the Speenhamland Act, was lucky to live on three quartern loaves a week. Even in the 1870s Henry Barkley wished that 'the labouring poor of England and Ireland were as well off, well clothed and well housed, as the Bulgars.'[1] The malcontents of rural England – the labourers, craftsmen and small tenant farmers and yeomen – were unaffected by travellers' tales of plenty or of uprisings of oppressed peasantry. They neither wished to restore the 'old open fields community' nor to massacre the landowners. The course they took, however, was as revolutionary as any being followed in Europe; they severed their ties with the soil of their homeland. So gradual and unobtrusive was their flitting that few recognised the significance of the movement. The tenant farmers and small yeomen were the first to move voluntarily; their trail had already been blazed by paupers removed by the overseers. Though he probably did not realise it, ten-year old George Hillier was fulfilling the aspirations of many when he was shipped by the overseers of Buckland Newton to Newfoundland. Later three young men belonging to the same unfortunate family were 'assisted' to Australia.[2] The fishing fleets of Poole had forged close ties with Newfoundland and many Dorset men, like John White of Dorchester and the released Tolpuddle Martyrs, favoured North America. The enthusiasm for emigration overseas was endemic rather than general, infecting groups of parishes rather than the whole county. Departures from the Halstock Vale were on a scale to draw comment in the summary of the 1851 census returns. The waterlogged gleys of the area and the broken terrain favoured small dairy farms. Railway connections brought new life to some of these little concerns but not to those around Halstock and Corscombe. The will to emigrate was most determined in districts where the odds seemed weighted against the small cultivator succeeding and where letters circulated the success overseas of some local family. Another factor encouraging emigration was the completion of some large-scale

[1] *Contrasts in Emerging Societies*, p. 143 and p. 222.
[2] Buckland Newton Apprenticeship Indentures, 1 July 1812 and Emigration Papers 1849, D.R.O.

operations such as drainage or road and rail building. Local men employed on these works found themselves with money in their pockets, and a disinclination to settle down at home, so they were admirably qualified for becoming successful emigrants.

Professor Arthur Redford has shown that in the early stages of the Industrial Revolution the pull of expanding towns in the Midlands and the North was not strong in the southern counties. To an agricultural labourer or a small craftsman a journey, without financial assistance, to Manchester was as impossible as one to Canada. Furthermore their skills were not those needed in industry where the child was 'more valuable to the manufacturer than the man'.[1] The townward drift from Dorset villages did not start until the 1870s when some improvement in their living conditions enabled labourers and small artisans to look around them and to take advantage of the railways. The weakest often prepared the way as they had done for overseas emigration; girls going into service set the pace for young men who reluctantly followed them to search for employment in towns.

Though their need was not so pressing well-to-do families were not unaffected by the general restlessness which followed in the wake of the repeal of the Corn Laws. Neither country business undertakings nor small estates had room for all the family, so sons of the Roberts family of Burton Bradstock and of the landowning Hawkins family of Martinstown sought opportunities overseas. In particular there was a steady flow overseas from Dorset rectories. The son of George Billington, rector of Chalbury 1861–1905, who emigrated as government botanist to the West Coast of Africa where he died at the age of thirty, was only one among the many enterprising sons from rectories which provided young men for every undertaking on land or sea.

As had always been the case the groups between the labourers and the great proprietors were the most flexible and ready to move. Although a slow townward drift of agricultural workers had started in the 1870s, the Dorset labourer remained, with the church mouse, a byword for poverty until after the First World War. With the peace came changes which shook the whole of rural society. Ironically the break-up of the great estates took place when Protection was in the air. It has been estimated that between 1919 and 1921 one quarter of the land of England and Wales changed hands, generally from landlord to tenant.[2] Old sale catalogues tell the tale for Dorset; on the Motcombe estate of the Grosvenors twenty farms,

[1] *First Annual Report of the Poor Law Commissioners*, 1835, p. 190, evidence of Dr. Kay of Manchester.
[2] F. M. L. Thompson, op. cit., pp. 332-333.

with an estimated rent-roll of almost £9,500, were sold. The great estates had gone the way of the open fields. When each of these systems ceased to be economically tenable, men dwelt on the moral qualities they had fostered, the independence and willingness to help his neighbour often shown by the copyholder and the affection and consideration that could mark the relations of long-established landlords and their tenants. Change in social and economic patterns is the life force in any healthy society; the danger comes when men believe that certain moral qualities are inseparable from a particular system and cannot be practised under any other. The same attitude marks man's relations with the soil. Because attempts to control the soil were, until the present century, both cautious and ineffective, cultivators and planners have often abandoned caution to undertake soil-improvement schemes which experiment has proved will be immediately effective though their long-term results are not always known. Taine thought in the 1860s that 'the whole country seems to be a fodder factory',[1] but scientists and farmers had only just started their attempts to control the soil. Only a century later did they begin to gain mastery over their environment. Bulldozer and plough have tamed Hardy's 'heathy, furzy, briary wilderness' of East Dorset and torn up centuries-old sward on Black Down and many other chalk hills. For the first time men in this island are tempted to think that they have freed themselves from bondage to the soil; but only the first round of the struggle has started. The results of over-intensive cultivation and the reckless siezure of agricultural land for building may remind men soon and forcibly that even industrial societies must live, if not in bondage to, in harmony with the soil. We cannot be so sure to-day, as Sir Humphrey Davy was a hundred and fifty years ago, that 'the soil offers inexhaustible resources'.

[1] H. Taine, *Notes on England 1860-1870*, ed. by E. Hyams, 1957, p. 128.

Old Quay, Poole

CHAPTER II

Arne:
The Spirited
Improvers

Description of Arne manor – ownership by the Pitt family – manorial cultivation and copyholding in the eighteenth century – the clay pits of Arne and their value to the Hydes of Poole – encroachments on manorial authority – family histories of the copyholders – possible agricultural improvements on Arne podsols – bankruptcy of Thomas Hyde – his successors at Arne – the end of the manor.

'Vast tracts of waste land that call aloud for improvements . . . What fortunes are here to be made by spirited improvers!'

> Arthur Young on the East Dorset heathlands,
> *The Farmer's Tour through East England, 1771.*

'For with the poor scared freedom bade farewell,
And fortune hunters totter where they fell,
They dreamed of riches in the rebel scheme
And find too truly they did but dream.'

> John Clare.

THE ANTIQUITY of manorial custom existing since 'time out of mind' had in the eighteenth century a particular charm for lawyers, scholars and land seekers. All these hoped to profit from brushing the dust of ages from dimly remembered uses and customs. Because

27

it was so protracted and inadequately chronicled the decline of the manor has commanded less interest than its heyday. Nevertheless from the stump of felled manorialism sprouted saplings which were to make vigorous growth in the modern world. The most obvious difficulty in any manorial studies is that of discussing the subject as a whole since customs varied from district to district. To follow the last days of Arne manor is not to watch the death struggles of manorialism throughout Dorset. Though references will be made to the decline of other manors, the slow eclipse of Arne deserves a central place. The manor, which included the hamlet of Slepe and covered the eastern part of the present parish, was one of contrasts. Its boundaries covered 3,364 acres of which over half was heath with patches of birch scrub and bog, yet this unpromising terrain contained clay pockets of considerable commercial value. The heath-encircled village, which seemed on the edges of civilisation, was within sight of Poole. Across a narrow strip of sea not only could adventurous youths gaze at Poole harbour crowded with merchant-men from the New World, but land-hungry Poole merchants could see the little fields of Arne. For prospering townsmen land had a value quite unconnected with its fertility, since landholding repre-sented social prestige and political power. So even plots, the very names of which – *Bitters Gall, Furzey Vineyard,* and *Stonyland* – suggest backbreaking and unrewarding labour were desirable. The borough of Poole was rightly named the devil's fish pool, since in its waters rival merchants battled as ruthlessly as pike. By the end of the eighteenth century three families, the Hydes, the Joliffes and the Titos, dominated the pool. The Hydes, like Young, believed that vast fortunes could be made from waste land, but in the case of this family the prophecy of Clare, rather than the prognostications of the agriculturalist, were fulfilled and Arne made and broke the fortunes of the Hydes, who, in their fall, helped to bring down the already crumbling structure of the manor.

Arne offered few attractions to the agriculturalist or to the travel-ler. Its long, indented coastline was repellent to eighteenth-century taste. A few seaside resorts were cautiously accepted for their salu-brity, but there was a strong prejudice in general not only against maritime districts but also their inhabitants. Crabbe considered them,

> '. . . a wild amphibious race,
> With sullen woe display'd in every face;'

while Cobbett eschewed the 'tarred, trowsered and blue-and-buff crew whose very vicinage I always detest'. The soil was hardly more promising than the terrain. Acid podsols with a humus-packed top horizon and often an unmanageable iron 'pan', two or three feet from the surface, predominated. On these soils, bell-heather, ling and mat-grass flourished but tillage, as Thomas Hardy observed, 'after holding on for a year or two . . . receded again in despair'. Pockets of pipe-clay were marked by a bog vegetation of purple moor-grass, sphagnum and cotton-grass which gave little indication of the potential value of the subsoil.

Despite Young's optimism the majority of eighteenth-century agriculturalists would have concurred with Claridge's opinion that the East Dorset heathlands were 'most dreary wastes'. In the six-teenth century they were viewed with an even greater distaste. As the acquisition of any lands, however unfertile, were essential 'steps to gentility' under the Tudors, George Pitt was not ill-pleased with the grant of Arne manor, although it was only valued at £1 16s. 3d. a year. As lords of a manor the Pitts were equipped to start their climb to a peerage, which was achieved in 1776 when George Pitt was ennobled as Lord Rivers. By this time he owned twenty manors scattered through four counties, but of these Arne, with its clay hovels set in paltry fields amidst heathland, was the last place to attract the interest of a handsome, fashionable and unstable peer;[1] but its contribution towards his income was not insignificant. Outwardly the manor did not seem a paying proposition; annual rents rose slowly from £10 10s. in the mid-seventeenth century to £13 19s. 6d. in 1772.[2] But these manorial rentals do not give the whole picture; by the mid-eighteenth century lifeholdings were beginning to change hands more rapidly and low rents were offset by high fines paid when the holdings were taken up by new tenants. At Arne, as in most Dorset manors, tenure was by lifehold, that is, land was granted for the life of the tenant claiming admission and for two other lives. The terms of admission included heriot, or payment in kind or cash when a new 'life' took over, the maintenance of manor court officials, generally the steward who presided over the manor court, his clerk and servants, in 'meat, drink and lodging for the space of two days and two nights' and 'other burthens, works, customs, suits and services', terms which even Williams Jeanes, who presided over the Arne manor courts during the years 1735-57, would have found hard to define. The very maintenance of 'immemorial customs' often hastened the dissolution of the manorial system which they were devised to sustain. These customs by allowing the taking up of copyholds at a low rent on the payment of a handsome fine provided an easy entry to landholding for the newcomer with ready money. A tenant, whose admission to the manor was generally inscribed in the court rolls, was that hybrid between a freeholder and a leaseholder, a copyholder. Failure to 'relive' due to the impoverishment, extinction of a copyholding family or to that lack of foresight described by Thomas Hardy in his story of 'Netty Sargent's Copyhold' meant that the copyhold fell in the lord's hands for disposal, if he wished, to the highest bidder. When in 1762 James Talbot took up a holding of 65 acres on three lives at an annual rent of 10s. he paid a fine of £300.

By the mid-eighteenth century there were six areas of cultivation in the desert of heath. The most fertile areas were the arable fields lying east of Arne church in a dip where a deep topsoil had accumulated through the centuries, and the grasslands now known as the *Moors* north of the Arne-Stoborough road. These pastures lie on

---

[1] Sir Tresham Lever, *The House of Pitt*, 1947, p. 182.

[2] Information on Pitt property in Dorset has been obtained from:
J. Hutchins, *History and Antiquities of Dorset*, Vol. I, pp. 98-99.
Notes and Queries for Somerset and Dorset, 1915, Vol. XIV, pp. 180-1; 1929, Vol. XIX, p. 229.
In Vol. XIX information concerning six of Pitt's Dorset manors is given from a MS dated about 1685, while Vol. XIV contains details from a MS dated 1772 of the rentals of George Pitt's Dorset estates.

alluvial soil and are intersected by narrow dykes, or lakes, all of which, according to Mr. Gerald Smith of Slepe Farm, contain salt water except one running from west to east through the whole area. West of the *Moors* at the mouth of the Frome lay *Arne Mead*, an open meadow of 44 acres which was divided into 149 strips. As the holdings of each tenant were scattered haymaking must have been a time of confused activity. At Slepe, Gold Point and Coombe even plot cultivation could only have been maintained by an unending struggle against heather, furze and reed. The arable fields were all enclosed. It is doubtful if open arable farming was ever practised on the East Dorset heath soils. Reclamation, as in forest districts, was an individual enterprise. From the beginning of cultivation the little ploughed plots were wrested from the heath by the individual rather than the community and continued to be held severally; while, contrary to the general rule that meadow land was early enclosed, fertile grasslands in predominantly heath areas, because of their great scarcity, long remained open but shared by a few cultivators not by the whole community. No Dorset parishes are completely on heath soils; Wool, East Stoke, West Parley, Arne and even the heath-encompassed hamlet of Hyde, south of Bere Regis, all have the saving agricultural grace of some alluvial meadow land which was mown communally by the leading parish farmers. A survival of these open meads existed ten years ago in *Everybody's Mead*, West Parley, although the common holders were reduced to three.[1] As heathland was ill-suited to open farming it is not surprising that of the 209 Enclosure Acts for Dorset only four were for parishes in Bagshot Sand areas.[2]

Although enclosed the arable holdings of tenants at Arne were not amalgamated until the mid-nineteenth century. While a few copyholders had the majority of their fields in a compact area, no tenant had all his fields together and most tenants had their holdings scattered in the four main areas of arable cultivation (see Figure 3 for holdings east of Arne church). Clearly this was the land neither for wheat nor for barley which is intolerant of acid soils. Rye, oats and potatoes were more likely to have thrived, but these crops were not popular in south England. In Dorset potatoes were mainly grown by commercial cultivators who had no intention of eating the 'base root' which was destined for the ever increasing urban populations. Determined to ensure profits these growers raised their potato crops on the rich brown earths around Bridport, Beaminster

[1] Information kindly given by Mr. J. King of West Parley, one of the common holders, in June 1957.

[2] G. B. Endacott, *The Progress of Enclosures in the County of Dorset in the Eighteenth and part of the Nineteenth Centuries*, 1938, p. 81. MS thesis in D.R.O.

and Abbotsbury[1] and so were able in some measure to face the
drop in demands for home-grown hemp and flax after 1815. Oats
were regarded by southerners as food for horses not for men – except
in outlandish Scotland. Arne with its 31 small arable fields scattered
amidst pasture and rough grazing did not have a large horse population. That the acid podsols were ploughed and produced some
wheat and barley crops was due to the labours of the cultivators.
John Hutchins, who as rector of Holy Trinity, Wareham, visited

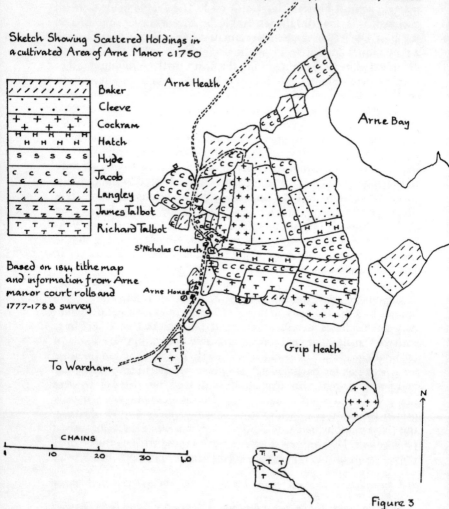

Sketch Showing Scattered Holdings in
a cultivated Area of Arne Manor c1750

Baker
Cleeve
Cockram
Hatch
Hyde
Jacob
Langley
James Talbot
Richard Talbot

Based on 1844 tithe map
and information from Arne
manor court rolls and
1777-1788 survey

Arne Heath

Arne Bay

St Nicholas Church

Arne House

To Wareham

Grip Heath

N

CHAINS
10   20   30   40

Figure 3

[1] W. Stevenson, *General View of the Agriculture of the County of Dorset*, 1812, p. 267.

the chapelry of Arne regularly, remarked on the great benefits from chalking since the early eighteenth century. From grumbling undertones in the manor-court proceedings about rights of way for dung puts, it is clear that these heavy two-wheeled carts were constantly lumbering from yards to plots.

Dairying was more profitable than arable farming as Arne was within easy distance of markets at Wareham and Poole. Grazing rights over the heath may once have been general, but they can only have contributed to subsistence not profit, and by 1778 the Common consisted of only four acres of maritime scrub in the extreme north of the parish. The 44 acres of *Arne Mead* were apportioned between lifeholders, some of whom exceeded their grazing rights, which amounted in all to 54 beasts; so that this fertile grassland, bright in late summer with sea asters, was often over-stocked. Swine were ubiquitous in eighteenth-century villages and Arne was no exception as pigs were regularly 'presented' at the manor court for roaming unyoked or unringed.

Shrewd Poole merchants might have thought twice about struggling for infertile Arne lifeholds if it had not been for the clay pits. From the time that potters first started work the value of East Dorset clay, strong, plastic and nearly pure white in colour, has been recognised. By the seventeenth century the exploitation of natural resources had become increasingly profitable to individuals, who were often prepared to face risks from which corporate bodies drew back. These industrial pioneers were tempted by the development of overseas trade and of home needs, often increasing as a result of the greater volume of foreign trade. Larger imports of tobacco and tea meant a corresponding increase in the demands of clay for pipes and teacups. Clay pipes were generally sold in public houses where earthenware beer mugs began to take the place of pewter ones. Clay mining became more profitable than ever before, and it attracted Thomas Hyde of Poole and Lewis Cockram of Swanage to enter a partnership for excavating clay in Arne and other Purbeck parishes. This partnership foundered in 1698 on the rocks of financial difficulties,[1] but Hyde was not deterred from continuing on his own, and the heavy spades that cut the slabs, or balls, of clay were kept constantly at work. Clay mining built the fortunes of the Hydes of Poole and the activities of this family overshadowed, at one time or another, the lives of every Arne parishioner.

As an exporter of pipe-clay Thomas Hyde gained a foothold in Arne by the end of the seventeenth century. His fellow townsmen

---

[1] F. J. Pope, *Dorset Suits*, Vol. XI, pp. 225-6 and XII, p. 22, MSS in library of Dorset County Museum. I am indebted to Mr. H. Johnstone of Poole Library for this reference.

were not blind to the profits to be dug on their doorstep and by 1737 Robert Cleeves, also a merchant of Poole, was established as a copyholder of the manor of Arne. His eighty-four acre holding, which included some land in the bleak north tip of Arne promontory, cannot have been an agricultural investment; so as well as prestige Cleeves had an eye on clay prospecting and probably was not blind to the advantages of some discreet smuggling. Well into the nineteenth century smuggling could be accounted one of Poole's main industries. The leading merchants of the borough were in a dilemma; as individuals they benefited from the illicit running of goods but as bailiffs and burgesses they feared 'the great decay of their town's manufacture by reason of the great quantities of goods run'. So they blew hot and cold; first petitioning the government in 1720 and 1722 for greater vigilance in checking smuggling and then, a few years later, begging that the stricter measures might be relaxed as the town was 'very much impoverished' because so many of its 'unhappy inhabitants' found themselves in prison.[1]

However much they buttressed their fortunes by a multiplicity of trading activities, both legal and illegal, eighteenth-century merchants were extremely vulnerable. The fall of mercantile houses was a recurring but little-publicised tragedy, easily disregarded as so many new men surged up to fill the gaps. In 1753 bad harvests distressed the poor and a trade depression pulled down many of the rich including Robert Cleeves of Poole who, in the cheerless August of that year, had to relinquish his Arne copyhold in favour of a fellow citizen and merchant, Thomas Hyde; while his handsome house in West Street passed to a member of a rival trading family, the Titos.[2]

The Hydes were established at Poole by the end of the seventeenth century. The partnership between Thomas Hyde and Lewis Cockram illustrates not only the restless drive of the urban, mercantile class but also that the land-owning gentry were not so deaf to 'the enticements of manufacture' as they professed to be. To the manor of Newton, which they held since the sixteenth century, the Cockrams added numerous other holdings in the neighbourhood of Swanage. Lewis Cockram reversed the usual procedure by which merchants obtained land for social distinction, for he took up his Arne copyholding in 1697 to add financial profit from clay mining to his already considerable estates. The experiment was not altogether encouraging for Lewis and though the Swanage Cockrams branched out into stone quarrying at Herston, the more retiring branch of the family at Arne dropped their clay-mining interests and

[1] J. Sydenham, *The History of the Town and County of Poole*, 1839, pp. 140-141.
[2] Church and Marshalsea Rate Book, 1751-1768, of St. James, Poole.

devoted themselves to agriculture and the protection of their life-holding rights by regular attendance at the manor court meetings.[1]

Thomas Hyde's connections with Arne were continued by his descendant George who, as he was an assessor at the 1737 manor court, had probably acquired a lifeholding though it has been impossible to identify it. Though his forbears had given him a good start, Thomas, the son of George, must have the credit of putting the Hydes to the forefront of Poole and Purbeck affairs.[2]

A network of family connections, a thriving business and his own energy enabled Thomas Hyde (1731-1795) to dominate the corporation for twenty years. As in Poole the franchise rested with about 100 freemen most of whom sat on the corporation, this body controlled not only borough affairs but also the destinies of parliamentary candidates. The influence of the Hydes was not only solicited but paid for by successive administrations who could ill afford not to woo a borough where the mercantile prosperity of the electors could render them intransigent.[3] The political ineptitude of George III and Wilkes' genius for turning personal injuries into national crusades made the year 1768 remarkable for a general airing of grievances throughout the country. Among those dissatisfied were many of the Poole electors who feared alike the stirrings of colonial independence which threatened their transatlantic trade and the autocratic direction of borough affairs by the Hydes. The dissidents invited Joshua Mauger, recommended by his wealth, his trading interests in North America and his family connections in Poole, to oppose Thomas Calcraft and Joseph Gulston supported by the Government and the Hydes. Both Calcraft and Gulston were young men with fashionable tastes ill-suited to the drudgery of canvassing 'a plodding trading town';[4] so that the work was undertaken by a local attorney, John Oliver, and Thomas Hyde. The money was put

---

[1] Information concerning the Cockram family has been obtained from J. Hutchins, op. cit., Vol. I, pp. 672-673; W. Hardy, *Old Swanage*, 1910, pp. 100-101; Manor Court Rolls for Arne and Slepe (after referred to as M.C.R.), D.R.O.

[2] The baptism of George Hyde does not appear in the Poole registers, only his marriage in 1730 to Anne Weston and his death in 1763. George may have been a younger son of Thomas Hyde (1681-1718) who, in Poole affairs, was overshadowed by his forceful father, Thomas (c. 1640-1714).

[3] Sir Lewis Namier and J. Brooke, *History of Parliament, The House of Commons 1754-1790*, 1964, Vol. II, p. 175 for reference to Shelburne's application to Bute for a continuation of the pension to the Hydes.

[4] J. Nicholls, *Illustrations of the Literary History of the Eighteenth Century*, 1828, Vol. V, p. 29, describing her brother's activities as a parliamentary candidate, the author of a sketch of the Gulston family wrote of Joseph 'his failings were the last in the world that should have been dragged into the full view of a plodding trading town, where in those days they dined at eleven o'clock, long before Mr. Gulston was out of bed'.

up by John Calcraft whose fortune, made from trafficking in government contracts and army commissions, enabled him to purchase a Purbeck estate and finance a brother as parliamentary candidate. There was little that Hyde did not know about the hopes and ambitions of the Poole electors, and notes in the Calcraft MSS show how thoroughly he used this knowledge, backed by Oliver's payments, to secure votes.[1] The 1768 election cost Calcraft and Gulston about £1,000 each, and Mauger more as he had to rely on money rather than his standing in the borough. Conscious that he was not personally well known, Mauger insisted that his offer of £1,000 to the corporation if he had 'the honour to be elected . . . member of Parliament' should be made publicly. Hyde was in the unfortunate position at this meeting of only being able to hint that he 'did not doubt that [the] other gentlemen would do as much'. An offer has more weight than a hint so Mauger and Calcraft were elected. As Gulston had started his great collection of books and prints, he was less ready with his money than the other two candidates, so took the line of upholding the rights of the free and independent elector and succeeded in unseating Mauger by a petition alleging corruption. In the spring of 1769 the inhabitants of Poole again enjoyed the treating, the flow of orders, and the distribution of favours and cash that accompanied contested elections in boroughs with a restricted franchise. Hyde feigned great alarm at the attention which the Poole election drew, especially as Mauger had presented a counter-petition against Calcraft for improper electioneering practices. But, like a true provincial, Hyde gloried in the disturbances at Poole, where his house had 'door and windows all smashed', as rivalling any election scenes in Middlesex. Mauger was returned by the 'friends of liberty and independence' in Poole, but Calcraft retained his seat, largely through the efforts of Hyde who recognised his old enemies on the corporation in their new guise as 'friends of liberty'.

Because of the disturbances at Poole or to secure the dignity of a country residence, Hyde established himself in the 1760s at Arne. Here his house probably stood on the site of the present Arne House, a mid-Victorian building which stands on an eminence commanding a magnificent view of Poole Harbour. Clay drew Hyde to Arne, where in 1772 he was paying £30 a year for mining rights, and the pleasures of being a country gentleman did not deflect him from business. In 1771 Hyde was negotiating for rights to dig potters' and

[1] Calcraft MSS, D.R.O. The papers of John Calcraft, 1768-1771 contain full information concerning Hyde's activities during the 1768 and 1769 elections, and also his clay-mining negotiations with John Calcraft and Josiah Wedgwood.

sugar bakers' clay on John Calcraft's estate, and he also made an agreement whereby Josiah Wedgwood agreed to take 1,400 tons yearly of this clay, which was not to be sold to any other potter. Hyde had the confidence of a man who thoroughly understands his business; and, like Richard Roberts of Burton Bradstock, who was ready to sell Bridport flax in Belfast, was not going to allow long-established traditions and the prestige of a renowned name hinder his search for new markets. In the eighteenth century the profits from expanding production to meet increasing demands were often reduced by the bottleneck of poor communications. Hyde busied himself at Arne with improving the trackways across the heath and he also built a small quay on the west coast of the promontory. Hyde's Quay is still marked on the 2½-inch Ordnance Survey map, but all that remains is a little inlet where tufts of purple moor-grass grow down to the flint-scattered shore. Inland tracks are still discernible connecting the former quay with the now disused clay-pits.

Hyde took over Cleeves' copyhold in 1753; by 1790 he owned or occupied over half of Arne manor. To understand how this could happen it is necessary to see how manorial use and custom were faring towards the end of the eighteenth century.

In every age the situation arises where long established organisations are accepted as fulfilling functions which, in fact, they have long ceased to perform; this was often the case with the manorial system in the eighteenth century. The original basis of the system was that every village householder had a share in the arable, grazing and meadowlands of the manor. The rights and duties of lords and tenants were defined and given form in the manor courts. The maintenance of these 'immemorial customs' in the eighteenth century helped to accelerate the dissolution of the manorial system. The three main causes which had hastened the end of the manor were the encroachments of unofficial enclosures, the amassing by individuals of large numbers of open-field strips and the taking up of copyholds, often by absentee tenants, as a speculation.

The enclosing of plots by individuals, anxious to evade manorial cropping and grazing regulations, must have started with open-field farming itself. Some areas of the great open fields were necessarily distant from the village and often bordered on waste. In these remote spots the stealthy enclosing of strips and nibbling away of waste were most easily achieved. Hovels were often thrown up near the small closes and these account for the groups of cottages which often cluster round the main village, such as Culeaze, Bucket Hill and Town's End in the parish of Bere Regis. Sometimes official sanction was given to temporary, or inhoc, enclosures in open arable fields. It was only a matter of time before the movable wattle was replaced by more permanent fencing. At the same time that lesser tenants were nibbling into the open fields more powerful ones, for the principle of equality was hard to maintain once the pioneering days of village settlements were over, were enclosing larger areas particularly of rich alluvial meadow land. The small and the large enclosures, though unofficially made, were gradually accepted by the community and sanctioned by the manor court as 'ancient enclosures'.

If a tenant wished to evade the manorial control of the open fields it was not always necessary to draw public attention by attempting enclosure. Tenants who made profits from some craft or cash crop were able to take up copyholds as they fell in. Providing the entry fines were paid the manor courts put no obstacle to the amassing by individuals of strips, which might eventually cover a large portion of the open fields. Winterborne Monkton is cited as a parish that was completely open at the time of its parliamentary enclosure in 1808.[1] but a façade of open-field cultivation was often a convenient cover behind which individuals could increase their holdings without raising a village outcry. So long as these holdings were neither fenced nor lying in a consolidated block, the field was technically open. Of the three open arable fields at Monkton, half of *North Field* and of *West Field* and a quarter of *East Field* were in the hands of individual tenants who certainly had to employ labour to work their tenements which, since they were unbounded by hedge or fence, could be described as open. All Dorset enclosure acts were primarily concerned with completing enclosures which had long been eating into the open fields and with the exchange of holdings, already in the hands of leading tenants, so that a consolidated block could be conveniently fenced.

In the late seventeenth and early eighteenth centuries tenements were gradually drawn into the hands of well-established local families whose activities were welcomed by the lord, anxious for fines, and unopposed by the peasantry, whose world had always been dominated by the 'ancient families'. But after 1750 'the spirit of migration' was abroad; new tenants appeared at the manor courts and aroused an indignation that had hardly been voiced earlier. These newcomers were the scapegoats for all the evils of rural distress; they were John Clare's 'o'erbearing fools' out 'to cheat plain honesty by force of might' and Cobbett's sharks swallowing small holdings like caplins. Sometimes the holdings were taken up by men who were never likely to see their land. The most outstanding of

[1] G. B. Endacott, op. cit., p. 58.

these transactions by absentees was that of William Grant of Motcombe. Through the hard work of his father, a partner in Sir Benjamin Truman's brewery, Grant was left a copyholding of 200 acres in the manor of Gillingham and enough money to foster, without satisfying, expensive tastes. He was soon in difficulties and pages of the Gillingham Manor Court Rolls for the last decades of the eighteenth century are filled with the manoeuvres of this fast-living and insolvent tenant, who lived first in Surrey then in Hampshire, to raise a little money on his copyhold.[1] This holding passed through the hands of Abraham Pascoud of Lower Grosvenor Street, of Myles Atkinson of St. Paul's Churchyard and of John Pearce of Standen Hussey in Wiltshire, with Robert Smith, a plumber, and Robert Coster, a miller, both of Hungerford in Berkshire, gaining a part interest as the copyhold passed from hand to hand. These changes were not exceptional, so that by the nineteenth century the possession of a copyhold was regarded as an investment rather than a means of subsistence.

The manor could hardly have survived the eighteenth century if it had not been for the taking up of copyholds by men of substance. Their heavy entry fines enabled the lord to maintain the manor; while, as the holdings of newcomers were often sub-let, the smaller tenant was not immediately deprived of land. When Thomas Hyde acquired Cleeves' holding at Arne, the small lifeholder had almost disappeared. Some scrutiny of the land tenures in Arne manor in the mid-eighteenth century and of subsequent changes may enable us to understand how newcomers, whose entry initially benefited the manor, undermined the manorial system so that it slowly subsided in the early nineteenth century.[2]

Little information has been found concerning tenants in the first decades of the eighteenth century. When the available manor court rolls start in 1735 some old families of substantial standing had already disappeared. The only traces of the Vyes are a memorial stone in the parish church of St. Nicholas and the field name *Hill Vieland*. Field names also indicate that the Culls and the Pooks, both Purbeck families, held Arne lifeholds; Corean, too, can only be traced by his fields. Whatever might once have been the small man's share of manorial land, by 1750 only one of the fourteen holdings belonging to the manor of Arne is known to have been in the hands of a family of 'labouring poor'. The Langleys, taxed for

[1] Gillingham Manor Court Rolls, inspected by kind permission of Mr. W. P. Farnfield of Gillingham. Some information concerning the Grant family is given in Lady Theodora Grosvenor's *Motcombe Past and Present*, 1873, p. 43.

[2] The changes of ownership of lifeholds at Arne between 1750 and 1815 have been summarised in Appendix A.

only one hearth in the seventeenth century and a century later owning but two acres, are an example of precariously placed tenants with no means to tide them over a single bad harvest or any other reverse, who were early casualties among copyholders. Probably the death of Thomas Langley in 1766 was a misfortune which his family were unable to survive. Even with larger holdings it frequently happened that land occupied by a widow or minor soon fell into the lord's hands. Of the two other small lifeholders, Whitelake and Hatch, no trace has been found in the available Arne records, so it can be assumed they belonged to families of unknown status outside the parish. Except for the holdings of Langley and possibly Whitelake and Hatch, manorial land at Arne was by the mid-eighteenth century in the hands of the gentry and yeomen.

A curious belief prevailed, and still exists, that a yeoman was permanently anchored to a medium-sized holding of 100-500 acres, embalmed as it were in his virtues of diligence, prudence and shrewdness. Clearly a man so noteworthy for sense and thrift would soon better his position. Once a yeoman amassed enough capital to pay the entry fines there was nothing to stop him accumulating lifeholds, especially before 1750 when there was less competition from townsmen.

Two yeoman families, the Bakers and Chismans, held copyholds in Arne manor in the mid-eighteenth century. The position of William Somner, incumbent of St. Michael's Wareham, the extensive property of the Cockrams and the long and respectable lineage of the Loops suggest that, whatever the size of their holdings, these families would not have considered themselves as yeomen. Alice Mercer and Martha Turner were little concerned with Arne affairs, as they were absentee copyholders. Mrs. Mercer had married into the mercantile family of Mercers at Poole, while Mrs. Turner was the well-to-do widow of a prominent Wareham citizen. After Mrs. Turner's death in 1789 her holding was taken up on behalf of young Elizabeth Harris of Morden, whose long life, stretching into the second half of the nineteenth century greatly fretted waiting claimants for Arne lifeholds. It was in the interest of the lord of the manor to allow sub-letting, generally for seven or twenty-one years, as this encouraged wealthy persons able to pay large fines to take up lifeholds which could be profitably let. The practice of sub-letting could also benefit men of moderate means as they were able by renting a lifehold to obtain a footing in the manor. Good seasons and hard work sometimes enabled them eventually to take up the copyhold as James Talbot did Widow Mercer's.

The tenure of lifeholds by the Bakers and Chismans conferred no feeling of carefree security; these families rose or fell by their farm-

16. The Moors at Arne. Lakes provided boundaries for many Arne fields, grounds for lengthy manorial disputes as to clearing and paupers with winter employment of scouring.

SOURCES OF WEALTH IN EAST DORSET. **17.** Corfe Castle. This town dominated the quarrying and clay-mining area of East Dorset where fortunes were made from digging the subsoil rather than ploughing the topsoil.

18. Disused Clay Pit at Arne. This pit, like many others rented by Thomas Hyde, was near the coast so pipe-clay could easily be shipped to Poole.

19. Stoke Heath. The East Dorset heathlands could support a few cattle, but Arthur Young's hope that their reclamation would provide 'fertile fields loaded with corn, and giving food to numerous herds of cattle' was over-optimistic.

THE FORAGE REVOLUTION IN DORSET. **20.** Water Meadows between Bockhampton and West Stafford, 1895 (*above*). The claim that Dorset led the country in the management of sheep and of water meadows was dismissed by Arthur Young as the dream of farmers accustomed to 'sleep through an inactive life'. **21.** Haymaking at East Stour *c* 1890. The grass-land improvements of the 1860s were not maintained during the depression of the 1880s when many meadows had the appearance of 'a nasty rug that won't feed'.

22. The Char Valley. West of the wooded banks of the winding Char lie the typical isolated farmsteads of the Western Vales; to the east lies the semi-circular sweep of Whitechurch Canonicorum.

FARMHOUSES OF THE WESTERN VALES. **23.** Woodcombe, Netherbury
(*above*). Built in the seventeenth century as a single storey dwelling of the
long-house type, a second floor was added as farming profits rose in the
eighteenth century and can be distinguished by the more evenly cut stones.
24. Camesworth, Netherbury (*below*). The rubblestone farmhouse was
built around the cob-walled dairy in the seventeenth century; a new dairy
house was added (to the right) later used for cider-making.

WESTERN VALE ACTIVITIES. **25.** The Bellringers, 1910 (*above*), Charles Knight (1859-1937) and his son (fourth and third from the right). Families like the Knights with a long record of parochial activity came into their own with the establishment of parish councils in 1894. **26.** Pymore Mill, Allington. By the mid-nineteenth century, the small flax shops were closing. Imported fibres were processed in the large mills, like Pymore, around Bridport. **27.** Charles Knight, 1960 (*right*). As winner of many prizes for basket making and embroidery, Mr. Charles Knight inherited the skill of his father who at the age of eight made his first waistcoat.

ing activities. Since the early eighteenth century the Bakers had filled a succession of burdensome local offices; they acted as jurors at the manor courts, land-tax assessors and overseers of the poor. Too much depended on the exertions of the head of the family; the Baker fortunes declined when Christopher's death in 1795 was followed rapidly by the decease of two other leading members of the family, Joseph and Thomas. By the 1830s the family followed the classical pattern for decayed yeomanry and drifted to the nearest town, Wareham, thankful to find employment as servants and small traders. Not a single Baker was left in Arne by 1841.

The day of the Chismans as yeomen was shorter than that of the Bakers and their decline more spectacular. By the mid-seventeenth century the Chismans were well established at Wareham, and the family took part in the two-way migration whereby well-to-do townsmen went out to acquire land while broken-down yeomen crept into the town to find work. William Chisman's acquisition of a hundred-acre holding, which probably included 23 acres formerly belonging to Corean, illustrates the truth of the criticism that life-hold tenure tended to encourage reckless individuals to risk all on taking up a holding. By about 1748 William Chisman had ceased to own, but not to work, his lifehold which had passed to John Jacob, probably from Poole. Objection was raised to Chisman's attendance at the manor court on the grounds of his being only a tenant not a lifeholder; but, if over-hasty, he was a man of spirit and not only continued to attend the court regularly but also defied for ten years its injunction to replace a hedge and bank in Goddess Lane which he had 'digged down'. In 1778 the fiery William died and with him was extinguished the family drive. His prolific descendants dragged on at Arne into the second half of the nineteenth century trying to eke out their miserable wages as labourers and boatmen by recourse to poaching and the poor rates.[1] Neither the Chismans nor the Bakers, both with mixed arable and pasture holdings, ever accumulated enough capital to tide them over any serious setbacks. William Chisman embarked on farming with too large a holding and never shook himself clear of debt; while the smaller holdings of the Bakers, mainly at Slepe, included too much marsh and heathland to allow the accumulation of reserves in good years. As the manor courts were concerned with maintaining a certain standard of agricultural efficiency, they welcomed substantial tenants not only because of their entry fines, but also so that capital would be available for the repairs to outhouses, hedges, roads and fences customarily undertaken

---

[1] Register of Prisoners in the County Gaol, 1818, D.R.O., John Chisman, fisherman, was imprisoned for poaching. The Arne Poor Rate Book, D.R.O., Henry Chisman received monthly poor-rate payments in 1801-2.

by copyholders. The Talbots were ideal manorial tenants, for as well as having financial assets they were a steady-going, prudent family unlike the Hydes who had a dangerous number of irons in the fire. When Richard Talbot took up his first holding in 1750 he was already a substantial tenant of the Cockrams at Swanage, and the taking over of part of Joseph Bakers' holding at a fine of £220 was not crippling. By the end of the eighteenth century the Talbots had not only increased their holdings to over 200 acres, but socially the family were, like the Musgraves in *Persuasion*, in 'a state of alteration'. James, Richard Talbot's brother, could only make his mark when he had to sign the overseers' acounts for 1792-3, but another member of the family had become an attorney.[1] He had found his way into a profession that in the eighteenth century was helping ambitious men 'to find a place in society more commensurate with their abilities than that to which they had been born'.[2] Although not always able to avoid debt,[3] the Talbots built up enough reserves to weather the post-war depression and sail into the comparative calm of a tenancy on a yearly lease. In 1826, Hezekiah, the eldest of James Talbot's six sons, rented North Farm which was as typical of the new age as its go-ahead tenant, since it incorporated the greater part of the lifeholdings north of Arne church.

The new manorial tenants were blamed for effecting the amalgamation of numbers of scattered holdings into farms of over a hundred acres which could only be rented by well-to-do men. The newcomers were also attacked for causing unemployment and consequently for the rising poor rates. The study of Thomas Hyde's activities at Arne may throw fresh light on these general accusations. In 1753 Hyde took over 24 acres of Cleeves' lifeholding at a yearly rent of 12s. and a fine of £50. At this time the land of Arne manor was, except for three smallholdings amounting to 33 acres, in the hands of well-to-do families. The small men had already lost whatever rights they once possessed as lifeholders with leases in the common meads. We only know that the grazing rights of substantial tenants in *Arne Mead* were extinguished in the mid-nineteenth century from an agreement made by the lord of the manor with the clay-mining Pike family. By this agreement the Pikes rented 95 acres

[1] M.C.R. Arne and Slepe, 1794, Richard Talbot attended the court as attorney in connection with the bankruptcy of Thomas Hyde.

[2] R. Robson, *The Attorney in Eighteenth Century England*, 1959, p. 58.

[3] M.C.R. Arne and Slepe, 1797. A 51-acre holding was mortgaged to a butter-factor of Wareham, William Gillingham. This unfortunate man was drowned, with twelve others, when the Wareham-Poole passage boat sank in October, 1806.

in Arne 'with the liberty to make and extend their present railroad across the piece of ground called Arne Mead to the sea . . . for the purpose of carrying clay'. This example, which could be multiplied throughout Dorset, shows how easily and imperceptibly common grazing rights often disappeared.

When Hyde extended his holdings in Arne he did not 'dispossess the swain'. He took over the lifeholds of the Loops and the Cockrams, both families once active in Arne, only after the death of Widow Loop and of Thomas Cockram, and he occupied as tenant the holdings of the Somners, John Jacob and Mrs. Turner, all absentee lifeholders. But if Hyde did not take over lands held and worked by the small man, he did prepare the way, by getting eight of the fourteen Arne lifeholds under his control, for the consolidation of these holdings. In the early nineteenth century six compact farms had been established in the place of the scattered lifeholdings, the memory of which was only kept alive by field and farm names. Thus Sumblers Farm was a corruption of Somners, but to the original living had been added Hatch's fields. By 1849 the six farms had been reduced to three, North and South Farms and Slepe Farm, all held by tenants with yearly leases.

If the new tenants had ousted small holders they would have obviously caused unemployment, but when Hyde took over his Arne lifeholds they were already being worked by hired labour. Since Hyde lived at Arne and, as overseer and manor court juror, took an active part in local affairs, there is no reason to suppose that he neglected his fields; it can be assumed that he employed the same number of labourers as his predecessors had done. The provision of employment was a question of some importance to Hyde who in 1791, when he held or occupied more than half the manorial lifeholds of Arne, paid £1 0s. 8d. out of the total parochial poor-rate assessment of that year for £1 11s. 2d. By preparing the way for the consolidation of his holdings Hyde did lessen the chances of a tenant, at some future date, taking up a small holding. But after 1815 few tenants had either the inclination or the financial incentive to continue the unending struggle of plough against heath. Many of the arable fields of the old lifeholds were allowed to revert to a state flatteringly described in the tithe apportionment of 1845 as 'rough pasture' and 'meadow'. The reduction of arable and the neglect of some meadow land, where the cutting of rush and the clearing of watercourses had once provided regular employment, meant that the large farmers employed fewer men than the lifeholders had done. In 1841 out of a male population of eighty at Arne only seventeen men were described as agricultural labourers, and some of these may have worked in Corfe Castle or Wareham. Joseph Boyt of South

Farm cultivated 252 acres, of which 98 were arable, with four labourers. Even taking into account Boyt's large family, this was a low figure and it is unlikely that the arable fields of South Farm were kept as clean as they had been when they formed part of the lifeholds of the Cockrams and Talbots.

With drive and capital at his back and no lack of benevolent intentions,[1] Hyde would seem to have been cut out for Young's 'spirited improver'. The co-existence of hungry multitudes with stretches of unoccupied land has always aroused indignation. In the 1830s Carlyle brooding at Craigenputtock blamed the government for not directing poverty-stricken Irish immigrants to the moors containing 'thousands of acres which would give them all meat'. He overlooked the fact that most of the immigrants had left similar desolate stretches in Connacht which had not produced even enough potatoes to support them. Arthur Young should have been more realistic about the possibilities of improving heathland but his whole outlook was coloured by the outstanding response of the thin, sandy soils around Holkham to improved drainage, manuring and cropping. A similar result was to be achieved in the East Dorset heathlands by paring off the turf and burning it on the spot. The land would then be ploughed for Young's agricultural panacea, turnip growing, which would clear the ground for oats undersown with 'white clover, rib-grass, burnet and trefoil'. These ambitious plans were to be encouraged by 'long, improving leases' and higher rents which Young considered the only means of arousing Dorset farmers from their tendency to 'sleep through an inactive life'. Young's trumpet calls had little effect in East Dorset; Humphrey Sturt took a step in the right direction by shipping from London the much prized ashes from soap factories to enrich the soil for fir plantations on Brownsea Island in Poole Harbour, but most other landowners and farmers, including Hyde, continued their old ways paying homage to the new methods with a few turnip fields. On the whole they were wise in their moderation; at Arne, in particular, vast reclamation schemes would have been of doubtful value.

The hard iron 'pan' often found in podsols makes even tractor ploughing hard going and, if successful, unmanageable slabs of subsoil are brought to the surface where they lie as desolately as fallen gravestones. Even if a reasonable tilth could have been obtained by horse ploughing, the battle for cultivating heathland would only have been half won. Heath soils are acid and deficient in potassium. This deficiency was only partly overcome by the scattered ash of 'burnbaking' when the turf was pared and burned

[1] Hyde on behalf of the poor protested at a public vestry meeting against enclosures at Canford. Poole Church Rate Register, 1783.

before ploughing. Eighteenth-century liming where 'undissolved lumps' of chalk were spread to 'lie the whole winter exposed to rain and the frosts'[1] was largely ineffective as chalk does not break up easily on heath soils.

Young's despised 'old path' was perhaps the most profitable one at Arne. The areas in dips, where a good depth of topsoil had accumulated, were ploughed and the small enclosed fields were protected from the wind, generally an unfriendly element on heathland, by hedges. More than anything else, heath soils need the constant feeding and weeding which only a small cultivator, be he lifeholder or tenant, can give. Farmyard manure, the main fertiliser before 1750, was excellent for providing potassium and for improving the structure of the topsoil. As good meadow land at Arne was confined to alluvial soils it was to the advantage of all the cultivators to keep it in good heart by cleaning the dykes which drained the land and cutting the rushes. The heath uplands of Arne were left untouched except for turf cutting in boggy depressions. The increasing cultivation of roots and clover should have strengthened the position of the small cultivator who, if his land was enclosed as at Arne, was ideally suited to intensive farming based on livestock fattening. Oats and leys in which white clover, tolerant of acid soils, predominated should, with the fescues and timothy of the alluvial meadows of Arne, have contributed to the increased production of dairy products and meat for markets at Poole and Portsmouth easily accessible by sea routes. These markets could have absorbed also large quantities of potatoes which would have been more economically grown on the acid heath soils of East Dorset than the Bridport loams.

Hyde had too little time and too much on his mind to effect agricultural improvements at Arne. Had he done so his plans would have been unlikely to have favoured small-scale, intensive cultivation. The merchant was concerned with pipe-clay not with the potential agricultural value of the podsols of Arne. The multiplicity of Hyde's interests made him particularly vulnerable to trade fluctuations. In the spring of 1792 conditions were set fair for a boom when a bad harvest and rumours of war 'heralded a crisis of first magnitude'.[2] Hyde was among the numbers of bankers and merchants swept away by bankruptcy. He surrendered his Arne lifeholds in 1794 through George Filliter, known as 'the honest lawyer', whose connections with Arne were to become closer. From Arne House, where he settled in retirement, Hyde had a panoramic

---

[1] [David Henry], *The Complete English Farmer*, 1771, p. 88.
[2] T. S. Ashton, *Economic Fluctuations in England 1700-1800*, 1959, p. 133.

view of Poole and the harbour where he had given and received many hard blows. He lived long enough to see his son, George Hooton, established as incumbent of St. Mary's, Wareham. Many sons of trading adventurers enjoyed respectable security because their fathers had barred no weapons in the commercial rough-and-tumble of the late eighteenth century.

One aspect of this struggle for mercantile survival is well illustrated by the scramble for lifeholds at Arne after Hyde's death. John Davis, who secured two of Hyde's most profitable holdings, came from a mercantile family with property in the newly-developed suburb of Poole, Longfleet. By an advantageous match with a youthful heiress of Ashwick in Somerset, Davis established himself as a 'valued inhabitant' of that parish and enlarged this inherited estate, which is reputed to have stretched for twenty miles.[1] Davis is the first example at Arne of a lifeholder who took up lands with no intention of farming them himself or of securing a regular income by leasing them to a tenant farmer; he merely waited for an attractive offer. Terms of the agreement between lifeholder and the prospective purchaser remained private, the manor court rolls only recorded the actual surrender and the terms imposed by the manor on the new lifeholder. In any case the manor court officials threw in their hands after the confusion of changes in 1795, and no further regular meetings were held. So the terms on which the ubiquitous Talbots eventually took over Davis' holdings are not known. Speculating with lifeholds attracted small men as well as the merchant princes of Poole. The tenures of Thomas Abbott and George White, men of moderate means, were both short-lived and unprofitable. White was ruined by his gamble and reduced to working as an agricultural labourer.

The general post of lifehold changes during the years 1795-1807 did little to help agriculture at Arne. Those speculating with lifeholds had no concern with crops, while those like the Talbots, who managed to retain their land, feared to venture on improvements in times of such uncertainty. The slowing down of work in fields and clay pits caused unemployment and rises in the expenditure on poor relief. In 1801 the Poor House was built at Jackhams. 'Carryings' of paupers to the lonely house overlooking mud flats, covered at low tide by crying sea-birds, must have seemed like journeys out of life itself.

[1] Information concerning the Davis family has been obtained from: Land Tax Assessments, Hasilor Hundred; the Marriage Register of St. James, Ashwick, seen by kind permission of the rector, Mr. G. Ridler, and verbal statements kindly made by Mr. Roberts, verger of St. James, and Mr. James of Ashwick, in December, 1959, when both were in their eighties. In the church of St. James there are stone memorials to the Davis family.

By 1807 all the Arne lifeholds except those of the limpet-like Talbots were in the hands of John Barker. The willingness of Barker to pay fines amounting to £1,114 was a godsend to Lord Rivers whose financial difficulties soon forced him to mortgage the estate. The frugal and industrious habits of the yeomen were not always the only passports to success. Sometimes a prudent marriage proved his 'pleasantest preservative from want' and such was the case of John Barker. He was descended from a farming family at Broadwell in Gloucester where he owned a moderate estate of 178 acres.[1] Barker's horizons widened when he married the only daughter of Sir Charles Mill of Mottisfont in Hampshire. He settled at Stoborough near Arne where he enjoyed his improved position by farming for a short time some of his Arne lifeholds, acting as overseer and by busying himself with local charities. Such humdrum ways were not to the taste of his son, who took over his father's estates in 1819 and, a little later, those of his maternal uncle and also the title of Sir John Barker Mill. He also filled the family living at Mottisfont in a carefree manner not wholly acceptable in the mid-nineteenth century. When Lord Rivers was considering the sale of the Arne estate, enquiries as to the possible 'duration' of Barker's lifeholds elicited the hopeful reply 'that Sir J. B. Mill was forty-six on November last and it is believed that his health is much broken with hard living'.[2]

As might be expected, Sir John, though spirited, was not an agricultural improver. He disposed of most of his lifeholds to George Filliter who eventually held all the Arne lifeholds save those of Cockram's, Cleeves', part of Baker's and Talbot's which he only occupied. George Filliter, whose family had been practising law in Wareham since the early eighteenth century,[3] was an excellent example of the new type of lawyer who took a respected place as leader of local society. Growing addiction to commercial and financial speculation made the late eighteenth and early nineteenth centuries a golden age for lawyers of discretion and integrity like the Filliters. It was only a matter of time before over-speculating or spendthrift lifeholders had to relinquish their holdings, as happened at Arne in the case of Hyde and Barker. The way was then open to legal families who, like the Filliters, specialised in conveyancing work to take the pick of the property market. Viewing his new

---

[1] Information kindly supplied by Mr. Irvine E. Gray, Records Officer, Shire Hall, Gloucester.

[2] Unsigned statement dated 22 January 1850 in Scott collection, D.R.O.

[3] Information concerning the Filliter family was very kindly supplied by Mr. D. F. S. Filliter of Parkstone.

property at Arne as a lawyer rather than an agriculturalist, Filliter determined to continue Hyde's work of consolidating lifeholds. No one could have known better the harvest of legal disputes often produced by small, scattered holdings. In failing to realise the agricultural possibilities of heath soils in the hands of small cultivators Filliter shared the outlook not only of his contemporaries but also of agriculturalists today. The emergence of Slepe Farm and North and South Farms at Arne seemed the hopeful dawn of progress after a night of lifeholding confusion. As Filliter grew older the anxieties of landowning loomed larger than its pleasures. His weariness coincided with Lord Rivers' wish 'to get the estate into his own management' so he took an underlease from Filliter and in 1850 sold the Arne estate to John Scott, second Earl of Eldon, whose descendants own it today.

The manor court of Arne and the mercantile fortunes of the Hydes subsided together; but the amassing of copyholds by Hyde did not cause but accelerated the downfall of manorial authority. This had been repeatedly flouted throughout the eighteenth century. The well-to-do tenants, who held the majority of the lifeholds at Arne and Slepe, were disinclined to heed the injunctions of the presiding steward, but anxious to maintain the 'immemorial customs' by which they had taken up their holdings. The old ship was carrying a new crew who were not ill-pleased with the unseaworthiness of their craft and the ineptitude of her captain which gave them the opportunity of charting her course. From the eleventh century to the sixteenth the manor courts played an essential part in village life; but unless constantly modified long established institutions cannot hope to survive. During the eighteenth century it was in the interests of neither the lord nor the tenants that modifications should be made. Some courts lingered on well into the nineteenth century. Richard Brinsley Sheridan maintained the manor court rolls of Frampton as a record of his personal and farming activities. He only closed them in 1881 on being told by his steward 'that to hold a Court Leet was illegal and unnecessary'.[1]

The steward was right, the work of the manorial courts was finished. By regulating allocations of land and farming practices the courts had ensured the survival of village communities through hungry and warring centuries. This tutelage and the protection of the lord enabled tenants to stand on their own feet and eventually assume control of their agricultural destinies. Paradoxically this independence was achieved in the eighteenth century under the aegis of the manor. The last service of the manorial courts was to

[1] Manor Court Rolls for Frampton, 1765-1881, D.R.O.

foster the growth of a new land-owning class, a prototype of which was Thomas Hyde of Arne.

NOTES ON SOURCES USED FOR CHAPTER II

Verbal sources

As the continuity of village life was disrupted by evacuation during the Second World War, only a few people can remember conditions in Arne at the turn of this century. I am very grateful for information from:

Mr. H. Gover of Ridge. The Gover family was in Arne by the end of the eighteenth century.

Mr. G. Smith of Slepe Farm.

Written sources

I am greatly indebted to Colonel H. E. Scott of Encombe, Corfe Castle, for kind permission to inspect estate documents without which a survey of Arne would have been impossible. These documents are now in the Dorset Record Office. Colonel Scott also kindly allowed photographs of Arne to be taken.

The Arne Registers, now in the D.R.O., were inspected by kind permission of Canon Maddox, lately incumbent of St. Mary's, Wareham.

The Poole Registers and Church and Marshalsea Rate Books, 1751-1802. These were inspected in St. James' church, Poole, by kind permission of the late incumbent, Mr. G. H. W. Bevington, and of the present incumbent, Mr. B. Bell.

CHAPTER III

Whitechurch Canonicorum: The Remarkable Tool

The grasslands of Dorset – the manuring and drainage of pastures in the eighteenth century – the sheep runs – the water meadows – dairy management and the system of letting out cows – butter and cheese making – description of Whitechurch Canonicorum, a typical dairy-farming parish of West Dorset – changes in land tenure in eighteenth and early nineteenth centuries – the disappearance of the cottage cultivator.

'Grass is a remarkable tool for work for those who love it and know how to use it best.'
André Voisin, *Rational Grazing: The Meeting of Cow and Grass*, 1962.

IN THE late eighteenth century the poet and the farmer both became increasingly attentive of the 'esculent herbage' beneath their feet. The one awoke to 'the tender green' of 'the soft bladed grass', the other realised with much less enthusiasm that, to be profitable, their pastures were going to need the same care as their fallows. This realisation came particularly hard on the farmers of West Dorset, which had been from 'time immemorial, a Dairy district' and was reputed to contain 'a greater number of yeomanry

. . . than in any other part of the country'.[1] Whether owner or tenant, the small farmer was the last man to have time or capital to improve his meadows, where some sort of grass would grow without expenditure on seed, fertiliser or drainage. The burden of grassland improvement on the small cultivator is unquestioned, but that dairy farmers of the Western Vales were yeoman in the early nineteenth century is not so certain.

Marshall, the most observant of the travellers in eighteenth-century Dorset, realised that the small size of the farms, necessitated by the topography of the district, did not preclude a number of these scattered homesteads being in the hands of a single owner. Already by the end of the eighteenth century old yeoman families who had cultivated their own farms of 30 to a 100 acres for generation after generation, like the Axes of Loders or the Coxes of Whitechurch Canonicorum, were becoming scarce in West Dorset. As early as the seventeenth century large landowners, like the Roses of Wootton Fitzpaine and the Arundells of Chideock, were not unknown. By the second half of the succeeding century new landowning families, the Colfoxes, Gundrys and Udals were determinedly on the march. How did the small farmers of the Western Vales withstand the onslaughts of these land-hungry families? There is no simple answer to this question, which can only be studied by trying to trace the fluctuations of land ownership in a single parish. Except for its large size, Whitechurch Canonicorum in the Char valley is a typical West Dorset parish where parish records and the tranquility of the terrain alike attract investigation. As the farmers of the Char valley looked to their cheese lofts and churns for profit rather than to their barns, some idea must be gained, before making the survey of Whitechurch, of the state of grassland management throughout Dorset at the end of the eighteenth century.

Voisin's three great enemies of a good sward, impeded drainage, deficiency of nitrate elements in the soil and bad management in allowing 'excessive and continuous grazing'[2] menaced to an even greater extent eighteenth-century pastures. Little could be done to improve drainage until manufactured pipes came into use after 1850. If the lie of the fields was suitable an energetic man might try to overcome waterlogging by digging ditches which were filled with stone, furze and bramble and then covered with turfs. But on the whole, drainage was neglected throughout the county. This neglect was particularly harmful in the Western Vales, where Marshall threw up his hands in despair at the state of the pastures and advised

---

[1] W. Marshall, *The Rural Economy of the West of England*, 1796, Vol. I, p. 48 and W. Stevenson, *General View of the Agriculture of the County of Dorset*, 1812, p. 75.

[2] A. Voisin, *Rational Grazing: The Meeting of Cow and Grass*, 1962, p. 68.

the sowing of grass, like corn, on ridges to 'shoot off the superfluous rain water'. The grassland most in need of drainage, however, was the permanent pasture that bordered the rivers winding through the 'succession of sheltered valleys' of West Dorset. Even a substantial landowner would have hesitated to disturb these meadows for reseeding with artificial grasses, and would have asked 'why the antient fundamental course which has been found profitable and useful for so many ages be expelled to make way for these outlandish usurpers?'[1]

The application of fertilisers involved less expenditure of time and capital than the laying of drains, but once again farmers found good reasons for leaving things as they were. Just as some die-hards feared that draining removed life-giving sap from the fields, so others held that 'guano, bone-dust and most of those concentrated manures . . . stimulate the soil so much that its exhaustion succeeds'.[2] This school stoutly maintained that 'muck's your man' and let their cattle do their work for them. But in many of the Western Vale grasslands only heavy application of phosphate and of nitrogenous top dressings could save the more valuable grasses such as meadow foxtail and timothy from being ousted by yellow rattle, fleabane, Yorkshire fog and couch. The man with riverside permanent grassland might shrug aside the need for fertilisers, but the farmer who was attempting to sow temporary grasslands, or leys, on the better drained, hillside fields of the Western Vales, had to acknowledge their importance. Before the use of manufactured fertilisers, which slowly gained grudging acceptance after 1850, fields of 'ley herbage' often became the depositories of every sort of waste. Pigeon dung, ashes, rotten fish and broken-up ant hills mixed with lime were all used by the zealous farmer determined to make two blades grow in the place of one.

The effective meeting of cow and grass by controlled feeding was considered in the eighteenth century and some conclusions reached tally with those accepted today. For successful grazing management, André Voisin advocated paddocks of about two acres in size. This advice echoes that given by the mid-eighteenth century writer to the effect that 'enclosures should be small; for cattle delight in frequent change, and thrive much the faster when often feeding in fresh pasture'.[3] In the valleys of the Axe, Char and Brit pastures of under five acres were usual. Herds were correspondingly small; Ottan of Wootton Fitzpaine, who let a dairy of 50 cows, was an

[1] [David Henry], *The Complete English Farmer*, 1771, quoting from an unnamed work of the early eighteenth century.

[2] *The Family Economist*, 1850, Vol. III, p. 39.

[3] [David Henry], op. cit., pp. 53-54.

exceptionally large owner for West Dorset where 20-30 cows, advocated as the ideal number for a herd,[1] were usual. Many farmers had far fewer cows, and the best impression of these typical herds of nondescript cows is given by eighteenth-century landscape painters. In the fields and lanes painted by Gainsborough and Standby four to five cows are usually roaming. Even at the end of the nineteenth century Thomas Hardy noted that, except in the Frome meadows, 'families' rather than 'tribes' of cattle were usual in Dorset.

Despite the small herds, over-grazing caused some small, favoured pastures – the *Milkwells* and *Clover Closes* – to deteriorate. But on the whole it was under-grazing that allowed yellow rattle, thistle and knapweed to suppress the 'tenderer of the grasses'. A large landowner like Gregory Syndercombe of Askerwell could afford to pay a few pence daily for women to spit thistles and to draw 'charling';[2] but even these small sums would have been considered wasteful by the man farming under 100 acres. Here the small farmer was right, for weeding would have been unavailing unless followed by better grazing management.

On the Chalk-derived soils of the central uplands the management of grassland was on a more lordly scale than in the little meads of West Dorset. The vast hilltop eweleazes where sheep had grazed 'for thousands of years without obscuring those chance hieroglyphs scored by men on the surface of the hills', were left virtually untouched. As French victories forced England to develop her own resources, some farmers reluctantly attempted ploughing, which only nibbled into the periphery of the maiden downland with its sward of sheep's fescue, crested dog's-tail, bent grasses and attractive herb population of thyme, burnet and birdsfoot-trefoil. Some of the lower slopes of the chalk downland had been ploughed for corn growing since Neolithic times, so the introduction of leys into the crop rotations was not so revolutionary as ploughing up the eweleazes. Already in the mid-eighteenth century three successive corn crops followed by ryegrass was a well established rotation. Some modern agriculturists would not agree with Young that this rotation was 'truly vile' since continuous corn cropping has been described as 'free-wheeling', or a process that can be continued indefinitely unless an obstacle appears in the form of soil organic matter falling below a critical level. Nor would grass experts today accept the Dorset farmers' 'rage for ray-grass' as entirely erroneous,

[1] *Communications to the Board of Agriculture*, 1804, Vol. I, p. 59.
[2] Gregory Syndercombe, Accounts, Vol. I, entries for July 1759 and October 1760. There was a marked difference in the rates of wages paid; the woman spitting thistles earned 5d. a day, while Hannah Taylor only got 1d. a day for pulling charlock.

since clover in a short ryegrass ley only 'contributes' when the ryegrass is ploughed.[1] Stevenson noted that many farmers did sow
ryegrass with both wild white and red clovers, also with trefoil;
burnet and ribgrass (*Plantago lanceolata*) were added according to the
taste of the grower for experiment. Of the 'outlandish intruders' two
gained a lasting hold in English grasslands, lucerne and sainfoin.
Lucerne was an intruder but sainfoin was indigenous, little noticed
until, like timothy, fiorin and white clover, it was re-introduced
from abroad with a new name and an enhanced reputation.

The French grasses, sainfoin and lucerne, were in the late eighteenth century crops for well-to-do landlords. Lesser men regarded
the fields of pink and blue flowers enviously when they saw how the
grasses flourished in times of drought and provided one cut after
another; but felt they were well clear of troublesome crops when
they realised the care needed in preparing the seed bed for lucerne
and how promising sainfoin, the seed of which cost £2 to £3 a
quarter, dwindled after overgrazing in the first year. Even clover
leys on which small farmers ventured to embark had their hazards.
Bathsheba Everdene in *Far from the Madding Crowd* was not the only
farmer to complain that 'sheep are such unfortunate animals!
There's always something happening to them!' when her flock
broke into a field of young clover which they devoured till they
'blasted theirselves'. Despite such mishaps clover and ryegrass leys
had come to stay, a fact that did not escape Shadrach Dunn of
Gillingham, a shrewd seedsman who acquired a short-lived fortune
and established a lasting name by putting Dorset marlgrass clover on
the market.

On Chalk-derived soils, or rendsinas, sheep set the farming clock.
For them were left untouched the vast eweleazes. Fields on the
lower slopes were sown with leys and sometimes turnips for autumn
and winter feed, while the meadows bordering on the quick-
flowing chalkland streams were flooded mainly to provide an early
bite for ewes and lambs. Only the stumps of wooden hatches and
the depressions of carriers and gattles remain to tell us of the management of water meadows, that 'business of great importance in the
agriculture of Dorset'.[2] The flooding of meadows, the folding of
sheep and the management of copse were all time-consuming and
skilled activities which landowners and farmers could carry out at
a low cost because of the seemingly inexhaustible supply of labour.
The initial cost of digging carriers, gattles and drawns, the channels
by which the stream water was spread or withdrawn, and con-

[1] *The Farmers Weekly*, 22 November 1963, pp. 88-91, and 8 November 1963,
pp. 63-65.
[2] J. Claridge, *General View of the Agriculture in the County of Dorset*, 1793, p. 34.

trolling the flood of water was estimated at £4 to £6 an acre, but the upkeep of the meadows was 'attended with but small expense',[1] given more precisely for the neighbouring county of Wiltshire as 5s. an acre yearly. Yet work on the water meadows seldom ceased. In winter hatches were repaired and water courses cleared ready for the spring flooding when water was spread at intervals over the meadows to lie for periods lasting from two to three weeks. By March the herbage, in which flote-grass, fiorin and timothy were predominant, provided an early bite for ewes and lambs which grazed till May. Water was then spread again to cover the land for a few days at a time so as to speed the growth of grass for July mowing which yielded $1\frac{1}{2}$ to $2\frac{1}{2}$ tons an acre. Despite competition from lucerne and clover, water-meadow hay was selling at £3 a ton in the early nineteenth century. Dairy cows then grazed the aftermath until November when the whole cycle, which had produced no little profit for the owner, started again.

Except on the alluvial meadows along the rivers Frome, Corfe and Stour, grassland management in East Dorset needed not so much skill as determination to battle unceasingly against the encroachments of furze, heather and bracken. The natural grasses of the heath soils, wiry mat-grass and the spear-like purple moor-grass only provided pickings for ponies, scraggy cattle and rootling pigs. But even the meagre benefits of heath grazing had been greatly curtailed by the mid-eighteenth century. This limitation was chiefly due to the concern of landowners to protect their turf-cutting and clay-mining rights. But small cultivators, like William Chisman of Arne, also helped to limit common rights by stealthily pushing their little enclosures into the heath.

The chalkland farmers had their barley fields as well as their eweleazes, while Purbeck men besides their grazing rights in common riverside pastures, such as Arne and Luckford Meads, had wrested from the heath enclosures for rye and oats; but in the Char valley farmers relied almost entirely on their pastures. Rising in the rough country east of Pilsdon Pen the Char only leaves the hilly countryside when it enters the heavy, waterlogged loams of the Marshwood Vale. As the river flows south through Whitechurch Canonicorum these loams, except in the valley bottom, become lighter and more freely drained. Even the presence of these easily worked brown earths on the slopes of the hills north-west and south-east of the Char did not tempt Whitechurch farmers to abandon their pastures for fallows. In 1801 when the high wheat prices of the

---

[1] W. Stevenson, op cit., pp. 358-372 and J. Claridge, op. cit., pp. 34-35 give full information concerning the irrigation of water meadows; Stevenson quotes widely from George Boswell of Puddletown, the Dorset authority on the subject.

two preceding years might have set the ploughs moving, only 303 acres of the total 5,420 acres in the parish were ploughed for corn.[1] Over half a century later the prospect of prolonged hostilities in the Crimea caused the breaking up of grassland for wheat on the lower slopes of Berne Hill: but farmers of the district never felt at home with corn growing. The general feeling about the man who refused to sell his wheat at 14s. a bushel in 1846 hoping, vainly as it turned out, to get 21s., was that he deserved his fate not for attempting to profiteer but for meddling in corn growing at all.[2] Strengthened by the knowledge that flax and hemp had been grown in the Western Vales for centuries and by the fact that jobbers often took over the management of the crop, farmers were a little more venturesome about flax growing. In 1794-5 bounty was claimed on 13,885 stones of flax produced in the whole county; of this total 1,201 stones were grown in Whitechurch Canonicorum.[3] With Napoleon on St. Helena and the exponents of tariff reductions gaining ground at Westminster, fields like *Poison Close* and *Nappy Close* were no longer ploughed for flax. Sometimes temporary leys were sown, but, as expenditure on good seeds, weeding and manures was stinted, these were often 'foul, weak and thin of herbage'. If the fallows were allowed to revert to permanent grassland, the pasture soon presented the depressing 'hide-bound, poached and poor' appearance that Young considered characterised much of England's permanent pastures.

Many reasons account for the determination of the farmers of Whitechurch Canonicorum to stick to their pastures. The terrain with its 'most broken and *troubled* surface' made ploughing difficult for the oxen which Stevenson noted still worked 'in the west, and north-west parts of the county'. Unwillingness to break with old ways or 'the rust of prejudice' often kept oxen working even when it was generally agreed that they were not suited to hilly ground. Dairies could, until the last decades of the nineteenth century, be successfully managed without expenditure on expensive machinery. Chestnut-wood pails and churns and cheese vats of elm wood were within the reach of men with modest incomes, unlike the seed drills and threshing machines which were becoming increasingly necessary for prosperous arable farming. Running costs

[1] *Proc.*, 1955, Vol. 77, p. 166. Extract from 1796 agricultural returns quoted by W. E. Minchinton, 'Agriculture in Dorset during the Napoleonic Wars'.

[2] The account of wheat growing on Berne Hill and of the profiteering farmer appear in a MS, kindly shown me by Mr. Charles Knight of Whitechurch, entitled: *History of St. Candida and Holy Cross* by George Broom, a National School teacher in Whitechurch about 1850-60.

[3] Flax and Hemp Returns, 1797, Dorset Quarter Session Records, D.R.O.

were also kept down as women were largely engaged in dairy work. Even at the end of the nineteenth century, when agricultural wages were slowly rising, Mrs. Reed of Netherbury started work at the age of ten in the Camesworth dairy for 3s. a week. The low running costs of dairy management and the practice of renting cows, which was general in West Dorset, meant that an agricultural labourer might nurse some hopes of becoming a dairyman on a small scale.

In 1754 Syndercombe was letting out cows at £3 5s. each a year, but by the end of the century Claridge put the average price at £6 a cow. With the cows the farmer provided pasture, winter fodder and a house for the dairyman who made his profit from the sale of milk, butter and cheese. Two establishments were necessary even if the dairyman's lodging was only a room adjoining the dairy as at Camesworth Farm, which was originally the dairy to the main farm standing on the site of the present old Rectory in the parish of Netherbury. Mr. David Parsons, who has lived at Camesworth Farm for forty years, considers that the present farmhouse consisted originally of a single, cob-walled dwelling room east of the dairy with a low cheese loft running above both chambers.

In the same parish of Netherbury a similar pattern of farmhouses with separate dairy establishments appears at Ford, Perhay and Whitehouse farms; also in the neighbouring parish of Symondsbury at Denhay, where the stone farmhouse still stands but only the debris of cob walls remain of the dairy house. The Denhay group of farms and cottages is one of the most beautiful in Dorset; not only are Higher and Lower Denhay farms attractive seventeenth-century buildings but at Higher Denhay Farm the same graceful, temple-like cowsheds appear as at Moorbath.

The practice of letting out cows was condemned by Marshall on the grounds that the uncertain tenure of the dairyman deterred him from making improvements. There seems some basis for this criticism; the precariousness of the dairyman's position is illustrated by the fact that throughout the 1851 census returns for Whitechurch Canonicorum the term 'dairyman' has been amended to read 'agricultural labourer'. Also dairies which were rented yearly with cows changed hands frequently. But if the system had its drawbacks, it provided almost the only means whereby a labourer could better his lot. A lucky and an enterprising man could gradually increase the number of cows he rented until, like Dairyman Dick in *Tess of the D'Urbervilles*, he achieved the distinction of sitting 'in shining broadcloth in his family pew at church'. But the odds against success were heavy. With dairy products a speedy sale is essential; jobbers had little time for the small man who had to make his own time-consuming arrangements to dispose of his butter, milk and cheese. By the end of the eighteenth century the larger producer was, with the aid of the jobber, getting good prices in the London market even though transport expenses were considerable. The heavy, canvas-topped wagons carrying butter and cheese were 'four days in passage from Bridport to London'.[1] Butter packed in wooden tubs and hard cheeses, often weighing 100 lbs., could be carried by sea from Bridport; but profitable dealings with the captains of the small cargo ships were only likely to be made by substantial men, like Richard Roberts of Burton Bradstock, who was able to include 'tubs of very prime salt butter' with his regular monthly shipments of yarn and sailcloth to London. All these arrangements necessitated organisation and expenditure beyond the powers of the small dairyman who had to rely on his wife jogging to market and possibly meeting with mishaps like the woman in Stubbs' painting who lost her wares when her horse shied at the sudden appearance of a raven.

In 1740 the Syndercombe accounts show that West Dorset butter was selling at 4d. to 6d. a pound; by 1798 it had reached the 'shameful price' of 1s. 1d. and 1s. 2d. a pound. After a slight fall, prices then remained stable till the mid-nineteenth century when they varied between 9d. and 11d. a pound according to the season. Although butter, milk and eggs disappeared from the cottage board, where they had never rivalled bacon, bread and cheese for popularity, demands in the towns were steadily rising. By the end of the eighteenth century these demands, as Marshall noted, were drawing butter from the local markets to London so that many well-to-do country dwellers bewailed with Miss Mitford 'the trouble, almost impossibility of procuring the pastoral luxuries of milk, eggs and butter'. In the Char valley, as in the other West Dorset vales, only the large dairy farms abounded 'in all good things which may be made from milk, rich cream, sweet butter, curds, creams, syllabubs, and so forth'.[2]

West Dorset farmers made profits from their churns rather than their cheese lofts. The pride of Dorset cheesemaking, Blue Vinney, did not travel well. Old beliefs and family secrets invested the making of this cheese with an almost ritual significance. Some held that the cheese could only be made satisfactorily in dairies with old, thick walls, others believed that even a whiff of tobacco smoke or scent near the cheeses would spoil the purity of their taste. But perhaps the true secret of making good Blue Vinney, or any other cheese, was the absolute cleanliness of shelves and utensils insisted

---

[1] W. Stevenson, op. cit., p. 384.
[2] W. Howitt, *The Book of the Seasons*, 1836, p. 121. Description of farmhouse activities in the month of May.

upon by Alice Hawkins, a notable Frampton dairywoman at the end of the last century. Alice and Robert Hawkins built up a profitable connection with Bournemouth, an ideal market for dairy goods as the pine-encircled town was building a name as a resort for those in need of rest and recuperation. Not only was Blue Vinney despatched from the Frampton dairy, but also butter, eggs and carcases of dairy-fed pigs. Robert Hawkins had been head coachman with the Sheridan family and his shining and fast moving horses were well known on the Dorchester road. They were driven by the pigman who, as he earned 14s. a week, had good reason to overtake jauntily nearly all other vehicles on the road.

Blue Vinney from lesser dairies sold at much lower prices. Mr. Marwood Hopkins of Milborne St. Andrew recollects that his father bought unripe Blue Vinney at Dorchester market for 1d. to 1½d. a pound. Prices of the hard and more satisfying cheeses rose from 1¼d. to 3d. a pound in the mid-eighteenth century to 5d. a pound at the end of the Napoleonic wars. Though prices rose by only a few pence in the decade after 1815, cheese was going the way of butter by the 1830s and 1840s.[1]

Although West Dorset farmers made cheddar-type cheese, this did not rank with the Somerset products as Dorset cheesemakers, with an eye on their butter profits, were considered over-sparing with cream.[2] Caution in the use of cream for cheese making was not unavailing as Caird noted that Dorset dairymen, by relying mainly on butter making, escaped the depression of the early 1850s which hit the primarily cheese-producing counties of Somerset and Cheshire. At the end of the nineteenth century the advanced methods of Theodore Candy of Cattistock gave Dorset cheese a national standing but it was too late to build a thriving Dorset cheese industry as overseas competitors had already captured the market. Nevertheless Mr. J. Caddy of Higher Holway Farm, who trained as a cheese-maker under Candy, remembers how many young men and women were willing to accept crowded accommodation and sparse fare at Woolcombe Farm for the sake of learning under an acknowledged master.

For the marketing of butter and cheese jobbers were the essential links in the chain which bound the Char and other Western Vales

---

[1] Prices of cheese and butter have been obtained from: The Syndercombe Dairies 1744-55, D.R.O.; The Minute Book of the Shaftesbury Union, Vol. II, p. 371, Gillingham Museum; J. Claridge, op. cit., p. 15; W. Stevenson, op. cit., p. 388; *Evidence before the Select Committee on Agriculture*, 1833, p. 264; *Western Flying Post*, 30 July 1798; information given by Mr. Ernest Hawkins of Chilcombe. These prices can only be taken as an approximate guide as they varied from month to month and from district to district.

[2] *Annals of Agriculture*, 1784, Vol. II, p. 443.

with city markets. The jobbers rode around to farmhouses and markets to purchase consignments for the factors whose undertakings were on a more ambitious scale. Frank Hill, who was making 100 pound cheeses at Manor Farm, West Bourton, in the 1880s remembers the agitated bustle in the dairy when the regular visit of the jobber was expected. Butter and cheese factors were often men of substance who were in a position to become the merchant bankers of rural society. William Gillingham, a butter factor of Wareham, lent James Talbot £400 so that he could increase his copyholding in Arne manor.

Except for occasional sallies into corn and flax growing, their dairies and grasslands occupied the whole attention of Whitechurch farmers. The larger farms of the neighbouring parish of Netherbury often had separate dairy houses. The smaller homesteads of the Char valley contained the dairy 'situated in the lowest appartment of the house, neatly paved and partitioned off'. In Befferlands Farm on the Char is a good example of such a dairy with the low-roofed cheese loft above it. Both rooms are now used for other purposes. The sale of cheese, butter, eggs and pigs sustained not only the modest farmhouses of Whitechurch but also many cottage homes with enough land to keep a pig or two by scrap-and-swill feeding and some poultry. The interesting question is how was the land of this typical Western Vale parish apportioned between tenant farmers, yeomen and cottagers holding under ten acres.

While the size of their estates can be estimated, the exact extent of the influence of large landowning families is hard to assess. Our minds have been so conditioned by the fate of Goldsmith's 'Sweet Auburn' and the plight of swains dispossessed by 'trade's unfeeling train' that we recoil from unravelling the same story from the tedious and confused records of poor-rate and land-tax assessments and from the tithe awards. The parish of Whitechurch Canonicorum was so extensive that it had to be divided into separate areas for the assessment of taxes; unfortunately the divisions used for assessing the poor rate do not tally exactly with those used for land-tax assessment. For the poor rate the parish was divided into four quarters, Berne, Vale, Abbotts Wootton and Wild; while land-tax assessments covered a slightly larger area divided into the tithings of Griddleshay, Sarum, Stoke Atram, Wells, Wild and Wootton.

Vale speaks for itself and covered the countryside around the Char valley in the north of the parish, and the village clustered round the church which magnificently commands the vale. Most of the houses were built of cob and from flints quarried on Hardown Hill to the south-east of the parish. These flints are not immediately noticeable as in the 1880s and 1890s many landlords tried to put a brave face on the agricultural depression with brick, so that the older walls of cob or flint are often concealed as at Wakelys Farm, just east of the church. Also during the depression a large amount of rebuilding had to be done to make good the damage from fire which broke out in one farm after another. Whispers circulated that some farmers by collecting their insurance money were taking an advantageous short cut out of a doomed industry. Also it was hinted that young men in the 'severe and reckless' mood which William Barnes attributed to those 'assailed by a misfortune they cannot resist', were getting their own back on a way of life that offered them no prospects. So strong was this suspicion that Mr. Charles Knight, whose family has been prominent in Whitechurch since the seventeenth century, recalls how during those troubled times law-abiding young men did not dare to venture out on winter evenings for fear of being suspected as fire-raisers. Some farms such as secluded Oselhay, Little Bluntshay and Lower Cockwell have triumphantly survived from the seventeenth century.

The southern area of the parish, reaching within about a mile of Charmouth church, was named Berne after the old manor which had by the eighteenth century, like Chilcombe, declined into a farmhouse. In the 1920s fire from lightning destroyed the few remaining parts of the old building which once had housed a strange figure who, before the activities of Jesty and Jenner had attracted attention, used to receive children 'to insure them, by a certain line of treatment, against ever catching smallpox'.[1]

Only two farms, Higher and Lower Abbott's Wootton, and a few cottages remain of the once populous Abbotts Wootton quarter which straggled north-west to the rough bracken-covered country around Coney's Castle. In the valley west of this hill fort stretch a line of south-facing farms, Great Coombe, Little Coombe, Sheep-wash and Nettlemore. These farms are connected by a flint-strewn track, winding between banked hedgerows of hazel studded with oak, which leads to the most western quarter, Wild, now part of the parish of Wootton Fitzpaine.

The earliest indication of the numbers of holdings in Whitechurch Canonicorum appears in the poor-rate assessments. This guide is not a reliable one because, since tenants as well as owners paid poor-rates, it is impossible to distinguish the types of occupiers; also, the numbers of holdings were inflated as poor rate was levied on house property as well as on land. The greatest value of these assessments is that they act as a barometer to register the constant fluctuations in the size and numbers of holdings; the rate was

[1] G. Roberts, *The History and Antiquities of the Borough of Lyme Regis and Charmouth*, 1834, p. 315.

assessed on 176 holdings in 1761, 216 in 1771, 168 in 1814 and on 171 in 1831.

The assessments for the land tax in the years between 1783 and 1832 give a more reliable picture than those for the poor rate of land tenures. But even these give no indication of the numerous sub-letting activities which provided one of the main interests of village life at a time when more stirring news only filtered into secluded parishes by out-of-date papers, so that, according to Robert Surtees, news could be 'a year or two behindhand – sometimes more, in harvest time'.

In 1783 land tax was assessed on 97 holdings of which 41 were occupied by owners; by the end of the Napoleonic Wars the number had declined to 83 of which 33 were occupied by owners. After a slight rise in 1823 the number of holdings returned to 83 in 1832, but by this time only 22 of the holdings were occupied by their proprietors.

The variations in the number of holdings from year to year appearing in the assessment returns for both poor rate and land tax suggests the existence of a reserve or 'bank' of holdings which constantly changed hands. Some fields had always gone with the old farms existing in the seventeenth century; but throughout the parish were scattered individual fields and parcels of land which, for various reasons, did not remain long with a single occupier. Some were fields held in trust like *Cattlebury;* while others, such as *Handcock* and *Girdle Ring* on the slopes of Coney's Castle, were too inaccessible to become a readily accepted part of a permanent holding. Even when fields like *Purgatory* or *Stoney Close*, unpopular because of inaccessibility or of infertility, became part of an established farm holding, their occupiers were willing to sub-let so as to gain a little profit from a stubbornly difficult field. The decline of the numbers of owner occupiers during the period 1750-1850 did not immediately reduce the numbers of fields available for the small man.

Complete and accurate information concerning land tenure in Whitechurch Canonicorum is not available until 1844 when the tithe award was made at a tide in the affairs of Whitechurch. Two farming groups held the field; those cultivating under 10 acres had numerical strength while those farming over 50 acres had the greater chance of emerging victoriously from the struggle for land. The 'middling sort of men' tilling between 10-50 acres still held on, but were often fighting a losing battle. The large numbers of the small cultivators were the great weakness of this group, for the pressure on the land was too great. In 1841 the population of Whitechurch had reached its peak of 1,581 persons. Had the whole parish been given over to open arable farming with an equal distribution of strip holdings, it is unlikely that 5,000 odd acres could have supported a population of one and a half thousand. But in the Western Vales the broken terrain not the land-rapacity of individuals had inhibited the development of open farming. Field systems of the district suggest that, with the exception of the ancient manorial lands at Wootton Abbas which were open in the early fifteenth century, enclosures were, as Marshall observed, made directly 'from the unreclaimed forest state', save where they early developed from Celtic infields and outfields.

The tithe award shows that one-third of the whole parish was in the hands of three landowners, Lord Bridport and John Bullen, both belonging to families long connected with the district, and John Morse.[1] These landowners were not concerned so much to 'dispossess the swain' as to own the larger farms of over 100 acres. Even in the mid-eighteenth century the expectation that landed proprietors would maintain smaller holdings was dismissed as 'a hope founded in folly; and therefore unworthy of regard'.[2] In 1844 profitable farms of over 100 acres were not plentiful in Whitechurch. Of the 138 occupiers of land only 22, all but Lord Bridport, tenant farmers, cultivated over 100 acres. About half of these large holdings were single and consolidated units such as Cards Mill and the Abbott's Wootton Farms; the rest were made up of two or more separate holdings. Some of these holdings had formerly belonged to the 'ancient families', others had been long in the hands of small holders. In the mid-eighteenth century the dwelling house at Cards Mill was dismissed as 'being nothing more than a cottage'. The clay-derived soil lacked drainage so the meadows were valued at 10s. an acre and pasture at 5s.[3] But in the early nineteenth century improving landlords had been busy and the 'cottage' was replaced by the present handsome brick building.

Engrossing was well on the way, but not always to the immediate deprivation of the small man, for sub-letting (for which the tithe award gives no record) was general, especially of fields separated from the main farm holdings. If sub-tenants were taken into account the list of occupiers of 1-10 acres would probably be much larger. The list, even as it stands, suggests that in the mid-nineteenth century the 'bold peasantry' of Whitechurch were still holding on to a position that was fast becoming untenable. Sixty-four of the 138 occupiers of land in the parish were cultivating under ten acres; of these just under a third owned their land. By the 1840s much of the

[1] For summary of holdings as appearing in 1844 Tithe Award see Appendix B.

[2] [David Henry], *Complete English Farmer*, 1771, pp. 57-58.

[3] Information from 1769 agent's report kindly shown to me by the late Dr. W. D. Lang, F.R.S., of Charmouth.

joy had gone from possession. The ownership of a few acres by the four elderly unmarried Orchard brothers suggests a past of penurious prudence; while a desolate future stretched before owners, like the Walbournes, with numbers of children. John Walbourne's large family included twins while a relative, William Walbourne, who had not the security of owning land, was the father of triplets. Already in the 1820s the family had drawn near the precipice of pauperism as old Henry Walbourne had been a regular recipient of poor relief. After 1815 the children of smallholders had ceased to be regarded as the 'flower and strength of the state'; large families in Whitechurch, as in other Dorset parishes, provided recruits for that menacing army of the 'surplus population' that haunted the early nineteenth-century economists. The fears of these apprehensive men seemed to be confirmed by the 1841 census returns which show two lots of triplets and twenty-two pairs of twins in Whitechurch and the neighbouring small parish of Stanton St. Gabriel. When naming their children parents often let their imaginations stray beyond the cares and frustrations of their secluded parishes. Among the Christian names in Whitechurch and Marshwood appear Pasher, Orlando, Bento, Abendego, Asenith and Adonyah.

Whether the smallholder was an agricultural labourer or a craftsman, like Robert Pitfield whose descendant now farms at Oselhay, a smallholding for poultry, potatoes and pigs was an inestimable benefit. But some employers grumbled that the tenancy of a plot turned 'labourers to farmers'[1] as they failed to give the full value of their strength and energy in return for wages. Also after 1850 it became increasingly difficult for a cottager to rent or subrent a plot because the number of fields in the 'bank' of land available for renting decreased as farmers began to find it more profitable to improve their outlying or infertile small fields by drainage and manuring rather than to let them for small, and sometimes uncertain, rents.

The fact that many of the occupiers of land under ten acres were craftsmen or tradesmen did not ensure their prosperity. In Whitechurch as in Bere Regis this double insurance against destitution was not always effective as the agricultural depressions of the immediate post-war years and of the early 1820s and 1830s naturally affected rural industries. Richard Fookes probably managed to thrive with his six acres as he was landlord of the Five Bells and so connected with the perennially prospering brewing trade. Even Arthur Young, no friend to part-time farmers, agreed that farming and innkeeping could be managed together 'if a man have a taste for such work'; but many small cultivators were engaged in less financially stable

[1] *Report of the Select Committee on Agriculture*, 1833, p. 56, evidence from Wiltshire.

trades. George Rockett and Isaac Bevis were small-scale flax and hemp manufacturers, and in the 1840s their cottage activities had no future. Prospects were no brighter in the building trade. Though local materials were still plentiful, only four new houses were erected in Whitechurch Canonicorum between 1841 and 1851 and only seven in the following decade. Trade was not brisk for masons; by 1841 Edward Stape, aged fifty, might have provided for his old age by savings made in the flush of building improvements during the Napoleonic Wars, but it was not easy for young George Mills to do the same in the 1840s. The building depression also affected, although to a lesser extent, carpenters. If skilled jobs were not available, these craftsmen could fall back on 'hedge-carpentry', or rough work on farm gates and fences, which was generally available in a grazing district.

The tenants of farms over 100 acres may be described as professional farmers whose leases depended on their ability to pay the rent; while smallholders were working men who supplemented their wages by spare-time work on their plots. But the 'middling sort of man' between the large tenant farmers and the smallholders elude definition. In Whitechurch about a quarter of the occupiers of land in the early 1840s fell into this group, which included working farmers, the vicar, the village schoolmaster and craftsmen. Of the 34 occupiers of 10-50 acres 19 owned part or the whole of their land, while of the 18 occupiers of 50-100 acres only seven were owners. Once a cultivator acquired a holding of over 50 acres his land attracted the large landowners who disliked the irksome task of making fence meet fence but were not unwilling to profit from the efforts of others. Among these moderate farmers the starting point of success was often ownership of a few acres which enabled men like Robert Mills and Joseph Collier to increase their holdings by the occupation of additional fields. These rented holdings were often scattered so cultivation was laborious and time-consuming. In these cases large families came into their own, but perhaps Thomas Dare at Middle Wild had too much of a good thing with seven sons on a thirty-five acre holding. Despite the low running costs of dairy farming men had a hard battle to pay their way; by 1851 Robert Mills, James Hoskins and Joseph Collier had all relinquished their tenements which, since they do not appear in the census returns, had presumably been engrossed into larger holdings. The widowed Sarah Roper was able to retain her late husband's fifty-eight acre holding as the thirty-six acres which she rented belonged to a relative.

The frequency with which holdings changed hands during the period 1783-1851, for which records are available, dispels the illusion of the reposeful stability of life in the Western Vales. In 1841 of the landholders of 10-100 acres in Whitechurch only Mark Wakely and William and Charles Genge belonged to families who had owned land in the late eighteenth century. The other influential land-owning families of the 1780s, the Knights, Buddens, Garrads and Barneses lived only in the memories of old men who remembered better days. In the ebb and flow of changes in land tenure some of these families reappeared at a later date. In 1851 Robert Budden was farming, as a tenant, at Mandeville Stoke, and on April 13th, 1913 a special peal of bells was rung in honour of the ninety-third birthday of Granny Barnes still farming at Wakelys.[1] In 1841 Mark Wakely lived in state in lonely, hill-encircled Sheepwash Farm, attended by two men servants and two maids. The farmhouses of well-to-do farmers were sometimes a shelter for indigent families who, in a district where they were known, were able to find work together as servants. At Sheepwash were employed Harriet Bowditch and her two young relatives, George and Elizabeth.

The tithe award of 1844 and the census returns of 1841 for Whitechurch Canonicorum enable us to take a last look at a village community in which almost a tenth of the population occupied land. The comparatively low capital needs of dairy farming and the existence of numbers of remote and infertile fields enabled the small farmer and the cottager to cling to their holdings well into the nineteenth century. But almost imperceptibly, so slowly did the change take place, these holdings became tenancies rather than small freeholds. As he held the most unattractive fields the cottage cultivator was at first left undisturbed in his tenure, but once a man had gathered together over fifty acres his holding tempted prospective buyers as being one capable of development. Small owners were bound to go; the less efficient men dropped out altogether and generally became labourers, while the more enterprising or fortunate often saw their holdings fall to large landowners, although they might remain in occupation as tenants. It must not be imagined that before the eighteenth century the Char valley was farmed by a happy band of yeomen of more or less equal status. As in other parts of Dorset, the riverside fields and lower slopes were early enclosed, and only the rough, bracken-covered hilltops were left open for grazing until the end of the eighteenth century.[2] The later half-hearted efforts at enclosure in these areas provided the fields which so frequently changed hands in the early nineteenth century. At that time it could be confidently said that 'small farmers manage

[1] Information from Mr. Charles Knight of Whitechurch who was one of the bell-ringers on the occasion.

[2] W. Marshall, op. cit., p. 131.

their little dairies just as well in many cases as their greater neighbours'.[1] But the small farmer was not able to lay drains, buy
artificial fertilisers or install new dairy machinery. The agricultural
depression of the 1880s had made these changes essential if the dairy
farmer was to survive so, as Richard Jefferies observed, 'in the heart
of the meadows the romance has departed. Everything is mechanical or scientific'. As the smallholdings gradually disappeared, so did
many cottages, only identifiable today by unexpected mounds or
clumps of overgrown fruit trees in pastures remote from the village.
In many of these pastures shining rye grass and carefully-grazed
cocksfoot show how firmly many dairy farmers today have grasped
the 'remarkable tool'. It is still possible in some fields, like wood-
bound *Pottle Oysters* and neighbouring *Stoney Close*, to admire a sight
that must have abounded in the Char valley two centuries ago –
fields almost in the state of nature. On the uneven slopes of these
pastures rush and fleabane mark the numerous waterlogged dips
and hollows. Knapweed, yellow rattle, thistle and scabious vie with
tussocks of cocksfoot and drifts of Yorkshire fog; while wild roses
entwine the thick hedgerows and trail long branches over the grassland. Such fields saddened Marshall and the succeeding agricultural improvers, but today they provide little oases of natural beauty
among the increasingly well-regulated grasslands of the Char valley.

NOTES ON SOURCES USED FOR CHAPTER III

Verbal Sources
Information concerning Whitechurch Canonicorum has very kindly
been given by:
Mr. C. Knight of Whitechurch, Bridport. Mr. Knight, whose
family has been prominent in the parish since the seventeenth cen-
tury, also let me use his fine collection of cuttings and photos and
the MS History of Whitechurch by George Broom.
Mr. W. Barnes of Whitechurch.
Mr. S. W. Batten, Northay Farm, Whitechurch.
R. Pitfield of Oselhay, Whitechurch.
W. Smith (1883-1961) and Mrs. Smith, formerly of Befferlands
Farm, Whitechurch.
To Mr. L. Sturdy of Trigon, Wareham, I am indebted for infor-
mation about the management of water meadows; and to Mr. J.
Strang, formerly Chairman of the Dorset Down Sheep Breeders'
Association, of Bere Regis for information concerning the part
played by water meadows in sheep management.

[1] *Report to the Board of Agriculture on Enclosures*, 1808, p. 32.

Information on cheesemaking has been kindly given by:
  Mr. J. Caddy, Higher Holway Farm, Cattistock.
  Mr. E. Hawkins of Chilcombe, Bridport.
  Mr. D. Yarde, formerly of Coombe Keynes, Wareham.

Written Sources
                    Dorset Record Office
Overseers' Accounts for Whitechurch.
These are not complete and are only available as follows:
  Abbotts Wootton   1754–1824
  Berne   1783–1832
  Vale   1754–1795
  Wild   1754–1827
  A summary of all quarters 1771–1820
Poor Rate Assessments 1761–1814.

                Dairy and Grassland Management
S. F. Armstrong, *British Grasses*, 1937.
V. Cheke, *The Story of Cheesemaking in Britain*, 1959.
Sir E. John Russell, *The World of the Soil*, 1957.
Sir J. Sinclair, *Code of Agriculture*, 1817.
J. Twamley, *Dairying Exemplified or the Business of Cheese-Making*, 1784.
A. Voisin, *Rational Grazing: The Meeting of Cow and Grass*, 1962.
Communications to the Board of Agriculture, 1802, Vol. III. This whole
  volume is given up to the problems of grassland management and
  of the conversion of grasslands into tillage.

CHAPTER IV

Burton Bradstock:
The Brave Sons

The naval families of West Dorset – description of Burton Bradstock – the adventures of the Roberts family on land and sea – Richard Roberts and his mills at Burton Bradstock – domestic and labour troubles – flax and hemp growing – reasons for decline of some rural industries after 1815 – search for employment by sons of small industrialists.

Burton's sons were always brave
On the land or ocean,
Ready for to kill or save,
When honour's the promotion.

Verse from song of The Loyal Volunteers of Burton Bradstock. A MS copy of the song was found among the papers of Midshipman R. F. Roberts who served in the *Victory* at Trafalgar.

WEST DORSET not only grew the hemp and flax for cordage and sails but also provided the navy with men, a harder task in the eighteenth century. From Burton Bradstock, from the villages clustered around Bridport and from the Abbotsbury area men joined the Navy because their fathers had done so, or because they were pressed into it. Only a few like Thomas Masterman Hardy set their hearts in childhood on a seafaring life.[1] Hardy is the best known and most loved of the West Dorset naval officers, nearly all of whom kept a shore base either through the estates of their families or by holding land themselves. In the lulls between the French Wars and after the peace, the admiral ashore became a stock character summed up by Miss Mitford as 'a most excellent and kind person, although a little testy and not a little absolute; and a capital disciplinarian, although addicted to the reverse sins of making other people tipsy whilst he kept himself sober, and of sending forth oaths in volleys whilst he suffered none other to swear'.

Sir George Somers purchased Berne Manor in the parish of Whitechurch Canonicorum but the memory of the sweet airs and golden sands of Bermuda would not let him settle. Samuel and Alexander Hood passed their youth in a secluded valley to the west of the parish of Netherbury. Looking south down the vale, little has changed since the mid-eighteenth century when Higher and Lower Kingsland farms had already stood for a century. Elm, ash and hazel would have been growing more thickly in the hedgerows two centuries ago and in summer many of the meadows would have been blue with flax. Although they grew up in one of the most fertile areas of West Dorset where the sandy, well drained loam is derived from Greensand, Samuel and Alexander never established themselves as Dorset landowners on the scale of their cousin, Lord Bridport. Charles Bullen who commanded the *Britannia* at Trafalgar belonged to a family whose fortunes in the late eighteenth century were established with the help of their flax-growing fields in the Char valley. The Pitfields at Symondsbury also profited from this Indian summer of flax and hemp growing. Lieutenant Joseph Pitfield (1790-1858) escaped from a French prison in 1811 and later helped to free captives in a plight worse than his own had been by taking a leading part in the bombardment of Algiers. He retired to Symondsbury where he is buried beside John Taylor his 'faithfull attendant'.

The village of Burton Bradstock lies a little east of the mouth of the Bride. As would be expected from its maritime and hill-encircled position, the parish reared seamen and sheep. On the heavy, ill-drained gleys of the Bride valley only grass flourished. In the opinion of two amateur agriculturists, Richard Roberts and Admiral Ingram, these meadows were not suitable for flooding.

[1] A. M. Broadley and R. G. Bartelot, *Three Dorset Captains at Trafalgar*, 1906, p. 18. Hardy is reported to have refused his father's offer of ponies to him and his brothers saying that 'Joe and Jack might have horses, but that he wanted a wooden one'.

Even Roberts, who thrived on experiments, hesitated to try to improve meadows that had been undisturbed for centuries. Nevertheless the Bride served Roberts well by driving the mills of Burton Bradstock. Water power and the restless energy of the Roberts family made the village a thriving centre for spinning and weaving flax and hemp grown on the brown earths in the valleys of the Brit and Char west of Burton.

The chronicles of the Roberts family show how one family was concerned with growing the flax and hemp, with spinning and weaving those fibres and with serving on the ships for which the ropes and sails were manufactured. The family history does more than provide signposts to the byways of local history, it transports us to the world of W. H. Kingston and of R. M. Ballantyne where the reader is stunned by the rapidity with which adventure, disaster and triumph assail the hero. Travel, financial failures and dramas at sea never completely detached the Roberts sons from their birthplace. No less than the most homekeeping labourer in Dorset they were bound to the soil by economic as well as emotional ties.

The connection of the Roberts family with West Dorset started early in the eighteenth century when Francis and Mary Roberts travelled, with their seven sons, from Wales to the small parish of Chilcombe about five miles south-east of Bridport. Already the only building of significance, the sixteenth-century manor, was declining into a farmhouse. But with the adjoining chapel the old manor still dominated the cluster of cottages which made up the parish standing near the summit of south-sloping terraced hills like an outpost of the ancient fort on Chilcombe Hill. The heavy, slightly acid loam of the district and the hilly terrain made sheep farming a first choice and barley growing a second. Within a fifteen-mile radius of Chilcombe four generations of the Roberts family made, and lost, their fortunes and established homes from which, in every generation, some members fared forth to new worlds.

By 1734 Francis, the only son of Francis and Mary Roberts concerning whom information is available, had left Chilcombe and was settled at Hembury, one of the many stone seventeenth-century farmhouses which still dot the Asker valley. At Chilcombe the Roberts family was followed by the Strongs who managed to prosper on the difficult land. A testament to their tenacity is the stone barn built in 1816, a year when a wet summer, early snows, rising poor rates and a shortage of money beat many farmers to their knees. The immunity of Chilcombe Manor from the general distress may have been due not so much to hard work on the land as to quick communications with the coast which enabled smuggled goods to be moved inland.[1] The tragic death of the Strong heir in the 1840s left Chilcombe with a ghost and with new tenants, the Samways, who held the farm until after the Second World War. The Samways, cousins of the Strongs, were a Loders family who grew hemp in the late eighteenth century,[2] but not to the exclusion of other crops. Their balanced farming enabled them to survive the disasters of 1816, the depressions of 1821-22 and 1829-30 and to take up the tenancy of about 300 acres at Chilcombe. Here with the help of his Dorset Horn flock, Frederick Samways navigated the treacherous 1880s so that not only were his sheep prize winners at Poundbury Fair but he was one of the few West Dorset farmers who at that time owned a threshing machine.

From Askerswell Francis Roberts moved to the sleepy valley of the slow-moving Bride where he settled at Bredy Farm. Here the field names, *Nighthays, Bathays, Washfield,* and *Eweleaze* still tell their own tale of dairy and sheep farming. Roberts' consequence as a West Dorset farmer was increased by his marriage to Grace, the sister of Major Richard Travers of Loders Court who farmed extensively and made his home a centre for the social activities of the district. Francis' character was not unlike his brother-in-law's; even his epitaph, generally silent on such qualities, allows him to have had 'kind and convivial manners'. Also, as befitted a man who was churchwarden for twenty years, he 'bore the character of an honest man'. Her life at Loders Court had given Grace a taste for being at the centre of village affairs and in 1753 she signed the churchwardens' account for Askerswell; her fellow officials were Gregory Syndercombe of Symondsbury, who also held the living of Askerswell, and George Burt. In the eighteenth century women, the fame of whose discretion and ability had spread beyond their households, occasionally held parochial office. Honour Symonds, the great grandmother of the auctioneer Giles Symonds, signed the overseers' accounts for Dowlish Wake, Somerset, for the years 1770 and 1771.

The careers of four of the five sons of Francis and Grace Roberts stirred even their drowsy neighbourhood to wonder and, finally, to the comforting realisation that the bold ones were not in the long run better off than their stay-at-home neighbours. The eldest, Francis (1748-1794), had a lifelong and eventful career at sea. As a Lieutenant he was the only surviving officer of the *Quebec* set afire during her encounter with the *Surveillante* south-west of Ushant in

---

[1] In 1964 Mr. F. Samways, late of Chilcombe, remembered exploring in the 1890s part of a tunnel reputed to have been used for storing kegs brought from Abbotsbury.

[2] See Appendix C.

1779. Francis was picked up by the enemy wearing only a signet ring and his pigtail ribbon. He escaped from the French prison to become captain of the *Helena* in which he carried despatches to Gibraltar 'through the thick of the fire of the enemy's flotilla'.[1] Despite his lifelong devotion to seafaring, Francis Roberts kept a shore base first as tenant, then as owner for a short time, at Mappercombe Farm, in the extreme south of the parish of Powerstock. The site of this 300-acre farm was well chosen as the farm stands on a south-facing slope of light, well drained brown earth, excellent for flax and hemp growing. In 1811 Francis' brother, Richard, estimated the annual value of this farm at £200, but allowance must be made for the fact that he was endeavouring to sell the property. Francis could safely leave the management of the farm to his wife, Fanny, who 'reigned at Mappercombe', dispensing affection and help to poor parishioners and to her numerous nephews and nieces, for she had no family. In 1794 Francis' career was ended, as were so many others, by yellow fever in the West Indies. He left £1,000 to his illegitimate son, Francis Cately, who was not a Roberts for nothing. He sailed to the South Seas, had himself tattooed and settled with a daughter of the King of Otaheite. She was one of those islanders whose smooth skins, graceful carriage and eyes, 'full of sensibility and expression' excited the admiration of Captain Cook's companions, who also commented enviously on the happy lot of the islanders, 'in no way concerned with the ceremony of marriage which was a simple agreement between man and woman'. This nephew's existence was characteristically remembered by his mill-owning uncle Richard (1752-1820) when he backed his petition for Admiralty hammock contracts by assuring the Naval Board commissioners that his nephew 'was married to a princess in one of those islands of the South Seas where this sort of hemp [Sunn] is grown in great quantities and has offered to load several ships annually for scarce anything'.

Richard, Francis' and Grace's second son, had married prudently if not to his complete personal satisfaction. His bride, Martha Hoskins, was a well-to-do widow who owned Burton Farm and had built Grove House. The house, built of local limestone still stands, shadowed by a large mulberry tree, one of the most attractive small country houses in West Dorset. Towards the end of their lives Richard and Martha, to use the nautical term employed by their great-granddaughter, 'parted brass rags', or set up separate establishments in Burton Bradstock, contenting themselves with an exchange of courtesies after church on Sundays.

Richard Roberts, like Thomas Hyde of Arne, was a man whose

[1] A. M. Broadley and R. G. Bartelot, op. cit., p. 20, footnote.

talents were exactly suited to the cut-and-thrust commercial climate of the late eighteenth century. His character was fully described by his daughter whose filial enthusiasm left her without full stops.

'He was very clever, very fond of new things, deeply interested in every new discovery in science and fond of art, very musical played violin and flute and had a chamber organ, trained the Church choir, very fond of Scotchmen had two as overseers . . . a great speculator, at one time made £2,000 a year but lost it by speculation always having new machinery, a great lawyer, always in lawsuits for the pleasure of it and settling the disputes of all his neighbours'.

A less breathless estimate was made by a more distant relative, J. R. Roberts, who recorded 'he made everybody's fortune except his own'.

As regards Roberts' litigatious disposition, it must be remembered that in the early nineteenth century a manufacturer was obliged to fight his own battles for lack of clearly established legal precedents in industrial and commercial fields. In many disputes it was customary to rely on the judgement of an impartial and reliable third person. In 1812 Roberts complained that barrels of 'potashes' sent from London were damaged; whereas his neighbours would have been content with a survey by a single arbitrator, Roberts wanted to 'call in a regular attorney and have a survey of two or three manufacturers'.[1] Sometimes the integrity of an individual was such that he was selected as arbitrator in nearly all local disputes. As late as the end of the nineteenth century E. A. Vince of Charmouth acted as a professional 'umpire'.

Roberts was unlikely to have agreed with any outstanding, outspoken character like Vince, so he resorted to numbers of arbitrators and, as a lawyer was generally included among them, their decisions often resulted in lawsuits.

If he failed to maintain a stable income, Richard Roberts made his mark on the spinning and weaving activities of West Dorset. Roberts was not a man to under-estimate his successes, and in 1813 he described his position as owning 'two water-spinning mills on the newest of best principles that are at present known. I have wages as cheap or cheaper than in any part of the kingdom. I have ten or twelve villages that have plenty of people in them at present unemployed that are near me with plenty of friends to assist me with looms and weavers.'

[1] Richard Roberts, Letter Books, Vol. II, entry for 2 August 1912. Throughout this chapter frequent quotations will be given from R. Roberts, Letter Books, Vols. I and II, but separate footnotes will not be given as the quotations can be easily traced by their dates.

Roberts' swingling mill[1], where the hemp or flax fibres were separated, stood on the Bride a little east of The Grove and so conveniently under the master's eye. The erection of the mill in 1803 partly accounts for the unemployment in the surrounding villages as flax and hemp swingling by hand was, like flail threshing, a great winter standby for labouring families. The separation of flax fibres was undertaken by men, while women and children worked at hemp scaling at rates of 4d. to 6d. a day. Sometimes payment was by weight; in November 1744 Gregory Syndercombe, incumbent of Symondsbury, allowed 8d. for scaling sixteen pounds of hemp.[2] This payment compares favourably with the sum the rector set aside for teaching his daughter, Edith. With surprising versatility Anne Tucker worked at weeding, clod breaking, hemp scaling and, by way of a respite, she earned 2d. a week for 'Edy's schooling' (entry for 7 July 1755).

The spinning mill, which may also have been used for swingling as processes in early mills were easily interchangeable, was built on a tributary of the Bride south-east of the church. The long, low building with its rubble walls now falling into disrepair is eclipsed by the nearby row of handsome stone cottages built in 1800. These were built for weavers for whom, before 1830, the provision of good housing was an economic proposition. Handloom weavers and even the spinners in rural mills were not divorced from life on the land. Weaving was often undertaken by smallholders or tenants. At the end of the eighteenth century it was not difficult for an enterprising man to divide his time between land and loom as there were still numbers of small livings, and sub-letting of these manorial landholdings was general. The manor of Burton Bradstock belonged among many others, including Arne, to the Pitt family. Manorial records are not available but there is no reason to suppose that the pattern at Burton differed greatly from that in other manors where livings remained recorded as separate holdings, but after 1750 were gathered slowly into the hands of a few tenants who were often anxious to sub-let fields that were inconveniently situated in their scattered holdings. This adding of living to living had been achieved by 1843 when the tithe map and apportionment show that large owners such as James Brown and Benjamin Symes held numbers of livings, mostly under ten acres, still identified by their previous owners' names. The new farmers with their sights set on profits from more intensive cultivation were unwilling to lease fields unless

[1] This process is also described as scutching.
[2] W. Stevenson, *General View of the Agriculture of the County of Dorset*, 1812, p. 292 for rates of wages, and p. 481 for quotation from H. B. Way concerning flax production in Dorset. Way estimated that one acre would produce 14-18 weights; a weight was estimated at 32 pounds, a stone at 14 pounds.

it were to sub-tenants as substantial as themselves, such as Richard Roberts' nephew, William, who rented five little holdings of under six acres from Symes. The old shuffling arrangements whereby plots were let out partly for money and partly for services had no place in the more efficient farm organisation with which landowners sought to protect themselves against the threat of the repeal of the Corn Laws.

When the harvest was bountiful, as in the glorious summer of 1813, the independent weavers were often joined by spinners. In July 1813 Roberts hesitated to accept an order for hemp yarn as 'my people are now almost all at harvesting'.

Apprentices were generally lodged in sheds which are now not easily traced around Dorset spinning mills. Millowners were reluctant to erect solid and conspicuous buildings which would draw the attention of ratepayers who viewed every newcomer as a potential pauper. When local children, for whom no living accommodation was needed, were in short supply Roberts had to make enquiries among the overseers of large, over-populated parishes such as Cranborne, Shepton Mallet and Ottery St. Mary. In applying for children from the overseers of the poor Roberts found himself in the quandary common to all labour-seeking manufacturers. Overseers wished to remove for good the children out of the parishes supporting them, while millowners like Roberts wanted a contract for an agreed term and then 'to return them at ages stipulated and not make them parishioners or . . . take them till the age of twenty-one years as apprentices'. Roberts had the reputation of being a just master so could write confidently to the Cranborne overseer that the children would 'be taken as good care of or perhaps better than at home both for food and raiment and morals, and will not have hard work to do more than twelve hours a day. Girls are most preferable.' Roberts explained his preference for girls of eight to ten years by observing they were 'generally the best workers and the most obedient to command'. Arrangements for their morals possibly excelled those for their feeding. The children were 'sent to church every Sunday and taught to read and say their catechism every Sunday about two hours'. But they were unlikely to have escaped the 'old bacon and white herrings' which Roberts was anxious to secure at a bargain price 'for the poor of the parish'. Every age turns a blind eye to cruelty, whether the overworking of children or a high rate of road accidents, which it considers circumstances render unavoidable.

The real tragedy in the lives of pauper apprentices began when their term of employment was ended. They were turned adrift unfit for work outside the mill, where they had at least had companionship and the certainty of a roof over their heads. The chief openings for girls on leaving the mill were marriage, domestic service, where the greater skill of small farmers' daughters gave them the preference, or the workhouse again. To face the struggle before them girls needed courage beyond that displayed by Burton's bravest sons. The numbers of these girls was probably never high because, as Roberts explained to the Cranborne overseer, it was seldom he needed 'more children than my parish can furnish'. The 1841 census returns tell the tale of decline in flax and hemp spinning; out of the total female population of 330 only sixteen were engaged on this work and of these only two were not born in Dorset. The elder of these two, who were sisters, was thirty years old so might have been imported by Roberts just before his death in 1820. In 1851 the women employed as 'factory servants' mostly came from Burton Bradstock. A few came from villages like Little Windsor and Wootton Fitzpaine where home spinning had been general before 1815. We can only conclude that the fate of Roberts' obedient little girls was, like that of Jo in *Bleak House*, 'to be hustled, and jostled, and moved on'.

Adam Smith's confident belief that only the end of government control was needed for the individual to achieve his, and society's, ultimate good was propagated at an auspicious time. In the mid-eighteenth century England was so clearly obtaining mastery at sea by drive and individual aggression that this policy set the pace for adventurers in industry. Some, like Richard Roberts, could sustain the combat undaunted personally, if not financially; others, like Richard's younger brother, William (1757-1811), were not tough enough to survive the rough and tumble. In 1811 William's drapery business in Bristol went bankrupt and soon after he died. William's wife and two daughters were salvaged from the wreck by Richard, less perhaps from compassion than a desire to contribute 'to the shame and mortification of those who were the means of pulling him [William] to pieces so unmercifully'. Rather in the same spirit Richard seems to have rescued from bankruptcy Thomas Roberts, whose claim to be Richard's brother was never directly denied. Thomas was employed at Grove Mill in a capacity described by his brother as 'servant', but in his own estimation as general assistant. In either capacity Thomas displayed the Roberts enterprise in a fashion singularly inconvenient for his family by stealing the cash books and collecting for himself debts due to his brother amounting to £200. After 'a grand personal struggle' Richard finally wrested the books from Thomas who was forced to make a public declaration disassociating himself from all activities at the mill. His ill-luck with southern assistants explains Richard's liking for Scottish foremen.

The year before the trouble with Thomas, the foreman at Grove Mill, Samuel Hoare, after learning 'the secret part of the business' took the information and his services to rival millowners at Castle Cary. Hoare was even bold enough to try, after his departure, to force his way into Grove Mill for more information. Roberts could hardly find words enough to express his fury: ' . . . you went in and took a survey of the works in the second room and not content with that you went into the lower room and there took a survey also and with more daring impudence took a tool and made some attempt to work with it, this by way of bravado to your impudence'. It is not surprising that his outburst concluded with a demand for written and publicised apologies unless Hoare was prepared 'to try the issue at the next assize'. The stronghold of Richard Roberts' secrets was further breached in the same year, 1812, by 'a stout big man with a burley face' who claimed to have received instructions to undertake repairs and made 'clear off' with some of the Grove Mill heckling machinery. So the captains of industry copied, for their more humdrum activities, the resourcefulness and drive of those at sea.

Robert (1758-1827), the fourth son of Francis and Grace, put his energies into acquiring land. By the end of the eighteenth century investment in land, when an increase of 15 per cent to 20 per cent on the landlord's outlay was not unusual[1], was as tempting as that in industry. Robert did not stray far from the heavy, poorly drained gleys of the Bride valley; he farmed successively at Gorwell in Long Bredy, Bredy Farm and at St. Luke's in Shipton Gorge. Neither the lands around the valley farms nor the 'wild heath country' of Gorwell were favourable for corn growing even when prices were at their most tempting; but the prices of butter and mutton also rose, though less spectacularly than those for barley and wheat. Gorwell was much favoured by foxhunters, and early in the nineteenth century the farm was leased by William Symonds, an ardent sportsman. But even his enthusiasm was outdistanced by that of the Frenchman who remarked when the well-known hunting parson, William Butler, was taken ill at a kill near Gorwell, that it was a pity the parson 'had not died as we could cry who-whoop over de fox and de Billy Butler at de same time'.[2]

Like other members of his family, Robert felt extra exertions would ensure increased profits so he set off for Scotland. In the early nineteenth century just when Sir Walter Scott was extolling misty glens and clan loyalties, Cobbett's 'feelosofers' and 'feenanciers' were stepping briskly forward to tell the world how to make money.

[1] G. E. Mingay, *English Landed Society in the Eighteenth Century*, 1963, p. 183.
[2] H. Symonds, *Runs and Sporting Notes from Dorsetshire*, 1899, p. 23.

The lesson was not thrown away on Robert who returned to Burton Bradstock, and in 1812 leased on three lives Cogden Farm which he steadily built up into one of the most thriving properties of the district. The estate did not prosper on farming alone. Already in 1812 the perspicacious could foresee an end to the farmers' 'glorious war'. Wide-awake landlords looked to the land for alternatives to their crops and stock. Outcrops of Forest Marble on the Cogden property were quarried for building stone. Purbeck and Portland quarries had a national importance but throughout Dorset small quarries provided the only local building materials in those areas where clay and chalk were lacking. Burton Bradstock, like many other Dorset villages, was built largely from the rock on which it stood.

Cogden farmhouse, rebuilt in the nineteenth century, stands in a dip encircled by gentle slopes. Not only is the land well drained but contains areas of brown earth well suited to wheat and barley growing. In 1813 Robert had good cause to join in the 'general thanksgiving for an immensely productive harvest'.[1] This was the last heartfelt harvest thanksgiving for some time. Although the 1815 act protected home-grown corn, it could not protect the unproductive farmers from the consequence of their inability, whether through lack of capital, intractable soil, mismanagement or misfortune, to meet post-war demands. In this 'fierce but silent contest carrying on between the productive lands of England and the unproductive',[2] Robert was well equipped to succeed. His business abilities, sharpened by a stay in Scotland, enabled him to foresee the possibilities of Cogden which luckily was on the market. Not only was the soil productive and well drained, a great consideration before the factory production of drain pipes, but the fields lay in a compact block on the Bridport-Weymouth road. Good barley was always in demand as 'the nineteenth century proved to be the century of ale',[3] while road communication with Weymouth and West Bay made dairy farming and sheep rearing for mutton profitable. Wool, too, was easily marketed at Bridport whence fleeces were sent by carrier to Salisbury and then by canal to London; or, more profitably, shipped from West Bay to Poole. Thomas Collins Colfox was a leading woolstapler of Bridport and his writings illustrate how sensitive a barometer trade was to the social and political climate. In 1819, the year of Peterloo, Colfox was aghast, 'the times are looking altogether dreadfully bad – men seem to be at their wits' end and nobody knows what to do, they appear not to know what to think'.

[1] T. H. Baker, ed., *Records of the Seasons*, undated last entry 1883, p. 246.
[2] F. M. L. Thompson, *English Landed Society in the Nineteenth Century*, 1963, p. 233. Quotation from *Select Committee on Agriculture*, 1836.
[3] P. Mathias, *The Brewing Industry in England 1707-1830*, 1959, p. 12.

The 1830 revolutions in Europe seemed distant affairs, at any rate until the risings of distracted labourers in November and December, so Colfox could take a more philosophic view of the 'glorious revolution' in France which would 'go on until the nations of Europe *first* and *afterwards* the whole world is renovated'. But troubles came a little nearer home with the 1832 outbreak of cholera in Dorset which caused 'a great injury to the trade'.[1] These agitations had their effect on farmers but, come revolution or calm, the population consumed beer, bread and cheese.

In the early 1840s apprehensions concerning the continuation of the Corn Laws caused a slight reduction in arable land, but even at this time over half the 236 acres of Cogden were still under the plough. Alert as he was in agricultural matters, Robert Roberts would have stared to have seen in 1964 a fine stretch of barley growing on Burton Common. This once gorse-studded slope running to the sea was an unprofitable piece of land, but it had been enclosed and was grazed in the 1840s by the indefatigable James Brown. The Common allowed Roberts easy access to the shore for his great interest, seine-fishing. This activity was already popular in the district and it gave rise to the Burton saying 'a dry seine never catches a fish', a sentiment equally to the taste of publicans – there were thirteen public houses in Burton at the end of the last century[2] – and of barley-growing farmers.

Richard Roberts had not the patience to undertake farming on the scale that his brother had done, but his temperament did not allow him to remain out of any local activities. Furthermore, he grew tired of waiting for the farmers 'to begin to croak and give way' on the question of prices, so he rented, probably as a sub-tenant since his name does not appear in land-tax assessments, fields in the neighbourhood and grew some of his own flax and hemp.

The hemp growers were more easily browbeaten into giving way than the flax producers; for, even when the Navy's need for cordage was at its height, hemp growing was still a cottage activity. Discussing hemp, Arthur Young declared in the year of Trafalgar 'that by far the greatest part that is raised in England is by cottagers'. By the end of the eighteenth century the small grower had reached the end of his productive tether and his efforts, so far as hemp was concerned, were not immediately reinforced by those of larger farmers. They needed more than a bounty of 3d. a stone to be tempted into the time-consuming job of growing hemp, which in some areas took the place of poultry rearing as a recognised source of income for women.

[1] E.M.C.H. and C.A.H., *Colfox Family Papers*, D.R.O.
[2] *The Dorset Year Book 1951-2*, p. 117, M. Ousely, article on Burton Bradstock.

Detailed returns for hemp and flax growing in Dorset are only available for the years 1789, 1791, 1792 and 1794. These show that whereas fibre production for 'shirting and sheeting' had once been general throughout the country, it had by the end of the eighteenth century became concentrated in certain districts. The light, well-drained brown earths, or foxmoulds, on the valleys sloping to the Brit and Char rivers and their tributaries were ideal for hemp and flax growing. These soils could be worked again and again to provide a fine tilth for seed beds which had to be 'rich enough to make good gardens'. In 1794 the whole county produced 3,699 stones of hemp, of which just over half was grown in Bradpole and Loders. The fact that in these parishes the majority of those claiming hemp bounties do not appear as owners or tenants in the land-tax assessments suggests that the sub-letting of small acreages to cottagers for hemp growing was general. [1] In Bradpole and Loders hemp was widely grown in open fields which had been unofficially enclosed; while in the neighbouring parish of Walditch the whole of the 1794 output of 141 stone was produced by four growers from allotments in *Walditch Common Field*. The intensive cultivation needed for hemp growing made the crop an unsuitable one for planting in open fields. In hemp-growing parishes enclosure initially benefited the small man by making available allotments which could be sub-let. Speculators, like Richard Roberts and George Udal, sometimes rushed in where the 'opulent farmers' feared to tread. The year 1789, although it opened with the dismal prophecy of 'thirteen weeks' frost, a bloody riot and a dead king'[2], marked the beginning of a boom in English exports, including ropes and nets for North America. The former colonists could thrive without the institutions of the mother country, but not, until after the mid-nineteenth century, without her manufactured goods.

Despite the fact that the cultivation of flax, like that of hemp, demanded 'the greatest nicety', and that the bounty was only 4d. a stone some substantial farmers ventured on flax cultivation. The difficulties of growing the crop were overcome by letting out land to jobbers, who paid £4 to £5 an acre and took the whole charge of the crop expecting 'nothing of the farmer but ploughing and the discharge of parochial taxes'[3]. The insignificance of the bounty was counterbalanced by the high prices to be obtained when imported flax supplies failed to reach this country. It was to break the monopoly of the well-to-do farmers that manufacturers and dealers started to rent land for flax growing.

[1] For details of production in Loders see Appendix C.
[2] B. Sheridan, *Journal*, 1784-90, ed. W. le Fanu 1960, p. 144.
[3] J. Claridge, op. cit., p. 28.

Symondsbury was the leading flax-producing parish in Dorset and its output in 1794 accounted for about a quarter of the total flax output of the county in that year.[1] In this parish flax growing was far from being a cottage affair. Leading farming families like the Pitfields, Chicks and Husseys, took the plunge into flax cultivation. They were joined by Charles Fookes and Paul Whettam, both of whom had manufacturing interests, and by speculators who hastened to sub-rent land in 1789, the year of brightening economic prospects, and in 1792 when war with France seemed inevitable. Flax growing was centred around Broad Oak, a hamlet nestling in a fertile, bowl-like depression to the north of the large parish of Symondsbury. Now only the small chapel and the imposing farmhouses of Lower Barbridge, Moorbath and Broad Oak tell the tale of early nineteenth-century prosperity and of the benevolent despotism of three generations of Syndercombes who from the rectory directed village affairs during the years 1739-1863. The majestic proportions of the old rectory, the impressive entrance of Crepe, a glebe farm, and the graceful, pillared cowsheds of Moorbath all testify to the taste, energy and wealth of the Syndercombes, who conferred the further benefit on posterity of leaving accounts of all their farming activities, including hemp growing, in which not a farthing or a half day's work is overlooked.

Where others sought profits, Richard Roberts was seldom far behind, and by the early nineteenth century he had edged himself into Symondsbury with a little estate of twelve acres 'fit for a little farmer dairyman'. Roberts' regular shipments to London in the seventy-foot schooner, *Fly*, built at West Bay,[2] included not only yarn and sailcloth but butter and flax, hemp and clover seeds of his own growing. His firm conviction that his own products, whether from mill, field or dairy, excelled all others made Roberts an excellent salesman. He had no hesitation in carrying his coals to Newcastle and arranging for the 'annual disposal of some of our best growing flax seed' in Belfast. His smallholding at Symondsbury could contribute little in the way of dairy produce, so Roberts, though he suffered from constant respiratory troubles, found time to puff around local markets in search of salted butter. His neighbour and correspondent, Captain Hardy of Portesham, considered Dorset salted butter infinitely preferable to the so-called fresh butter of London and no hint of any new commercial opening was thrown away on Roberts. As he lived within riding distance of the dairy farms of the Char valley, it is strange to find Roberts travelling for his supplies so far afield as the Okeford Fitzpaine butter market.

[1] For details of flax production in Symondsbury see Appendix D.
[2] D. Payne, *Dorset Harbours*, 1953, p. 117.

This was probably due to the fact that regular butter factors were already combing the renowned Char dairies before Roberts arrived on the scene.

Richard Roberts' flax-growing activities were in 1811 supervised by his son, Francis. Even this seemingly inoffensive occupation involved Roberts in fierce disputes with the Tax Commissioners as he refused to be taxed for the horse used by Francis. Like resentful tax-payers of every age, he wrote: 'the money I do not regard, at the same time I am aware a great part of it is going into the pockets of very unworthy men'. He then played a trump card, peculiar to his time, of threatening 'to quit my country and set agoing my business abroad whereby I should become its enemy'. The French government, during and after the war, was not averse to English manu-facturers bringing to France their machines and some of their des-pised shopkeeping qualities.

Francis (1789-1858), Roberts' second son, had drifted into the business after starting with his elder brother, Richard (1788-1842), a career in the Navy. In turn both boys went to sea under Captain Hardy and so upheld the tradition that whenever possible West Dorset men served together. Hardy himself had been a midshipman under the boys' uncle, Captain Francis Roberts. Richard's first, and last, engagement was at Trafalgar. His family were more conscious of the honour, commemorated in the Burton song, than Richard whose letters show a pathetic mixture of confidence and uneasiness. 'We have forty men wounded, nine officers and (I think) as many killed, it was a much harder action than the Nile, several in our ship say'; then later: 'I was quartered to assist the surgeons and as you may imagine it was a disagreeable one, but that was nothing after the first'. Nevertheless, Richard left the Navy in 1806 and eventually joined the home-keeping brother, William (1797-1819), in assisting at the mill. Francis' naval career was cut short by ill-health rather than inclination for he served with distinction under Captain Hardy in the *Triumph*, and later had the honour of bringing home a captured merchant ship with a cargo of French wine. The ship was wrecked to the sorrow of Francis' relatives, but possibly to the entire satisfaction of Cornishmen living along the coast of Whitesand Bay where the *Jonge Fanny* sank. After such stirring times, life at Grove House with two brothers already in the business and a managing father soon began to pall. In 1829 Francis applied unsuccessfully to Admiral Hardy for a position 'in a packet or trans-port service'.[1] The decades after 1815 were often weary ones for naval officers ashore. It was one thing to return after strenuous

---

[1] A. M. Broadley and R. G. Bartelot, op. cit., p. 157 and p. 160 for account of *Jonge Fanny*, and p. 206 for application to Hardy.

voyages to a well-run farm, as Captain Francis Roberts of Mapper-combe did, but quite another thing to undertake the daily super-vision of property. While they often prospered as landlords, as did Lord Bridport and, later, Rear-Admiral Maurice Nelson, owner of Chilcombe, naval officers did not always succeed as practical farmers. Some vainly hoped to conduct their farming operations with the brisk regularity to which they had become accustomed at sea; others started too late to become absorbed in agriculture so fell into dawdling ways, being only steadfast, like Captain Vye in *The Return of the Native*, in straining their gaze seawards. Francis cannot have found full occupation in the management of thirty-two acres, of which over half was rented out, and of Grove Mill which by 1843 was grinding corn, as it was in 1964.

Well before the end of the war Richard Roberts had realised that for manufacturers peace could only bring a fiercer competitive struggle and he prepared for the fray which he did not live to enjoy. In 1811 he was making enquiries of a correspondent as to 'what repute the gas-lights are now held in Leeds . . . I mean if they continue in good repute to adapt my mills to them another winter. Are they safe and cheap?' In the same year he was writing to London for three bags of Roman Cement, a durable mortar patented in 1796. Not only was the cement in demand to disguise the despised brick of substantial houses, but it was often used in farmhouses to strengthen walls of crumbling cob. Two months after Waterloo William was in London 'to attend some of the processes in cleaning and bleaching flax and hemp'. Only four years earlier Roberts had prided himself that 'my bleaching will be all in the usual [way], no chemical processes at all with me'. But William did not live to put his new ideas into practise. Only men well-equipped with technical knowledge could face the challence of peace; neither Richard junior nor Francis had the business ability that enabled their father to grow the flax and hemp, organise the spinning and weaving of the fibres and market the yarns and cloth.

That Richard Roberts' sons failed to show their father's drive was due to lack of opportunity rather than of energy. After 1815 England eased herself out of the post-war depression by lowering tariffs on raw material imports so as to stimulate industrial production. Foreign competition and lessening naval demands had already dis-couraged home production when in 1836 the ending of the subsidies for flax and hemp growing removed the last incentive to fibre culti-vation whether for home or commercial use. Already by 1825 Cobbett was surprised to find a woman in Sussex 'bleaching her home-spun and home-woven linen', while about twenty years later Emma Hardy's discovery in Cornwall of 'a very old woman in a very old cottage' spinning flax had all the charm of finding a fairy-tale activity come to life.[1] Some mills continued to spin imported flax and hemp well into the nineteenth century. In the 1880s the yarns spun at Horsehill Mill in Stoke Abbott were woven into bags and sacking in the village where the rattle of cottage looms was seldom silent. Mrs. Reed of Netherbury recounts how her mother trudged three miles to work a twelve-hour day in Pymore Mill, Bradpole, for 4s. a week. Mrs. Reed followed in her mother's footsteps and worked at the turn of this century in Slape Mill. As an unskilled worker she was paid 2s. 6d. a week, a sum which rose to 7s. when she became skilled enough to use a double frame for spinning. Although by the early nineteenth century the work of separating, or swingling, the fibres and of combing, or heckling, them ready for spinning could be carried out in mills, until the end of the century flax swingling was often undertaken in small shops, the sites of which are sometimes indicated by field names. Mr. Oscar Gale, whose family has long been established at Powerstock where a John Gale claimed a flax bounty in 1794, remembers two huts in Powerstock where flax was 'skimped' or separated. In his father's time, acrid smoke drifted over the village from the heaps of burning waste outside these flax shops. At Bourton in North Dorset the wheels, driven by steam, in the mills belonging to the Maggs and Jesse families were turning within living memory. The Maggs family however, had taken the precaution of supplementing their spinning activities with engineering and the manufacture of agricultural implements. A descendant of this family still living at Bourton, Captain Daniel Maggs, has explained that capital was available for this venture partly because of the profits gained from the spinning business through information gathered by an erring son who had been sent to Riga to keep him out of further trouble at home. Because of his speculations Richard Roberts was not able to leave his sons sufficient capital to try new manufacturing ventures. Furthermore the late nineteenth century was to have little room for do-all magnates like Roberts who managed his fields, his mills and his marketing, or like Thomas Hyde, who farmed, directed quarrying and clay mining, and carried on a general trade with Newfoundland. Many industries were becoming localised. The hundreds of small mills, quarries, clay pits, tanneries and breweries, that had prospered in the early nineteenth century, gradually gave way before concerns which attained national pre-eminence because some individual possessed an acute understanding of the natural wealth of a district and of public demand. Wedgwood mastered not only the properties of his native clay but also the taste of his age; similarly

[1] E. Hardy, *Some Recollections*, 1961, p. 42.

the breweries of the Midlands using the vaunted gypsum-bearing waters of the Trent, met the needs of urban populations no longer bound by provincial patriotism to their home brews. Only a few old inhabitants now remember that Dorset ale was once 'particularly celebrated, and in some respects unequalled'.[1]

Had the heirs of small undertakings possessed demonic energy they could hardly have set the wheels in motion again, so they were obliged to seek other openings. Their fathers had often been land-owners as well as merchants and industrialists; but farming was not an attractive opening after the 1870s, even if the family estates had been retained; and work as a subordinate in a great industrial concern was hardly more attractive. Large undertakings, furthermore, were not plentiful in Dorset. The Gundry family of Bridport, the clay-mining Pikes, the quarrying Mowlems and the brewing Popes had built solidly enough for their concerns to support generation after generation, but the descendants of small, out-distanced, business families had to shift for themselves. Thomas Hyde's son found a calmer refuge in the Church than he had known in the storm-centred home of his childhood. The process was reversed with the sons of Francis Roberts who discarded the quiet, dawdling peace-time life of their father for service with the Peninsular and Orient Steamship Company. The directors of this company early realised that the screw propeller and the increasing numbers of eastward-bound travellers were changing the once-in-a-lifetime attitude with which eighteenth-century passengers faced long sea voyages. By the 1860s developing colonies were needing educated settlers; Martin Chuzzlewit, who arrived rather prematurely as an architect at an American Eden, was among the first of a long line of middle-class emigrants. The new types of settlers – schoolmasters, doctors, lawyers and missionaries – demanded quicker communications with England. The Cunard, the P. and O. and the Steamship Navigation companies all catered for the new emigrants who, unlike the earlier settlers, were more anxious to retain than to sever connections with their homeland.

Francis Roberts' two sons, William and Richard, became captains of P. and O. liners; in turn each commanded the *Valetta* running in the 1860s between Marseilles and Alexandria. William eventually became the P. and O. Company's agent at Suez until 1891.[2] His fifty years' service spanned a time of great increase in his company's activities and a change in the public attitude towards colonies which came to be regarded as cornerstones of the new imperial edifice

[1] J. Britton, *Beauties of England and Wales*, 1803, p. 324.
[2] Information kindly given by Mr. B. D. O. Jones, Librarian for the P. and O. Company.

rather than millstones round the taxpayer's neck. Richard died in 1861 from the effects of exposure at sea. He left a youthful son to the care of relatives who, mindful of the Roberts' background as well as the need to get the boy settled as soon as possible, entered him in the Navy. Whereas his great-uncle and namesake had made enough prize money to buy Mappercombe, Francis' moderate prizes from slaves released from traders off the coasts of Zanzibar allowed him to keep only Grove House which remained in the hands of his daughter until 1935.

The sluggish Bride no longer drives any water wheels, the Cogden quarries are overgrown and the brisk rattle of the carts of fish dealers, or 'jutes', is no longer heard on Burton cobbles; but the link with Trafalgar long remained. In 1964 Grove House was in the hands of Colonel Adair, descendant of Captain Adair of the Marines, who, during the engagement at Trafalgar, endeavoured to move the body of the mortally wounded Scott, Nelson's secretary, out of the admiral's sight.

NOTES ON SOURCES USED FOR CHAPTER IV

Verbal Sources

This chapter would have been impossible to write without the very kind help of Miss D. S. Roberts of Southsea. Miss Roberts not only gave me much verbal information of her family, she also allowed me to see family papers and portraits and a MS account of the Roberts family by J. R. Roberts from which I have largely drawn for material. Miss Roberts kindly allowed the reproduction of the photograph of her father, Captain Francis Roberts.

For information concerning hemp and flax spinning at Bourton I am greatly indebted to Mrs. D. Moore. As the late Mr. Robert Moore's mother was a Jesse, Mrs. Moore was able to tell me much concerning the Jesse family. She also kindly allowed me to see over her home, Ivy Lodge, owned by the Jesses since the 1760s. In some rooms few changes had been made during the last century, so the dwelling house is as interesting historically as the adjacent mill and rope walk. This unit, no longer in Mrs. Moore's possession, is unique in Dorset and should be preserved at all costs. Mrs. Moore also kindly lent me a book giving the sums paid to ball winders at the Jesse factory for the years 1851-53, and allowed photographs to be taken.

Captain Daniel Maggs was good enough to give information concerning the spinning activities of his family in Bourton.

For the Brit and Char valleys information concerning flax and hemp was very kindly given by:

Mr. Oscar Gale, Powerstock.

Mrs. E. Reed, Stump Cottages, Netherbury.

Mr. W. Wakeley, Stoke Abbott.

Written Sources

A. M. Broadley and R. G. Bartelot, *Three Dorset Captains at Trafalgar*, 1906.

As well as describing the careers of Thomas Hardy, Charles Bullen and Henry Digby, the authors in a long and discursive book give much information, for which the sources are not always quoted, of other naval officers, many of whom came from West Dorset.

Proceedings of the Dorset Natural History and Archaeological Society, 1960, Vol. 82, pp. 143-154, J. Pahl, The Rope and Net Industry of Bridport.

Dorset Record Office.

Letter Books of Richard Roberts, Vol. I, May 1807–Sept. 1815.

Vol. II, Jan. 1811–Dec. 1813.

Richard Roberts' personal affairs had a large place in his business correspondence; both home and mill activities were described with his characteristic vehemence. For this reason the letters give an excellent picture of Roberts' bustling and disputatious habits, but contain too few details of prices, wages and profits to provide a clear insight into the day-to-day economy of mill-owning in the early nineteenth century.

Records of payments of Hemp and Flax Bounties.

The records for 1789 and 1791 give the names of the bounty claimants, their place of abode and the sums paid. Those for 1792 and 1794 give in addition the locality and names of the fields where crops were grown. A summary of hemp and flax production 1786-1791 is given with the bounty returns but appears incomplete as, except for 1791, the estimates are far below those quoted in Claridge, op. cit., p. 30. The D.R.O. estimates for Loders and Symondsbury, hemp and flax-growing parishes, have been summarised in Appendices C and D.

The Syndercombe Accounts.

The two volumes of the accounts of Gregory Syndercombe senior cover the years 1740-1755 and 1755-1764, while those of his son, also Gregory Syndercombe, are for 1788-1799. These accounts are invaluable as they show day-to-day expenditure on eighteenth-century farms down to the very smallest items. Expenditure on education, clothing and household repairs is also entered. Luckily for posterity Gregory Syndercombe senior was not a clergyman who thought the world could be too much with him.

Castle Hill House, the Gothic bakery

CHAPTER V

The Blackmoor Vale:
Lives of Casualties
and Expedients

*Social unrest among all classes 1815-1830 –
beginnings of rural distress in the mid-
eighteenth century – description of the Blackmoor Vale – fertility and poverty – the agricultural riots of 1830 in Dorset – their
violence and suppression in the Blackmoor Vale
– the aftermath.*

'After all that Legislation has done, or may do, the Poor
must be left very much to the care and kindness of their
more wealthy and natural Protectors. The Poor must
live, to use their own forcible and homely expression,
"from hand to mouth". Their lives are lives of casualties and expedients; their Protectors must guard them
from the evils of the one, and guide them through the
difficulties of the other.'

> D. O. P. Okeden, *A Letter to the Members of
> Parliament for Dorsetshire on the Subject of Poor
> Relief and Labourers' Wages,* 1830.

THE BLACKMOOR Vale is like Fournier's lost domain; it is easier
to describe this valley 'where the fields are never brown and the
springs never dry' than to define its geographical position. William
Barnes and Thomas Hardy have made us so familiar with the elm-

studded pastures of the Vale that we are surprised to see them actually stretched before us. To those living in the Vale it is the world beyond the encircling chalk hills that is unreal; in its green remoteness illusions flourish as luxuriantly as the meadow grasses. Here a hundred and thirty-seven years ago men cherished the most dangerous of all illusions: the belief that the thriving will heed the cries of the downcast. Men, to whom the world outside the Vale hardly existed, had long years in the Antipodes to meditate on their error. Their crime was that they had sought too ardently the domain lost a century earlier; or, in their own words:

'Our venerable fathers remember the year
When a man earned three shillings a day and his beer,'

During the sad winter's tale of 1830-31 the labourers were not the only searchers for the dimly-remembered joys of the past. The Home Secretary, the squires, tradesmen, farmers and half-pay officers all found it hard to come to terms with contemporary society. If unable to adjust themselves, these men could at least ensure that their children were at home in a society which paid lip service to old values, while drawing sustenance from the new industrial society. The labourers could find no expedient by which their children might escape from the casualty of having to live as agricultural labourers in the mid-nineteenth century.

John Claridge was not the man to be under the spell of any lost domain; for him the Vale of Blackmoor extended 'from North to South about nineteen miles from Gillingham and Silton, to Duntish and May Powder; and from East to West from Compton and Sutton, about fourteen miles, to North Wootton and Long Burton, and contains upwards of one hundred and seventy thousand acres of very rich land, chiefly grazing, dairying, and about one tenth part in arable, with some plantations of orchards'. In this favoured Vale, enfolded by Hardy's 'langourous' atmosphere, were bred the most determined of the Dorset rioters who rose in 1830. Their world was a small one but they were driven by impulses which stirred men from the Shannon to the Danube. Revolutionaries are driven by double motives; their personal sorrows and frustrations, and anger that they belong to a class to whom society accords work but neither security nor responsibility. The shadowy lives of the Blackmoor Vale rioters gain substance if viewed against a background not only of Dorset affairs but also those of the Continent. Also, in studying popular risings it is just as important to ascertain the views of the established and quiescent sections of society as those of the men in revolt. These views were often expressed in local newspapers, which have been widely used in this survey.

As well as catering for the established classes county newspapers

met the needs of a larger section of the community, those aspiring
to a settled position in society. The outlook of school masters and
mistresses, of shop-keepers, of horse dealers and entertainers was
largely moulded by the newspapers in which they so frequently
advertised. More than anything else those struggling to achieve
security feared a social upheaval. Liberal newspapers like the
Western Flying Post, often known by its alternative title the *Sherborne
Mercury*, had to tread warily. Even so their views were often
violently attacked by editors of the conservative *Dorset County
Chronicle*, one of whom wrote of his rivals, much in the style of Mr.
Pott of the *Eatanswill Gazette*, 'we ask the few who look at their paper
if they have not made their journal a *hortus siccus* of Democracy? If
their pen does not leave on every page over which it passes, a slimy
trail of sedition and infidelity?' *The Times* reported the trials of
the 1830 rioters in greater detail than the local papers, but it was not
until the 1840s that this national newspaper became the champion
of the Dorset labourer. This advocacy was not altogether to the
taste of the county and on 7 January 1847, the editor of the *Poole
and Dorsetshire Herald* put *The Times* in its place as being 'an organ
we are obliged to say, fast taking up a position without authority,
without feeling, without good intent and without truth'.

The placing of the 1830 disturbances in Dorset against a wider
background in no way lessens the individual tragedies of the
labourers who came to the fore; but to direct the light of investigation only on the group of men participating in the riots is to throw
contemporary society into shadows which are too unrelievedly dark.
Today if we followed the broken lives of the seriously injured on our
roads every year or of the forgotten aged, our society would appear
unashamedly ruthless and lacking in humanity. The discontent of
the agricultural labourers was shared by all classes of rural society,
not only in England but throughout Europe. Town dwellers on the
Continent may have sighed for the order and opportunities fleet-
ingly enjoyed under French occupation, but countrymen dreamed
of a return to the carefree days of plenty enjoyed under some dimly-
remembered national hero. While few Englishmen sighed for the
golden age of King Alfred, landowners, farmers and labourers were
not at ease in the years between the fall of the first and second
Napoleonic Empires. Around these three basic groups, and often
belonging to one or other of them revolved the clergy, attorneys,
shopkeepers, craftsmen and servants. All of these save the clergy and
lawyers, felt in 1830 that their bright morning expectations of a
century earlier were giving way to a grey and long-stretching afternoon of frustration. The squires sighed for the profits and prestige
which landowning had ensured in the 1770s and 1780s; while far-

mers felt that harvest profits were doomed once the necessity for protection had been questioned. The labourers, too, had memories of the better days their grandsires rather than their 'venerable fathers' had known, when a man's whole energy and time were not expended on work under the eye of a master. If the men who maintained the economy of Dorset felt that the good times had passed, those who supplied them with beer, tea, boots, saddles and carts necessarily shared the view. In so steadfastly looking back all classes of rural society were in danger of being incapacitated from ever moving forward. Only the clergy, lawyers and manufacturers had firmly turned their backs on their tarnished images of the mid-eighteenth century and determined that their activities should assume a nobler aspect.

The predicament of landowners, farmers, and of rural shop-keepers and craftsmen was one of struggling to survive in a country which no longer looked to the soil for its wealth. At a time when his wealthier neighbours realised they might have to look further afield for profits, the agricultural labourer found himself bound to the soil which no longer offered him a living. This fact was only accepted after the back-breaking struggle to survive that lasted nearly a century.

This struggle started earlier than is generally imagined. The year 1750 is often taken as the high-water mark of village prosperity in England. It was widely believed that after that date the peasant gradually lost his land, his grazing rights, his independence and his self-respect. In times of stress what men believe to be true is as important as the actual truth, but the risings of 1830 will be seen in better perspective if some scrutiny is made of the alleged time of plenty in Dorset. By the mid-eighteenth century most large villages in Dorset had their Houses for the Poor and in every parish the community was pulling along landless labourers who could not find, or keep, regular employment. In Bere Regis, largely an open parish, the Poor House had to be rebuilt and enlarged in 1749. West Dorset was traditionally the area where the small farmer lived in good fellowship and rude plenty with his labourers. But in Whitechurch Canonicorum the House had its inmates by 1755 and later relief payments in Charmouth were increasing to such an extent that 'at a Special Vestry it was unanimously agreed that all persons, receiving any pay of the parish, who shall not attend some place of Divine Service both in the morning and afternoon shall be stopped of their pay'. In the extreme west of the Blackmoor Vale the overseers of Beer Hackett were repairing the Parish House in the 1760s. The small towns were no more able to offer all their inhabitants a living than the country parishes; the Sherborne workhouse opened in

1738, and Poor Cottages existed in Gillingham by 1753.[1] Had Ebenezer Scrooge made his misanthropic enquiry concerning the operation of the workhouses in Dorset in the mid-eighteenth century the answer would have been, as it was in London a hundred years later, 'very busy'.

The rebuilding or enlarging of workhouses and slowly mounting expenditure on relief tell their tale of poverty and, in villages, of the plight of the landless labourer. Some open land, for either tillage or grazing, still existed in 1750 in the majority of Dorset parishes, but rights in open fields had often become restricted, as at Arne, to a small number of manorial tenants who were well removed from the labouring class. Many manor courts continued to function into the nineteenth century, but small men had dropped from the jury as they had from vestry meetings. Jurors by the late eighteenth century were leading tenants increasingly concerned with maintaining their own rights and those of the lord against the infringements by cottagers, such as cutting turf at Arne and furze at Frampton. The courts, providing the customary forms were observed, put no obstacles to hinder a single tenant obtaining a number of arable holdings or grazing rights. No machinery existed to protect the interests of the smaller tenants once their lifeholds ran out. Even if such machinery had existed the courts lacked power to enforce their rulings. Already in the sixteenth century Tusser contemptuously observed that the jurors:

'Determined at Court what they shall,
Performed is nothing at all'.

In Tusser's day the small copyholder still had a say, however ineffective, at manor courts and also at vestry meetings. By the mid-eighteenth century the small man carried little weight in either manorial or church affairs. The right of all ratepayers to vote at vestry meetings had not always prevented the small ratepayer from being over-ruled by his more substantial neighbours. But a seal was set on his inferiority in 1818-19 when plural voting was established in favour of the man of property, and also the right to set up select vestries, always of substantial ratepayers, to appoint and direct the overseers of the poor.[2] The offices of parish clerk, sexton and bellringer remained in the hands of the villagers, but their scope was

---

[1] Information concerning workhouses has been obtained from: The Overseers Accounts of Bere Regis, April 1749; of the Abbotts Wootton Quarter of Whitechurch Canonicorum, January 1755; and of Beer Hackett, 1762. The entry in the Charmouth Vestry Book for October 1784 was kindly shown me by Mr. R. W. J. Pavey of Charmouth; The Memoranda Book of John Toogood of Sherborne, D.R.O.; The Manor Court Rolls of Gillingham, November 1753.

[2] J. L. and B. Hammond, *The Village Labourer*, 4th ed. 1927, p. 158.

limited by the new clergy who were aware of the spiritual needs of their humble parishioners but not of their need to play some part in parish affairs.

The fact that in 1750 the outward form of village life appeared to have hardly changed has deceived social historians, as it did contemporary observers, into believing all was as it had been. But new blood was coursing through the hardened arteries of manorial and parochial bodies. The Drax family had superseded the Turbervilles at Bere; as copyholders of the Gillingham manor the Matthews family had taken the first steps towards becoming landed proprietors. Open field strips were gradually amassed by a few families who, when they bothered to attend, dominated the manor courts. Similarly the influence of substantial ratepayers increased at vestry meetings, the direction of which was often delegated by eighteenth-century incumbents to their little-heeded curates.

The foundations of the village community seemed firmly set in the mid-eighteenth century. Although shaken in the second half of the century, these foundations only cracked under the unprecedented strain of the population increase in the early nineteenth century. This increase came at a time when tenant farmers had little interest in manorial courts and many landowners were ready to kick down the ladder of manorial copyholding which had often helped them to rise. Meetings of vestries, unlike those of the manor courts, were of importance to both rate-paying tenants and landowners whose influence moulded parochial decisions. There was, therefore, little chance of the rising numbers of labourers finding any part to play in the village community. This absence of responsibility was as keenly resented by labourers as the fact that the rising value of land lessened their chances of keeping any remaining common rights or of renting plots of land. Labourers had to live by work alone, and Caird considered that in 1850 the wages for this work had hardly risen since 1770.

The strains and stresses on rural economy in the second half of the eighteenth century were largely due to rises in grain prices. In 1756 the general depression over failures on land and sea was intensified by a bad harvest and food riots which caused William Toogood of Sherborne to warn his sons not to let 'a covetous eye tempt you to be foremost in advancing the price of corn'. The war which England entered so inauspiciously ended triumphantly in 1763. Peace brought an extension of English possessions overseas and the inevitable dislocations at home. The cider tax remained to the 'great uneasiness and discontent' of the West; in November 1764 the poor of Beaminster rioted because of the 'exorbitant and unnecessary price of corn'. Discontent was still rife in the spring of the following year when rioters destroyed a bunting mill at Stalbridge, but were driven out of the Market by wool-combers, and attacked a mill at Marnhull. Here the crowd was repulsed by 'sixteen stout young fellows of the parish, famous for good back sword players'.[1] The crowds were overcome by chance rather than conviction. The wool-combers, a remarkably independent body of men, and the 'stout young fellows' were as likely to have accounted for 'many broken heads and bruised limbs' among the constables as among the rioters. The ineffectiveness of parish constables was apparent in the sixteenth century when the Tudors saw the shadow of a rising behind every group of wandering beggars, but no better system of maintaining order had been found two hundred years later. The pride of the Frenchman who observed that the horrors of the 1780 Gordon riots in London 'would be inconceivable in a city as well policed as Paris'[2] was understandable if not substantiated by subsequent events.

The disturbances of the 1760s were temporary outbursts. Only in the 1780s did the gentry, clergy and parish officials realise that discontent, previously attributable to some specific cause, had become an ever-present Banquo's ghost at the national feast which was being enjoyed by landowners, farmers, merchants and manufacturers. Steam was not yet the Englishmen which Emerson declared it to be in the 1830s, but the increasing use of power-driven machinery, expanding overseas trade and improved farming methods brightened the prospects of all classes save the agricultural labourers. We seldom give the eighteenth century credit for the reflective earnestness and sense of moral purpose which so many men displayed. Aided by economic theory, Victorians often came to terms with the misery and poverty of the labouring classes more easily than their fathers and grandfathers had done. From 1780 onwards poured forth a steady stream of pamphlets offering every possible solution to the paradox of one section of the community becoming more poverty stricken and hopeless as the nation bounded into greater self-confidence and wealth. The appearance of these badly printed publications and their frequently ill-arranged contents have caused them to be overlooked. But many squires, parsons, professional men and minor officials put their very hearts into these little books now collecting dust on library shelves. The good feeling

---

[1] Accounts of disturbances appeared in the *Western Flying Post*, 4 December 1764; 6 November 1764, and 25 February 1765 and were quoted in the *Western Gazette* under 'News from the Past'. The dates were kindly verified by the Editor of the *Western Gazette* which was amalgamated with the *Western Flying Post and Sherborne Mercury* in 1867.

[2] G. Rudé, *The Crowd in the French Revolution*, 1959, p. 26, referring to the view expressed by L. S. Mercier in *Tableau du Paris*, 1783, pp. 22-25.

that prompted these efforts was often more commendable than the solutions offered. Pamphlets for and against enclosures winged their way like envenomed darts from study to study; morals, education and household economy were also considered, though not with the crusading zeal with which men of the mid-nineteenth century approached these subjects. Nearly all pamphlet writers carefully skated round the thin ice that covered the possibility of increasing wages.

The government of Pitt the younger at last got its head above the sea of suggestions and advice; the Speenhamland Act of 1795 was passed and the laws of settlement were relaxed. These measures enabled the poor to exist if not to live, the government to turn its attention from revolution at home to war abroad and the controversialists to break out again into full cry. The Speenhamland Act provided the magistrates with a standard, to be used at their discretion, by which relief was granted on the basis of the price of bread and the size of the family. A fatal provision was included enabling wages, which fell below the accepted standard of relief, to be subsidised from the poor rates. A man could exist if he stayed in his home parish, but he was not encouraged to better his prospects further afield even by the new Poor Removal Act. By this act a migrant could only be bundled back to his place of settlement if he actually became chargeable on the rates of his new home. By the 1830s it was at last obvious that no further tinkering could improve the parochial machine so that central authorities were instituted in the place of the old parish management. Professor Redford has shown that the modification of the Settlement Laws did little to encourage long-distance migration from depressed areas to those of industrial expansion. Of the 4,323 migrants moved under the auspices of the Poor Law Commissioners during the years 1835-37 the majority were drawn from Suffolk and those counties stretching south-west from Norfolk to Wilts. Only ten came from Dorset,[1] a number of which included the Painter family from Iwerne Minster. The date when Samuel Painter, a carpenter, took the plunge of moving to Manchester is not recorded, but he obviously soon regretted his temerity for appeals to his home parish in October 1836 were met with £4 from the Shaftesbury Union guardians. Once a countryman is really adrift in a city there is little likelihood of tiding him over his difficulties. In March 1837 the Painters, who must have been exceptionally clamourous, were helped back to their home parish. The result of the whole venture was that, whatever their economic position, the travelled Painters had a tale to tell for the

[1] A. Redford, *Labour Migration in England, 1800-1850*, 1926, pp. 92-93, referring to figures of assisted migrants from *Accounts and Papers*, 1843, XVI, No. 254.

rest of their lives, and the Shaftesbury Union guardians were out of pocket to the tune of £14 5s. 1d.[1]

New ideas easily reached villages like Iwerne Minster, which stood on main thoroughfares, but they seldom penetrated remote areas like the Blackmoor Vale. In this district outside views were unheeded and the ways of the Vale would have been equally unknown to the outside world if it had not been for the acrimonious, and published, exchanges of opinion between Henry Walter, rector of Hazelbury Bryan and a neighbouring magistrate and fellow clergyman, Harry Farr Yeatman.[2]

Within the half-moon marked by Hazelbury Bryan – Stoke Wake – Mappowder – Pulham were found some of the finest grasslands in Dorset and the most determined of the 1830 rioters. In early summer the heavy waterlogged gleys and brown earths of this area produce a prodigious flush of herbage. Reed grass forms a swaying wall on either side of the Mappowder – Stoke Wake lane; to walk through the fields from Stivvicks to Povert Bridge is to recapture the childhood sensation of being imprisoned by waist-high grasses and smothered in clouds of pollen. Only the nightingales and the squelching tread of cows beside the stream break the mid-day silence of these meadows. Claridge considered that the pastures watered by the Lydden and its tributaries were 'rich enough for an acre and a quarter to carry a full-sized Devonshire ox through the summer', and the meadows produced 'excellent hay' worth 40s. a ton to farmers. Even today the villages of Hazelbury Bryan, Stoke Wake and Mappowder are small islands in a sea of grassland, but much of the far-reaching parish of Pulham lies along one of the highways from Dorchester to Sherborne. At a cross roads still stands the rambling Green Man which was one of the Vale's main points of contact with the outer world.

An acre and a quarter of Blackmoor Vale pasture may have supported a Devonshire ox, but a labourer could hardly earn his keep. Of the 2,454 acres covered by the parish of Hazelbury Bryan 2,020 acres were grasslands which barely supported 77 agricultural labourers in the summer. Henry Walter in his *Letter to the Reverend H. F. Yeatman* has described how these labourers could earn 9s. a week with beer while mowing and haymaking, but this allowed little

[1] Minute Book of the Shaftesbury Union, Vol. 1, 1835-37, pp. 223, 237 and 303-4. Gillingham Museum.

[2] H. Walter, *Letter to the Rev. H. F. Yeatman acting magistrate for Dorset and Somerset*, 1833 (65 pp.) and H. F. Yeatman, *Answer to D. O. P. Okeden, Esq.*, 1839 (97 pp.). Walter supported Okeden's views published in *A Letter to the Members of Parliament for Dorsetshire on the Subject of Poor Relief and Labourers' Wages*, 1830 (19 pp.), based on the belief 'that full and fair wages . . . would go far to obviate all necessity for parochial relief'.

margin for saving against the winter months when those lucky enough to find employment earned 7s. a week. Walter reckoned that the dawn-to-dusk work of a man and his three sons under fourteen in the fields, and of his wife making buttons only produced 13s. 4d. a week, the minimum sum which, under the Speenhamland regulations, the family would have received if they had all stopped work and drawn relief. Farmers found it less burdensome to pay increasing poor rates to subsidise wages and to support paupers, who might with luck die or move on, than to establish the dangerous precedent of paying a living wage, which they feared might have to be increased with time. Only a panic like that caused by the 1830 riots reminded landowners and farmers that their rents and profits depended on labourers being able or willing to work. With the apathy of undernourished men the labourers tolerated a system which just enabled them to exist but bound them to a servile dependence on their employers and the parish overseers. A man whose diet over the years has been chiefly potatoes and tea[1] is bound to have a poor opinion of himself. The bad season of 1845 forced William Soper of Maiden Newton to beg for relief until 'the potatoes were round again'. This phrase sadly echoes the reputed saying of Irish peasants when crop failures forced them to beg at Protestant mansions, 'Good-bye, God, until the potatoes grow again'. With the same listless resignation labourers accepted the overcrowded, two-roomed cottages with their earth floors and damp walls and the humiliating visits to overseers who 'talked very rough'.[2] How this almost stupefied submission gave place to the outburst of November 1830 can be followed in the accounts of local papers, but the reasons why the labourers of Southern England reached the end of their tethers in the summer and autumn of 1830 are harder to discern. To follow the events of the year is to find possible causes, but in the last resort we are faced with the truth that, 'The wind bloweth where it listeth, and thou hearest the voice thereof, but knowest not whence it cometh and whither it goeth'.

In Dorset the spring months of 1830 cheered the farmers as the weather was 'most propitious to all growing crops';[3] but the

---

[1] H. Walter, op. cit. p. 15.

[2] *The Times*, 7 May 1846, for the account of William Soper in a letter from R. Sheridan on the Dorsetshire Poor and the *Poole and Dorsetshire Herald*, 7 February 1847, for an account of Susan Galpin's unsuccessful attempts to get relief for a dying brother and father, see p. 116 *infra*.

[3] As quotations from newspapers will be frequently used, a separate reference will not be given in each case. The extracts have been taken from the *Dorset County Chronicle*, June 1830 to February 1831; *The Western Flying Post*, June to December 1830; *The Sherborne Journal*, January to February 1831; *The Times*, 12 to 14 January 1831, gave a particularly full report of the activities of the Special Commission sitting in Dorchester.

sunshine brought little profit to dressmakers and milliners since their clients, daily expecting to go into mourning for George IV, deferred making their spring purchases.[1] The rejoicings on the accession of William IV in June were heartfelt, partly on the principle that any change must be for the better, and also because rumours of the new king's benevolence had spread so that it was firmly believed that he desired the destruction of threshing machines and the payment of 2s. a day to agricultural labourers.[2]

In Dorset the rejoicings were slightly overcast by a small cloud in the west where 'alarming destruction' by incendiaries in Bridport caused a hundred gentlemen to patrol the streets nightly. By August the whole European sky was 'shaded and cloudy'. In England haymaking was delayed and the 'exuberant' wheats had run to straw; in France the aspirations of the Bourbons had come to an equally untimely end. Forced to leave the country, Charles X, looking 'very unwell and . . . quite disconsolate', eventually landed at Poole. The harassed monarch, alarmed by the crowds at the quayside, disembarked most unwillingly and was hurried with his family and *entourage* to Lulworth Castle; the overflow had to be accommodated at Hethfelton House in East Stoke. The Prince of Orange also arrived in England 'looking pale' and with a large amount of luggage, but his stay was only a short one. This coming and going of agitated royalty was, in the Duke of Wellington's opinion, a 'bad and mischievous example' to English malcontents. But the atmosphere in the southern counties was already so charged that hearsay and rumour only intensified existing unrest and expectancy. The sight of a Bourbon flinching from a gaping Poole crowd may well have afforded Dorset labourers food for thought, but it is doubtful if they grasped the significance of the encounter.

By September the skies seemed to be clearing. Harvest fears were allayed, and the late King of France ventured out shooting in the Weld preserves. The cottagers on the Weld estate received the remnants from the lavish Bourbon board, but complained 'that the meat etc. was boiled to a *poultice* and they could not therefore enjoy it'.[3] All seemed set fair for a plentiful autumn and a festive winter. The gaiety of the Weymouth season made up for the spring losses of the milliners who presented a novelty in the form of 'a *beret*, composed of shaded blue gauze . . . ornamented only with a very broad gauze ribbon to correspond, which is fastened in two short bows,

[1] *Journal of Mary Frampton 1770-1846*, ed. by Harriet G. Mundy, 1885, p. 344. Mary was the sister of James Frampton of Moreton, near Dorchester, best known in connection with his zeal in apprehending the Tolpuddle Martyrs.

[2] *The Times*, 14 January 1831, Richard White, a constable, in his evidence of the disturbances at Handley said this belief was held in the district.

[3] M. Frampton, op. cit., p. 358.

with ends that fall nearly to the knees, on the left side'. Short reports of disturbances in Kent and Sussex first appeared in the *Western Flying Post*, but made flat reading beside accounts of the 'extra-ordinary state of fermentation' in Italy, in Belgium and the Iberian Peninsula. The destruction of threshing machines in distant Kent could be treated as a joke; a Dover man was warned of an impending attack on his threshing machine which proved to be an allusion to his forceful wife, so this 'eclaircissement turned all the serious apprehensions into merriment'. The laughter subsided when Kentish labourers 'hoisted the tricoloured flag'. In Dorset it was noted with anxiety that 'the plentiful harvest, good potato crop, remarkably fine autumn weather without frost to impede the labours of husbandry, appeared to have no effect in lessening the murmurs of discontent'. Apprehension turned to alarm when disturbances broke out in Hampshire and the *Western Flying Post* gave second place to the excesses of the 'vindictive and blood-thirsty' Conde d'Espana in Barcelona. On 22 November sullen crowds gathered at Bere Regis where they were ineffectively harangued by the magistrate, James Frampton (1769-1855), who eventually read the Riot Act at the neighbouring village of Winfrith Newburgh. Here Frampton took the spirited action of seizing a handy labourer by his smock.[1] The man wriggled out and the magistrate was left, like Cinderella's discomfited prince, holding a garment without its wearer; but a young man and two boys, who proved less agile, were arrested. The prominent part he played during the 1830 disturbances went to Frampton's head and during the next decade he peppered the Government with reports from the Dorset front[2] which began to vie with Ireland as the storm centre of the United Kingdom.

On 23 November disturbances began to erupt throughout the county. There was no concerted plan though the name of Hunt, an alias for Cooper, prominent in the Hampshire rising, cropped up during the evidence before the Special Commission; but rumours spread of two mysterious men seen riding fast through villages and towns, 'with something different from a common riding-stick' supposed to be 'some unlawful weapon or engine'. The risings in Dorset were essentially protests against unpopular individuals whose activities had long been resented but a stimulus had hitherto been lacking to goad undernourished men into action. Where the sandy heath soils give way to the rendsinas around Dorchester, Frampton

---

[1] M. Frampton, op. cit. pp. 360-362, for account of the outbreak of disturbances in Dorset.

[2] P.R.O. HO.40/36 see also R. F. Wearmouth, *Methodism and the Working Class Movements of England 1800-1850*, 1937, p. 217, for reference to Frampton's despatches to Melbourne.

had been particularly active since the end of the Napoleonic Wars. He was the Draco of the fields and idling labourers, skylarking girls and women labourers attempting to take away a few turnips all found themselves in prison. That the labourers around Bere, Wool and Winfrith were so moderate was due partly to their habits of fearful submission and partly to the sympathetic attitude of John Sawbridge Erle Drax. This sympathy was considered most ill-placed by his fellow landowners, one of whom alluded to 'the most *defiant conduct* of Mr. Drax'.[1]

The villages on the chalk downland near the Dorset-Hampshire boundary were particularly open to rumours of disturbances in the neighbouring county. These rumours added to their own particular grievances inspirited men in Cranborne, Edmondsham and Handley to rise on 23 November. A group of men, whose numbers were blown by hearsay into 300-400, followed Joseph Pope of Edmonsham and took 6s. from Richard Broncker. At his trial the bewildered Pope said he 'was to have had several characters, but he did not see any of them were come'; only a voice called out from the gallery that Mr. Sanderson Robins, rector of Edmondsham, had intended coming to give the prisoner a character 'but that he had been prevented'. Pope was transported for seven years, and his twelve children struggled on as best they could.[2] In fairness to Robins it must be added that he had an invalid wife. When dusk fell a group of Cranborne men under James Wilkins were emboldened to take 8s. 6d. from a land surveyor, a man whose profession was popularly associated with enclosures. Even more to the immediate purpose, the rioters secured 'a large quantity of beer, about three or four gallons, and some bread and cheese'. The drink made James Thick incapable, rendered Robert Zillwood 'particularly civil' when he relieved Farmer Dixon of a sovereign, and confused John Read who was not certain whose side he was on. Read was returning to Cranborne with three stolen sovereigns in his pocket when he hurried to the assistance of Lord Salisbury 'struggling with a man who had a bar of iron in his hand'. A widower of twenty-four, Read was probably as bewildered by grief as by drink; but his instinct to help an attacked man saved him from transportation. The man with the iron bar disappeared in the dark and was never arrested. Here it must be stressed that the men apprehended were not necessarily the ringleaders or the most violent, but those who were identified in the confusion by witnesses willing to come forward with evidence,

---

[1] *Proc.*, 1930, LII, pp. 84-5, W. M. Parry Okeden, 'Agricultural Riots in Dorset, 1830'.

[2] For list of prisoners and their sentences see Appendix E.

those who came within reach of the constables, and those with characters well known to the magistrates.

The village constables and tithing men had a breathless time of it during November. Chosen at the manor courts or vestry meetings, these unpaid officers hoped to pass their year of office with nothing more unnerving than a scare about lost chickens. They suddenly found themselves called out night after night to face crowds who accepted the constables' own low estimation of their authority. When a crowd gathered at Iwerne Courtney no one was inclined to take seriously the familiar shopkeeper, Thomas Burge, just because he brandished his staff of office. Constables and tithing men put all their faith in this staff for they believed with the constable in Thomas Hardy's story 'The Three Strangers', 'When I raise en up and hit my prisoner, 'tis made a lawful blow thereby. I wouldn't 'tempt to take up a man without my staff – no, not I. If I hadn't the law to gie me courage, why, instead o' my taking up him he might take up me!' George Newell 'forcibly wrested' Burge's staff from him. In the scuffle Newell's younger brother of eighteen, William, came to his rescue, but was overpowered by two men, one of them a captain in the Navy. No charge was finally brought against George, but William was sentenced to three months' hard labour for his brotherly action. He must have been a man with a strong sense of family responsibility, as twenty years later he was supporting not only six children and his own mother, but also his mother-in-law. A more daring attack was made on Walter Snook, farmer and constable at Stour Provost. On 29 November disturbances broke out in two neighbouring but quite dissimilar parishes, Stour Provost and East Stour. The manor of Stour Provost was in the hands of the Provost and Scholars of King's College, Cambridge, who still maintained in 1830 small lifehold tenements and pastures open to common grazing. Engrossment and enclosures were not among the grievances of this village which keeps, even today, a dignified and academic aloofness from bustling, down-to-earth East Stour. This parish also contained many smallholders and an exceptionally large number of craftsmen, particularly basket makers and wheelwrights. Walter Snook made some arrests for machine smashing at Stour Provost and conducted his prisoners to Shaftesbury where 'the keys of the lock-up house could not be found'. The confusion, the early dusk of a November evening and Snook's feeling that everything had been too much for him, all made the rescue of his prisoners an easy matter even by unorganised men. Where lock-up houses were not available, as at Sturminster Newton, 'the town constables had to take their prisoners to the public house and remain guard over them', or to their homes where it was 'not pleasant work to sit with a man hand-cuffed all night or to turn your children out of their beds to make [way] for the burglar, the drunkard or other bad characters'.[1]

From Stour Provost came the only farmer who joined the rioters in Dorset. The Hammonds noted that an 'interesting feature of the trials at Winchester was the number of men just above the condition of agricultural labourer who threw in their lot with the poor.[2] This was not the case in Dorset. John Dore with a strong sense of his own importance, a farm of under fifty acres and a beer-shop, in the interest of which he was accused of fomenting trouble,[3] was the nearest the peasantry got to a knightly Götz von Berlichingen to lead their cause. At the Stours machinery seems to have been attacked from wantonness rather than desperation; one of the prominent rioters was himself a wheelwright who undertook machine repairs.

The fertile brown earths around Shaftesbury tempted farmers to increase their holdings. Almost the whole of the once-open Cann Field fell into the hands of David Gillingham. He was a man of substance who built an imposing stone farmhouse, bought a threshing machine and took the lead at Cann vestry meetings. Though they were determined to prevent waste and refused relief to able-bodied men in the bleak, work-short winter of 1817-18, the Cann vestry men were not sharp enough to prevent the overseer making off in 1819 with his pockets well filled.[4] The destruction of the threshing machine which Gillingham, like many other farmers during the disturbances, left temptingly in the open to save his farm buildings, gave a focus to long suppressed resentment. The successful attack was led by the Elkins family, two of whom had prison records. George Elkins the younger saved himself from transportation by turning King's Evidence. Of the fifty-five men who came to trial at Dorchester the only other prisoner to do the same was William Stokes, a Wiltshire man involved in the Cranborne disturbances.

The riotous assemblies in the villages on chalk and those of the rich alluvial and brown earths around Shaftesbury were periphery disturbances; the heart of the rising was in the Blackmoor Vale. This judgment can only be based on the numbers apprehended, so the possibility cannot be overlooked that the Vale magistrates and constables were more zealous than elsewhere.

[1] Anonymous, Recollections of a Sturminster Newton Man, dating from about 1815. MS in D.R.O.

[2] J. L. and B. Hammond, op. cit., p. 259.

[3] The Times, 14 January 1831.

[4] Minutes of Cann Vestry Meetings, Vol. I, D.R.O.

CHILCOMBE. **28.** Sheep shearing *c* 1880 (*above*). Mr. Frederick Samways (*child extreme right*) remembers the itinerant shearers worked from 5 a.m. to 8 p.m. and expected beer and cider to be provided for nightly dances. **29.** Manor and church. Well situated for sheep rearing, barley growing and smuggling, Chilcombe launched the Roberts family in Dorset and supported later occupiers through the agricultural crises of the nineteenth century.

THE ROBERTS' DOMAIN AT BURTON BRADSTOCK. **30.** Grove Mill
(*above*). A water wheel was used in Roberts' swingling mill, built 1803,
until 1949 when it was replaced by a turbine engine. **31.** Grove House
(*below*). Except for the dormer windows, added in 1906, the house has

changed little since it was occupied by Richard Roberts. **32.** Cottages, Burton Bradstock (*above*). No friend of dissent or time-wasting, Richard Roberts squeezed in four weavers' cottages between the church and the spinning mill.

33. WEST BAY, BRIDPORT (*above*). Shipbuilding developed under the stress of the French Wars and declined with the increasing use of steam power. The launching of the 272 ton *Swift* in 1864 was the swan-song of the shipyard. **34.** Captain Francis Roberts (1850-1915) (*right*). The last of the seafaring Roberts.

THE CENTRE OF THE 1830 RISINGS. **35.** The Blackmoor Vale (*above*). Four men were transported from Stoke Wake, the village in the foreground, for their determined part in the risings. **36.** Sturminster Newton (*below*). Beside the Stour and its tributaries stretched the most fertile grasslands in Dorset.

DORSET WORKHOUSES. **37.** Cerne Abbas. Built at the foot of Wearm Common Hill, the barrack-like building towards the top left stood in bleak contrast to the supposedly carefree days before enclosure. **38.** Stoke Abbott. '*A hopeless race, that owns yon bleak abode, Of grief and care, beside the public road.*' W. Holloway.

OUTLYING AREAS AFFECTED BY THE 1830 DISTURBANCES. **39.** Cranborne (*above*). Conditions had not improved by the 1840s when Lord Ashley was distressed by 'the same vice, the same misery'. **40.** Mill, Stour Provost (*below*). Unrest quickened the pace in this slow moving parish; John Dore, innkeeper and farmer, encouraged the rioters, the rector wanted to fight them and the constable eventually arrested five men of whom one was transported.

With the Seasons Greetings

41. A smallholder of East Stour, *c* 1900. Three acres and a cow remained a Christmas-card dream, as by the 1880s agricultural labourers were determined to leave the land.

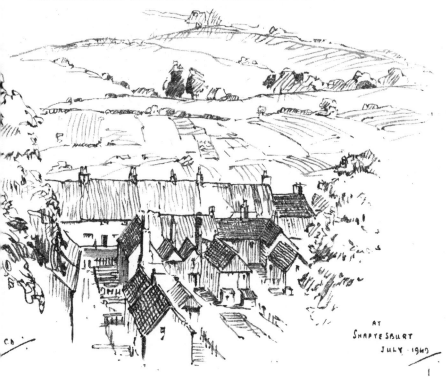

AT
SHAFTESBURY
JULY 1949

Talk in The Green Man at Pulham became increasingly spirited as November wore on, and the rumours passed from cottage to cottage along the heavily rutted lanes of the Blackmoor Vale. The new king was on the side of the labourers, payments would be made for destroying threshing machines, just as, in the good old days, churchwardens had paid for heads of vermin; 'Peel's bloody gang' had been armed with 6,000 cutlasses from the Tower: 'Englishmen, will you put up with this?'[1] These stories spread rapidly in November which was a slack month. Even without the use of threshing machines there was not enough corn grown in the Vale to provide a significant number of labourers with winter flail threshing; the meadows were not flooded so no water courses had to be cleared. Many men had to undertake parish work on the roads, and

[1] *The Times*, 13 January 1831, reported the evidence of James House of Stoke Wake in which he said that labourers believed the Government would pay them for the destruction of machines. Information concerning the new police is in a small pamphlet in P.R.O., HO. 46/25.

labourers in the gangs readily exchanged news and grievances.
Almost all the grievances of the Blackmoor Vale peasantry in
1830 might have been voiced any time in the fifty preceding years.
Henry Walter, who knew the area and sympathised with the labourers, was certain that before the risings 'the population of this
district had not been . . . in a particularly dissatisfied state'. Walter
would have dated the grievances of the peasantry from the passing
of the Speenhamland Act in 1795. Farmers asserted that chances of
increasing wages had faded with the end of the 'glorious war'. The
labourers themselves would have been hard put to say exactly when
potatoes and barley cake took the place of wheaten bread, cheese
and fat bacon and when home-brewed beer gave way to tea, or
infusions which passed for that beverage.[1] The Game Law of 1816,
by rendering a man liable to transportation for even suspected
poaching, made any attempt to vary a monotonous diet by snaring
a rabbit or pheasant a dangerous undertaking. In 1814 there were
six convictions at the Dorchester Quarter Sessions, 22 in 1815, 27
in 1816, 41 in 1817 and the same number in 1818.[2] While making
the westward descent from Bulbarrow the traveller is struck by the
charm of the valley scenery which depends on the patches of woodland breaking the patchwork regularity of the pastures and meadows. These were the coverts where pheasants were reared on food
which sometimes consisted 'with due alteration of diet for their
health of boiled rabbits chopped up small, sago, milk, rice, hard-
boiled eggs (well minced, of course), Indian corn and other suitable
delicacies.'[3]

Many centuries earlier the same loving care had been given the
deer which roamed throughout the Royal Forest covering the
Blackmoor Vale. As the woodlands gradually passed from forest
land, the assarts, or clearings for cultivation, were generally made
by individuals. The laborious felling and clearing by the family
rather than the community meant that open-field farming in the
Vale was largely restricted to stretches of land of little agriculture

[1] Mr. F. Browning of Bloxworth and Mr. W. Hardy of Longthorns both remember that, at the turn of this century, their mothers made an infusion by pouring
boiling water on charred bread crusts.

[2] Dorchester Jail Registers, D.R.O. These convictions were for poaching and
allied offences such as deer stealing and attacks on keepers.

[3] Beeton, *Field, Farm and Garden*, c. 1880-1881, p. 68. Quotation from a letter by
Reverend F. O. Morris dated 1879 on the evils of battue shooting in
Yorkshire. Francis Morris (1810-93) grew up at Charmouth, Dorset. He
luckily obtained the cure of 240 souls at Nunburnholme, Yorkshire so could
easily direct his energies to conducting massive campaigns in the press for
protecting birds from the onslaughts of gamekeepers, sportsmen and milliners,
and the public from the heresies of Charles Darwin and John Bright. His books
on British birds and moths were among the first works on natural history to
reach a wide reading public.

value, like Stoke Common, which were left open for common grazing. About 300 acres of common in the north and west of Mappowder parish were enclosed in 1807; while much of the common land
around Buckland Newton and Hazelbury Bryan was not enclosed
until the middle of the nineteenth century. But by 1830 grazing
rights on these commons had fallen into the hands of a few proprietors. In Buckland Newton about twenty-seven acres were left
for the 'exercise and recreation of the labouring poor' who certainly
had enough exercise and would have preferred the right to keep a
few geese or cows. An attempt was made to offset enclosures at
Hazelbury Bryan, some of which are still easily distinguishable on
the pleasant, elm-bounded plateau north-east of the parish church,
by letting out some five-acre plots, rent and tithe free, to labourers.
In the 1820s the rector also let out thirteen acres among thirty
labourers at £2 an acre, a considerable reduction on the £8 often
charged for potato ground.

Despite these concessions disturbances broke out so suddenly on
26 November 1830 that inhabitants of the Vale could only attribute
the eruption to foreigners.[1] In country parlance 'foreigners' could
only mean Irish labourers or gipsies. The employment of Irish harvesters was a grievance in Kent where 'every man who has ever
employed an Irishman is in constant dread of a visit'.[2] But Irish
migrants avoided Dorset and Wiltshire where they recognised a
poverty equal to their own. The 1841 census returns show that in
June, a haymaking month, only 605 Irish labourers were in Wiltshire and 645 in Dorset compared with 3,402 in Hampshire and
4,084 in Devonshire. The gipsies were also the scapegoats of rural
communities, universally blamed for thefts, fires and poaching; yet
the Dorchester jail registers show they were remarkably seldom
committed to prison. The dark looks and mysterious words of this
alien race inspired both squire and cottager with the dual feelings
of distrust and an anxiety to conciliate. Variations of the story told
by Mr. Alfred Macey of Gillingham occur throughout Dorset and
explain the circumspection of magistrates and constables. At the
end of the last century Mr. Macey was in the White Horse at
Gillingham when the publican refused to serve a gipsy woman
saying, 'We don't want any of your tribe here'. As the woman went
out she looked back to remark that the innkeeper would not long
need his licence; within the year he was dead. No one liked to accuse
the gipsies openly and by November Irish harvesters had returned
home, so the foreigners were reduced to mysterious strangers who,

[1] H. Walter, op. cit., p. 11, for account of the rector's allotment scheme, and
p. 20 for description of the outbreak of rioting.

[2] *The Western Flying Post*, 18 October 1830.

unlike the Vale men, wore 'white hats and blue smock-frocks'.[1] Perhaps the truth is that the atmosphere was so charged with old feuds, personal frustrations and long-standing grievances that the lightest rumour was enough to set all these smouldering emotions ablaze. A now-or-never feeling made men behave in unexpected ways. George Legg of Mappowder, 'as honest and as quiet a man as any in the Kingdom', found resolution and voice to declare when the Vale men rose that 'the land and tithes should come down and they [the labourers] would have higher wages'. Legg knew what he was talking about as, according to the evidence of the curate at Mappowder, he had brought up five children on 7s. a week, though his employer declared that he earned 9s. with a little extra in summer. Legg started work for this farmer at the age of about six when he must have been employed bird scaring. This was lonely work for a child; Mr. Herbert House of Buckland Newton recalls how he started bird scaring at Fifehead Neville at the age of ten in 1880, when he earned 3s. 6d. for a seven-day week. He dreaded being alone from dawn to dusk and eagerly watched for a passer-by to tell him the time so that he could place a stick in the ground and, on sunny days, have the comfort of seeing its shadow mark the passing hours.

The first act of the group which Legg joined was to destroy the threshing machine of William Coward at Woolland. Here as in all other similar cases, it is difficult to determine whether the men arrested were outstandingly determined, too slow to avoid detection and arrest, or very honest, for some rioters gave themselves up voluntarily after the outbursts had subsided. The men who took the lead in the groups which hurried from village to village on 26 and 27 November were followed by numbers of spectators who melted away when they smelt danger. The attack on Coward's machine was led by James Thorne, who was foolish enough to boast at the King's Arms, Buckland Newton, that he and Adam Thorne 'were the first two men who rose'. James Thorne may have been crossed in love; in 1822 the banns of his marriage with Susannah Legg were stopped by one of the parties, and two years later he married an illiterate Mappowder girl.[2] Both James and Adam were determined men bent on redressing their personal or economic grievances and would have proceeded to Woolland even if Coward's brother-in-law, Joseph Blandford, had not spitefully assured the crowd that 'the machine was brought out to the field for the purpose of having it broken and that the mob might go down to the house'. A local

[1] *The Western Flying Post*, 29 November 1830.
[2] Stoke Wake Marriage Register, inspected by kind permission of Mr. F. N. Kent of Stoke Wake.

magistrate, Charles Byam Wollaston, corroborated the fact that such a statement was made. James House not only believed Blandford, but this guileless young man also swallowed the story that labourers would be paid for their trouble in breaking machines. He begged for mercy 'for the sake of his wife and family. He said he had two children and *almost* a third'. House was the only one of the five Stoke Wake men who escaped transportation. He was sentenced to a year's hard labour. When the year was up he returned home to die at the age of twenty-five,[1] leaving his wife to take his place in the fields to support her three children.

The Stoke Wake rioters joined the Mappowder men for a busy day on 27 November. In the turmoil George Legg and Joseph Sheppard determined to settle an old account with Christopher Morey, a small farmer and blacksmith. Morey denied that he had had any quarrel with Sheppard and that he had threatened to transport him if he could, but he admitted there had been a 'dispute' seven or eight years ago. The two men, followed by the usual crowd of admiring yet apprehensive onlookers, knocked up Morey and demanded the pitiful sum of 1s. 6d. At first Morey blustered, asking Legg 'What do you do there with your sauce?', but eventually produced 2s. to which his agitated wife added 1s. From the newspaper reports George Legg himself seems to have been the only one of the accused men able to stand up for himself in the court. His employer and other farmers, as well as the curate of Mappowder, all spoke warmly of Legg's industry and honesty, but even without this support we have the impression that he would have been master of the situation. When Mr. Justice Alderson was in full swing of a moral homily on the benefit to a prisoner of a good character, Legg interrupted him to declare, 'I would rather that your Lordship would put twenty-one years transportation on me than be placed in the condition of the prosecutor [Morey]'. Legg's tragedy was not that he was sentenced to six month's hard labour for his part in the disturbances, but that with so many good qualities that the judge himself was moved to say, 'I have never heard a better character given of any man', he had no part to play in the community. The labourer's voice was only heard in village life when he applied for relief. Poverty excluded him from vestry meetings and from manorial courts, where these still assembled, and delayed the development of Friendly Societies which gave the humble subscriber some chance to voice his opinion. In 1831 it was estimated that the ratio of the number of persons in Friendly Societies to every 100 of the population was 5 in Dorset, 8 in Wiltshire, 12½ in

[1] Stoke Wake Burial Register for 31 January 1832.

Devon, $4\frac{1}{2}$ in Hampshire compared with 17 in Lancashire.[1]

George Legg was also in the crowd that surrounded John Pount's farm at Buckland Newton, 'with a great noise and blowing of horns', and smashed the threshing machine. James Venables, vicar of Buckland Newton 1805-50, tried to disperse the men with the soothing words that he would call a vestry meeting 'and make everything agreeable to them'. By this time villagers had no faith in vestry meetings and the crowd swept onwards. Although a magistrate and responsible for committing most of the Blackmoor men, Venables was staunch in his support of local men. He told the court the 'Mapperdown men behaved themselves better than men of most disturbed villages'. Venables was buried within a stone's throw of his rectory and his table-stone bears the curiously ambiguous epitaph: 'What he is what he was and what he shall be will best be known at the day of judgement'.

Machines were attacked in the Vale not so much because they caused serious unemployment in this pastoral area but because they symbolised the impersonal power of the farmer over his labourers. He could harness their energies to a machine which, as Tess of the D'Urbervilles found, 'kept up a despotic demand upon the endurance of their muscles and nerves'. While young married men may have feared the loss of winter work, older men primarily dreaded the speed of the machines. Few of the men committed to prison in connection with the 1830 riots had escaped injuries to their hands. These were mostly from the slipping of bill hooks, but James Hobbs, a basket maker of Henstridge, was surprisingly marked by 'a codfish bite in the hand', probably due to a spell in the Newfoundland fisheries. Injuries from hooks and scythes, from falls and from attacks by livestock were known and accepted hazards; but the whirring knife of the chaff cutter, the rapidly rotating drum of the threshing machine and, later, the exposed blades of the mowing and reaping machines, presented new and more alarming dangers. Both Mr. Walter Tucker of Stour Row and Mr. Frederick Wills of Beer Hackett described how, at the end of the last century, old men tried to halt the use of mowing machines by hiding stones in the grass to break the blades and turn farmers against machinery. In 1830 George Jesty of Puddletown was convinced that his labourers at Druce Farm were anxious to be freed from 'the slavish work' of flail threshing. Young single men may have felt the fascination of machinery, but fathers, thinking of the family's winter bread, and elderly men, preferred the old ways. These might have proved less

[1] P. H. J. Gosden, *The Friendly Societies in England 1815-1875*, 1961, p. 23, quoting from *The Select Committee of the House of Lords on the Poor Laws*, 1831.

troublesome in the long run for Jesty too, as he was sued for the payment of his threshing machine.[1]

Except for the rotating drum and the bars of the stationary concave the threshing machine was mainly constructed of wood. This explains how machines were so easily destroyed and why their maintenance was entrusted to wheelwrights and carpenters. John Major, carpenter at Pount's Buckland Newton farm, must have loved his machine, as he hid the iron work in a withy bed when he suspected trouble. Charles White, in his evidence, denied revealing the hiding place despite James New's assertion that 'ne'er a man would have known where the machine was' without White. But as James New, who had a previous conviction for felony, and Charles Coombs smashed 'the Great Wheel' they were transported, while White was not even arrested. In their committals of rioters magistrates were as anxious to rid their districts of suspected characters or potential trouble makers in the future, as they were to ascertain exactly who was responsible for damage or for robbery. Among the thirty or so men trampling round Pount's farm in the early dusk of a November afternoon were two middle-aged labourers, George Jackson and John Durrant. Both men were given excellent characters by James Venables and their participation in the disturbances was more on their children's behalf than their own. Their efforts failed, for the children of both men led the same life of grinding poverty that their fathers had done. Jackson battled into old age with the help of a charity blanket and button-making daughters, while John Durrant, despite his ten children, died a pauper at eighty-one. Even the irrepressible George Legg may have subsided at last in a charity blanket.[2]

Energy, honesty and skill could earn a labourer no reprieve from a life sentence of labour; and his attitude is best expressed by Mr. William Hardy of Longthorns who, looking back on his life as a farm worker, declared, 'however much you worked and scrambled, the farmers just wiped their boots on you'. So far as their careers can be traced after 1830, neither the rioters who returned home nor their children bettered their estates. An exception was young John

[1] *The Dorset County Chronicle*, 13 January 1831, for G. Jesty's letter in praise of threshing machines and 17 March 1831, for the case of Raynard, ironfounder of Weymouth, v. G. Jesty.

[2] As there were two George Leggs, of approximately the same age, in Mappowder, it is impossible to be certain that the Legg who obtained a charity blanket in 1848 and died in the same year, was the man who stood up so firmly to both judge and prosecutor. Information obtained from the Mappowder Burial Register and a MS notebook giving the distribution of charity clothing and blankets, 1847-48, both in the Mappowder parish chest and inspected by kind permission of Dr. S. F. Jackson, lately rector of Mappowder with Plush.

Toms, arrested at Winfrith, who rose from a labourer to a mason.[1]

Before leaving Buckland Newton the crowd waylaid Robert Bullen and William James and demanded money. What the rioters secured from Bullen is unknown, though rumour put it at £1, as he refused to give evidence or to prosecute the men. The Bullens had been long established at Pulham as tenant farmers and local officers, so they well knew the plight of the labourers. William James of Mappowder had had to fight his way upwards and could afford little sympathy for those who were down. James was exactly the man to be unpopular in a village. Not only, as a Purbeck man, was he a foreigner, but he leased almost half the land in the parish which covered 1,887 acres. One of Cobbett's hated new men, James occupied Place Farm, once the home of the ancient family of Coker. As became a man of substance, James was a churchwarden and also, after 1830, one of the trustees for Mappowder *Charity Mead*. By the mid-nineteenth century land left for the support of the poor was often let on a purely commercial basis or the rent was, as in Mappowder until 1854, 'applied towards paying the Poor's Rate'.[2] James was disliked as a foreigner with a large holding and as churchwarden who at vestry meetings would be concerned with the niggardly relief allowances. He returned the feelings with which he was regarded and had no compunction in giving evidence which helped to transport four men.

Even a day like 27 November, when to the half-elated and half-frightened villagers the foundations of society rocked, had an end. At 8.30 p.m. the flagging crowd reached their final destination, John Young's farm at Pulham. If events of the day aroused mixed feelings in the villagers, the farmers felt consternation alone. The risings threatened all the efforts they had made to establish themselves since the disasters of 1816-17. Young, like Bullen, was a substantial tenant farmer at Pulham and also a churchwarden.[3] On the uneasy evening of 27 November he had been joined by a fellow farmer, Matthew Galpin. The two men, like other Blackmoor farmers, cannot have felt at ease when dusk fell and they heard the shouts of approaching men and saw the flicker of torches near barn and rick, but they airily passed the matter off when giving evidence before the Special Commission. Young 'was inclined to give' Henry

[1] Winfrith Baptism Registers. At his daughter's baptism in 1836 John Toms' occupation was given as 'mason'. Winfrith Registers were inspected by kind permission of Mr. E. Ramm lately rector of Winfrith Newburgh.

[2] Mappowder Vestry Book, entry for 23 March 1854. The question of letting of charity land was the subject of a bitter correspondence in the *Dorset County Chronicle*, 11 January 1844.

[3] Information concerning the parochial activities of the Young and Bullen families have been obtained from the Pulham Churchwardens' Accounts 1790-1932.

Spicer and George Legg six half-crowns, while Galpin more honestly said he parted with two sovereigns to protect his threshing machine. The twenty or so men who came with Legg and Spicer included several Mitchells. This family was one of the mainstays of the parish; for the previous half century the churchwardens had been paying Mitchells for activities which ranged from skilled building work to digging docks. To be well known by local authorities, providing there was no record of insubordination or crime other than in-sobriety, was a protection to rioters. The Mitchells were bound over to keep the peace, but Henry Spicer, a newcomer to Pulham, was transported for robbing Young.

By 1 December the rioters who, despite rumours putting their numbers at 600,[1] had gathered in groups of twenties rather than hundreds, had aroused the county. Gentlemen, farmers and leading tradesmen promised 'in the most handsome manner to follow the magistrates wherever they might please to lead them'.[2] Special constables were enrolled: 560 in Weymouth, 402 in Dorchester and 1,100 in Blandford, with a further 160 mounted men 'well armed with pistols and a sabre'. For further security in face of their formidable adversaries the magistrates secured a troop of the 9th Lancers, later relieved by the 3rd Dragoons.[3] Since 1815 the half-pay officers, who formed the backbone of the special constabulary, had been living on the memories of their campaigning days. The disturbances offered them no less than the labourers, visions of recovering their lost domain of consequence and hopeful prospects. Not only did the old war-horses eagerly scent the fray, but the un-tried longed to make their name. Major Verity, formerly of the 92nd Highland Cavalry, saw himself leaving the armchair to play his part in a special observer corps of half-pay officers who '(Proteus like) should assume every shape' and 'would feel an esprit and good-will in furtherance of the desired object which could not be expected from men of a lower cast in life'. While Mr. James Payton, Midshipman R.N., envisaged promotion as he scrawled a report on subversive activities around Wimborne, only begging for secrecy as the information, if known, 'would only subject me to the fury of the multitude'. Even grocers had their dreams, and Peter Marling of Blandford pointed out that a reduction in the price of licenses to sell tea, which had risen from 5s. 6d. to 11s. between 1820 and 1830, would go far to restore order. He also aired the old grievance that 'the little farmer or tradesman, who does his

[1] *Colfox Family Papers*, p. 88. D.R.O.

[2] *Western Flying Post*, 29 November 1830.

[3] H.O. 40/27. Reports to the Home Office of Captain Frederick Hovenden, half-pay officer in charge of defence arrangements in Dorset.

labour himself pays his poor rates to get the great man's work done'.[1]

By the time the county magistrates had collected their wits and the constables, the flickers of unrest had died down except in the Blackmoor Vale, the only place in Dorset where some attempt was made at sustained resistance to the authorities. Meetings were held on Castle Hill, where ancient earthworks, dotted with great beeches, provided cover, an outlook over the western approaches to the Vale and confidence to labourers who dimly felt that in this place they were carrying on an ancient tradition of defiance. On the lower slopes of this hill stood the home of the Williams family, Castle Hill House. Neglect not fury had by 1964 gutted this fine mansion as effectively as rioters could have wished. Jackdaws nested in the attics and starlings in the reception rooms, while sycamore and buddleia sprouted from the Gothic turrets which concealed the chimneys of the laundry and bakehouse. When the Lancers were moved in to protect this mansion the rioters unwisely left their stronghold and moved down on 4 December to Stoke Common where thorn thickets and scattered oaks provided their only protection. Mr. Williams, in charge of special constables from Cerne Abbas, and a detachment of Lancers prepared to meet the challenge of the rioters who by this time probably did not consist of more than fifty men. Cautiously a few constables approached the Common, leaving the main body of men hidden lest the crowd should disperse. Among the assembled men 'a loud shout of defiance was set up, and as they [the constables] got nearer, they addressed them in rough language, and declared their determination to persist in destroying machinery'. Then the constabulary horsemen spread out to surround the rioters and 'drawing the circle constantly closer, soon got them into a very confined space'. The labourers tried to make some resistance but when the main body of constables and the troops appeared 'they seemed dismayed and were quietly taken'. Seventeen men had been arrested when further contingents, one under the command of James Farquharson, arrived. Farquharson must have regretted not being in at the kill as the whole episode reads like one of his notable runs when the hunt 'met at Shortwood; a large field out; found, and went away to Humber, and over the brook to Pulham, and on by the "Green Man" Inn to Hazelbury Common and Deadmoor, then bore to the right for Fifehead Neville and Locketts; leaving Hazelbury Bryan on the right he tried to get over the hill at Woolland but strength failing (for the pace had been very fast) he struggled on to Stoke Common,

[1] During the disturbances the Home Office was flooded with suggestions; those cited came from bundles H.O. 44/22 and H.O. 40/25.

where he lay down, and the hounds soon polished him off'.[1]

Rumour put the number of men committed to Dorchester jail at two hundred, but only fifty-five men appeared before the Special Commission. As a result of two days' work by Mr. Justice Alderson and Mr. Baron Vaughan at the Crown and Nisi Prius Courts, six men were condemned to death and ten to transportation for seven years. Those under sentence of death were reprieved, three being transported; but petitions against the transportation of thirteen men, eight of whom came from the Blackmoor Vale, failed. The sense and sincerity of John Rutter, who organised the petition at Shaftesbury, commanded a hearing even from his opponents, but Henry Hunt who sponsored a general amnesty in the House of Commons was not so generally respected. The *Dorset County Chronicle* reported the fact that the Dorset prisoners were put aboard the *York* hulk on 4 February, but their commiseration was reserved for the removal of political prisoners in Portugal who 'presented in their wretched looking plight the most miserable spectacle that can be conceived'. The local press, like Mary Frampton, was happy to write off the riots with the consoling reflection that the agricultural skill of the convicts would probably render 'our disturbances here a blessing to our Antipodes'.[2] The blessing was doubtful as the Governor of Van Dieman's Land wrote concerning the rioters who arrived on the *Eliza* that 'several died almost immediately from disease, apparently induced by despair. A great many of them went about dejected and stupefied with care and grief, and their situation after assignment was not for a long time much less unhappy'.[3] If any Dorset rioters returned after seven years it has not been possible to trace them. We can only guess their feelings from the ballad, one verse of which runs:

'We labour hard from morn to night, until our bones do ache
Then every one they must obey, their mouldy beds must make.
We often wish, when we lay down, we ne'er may rise no more
To meet our savage Governors upon Van Dieman's shore.'

Luckily the Dorset disturbances were over well before Christmas so little shadow was cast on the festivities. At Moreton House, the home of the Framptons, the Christmas cheer was 'not inferior to former years'; only the mummers were lacking. For many years the gentry were to have a horror of the labouring poor gathering after dusk. The local press found new excitements to report. A member of

[1] *Western Flying Post*, 6 December 1830, for the account of the last stand of the men on Stoke Common, while that of the fox is described in H. Symonds, *Hunting Runs and Sporting Notes from Dorsetshire*, 1899, p. 40.

[2] Mary Frampton, op. cit., p. 366.

[3] J. L. and B. Hammond, op. cit., p. 300, quotation from Correspondence on Secondary Punishment, March 1834, p. 23.

a Dorset family seemed within reach of the Papal chair as 'it is considered almost certain that Cardinal Weld will be elected Pope'; while the English radicals were preparing a 'reign of anarchy' by supporting vote by ballot and so enabling 'servant to vote against master . . . can anything be more subversive to the social principle than this?'. Also a suggestion was made, and 'cordially' supported by the editor of the *Dorset County Chronicle*, 'that wives and families should be sent after the convicts'.

The press had applauded the efforts of a young and pretty girl, who had led the citizens in the Paris barricades[1]; but had no word of praise to spare for the wives of agricultural labourers whose lives were truly ones of expedients and of pitiful attempts to meet daily the minor crises of living. Their efforts are best illustrated by the story of Susan Galpin of Sutton Poyntz, who struggled to maintain her parents and three children on the 12s. earned weekly by her husband and brother. In the hard winter of 1846-47 her father and brother fell ill, so Susan walked four miles in the rain to try to get help from the relieving officer. This was refused, so from her brother's employer she obtained a cup of broth for the invalids who had been living on dry bread and tea without milk or sugar. The young man shared the broth with his father, and exclaimed when it was finished, 'Now my broth is done, I'm done'. A few nights later Susan's little son, huddled beside his uncle for warmth, called out, 'Oh, mother, William is cold and feels stiff'. The father died at the same time as the son, and both were buried in one grave. Yet less than a year earlier John Floyer, member for Dorset, 'could hardly remember a time when the condition of the labourers was better'.[2]

Since women felt the pinch more than men who, as the chief wage earners, had the largest share of food, they made the first efforts to solve the village problem of too many mouths for too little food: they left the villages. In the eighteenth century the daughters of small farmers were in great demand as servants; a century later the demand was less discriminating and unskilled cottage girls were welcomed, for a few months at least. Domestic work offered hopes of betterment as well as the certainty of drudgery; any girl in a town situation had friends and sisters waiting for a similar chance. They arrived to delight urban housewives by wearing '*such* a nice plain gown, of only one colour . . . and *such* a good strong serviceable half-a-crown Dunstable straw bonnet, trimmed very plainly; and *such* a nice clean quilled net-cap under it; and *such* a tidy, plain white

[1] *Western Flying Post*, 16 August 1830.
[2] *Poole and Dorset Herald*, 7 January 1847, for Susan Galpin's story; *The Times*, 9 May 1846, for Floyer's statement on the condition of the Dorset labourers.

muslin collar over one of the quietest black-and-white plaid shawls
. . . *so* thoroughly like what a respectable servant ought to be'.[1]
But followers, open-worked cotton stockings or ill-health often caused
the girls to be soon cast adrift by employers whose enthusiasm for
quiet country girls had cooled. Not all employers were as neurotic
as Thomas and Jane Carlyle who had five servants in six months,
but the turnover was great and the demand seemed insatiable. In
every Dorset village eager girls with small corded trunks awaited the
carrier's cart to take them on the first lap of their townward journey.
Some, like Annie Langdown of Bere Regis, who went to a relative,
found their feet; others, like Annie's cousin, returned home to die of
consumption.

The girls blazed the trail and by the 1870s the younger men were
prepared to follow them. The pattern remained the same, one successful migrant prepared the way for others. Mr. Gillam of Netherbury remembered how one man encouraged others from the parish
to follow him to the South Wales coalfields. Often the move was
achieved in two steps; by finding in the district non-agricultural
work which led to distant employment. The first step was the
hardest because country boys, as early wage earners, had less
education than the girls and were also less quick to pick up new
ways. They seldom lost their typical gait 'as though they have a
heavy weight tied to each leg, so that it can only be moved by a
heave of the whole body in the opposite direction'.[2] This weight
which bound them to the soil had fettered them too long to be
readily cast off. Some of the ways by which young men set forth on
new ventures are well illustrated by the story Mr. William Hardy
tells concerning the careers of his father and uncles. Frederick
Hardy, born about 1857, grew up with his brothers, George and
Thomas, in Maiden Newton. The railway had brought to this town
a short-lived, sunset prosperity which hardly illumined the lives of
labourers who in the 1870s were still only earning 10s. a week. One
day the young men discussed their prospects. Frederick, who had
married a local girl and was happy in his work as a carter, had no
desire to change. Perhaps he chose wisely, as at eighty-six he was a
hearty old man well able to spring backwards and forwards over a
broomstick in the popular village Broom Dance. George and
Thomas told Frederick to 'bide with his horses but they intended to
better themselves'. Thomas' first step off the land was a cautious
one, he became groom to Dr. Robert Rendall and helped on his

---

[1] *The Greatest Plague of Life*, ed. by the Brothers Mayhew, c. 1840, p. 86.
[2] *Girls' Own Paper*, 11 November 1885. This description appears in an article
advocating evening classes in villages, including those for teaching boys
gymnastics.

thirty-acre holding. At first sight this work seemed even harder than the labourer's round as there was often no respite at night, when the doctor had to be driven along the windswept roads of the chalk uplands. Thomas worked well and conscientiously and by recommendation obtained a responsible situation in the Duke of Connaught's establishment at Bagshot. George was more adventurous and by going to sea took a way off the land that was not unusual with Dorset men. Fifty years earlier young men could sign on at Poole for the Newfoundland fisheries, but Southampton had now eclipsed the Dorset port, and George became a steward on a transatlantic liner. The shambling walk and the Dorset dialect were soon dropped for crisper, nautical ways and George married a well-to-do passenger. He occasionally returned home 'a great dandy with a bow-tie and very well-spoken'. This possibility could hardly have been envisaged by George's grandfather, as the men of 1830 sought no new way of life but were obsessed with a return to the past as it appeared to them from the glowing accounts of their grandparents.

Why did this lost domain especially attract the men of the Blackmoor Vale? Two reasons chiefly account for the zeal with which the Blackmoor men took part in the disturbances; one was common to the whole county, the other peculiar to the Vale. The population increase affected nearly every Dorset parish, but some villagers were helped in their search for employment by proximity to towns, ports, quarries or spinning mills. The people of Blackmoor depended on the land alone for their livelihood. It was impossible for fathers in 1830 to imagine different lives for their children, so they demanded higher wages and more opportunities for renting land. It was hard for these parents to realise that if their aims had been achieved their children might have benefited but not their grandchildren. After 1850 it was clear that the Vale could no longer support large numbers of labourers. Winter work had always been scarce in this pastoral area; machines had come to stay in the hayfields and farmyards. Young cottagers in the 1870s had little sympathy with the dreams of their grandparents and Jesse Collings to restore a golden age of cottage farming, or with those of Joseph Arch to improve working conditions through unionism. By 1881 the Blackmoor men had risen again, this time never to return; the population figures of Mappowder, Pulham and Stoke Wake were lower than they had been in 1831, while those of Buckland Newton, which reached a peak in 1871, had fallen sharply.

The remoteness of the western Blackmoor Vale made the struggle for survival even harder than in other districts, since there was little outlet for the increasing population. This isolation also helps explain the fierceness of the labourers' determination in 1830 to make their lives easier. The villages of Mappowder, Pulham, Hazelbury Bryan and Stoke Wake were connected by sunken tracks and paths through the fields; their communications with the outer world were barred by a chalk wall to the south, and to the north the melting blue horizon indicated far-stretching grasslands unbroken by roads or towns. The inhabitants of this cluster of villages enclosed by hills and a sea of grass, were thrown upon their own thoughts. Political issues did not concern them; the messages of the Established Church were dulled through familiarity, while those of Dissent had not penetrated into the Vale. In 1836 the Home Missionary Society of the Congregational Church found the district 'exceedingly dark and benighted spiritually', and sent a preacher who did much good 'among a poor, scattered and neglected people'.[1] The fruit of his labour is the meeting house at Duntish, today one of the best kept chapels in Dorset. The men of the Vale had few interruptions to their brooding thoughts of the past. As children they had absorbed the stories of their grandparents who tended them while parents worked. No school inspectors, who were to 'deal Dorset its death blow',[2] woke young people from their dreams. Wherever a man worked in the western Blackmoor Vale the landmark of Castle Hill was before him. Here men had once made a stand, and to this fort the rioters hurried when the echoing horns called them to action in November, 1830. The rising failed and one more regret was added to the labourers' store of memories. Their sorrow was chiefly for their children whom they watched following the hard and hopeless ways of their forefathers.

NOTES ON SOURCES USED FOR CHAPTER V

Verbal Sources

At the turn of this century W. H. Hudson talked to an old woman who remembered the 1830 risings in Wiltshire. Hudson recounted these and other stories of the troubled times in *A Shepherd's Life*, 1910. No such memories, handed down by grandparents, have been traced in Dorset. An understanding of conditions under which labourers lived in 1830 can, however, be gained from descriptions of village life at the end of the last century. For those who remained on the land conditions changed little between 1830 and the end of

[1] W. Densham and J. Ogle, *The Story of the Congregational Churches*, 1899, pp. 67-69.
[2] This was the opinion of William Barnes given during an interview at Winterborne Came and reported in an unnamed and undated newspaper cutting in Gillingham Museum, Book 144, Box 56-170. Barnes was discussing Dorset dialect.

the First World War. For accounts of village life I am grateful to:
Miss A. E. and Mr. F. Beck, Buckland Newton.
Mr. F. Browning, Bloxworth.
David Gould (1876-1965), Thornford.
Mr. W. Hardy, Wool.
Mrs. A. Hawkins, Bere Regis.
Charles Hawkins (1874-1964), Martinstown.
Mr. H. House, Buckland Newton.
Mr. J. Mitchell, Hazelbury Bryan.
Mr. W. Tucker, Stour Row.
Mr. F. Wills, Beer Hackett.

Written Sources
Working-class conditions in the nineteenth century have not lacked chroniclers. The authorities most consulted in connection with this chapter have been:
J. L. and B. Hammond, *The Village Labourer*, 1st ed., 1911.

It is now generally agreed that the Hammonds saw the Enclosure Acts in the light of the expulsion from Eden: with unbroken light and happiness before, and afterwards only toil and darkness. But whatever criticisms can be made, the sustained moral fervour of this book will ensure its remaining one of the great works of the period. The 1830 risings throughout the southern counties are described in considerable detail.

A. Redford, *Labour Migration in England*, 1800-1850, 1926.

Though this book deals primarily with the growth of industrial towns, the full account of the operation of the old and new Poor Laws bears directly on conditions in Dorset.

E. P. Thompson, *The Making of the English Working Class*, 1963.

Rural conditions are described in Chapter 7 on 'The Field Labourer', but the chapters on 'Christian and Apollyon' and 'The Transforming Power of the Cross' have much to say concerning the effects of dissent on urban populations that is also applicable to Dorset villagers.

R. Wearmouth, *Methodism and the Working Class Movements of England*, 1937.

The effects of Methodism, not always identical with those described by E. P. Thompson, are outlined in general. Particular attention is paid to Methodism in Dorset in connection with the Tolpuddle Martyrs (pp. 208-221).

Extracts from ballads have been taken from *Victorian Street Ballads*, ed. W. Henderson, 1937.

Parliamentary Papers
Reports of Select Committees on the State of Agriculture, 1821 and 1833.

Reports of Special Assistant Poor Law Commissioners on the Employment of Women and Children in Agriculture, 1843.

The 1843 reports contain full information on conditions in Dorset. Among those giving evidence was the Reverend Sydney Godolphin Osborne, rector of Bryanston and Durweston, whose efforts were shamefully denigrated by the *Dorset County Chronicle,* 21 March 1844, as being undertaken because of Osborne's aim 'to become a public man'.

Parish and County Records

Light is thrown on the lives of the men implicated in the 1830 disturbances by parish records, census returns, land-tax assessments, for ascertaining whether any of the rioters came from families who had once occupied land, and, most important of all, the Dorchester jail registers. These are available in the Dorset Record Office for the years 1782-1878, where information is given concerning the age, occupation, marital status, number of children, height and distinguishing marks of the prisoners. The names of the committing magistrates and the offence are entered as well as the sentence and notes on behaviour and dates of release.

Records have been consulted for the following parishes:

Buckland Newton Accounts of Overseers 1751-1795, D.R.O.

Apprenticeship Indentures 1664-1812, D.R.O.

Cann Churchwardens' Accounts 1793-1844, D.R.O.

Minutes of Vestry Meetings, D.R.O.

Hazelbury Bryan Minutes of Vestry Meetings 1813-1839, D.R.O.

Mappowder Baptism, Marriage and Burial Registers.

MS notebook giving account of Shipley and Beauchamp charity distributions, 1847-48.

Vestry Book 1847-48.

These were inspected by kind permission of Dr. S. F. Jackson, lately rector of Mappowder with Plush, to whom I am also indebted for much information concerning the west Blackmoor Vale.

Pulham Baptism, Marriage and Burial Registers.

Churchwardens' Accounts 1790-1832.

These were inspected by kind permission of the Reverend W. Duncan Oddie, rector of Pulham.

Stoke Wake Baptism, Marriage and Burial Registers.

Churchwardens' Accounts.

These were inspected by kind permission of Mr. F. N. Kent, Manor Farm, Stoke Wake.

Public Record Office

Communications from every part of the United Kingdom poured

into the Home Office during the troubled 1830s. These documents are in packages in the series HO.40 and HO.44. The material in these packages is useful for conveying the general state of alarm at the time rather than any specific information.

The names of the jurors at the Crown and Nisi Prius Courts, 11 and 12 January 1831, are given in Assizes 24/18.

CHAPTER VI

Bere Regis:
Various Species
of Trade

*The respectable revolutionaries – the overthrow
of small tradesmen, craftsmen and copyholders
– description of Bere Regis – the Drax family
in the place of the Turbervilles – decline of
open-field farming on Chalk – overstocking of
trades in the mid-nineteenth century – the
arrival of grocers in villages – dressmaking and
button making – the vicissitudes of the Langdown family – election violence – opportunities
as well as misfortunes brought by changes in
village society.*

'There often appears among farmers a great disposition
to embark in various species of trade and manufacture
and commerce.'
Arthur Young, *The Farmer's Calendar*, 1805.

MANY WOULD agree with Thomas Huxley that chalk downland
has a 'peacefully domestic and mutton-suggesting prettiness'. That
the serenity of the countryside is often at variance with the turmoil
of human lives is also a generally accepted proposition. When he
stressed the calm domesticity of the chalkland scene Huxley might
have had in mind Bere Regis, set at the foot of his 'undulating
downs and rounded coombs'. The whole atmosphere emanates an
air of tranquility or, in Sir Frederick Treves' opinion, of dullness.
But Sir Frederick found 'curiously ridiculous' the arresting carving
of a cynical-looking angel on the outer wall of St. Michael and All

Angels at Winterbourne Steepleton. Yet by 1848, the year when 'the old depths of chaos were unsealed', the fields and lanes of Bere had witnessed revolutionary struggles as fierce, in terms of human effort and anguish, as those which were raging in Paris, Naples or Vienna.

It had long been the conviction of Englishmen that revolutions, like eating rye bread and wearing wooden shoes, were amongst the many peculiar and undesirable activities of foreigners. Nevertheless, in a garb of broadcloth respectability many manufacturers and land-owners were in the early nineteenth century bringing about changes which were to shatter the old society far more effectively than the violent assaults of the intellectual *sans-culottes* throughout Europe. Factory production and high farming, or the massive use of man-made fertilisers and feeding stuffs, loosened the ties which bound men to the soil. That a man should no longer be bound to his lord, his soil and his neighbourhood for the supply of all his needs was among the chief aims of revolutionary patriots in Central and East Europe. But such freedom was achieved in England largely by the efforts of men like Arkwright, Cobden and Sir Humphrey Davy, pillars of established society.

Though seldom reaching gale force the chilling winds of change blew through remote valleys and across 'the open, draughty downland' of Dorset and spared neither the mighty nor the humble. In Bere early in the eighteenth century the Turbervilles, whose swords founded their fortunes in the Middle Ages, gave way before the plantation-owning Drax family. Lesser gentry like the Ekins and Williams families were swept aside by efficient, progressive farmers like the Scutts. Yet when in the winter of 1830 ricks were burned at Bere the incendiaries, not the Scutts, were proscribed as revolutionaries. But these poverty-stricken labourers were endeavouring, no less than Metternich and the chancelleries of Europe, to hold back the forces of change so as to maintain in society the place which they believed was theirs by tradition and right. Following the trend-setting Romantics, literary society paid its sorrowing last respects to the dispossessed ones, whether ancient freeholders or landless peasants. Although few public speeches were complete without some reference to 'the peaceful industrious communities of our island home', the fate of the small craftsmen and retailers, as integral a part of rural society as the tillers of the soil, was unmourned. The fact often escaped contemporary observers that the admired 'upright, downright yeoman' might equally justly have been described as 'cheese-paring', the adjective usually designating those concerned with small business undertakings. Many farmers, as Arthur Young observed, had second strings to their bows, and this oscillation between agriculture and trade produced a comfortable way of life provided that plodding methods of farming were not disturbed and the demands for shoes, bricks and farm implements remained steady. But steadiness of supply and demand was not a feature of the early nineteenth century. Furthermore it was just during this period that landlords were most busily drawing in lifeholds for amalgamation into consolidated holdings which could be leased for years. The less efficient farmers, generally those heavily involved in sideline activities, were the first to lose their lifeholds. Numbers of small craftsmen and dealers, therefore, were throwing all their energies into concerns which, in the face of increasing competition and decreasing demands from impoverished villagers, could hardly prove profitable. Buttermen, cobblers, grocers and carpenters were not cast in heroic moulds and their desperate efforts to obtain tools and raw materials so as to satisfy customers, more concerned with getting credit than paying cash, aroused little popular sympathy.

The full records which are available for the large village of Bere Regis make it an ideal parish from which to learn the sad stories not only of declining gentry but also of bewildered artisans and shopkeepers clinging to their undertakings long after all hopes of profit had died. Both the gentry and the traders gave way before men determined to run their farms and other undertakings not as community activities within the framework of manor or guild, but as independent profit-making concerns. But first some account must be given of Bere itself, of its parish activities and of the farming methods in the hills and vales surrounding the village.

Bere, although failing to fulfil its early promise of developing into a thriving borough and market town, never quite lost the lustre shed in the Middle Ages by royal favour and by courtly patronage. Although by 1750 the stones of King John's hunting lodge buttressed up the walls of Court Farm and the last of the Turbervilles lay in a Putney churchyard, Bere still had expectations of consequence as a town. These were partly due to its position at the intersection of roads running from Dorchester to Wareham and connecting Blandford with Weymouth, and partly to the village's early association with crown and court which enabled it to take the lead over the smaller chalkland parishes to the north and over the hamlets on the sandy heaths to the south. Bere had further claims to fame on account of its market and of Woodbury Fair, both of which functioned within living memory. For three days in September the fair on the ancient earthworks of Woodbury Hill attracted great attention. Farmers came to deal in sheep and, above all, in horses; young people sought entertainment and the first oysters of the season, while old people were content to sit and 'to hear the news' at the two inns and the restaurant on the hilltop. Gentlefolk came on the first day and bargain-hunters on the last or 'pack and penny' day. Now only memories of old inhabitants, half buried piles of oyster shells and small china models of the oyster vendors and their stalls remain to recall this great fair renowned throughout Wessex. So Bere achieved the status of a small town on account of its position, its market and fair, and of its memories of kingly condescension.

The 8,313 acres of Bere parish covered the common West, Middle and East fields on the chalk; the fertile, alluvial meadows bordering on the river Bere, flowing south-east through the parish, its course marked by a chain of ancient farmsteads, Roke, Court, Dodding's and Philliols; and stretches of heath on the sandy, gravelly podsols south of the village.[1] This last area once supported a scattered, impoverished population who, together with the seafarers passing frequently through the village, gave the inhabitants of Bere a reputation, which still clings, of displaying a certain nonchalance towards the law.

As in nearly all other chalk parishes of Dorset, the open arable fields of Bere were, by the mid-eighteenth century, confined to areas which, because of poor soil or difficult terrain, were too unattractive to invite enclosures. Wherever patches of brown earths occurred in the thin Chalk-derived loams of the open fields, enclosures, such as *Muddox Barrow* and *Rentcroft* closes, had appeared. The continual turning over of light rendsinas and the weary journeys between the strips scattered throughout the open fields repaid the cultivator so long as the prices of wheat and, even more important for Bere, those of barley, held firm. While age-sanctioned methods of open farming did not achieve the 'great gains to be made . . . by going out of the common road', they did protect the cultivator from the losses of over-speculative farming. Bad harvests, like those of 1756 and 1766 affected the whole community; but although the small farmer faced a serious setback at such times, a better season filled the little barn in his 'backside' no less than the great barns of Roke and Philliols. The seasons rather than the system of farming determined the profits, a comforting thought for the small man, and 26 of the 46 tenants of Bere manor in 1776 held under 30 acres.[2] The demand for wheat rose steadily and, after 1773, began to exceed home production; while the needs of brewers and maltsters for barley seemed unlimited. Barley, rather than wheat, brought cash to the small man, but, as he generally held most of the land in the open fields and so followed the common practice of sowing long-eared barley after wheat, his yields from an exhausted soil were not such as to bring

[1] See Figure 2.　　[2] See tables in Appendix F.

him great profits. By 1796 when 206½ acres in Bere were sown to wheat the acreage under barley was almost double,[1] and many of the strips in the open fields had been merged together.

More intensive farming meant an increasing use of sheep as 'the tools of husbandry',[2] but already by the mid-eighteenth century common pastures had been restricted and by the end of the century even those manorial tenants with leases, or right of stockage for sheep on Bere Down, found that they could only increase their flocks, and consequently their cereal yields, by growing turnips and by flooding meadows to provide an early bite for ewes and lambs. Neither of these activities could be easily undertaken by farmers relying mainly on open holdings. When Arthur Young attacked Dorset farmers for not regarding 'sheep and turnips as synonymous terms',[3] he disregarded the fact that farming in the greater part of the chalk, or sheep, districts were still open and there-fore unsuitable for the 'sheet anchor' of the new farming. By the act of 1773 greater crop variations in open fields were possible, but progressive farmers were more anxious to enclose their strips than to take advantage of the act.

The blessings of peace in 1815 were far from being unmixed. In Bere, as in other parishes, only farmers with financial reserves managed to weather the storm of falling prices, rising poor rates and the uncertainty of the Government's policy as regards protection. This uncertainty caused greater hardship than the actual repeal of the Corn Laws; for, after the blow fell in 1846, those who had man-aged to survive the buffets of post-war years adjusted themselves to changed conditions. New manures, particularly bones and guano, began to take the place of the 'golden hoof' and water meadows provided pasture for dairy cattle rather than an early bite for sheep. Although wheat prices dropped there was no decline in the demand for barley.

New methods made not only whole-time farmers but also leases for years rather than lives inevitable. To offset the low rents usual with lifeholds the landlords could, as was done at Arne, increase the fines for 're-living', but the falling-in of lives was unpredictable so that leases for years became fashionable. Landlords preferred short tenancies when grain prices were rising and long ones when prices

---

[1] *Proc.*, 1955, Vol. 77, pp. 169-170, W. E. Minchington, 'Agriculture in Dorset During the Napoleonic Wars'. After Fordington with 430 acres, Bere with 382½ acres had the highest acreage sown to barley of all the coastal-belt parishes making the 1796 return.

[2] *Agricultural History Review*, 1960, Vol. VIII, pp. 5-19, E. L. Jones, 'Eighteenth Century Changes in Chalkland Farming'.

[3] A. Young, *The Farmer's Tour through East England*, 1771, p. 345.

fluctuated, while the tenants' desires moved in an exactly contrary direction. A few landlords moved in their own orbits remote from the rough-and-tumble world; the sixth Earl of Shaftesbury refused granting any written leases and many bishops, chapters and collegiate bodies resisted the new-fangled innovation of leases for years until the last decades of the nineteenth century.

The manor of Bere was, until the early eighteenth century, in the hands of the Turbervilles. When this family died out Roke, one of the largest Turberville farms, once forming a separate manor, was taken over by Henry Drax. He possessed a fortune from sugar plantations and an estate in Yorkshire, so was an eligible suitor for Frances Elizabeth Ernle, heiress of the Erles of Charborough Park, about six and a half miles north-east of Bere village. The Erles had taken a leading part in securing the Protestant succession in 1688 and this propitious union of wealth from the New World and liberal principles from the Old prospered. Within ten years more land, including two Bere mills and Court Farm, had been added to Roke. Increasing demands during the French wars quickened the pace of production beyond the powers of small farmers so more livings and farms fell to the Drax family and these finally devolved on the heiress, Jane Frances, who married in 1827 John Samuel Wanley Sawbridge, a grandson of the John Sawbridge who ardently championed the cause of Wilkes by promoting the Bill of Rights Society. John Samuel Sawbridge assumed the surname and arms of the Erle-Drax family and in return for the acquisition of an heiress and a well-respected name he brought the Sawbridge wealth, drive and business ability.

The ground had been prepared for John Sawbridge's long career as an active, despotic and improving landlord. Land-tax assessments show that the consolidation of lifehold tenements was well under way in the first decades of the nineteenth century. This process of consolidation followed a clearly defined pattern which can be traced since maps are available showing the small lifeholds and open-field tenements as they existed before unofficial enclosure changed both the field and the social systems of the parish.

Between 1773 and 1776 Isaac Taylor drew detailed maps of the manor of Bere which by the eighteenth century covered the whole parish, with the exception of the small hamlet of Shitterton. With painstaking care Taylor gave the acreages of the closes and of the hundreds of tenements in the open arable fields and common pastures, the names of the occupiers and, in most cases, the tenure by which they held their lands.[1]

In 1776 of the 2,037 acres of agricultural land in the manor of

[1] Isaac Taylor, maps of the town and manor of Bere Regis, 1773-76, D.R.O.

Bere only about 300 acres were freehold. Except for Sarah Clark's copyhold of 66 acres and about 230 acres of leasehold, all tenure was by lifehold. Leasing on lives assured the occupiers security and protection against excessive rent fluctuations, but was not popular with improving landlords. Ten years later more competitive farming and the hazards of life had caused casualties among the lifeholders. When the livings fell in, through deaths and failures to 're-live', open-field tenements were often consolidated and let, it must be presumed in the absence of manor court rolls for Bere, at increased fines. Only well-to-do tenants, like the Homers and Woolfreys, were able to take up these larger holdings. Clinging to 'precedence and established ways' many old families were temperamentally as well as financially incapable of adopting the new farming methods which might have helped them when peace brought those short, sharp agricultural crises so disturbing for the small farmer. The years 1815-30 saw not only the further consolidation of small, scattered tenements but also their leasing for years, not lives, to tenants able to pay a regular and economic rent and prepared to devote their whole time to increasing their own and their landlord's profits. The days of jogtrot farming to supply the family, with a possible barley surplus for the maltster and the comfortable oscillations between trade and agriculture were passing. If the parish could not provide suitable tenants the 'spirit of migration' was abroad and, even in unsettled times, enterprising men were prepared to travel across the county to take up promising holdings. Thomas White Ingram who rented Philliols, long owned by the Ekins family, not only came himself from Milton Abbas but brought some of his labourers with him; while Henry Ears of Doddings Farm came from the same district.

The 1846 Enclosure Act completed the work which had been steadily progressing since the late eighteenth century. In the open arable fields, where many arable strips had already been un-officially thrown together, the act was mainly concerned with the re-arrangement of holdings already created by the amalgamation of strips. Where new allotments were made the commissioners far from allocating the land 'in little parcels little minds to please' threw together the little strips into large fields which were eventually divided between three new holdings; West, Muddox Barrow (now Skippets) and East farms. In the heather and gorse covered stretches of Bere and Middle Heaths, enclosure took a different course. As well as the establishment of two new farms, Lower Woodbury and Middle Heath, some small allotments, carried out by individual enterprise while the heaths were still open, were officially recognised. The lord of the manor kept in hand a large part of the heath where the once despised gorse was cherished to provide cover for foxes.[1]

The acres and the social standing of the freeholders of Bere in 1776 varied greatly. There was little in common between the armigerous Pleydells with their large estate in Milborne St. Andrew, the Ekins family, 'ancient freeholders', who turned to malting in their struggle to hold Philliols, the yeoman Manuels of Bloxworth, where a clump of firs perpetuates their name, and the Mates and Spears with their modest holdings.

The forty-one manorial tenants whose land was chiefly lifehold had more in common since nearly all of them, at one time or another, were connected with a craft or trade. The exceptions were humble families, like the Stockleys and Barneses, and flourishing ones like the Homers and Woolfreys. By the 1850s the Homers were able to look back over a century of steady advancement; the Woolfreys had also been able to hold their own, thanks chiefly to their occupation of the corn mill at Broadwater. A concentrated application to farming, frugal habits and luck in the matter of male heirs, all contributed to their success. Rejoicings over the birth of an heir were too often short lived. The memorials in and around any Dorset church show how formidable were the hazards of growing up until the turn of this century. The eighteenth-century registers of Poole show that the ink can hardly have been dry on many baptismal entries before the infant's burial was recorded. In Martinstown parish church Charles Hawkins (1797-1866) and his wife Frances mourn the death, before their early thirties, of seven of their ten children; in Bere many parents were bereaved by the diphtheria epidemic of 1890.

By the mid-nineteenth century the new pattern, which was to endure for almost a century, was firmly established in Bere. The tenements in the open arable fields had been amalgamated to form consolidated holdings, a process which was rounded off by the Enclosure Act of 1846. Except for lands around Shitterton still owned by the Pleydells, the whole parish was in the hands of the Drax family who leased to tenants the newly enclosed farms on the once open fields, and the old enclosures of the valleys. More land was brought into agriculture, the tithe apportionment gives 3,371 acres under cultivation as compared with Taylor's estimate of 2,037 acres of agricultural land. The increased acreage of cultivated land was due to enclosures and to more effective ploughing and draining rather than to new crop rotations. Sheep grazing on the downland,

---

[1] E. W. Bovill, *The England of Nimrod and Surtees*, 1959, p. 51. Though no locality is specified the author states, 'Down in the West, Drax spent much money on planting gorse, doubtless to provide safe harbourage for the scores of foxes he was turning down'.

only rights of stockage were now limited to ten persons, and fields of barley, now producing thirty-two bushels to the acre compared with twenty-eight fifty years earlier,[1] gave the impression that a century had rolled by without disturbing the traditional methods of farming and way of life in Bere. But hardly a family in the parish was untouched by the changes between the years 1750 and 1850. All are familiar with the social and economic strains of this period on a national scale. These tensions acquire a new meaning when studied in a small area where descendants of the families, whose fluctuating fortunes can be charted from the parish records, are still living.

Bere in the mid-eighteenth century was a thriving parish though pauperism was not unknown. By 1741 the Poor House had been erected on Warren Heath remote from the village centre. Its site is now indicated by an unexpected and marked bend in the road. But the House did not yet overshadow the inhabitants of the parish where relief aided temporary distress rather than chronic pauperism. The needs of its inhabitants, estimated at 936 in 1801, were met by the fourteen tradesmen on whose stock poor rate was levied in 1750. These needs were modest as many families grew their own wheat and baked their own bread at home using furze as fuel; and home weaving of linen and wool had not died out. Of these fourteen tradesmen seven belonged to families holding land.[2] The Chips, Satchells and Burgesses were connected with brewing. Besides these families regularly connected with brewing and innkeeping, the fluctuating numbers of householders rated on their stocks of beer suggest that many small farmers must have brewed beer for sale when their barley yields were exceptionally high. Brewing for home consumption was normal in cottages as well as farmhouses so that most families were able 'to brew their own beer and enjoy it by their own fireside'.[3] Even in the 1890s Mr. Marwood Hopkins of Milborne St. Andrew remembers how 'most farms had their own brewhouses' and at harvest time one man was kept at home for brewing. Inns had more the character of clubs for the well-to-do and resting places for travellers than of mere drinking houses. Innkeepers were often substantial men farming on a considerable scale as was the case with the Chips, the Burgesses, the Kitcats and the Mates at Bere.

[1] Enclosure Award, 1846, for rights of stockage; W. Stevenson, op. cit., pp. 232-3, and J. Caird, op. cit., p. 61 for estimated barley yields. Mr. John Strang, formerly of Bere Down Farm, considered that in the 1960s a yield of 40-45 cwts. (approx. 80-90 bushels) to an acre was not unusual.

[2] Battrick, Burgess, Chip, Clench, Ekins, Satchell and Fry; James Kitcat and John Mate appear as innkeepers in the land-tax assessment for 1783.

[3] *Select Committee on Agriculture*, 1821, p. 61. The witness was describing a Sussex parish but the same conditions prevailed in the south-west.

The Chip family seem to have left Bere in the late 1770s but the other three families struggled on into the nineteenth century, despite many vicissitudes. By the 1820s beer shops started to take custom from the established village inns. These 'low publics' provided solace for labourers whose increasing poverty made home brewing out of the question. While the consumption of beer steadily increased between 1750 and 1850 the methods of purveying it changed. By the mid-nineteenth century Surtees was lamenting the disappearance of 'the large comfortable old posting houses' where 'the landlords were generally sportsmen themselves, and also large farmers'. This was true in the case of the Mates in Bere who, in their heyday, were not only tenants of Court Farm and of the Royal Oak, but also owners of the New Inn. By the 1840s there was little place for part-time farmers or for lavishly-living innkeepers and the Mates were reduced to woodmen and agricultural labourers. In her old age, Margaret, widow of the last of the Mates who had been able to live independently, was supported by the poor rates.

Closely connected with brewing is milling, which was the industry least affected by the upheavals of the period 1750-1850. Whether corn was produced by a number of small lifeholders or by a few large leasehold tenants, the sacks of grain still came to the mill for grinding. The Woolfreys, whose holding in 1776 was more than half in open-field strips, would not have survived had it not been for their mill at Broadwater. In the mid-eighteenth century there were four mills in Bere and a century later the industry was still flourishing enough to attract young men from outside Dorset.

Brewers and innkeepers frequently shared the upper ranks of the village hierarchy in the mid-eighteenth century; close below them came the blacksmiths and carpenters. The latter were skilled men who specialised in wagon making, church repairs, and the making of cabinets and coffins. Rough, or 'hedge', carpentry was undertaken by the farmer himself or by his workmen, just as the cottager often made his own window-frames, doors and bedsteads. As whole-time carpenters were needed only for skilled work it is not surprising to find only two in the parish records. Both belonged to families, the Comptons and the Ashes, holding over fifty acres of land. One of the Comptons was responsible in 1772 for erecting 'a place in the market house for the fire engine'. The Comptons held their land until 1815 when all records of the family cease so it is impossible to say whether they were casualties of the peace or left Bere to better themselves further afield. The Ashes struggled on at Bere, farming, making coffins at 8s. a piece[1] and selling 'hessings' for paupers'

---

[1] Prices varied throughout the county; the Gillingham overseers were lucky enough to buy workhouse coffins at 6s. each.

bedding. This multiplicity of activities did not save them from destitution and by 1851 old carpenter Ash was a pauper. His fate is not surprising as in 1841 the number of carpenters in Bere had increased to nineteen. These included men from families like the Whennels, Poors and Browns, who had entered the trade not so much because the demand for craftsmen in the parish was pressing but because their small family holdings had gone, and carpentry was a craft which had been mastered by most small farmers.

Carpentry, tailoring and shoemaking all suffered from overcrowding in the mid-nineteenth century. Craftsmen in building, iron working and saddle making fared better and as a result of less competition were enabled to keep up their prices.[1] Their restricted numbers were due to strict apprenticeship regulations, often waived in less highly skilled trades, the capital needed for equipment and premises and the fair degree of book-learning required for running a business which did not depend on the needs of poor neighbours but those of well-to-do farmers. If tenants of newly-enclosed downland, where numbers of furze covers were planted, grumbled about the 'scores of foxes' Drax was turning down, saddlers welcomed his enthusiasm for building the area around Bere into one of the most notable hunting districts in the county. In 1841 the Shaves, father and son, had the monopoly of saddle and harness making and in ten years they were only joined by one newcomer. The Shaves early illustrated that ability for keeping a constant watch on the market which, more than any other quality, enabled men to bend rather than break in the recurrent crises of the early nineteenth century. In the mid-eighteenth century the Shaves only rented two acres of land around their corn-mill at Elders; as a profitable sideline to milling they sold hardware. A century later the family not only had the monopoly of harness making in Bere, but they were also able to rent over 100 acres and have maintained their connection with the land into the 1960s.

Of the four blacksmiths working in Bere in 1841 only William Biles came from the immediate neighbourhood. This stresses the fact that once the prosperity of an essentially agricultural community waned, few members of distressed farming families were able to better themselves by engaging in the more profitable crafts.

Bere, like other parishes covering some podsols with pockets of clay, had its own brick kilns. Bricks were cheap, selling at 2s. 6d. a hundred in the mid-eighteenth century, and an expansion of brick making might have salvaged numbers of families turned adrift after the peace. But in 1841 there was only one old brickmaker, with a young assistant, in the parish. The clay and the kilns were available

[1] *Select Committee on Agriculture*, 1833, p. X.

but between the years 1815 and 1850 the building of small houses, for which local materials might have been used, was so restricted as to be, in some districts, almost at a standstill. Builders who managed to struggle through these hard times came into their own after 1850 when the erection of rows of cottages, church restoration and the modernisation of farmhouses became fashionable. Before the end of the nineteenth century Bere enjoyed a short Indian summer of prosperity. Brickmaking was extensively carried on at the old Dodding's and new Black Hill kilns; old inhabitants remember how the drays of Johnson's brewery blocked the narrow lanes leading to the surrounding villages, and blacksmiths found that the use of horse-drawn machinery greatly increased their business. Master blacksmiths prospered but workmen, paid 6d. an hour in the early twentieth century, found it hard to rise. Nor did the sun shine for agricultural labourers and many of the younger men were gradually and sadly leaving the parish in search of work further afield.

The trading interests of numbers of eighteenth-century lifeholders, such as the Battricks, Frys and Clenches, fluctuated between mercery, hardware and shoes. Their speculations, however, were on such a limited scale that when the demand slackened the little businesses could easily be closed and the family depended again on farming as their sole livelihood.[1] The little eighteenth-century storekeepers anticipated by two centuries the super-market proprietors in their efforts to satisfy all the needs of their customers under a single roof. The Battricks and Clenches managed to retain a few acres of their holdings until the 1840s. This achievement was only possible by ceaseless work and saving. The Battrick family were connected with shoemaking for over a century so built up a reputation for sound craftsmanship which enabled them to hold their own in face of competition. Shoemaking, wrote Cobbett, certainly with an eye to the future circulation of his publications, was 'a trade which numbers more men of sense and public spirit than any other in the Kingdom'. But in 1841 Bere with its eighteen cobblers to a population of 1,394 must have had too much of a good thing. The Clenches had been dealing in linsey, at 2s. a yard in 1777, dowlas and pairs of stockings for almost a century when in 1787 John Clench had the call to leave Bere to devote himself to the Sunday School movement.[2] Part of the family continued the business but not the lifeholding. Also in the 1780s, but possibly for more mundane reasons, the Frys severed their connections with the land and their living passed to the Ekins family soon to be dispossessed themselves.

[1] In 1709 poor rate was levied on the stock of one tradesman, by 1750 the number had risen to 14 and by 1771 it had declined to 9.

[2] H. Lawrence Phillips, *Poole and its Rectors*, 1915, p. 48.

In the easy-going economy of the mid-eighteenth century the part played by the churchwardens and overseers must not be overlooked. They helped the funds of the community, in the shape of church and poor rates, to circulate among tradesmen and artisans. The churchwardens authorised not only the payment for materials and for the services of glaziers, painters and carpenters in the church but also until about 1750, small sums for heads of vermin. This money reached members of the community such as servants, farmers' boys and labourers who might otherwise have had no opportunities for earning a few extra pence. Nor did the 'ancient freeholders' despise these small sums. The Ekins and Spear families brought the heads of stoats, otters, polecats and hedgehogs for payment. Regular poor relief was generally given by the overseers in kind or in services such as chimney sweeping, thatching and the cutting and delivery of turfs. The staple goods purchased for the poor were shoes, coarse clothing and materials such as dowlas, linsey and hessian. Sometimes payments for other goods were authorised, such as 2s. paid to Mary Candy for a 'bottle of scurvy grass, drops, physick for Mary Young, water to wash her mouth'. In a relaxed moment overseers sanctioned the expenditure of 4d. on a quart of beer for 'wenches to appear at Privy [Petty] Sessions'. Naturally no business could subsist on its orders from overseers, but these demands, coming most plentifully in times of hardship, often helped small tradesmen over a difficult spell. Such spells became more and more frequent as debts increased when prices rose during the war years. After 1793 relief was generally paid in cash but, although in the first two decades of the nineteenth century poor rates doubled in many Dorset parishes, the custom of paupers was of little value to shopkeepers. The labourer's standard of living had fallen so low that his wants were centred on bread alone. After the Poor Law Amendment Act of 1834 rates no longer returned to the pockets of traders and artisans in small parishes. Relief, unless the case were exceptional, was only to be given in the Union workhouse. As Bere was in the Wareham Union the orders for the new workhouse, erected in 1835, went to Wareham shopkeepers. These orders were not, at any rate in the 1840s and 1850s, on a scale to make the fortune of any shopkeeper; but the effects of road and railway building did by the 1860s improve the prospects of tradesmen in small towns. The man with capital enough to rent one of the newly consolidated holdings in Bere was more likely to be seen 'fumbling at the bottom of his canvas bag for silver and gold' at Wareham or Wimborne than making his purchases in his home parish.

Parish records in the early eighteenth century are concerned chiefly with the purchase by churchwardens and overseers of clothing materials, shoes, hardware and limited quantities of alcohol. Groceries seldom appear because parish officials did not consider them to be necessities as the consumption of such goods was confined to the well-to-do.

The arrival in the 1830s of grocers in villages and working class districts of towns was a revolution in shopkeeping. The principle was recognised, with certain modifications as to quality, that rich and poor alike not only wanted, but were prepared to pay for, a more varied diet. The need was greatest among the poor who, since the late eighteenth century, had been subsisting largely on a monotonous diet of bread and potatoes. In vain did prudent economists suggest the infusing of currant or hop leaves and the keeping of bees rather than the squandering of money on tea and sugar. The labourer's wife needed the stimulus of tea, even if it were only the one ounce purchased weekly by Mrs. Hayward of Stourpaine,[1] as much as her husband needed beer. To their supplies of tea, sugar and spices, grocers were adding in the 1840s, when the political climate favoured free trade, cocoa, treacle, rice and coffee. In 1841 five grocers were established in Bere, three of whom were elderly men belonging to former landholding families, the Cokes, Goulds and Gallops. Ten years later a Scotsman and a Londoner had set up business, a sure indication that future prospects, even in towns like Bere, swept by agricultural crises, were hopeful. The cheating of customers by dairymen, corn chandlers and bakers was not unknown, but it was comparatively easily detected as most customers knew how fresh and unadulterated goods should look. This was not the case with groceries and vendors could not resist the temptation to profit by the sale of adulterated goods. Public-spirited men tried to warn people that 'when we are invited to try the "fine Java" at 1s. 11$\frac{3}{4}$d., we are simply asked to purchase some roasted potatoes and marigold . . . when potatoes are dull at $\frac{3}{4}$d., and marigolds may be had in the fields for the trouble of picking them' and that 'flaked cocoa is nothing but the refuse of better preparations'.[2] Very few customers had the time, the fuel or the equipment to roast and grind coffee beans or to boil cocoa nibs for two or three hours. Yet few small grocers made a comfortable profit. They themselves were often victims of the almost universal swindling which accompanied the increasing imports of foreign and colonial goods and received adulterated wares from the wholesaler. Much time was spent in weighing out minute quantities and, as ready cash was seldom available, in chalking up debts often only repaid in part.

[1] *Report on Women and Children in Agriculture*, 1843, p. 91.
[2] *The Family Economist*, 1851, Vol. IV, p. 153 and 1848, Vol. I, p. 53.

42. Bere Regis. View from Woodbury Hill looking south-west over the village and meadows beside the Bere to the heathland of Black Hill.

THE ECONOMIC PILLARS OF BERE
REGIS: FARMING AND BUTTONY. **43.**
Philliols Farm. The Ekins family built
the brick outhouses in the mid-eighteenth
century, but modernisation did not
enable these freeholders to keep their
land. **44.** The Button Depot at Milborne
St. Andrew. Established in 1803 by
Peter Case, the depot was 'crowded like
a fair' on Fridays when families from the
surrounding district brought in their
buttons.

45. Bere Regis. To the east lie small fields unofficially enclosed by the mid-eighteenth century, to the north-west the larger enclosures made a century later.

THE BERE SCENE. **46.** (*above left*). Believed to be William Barwell, Congregational Minister in Bere, 1871-74. **47.** (*above right*). The Oyster Seller. A popular china figure at the end of the nineteenth century. On Woodbury Hill can still be found the oyster shells thrown aside by those who came to the fair to enjoy the first oysters of the season. **48.** (*below left*). Annie Langdown, 1890. The first photograph from London with Annie wearing a maroon dress made by Elizabeth Boswell. **49.** (*below right*). Annie Langdown (Mrs. Annie Hawkins), 1964.

50. Honeycomb Wood. Woodmen were reluctant to leave their work, since they found: '*In whatever season it mid be*
    The trees be always company'. W. Barnes.

51. Bagber elms. '*Where elms from Nature's hand confus'dly thrown
With bushy trunks . . .*' W. Holloway.

52. Upper Farm, Lillington. A typical eighteenth-century farm with dairy, cider house, cottage and cowsheds clustered around the living quarters. **53.** Brimley Mill, Stoke Abbott. Of little economic value, the horse chestnut appears to greatest advantage as an ornamental tree when planted near buildings.

THE WOODWORKERS. **54.** Mixed cricket at Thornford, 1902 (*above*). David Gould seated third from left. **55.** David Gould spar making (*lower left*). **56.** Robin Stone, basket maker of East Stour, *c* 1900 (*lower right*).

By 1850 nearly all the families who had been lifeholders a century earlier had lost their land, though many hung on grimly to their trades. Their fall, though it caused a revolution in rural society, had not been a spectacular one. Smallholders gradually ceased their plodding journeys from strip to strip and took the harder road of sitting long hours at the bench making and repairing goods for which it was increasingly hard to secure ready payment. The larger landholders concealed their poverty as best they could, ashamed to let their neighbours know their wants. Dispossessed lifeholders were alike in that, whether cottagers or once 'substantial householders', they were forced to throw their wives and offspring into the defences against destitution. The numbers of women and children undertaking paid employment in agricultural work, in dressmaking and in the stitching of gloves and of buttons was the second revolutionary upheaval in the daily life of Bere. For those who could stand the life, field work was generally available, but many women tried to earn money in their homes.

The four dressmakers in Bere in 1841 could probably have earned a living, but in ten years the number had increased to sixteen dressmakers and milliners who were certainly battling for limited custom. The point to which earnings dwindled can be gauged from the fact that at this time a London seamstress was paid 1s. for making a dozen of 'the cheapest and coarsest coloured cotton shirts complete'.[1] These dressmakers came from a wide section of the community ranging from Mary Spear, an independent gentlewoman, to Harriet Moore who struggled to maintain a pauper grandfather. One of these dressmakers, young Elizabeth Boswell, succeeded in making her way. By the 1880s an apprenticeship in her establishment was eagerly sought, although it involved working without pay from 9 a.m. to 8 p.m. with breaks for lunch and tea. Time off was allowed for choir practice providing it was made up on Saturday.[2] By the last decades of the nineteenth century dressmaking had more profitable possibilities. The steady migration of girls to the cities in search of domestic work had started. Great efforts were made to provide daughters leaving home with a new dress. When they returned their small savings were often spent in having clothes made for their mothers and sisters.

Despite the spate of seamstresses in 1851 supposedly all needing tapes, needles, threads and materials only one drapery establishment, in the hands of the Case family, supplied their needs. The

[1] *The Woman's World*, 1888, edited by Oscar Wilde, p. 301, Clementina Black, 'Something about Needlewomen'.
[2] The information was kindly given by Katherine Lane who was herself an apprentice under Elizabeth Boswell, who later became Mrs. Griffin.

arrival of the Cases in the early eighteenth century was a landmark in the social history of Bere. The Cases were the great merchants who, for half a century, provided buttons for Europe and America and work for the women of central Dorset. The last of the Cases, who died in 1912, used to describe the bustling activity of the button trade with one of its chief depots, now the post office, at Milborne St. Andrew,[1] but his recollections must have been largely from hearsay. Among the wonders of the Great Exhibition of 1851 was Ashton's button machine which was to put an end to home button making and to the prosperity of the Case family. It was not until the 1820s that button making became almost a matter of life and death in the poor homes of Bere. From the time that their fingers were steady enough until their abused sight failed, girls and women filled in the wire button rings with intricate stitched patterns. The numbers of these desperate workers rose from fourteen in 1841 to sixty-seven in 1851, a sure indication of the numbers of families living on the starvation line in the 1840s. Grinding work as 'buttony' was, its disappearance would have been a terrible blow had not home glove-making taken its place. This activity continued in Bere until after the First World War.

Theoretically the burden of the hard mid-nineteenth century years was eased for agricultural labourers by the end of the century. The rains of the late 1870s washed the heart out of high farming and with it the determined resistance to wage increases. Furthermore, the boys were following the girls in the search for work outside their home parishes. But the effects of the depression and of the drift to the towns were slow in relieving the proverbial poverty of the Dorset labourer. The memories of a nonagenarian can recall, if not the actual years, the texture of life in the tough, hunger-ridden 1840s and 1850s. The recollections of Mrs. Annie Hawkins, born in 1873, furnish not only a fitting epilogue to a sad chapter in the history of Bere, but also illustrate the determination and energy that enabled her and so many of her contemporaries to overcome their hardships.

George Langdown, Mrs. Hawkins' father, came of a family of small landholders; the vicissitudes of this group were so constantly repeated throughout Dorset that the individual tragedies have been overlooked.

The early years of the eighteenth century, traditionally a time of plenty for farmer and labourer alike, were not altogether golden for the Langdowns. Either directly or indirectly Widow Langdown was assisted from the poor rates. In 1710 the sum of

[1] Mr. Marwood Hopkins of Milborne often heard William Miller Case talking about the thriving button trade.

9s. 5d. was spent on 'time and labour' for repairing her house, while two years later she was paid 6s. by the overseers for 'attending Mrs. Coles's family'. Poor-rate payments for nursing and for home-made remedies were life savers for many widows and poor wives, whatever they were for the patients. Taylor's map shows the Langdowns as occupying in 1776 a fourteen-acre lifehold consisting mainly of strips of less than an acre scattered throughout the open fields. The family continued on the fringe of parish relief, not always receiving it, but also selling small quantities of barley to the overseers for distribution among the needy. The parochial officials were valued customers of the small producer. As a rule the more prosperous farmers had little time for the petty quantities and services involved; nevertheless, Farmer Little with forty-seven acres did not spurn a few shillings for carting paupers out of the parish and furze faggots to those legally 'settled'.

The landholding of the Langdowns appears and disappears in the land-tax assessments with the apparent inconsequence of Alice's Cheshire cat. It is not surprising to find the family paying 10s. 11d. for their holding in the 1780s, but their absence from the assessment in the incentive-giving 1790s is unexpected. Even more curious is the reappearance of the Langdowns, still paying 10s. 11d., in 1815 and their maintenance of the tenement until 1830, years in which the knell sounded for so many smallholders. A possible explanation is that the family sub-let their lifehold at a profitable rent when grain prices were rising but, after the peace, found themselves burdened with a holding which was a source of neither pride nor profit. By the 1840s the money earned by his daughter in making buttons was more profitable to old Henry Langdown than the quarter of an acre in Middle Field that still remained to him. Henry did not spare himself and worked as an agricultural labourer into his seventies. The same hard life awaited his young relative Peter Langdown, born in 1821, and also Peter's son, George, who was Mrs. Hawkins' father. George was not given either to brooding over past misfortunes or to taking precautions to ward off future ones. He found saving hard, married young and had nine children. His wife, Hannah, was the daughter of a Langdown who had married into the Stickleys of Woodbury Hill. This family can be identified with the smallholding Stockleys of the mid-eighteenth century, and two centuries later they were still farming on Woodbury Hill, thriving, according to Mr. Maurice Stickley, mainly 'on the view and the air'. Annie, the eldest child of George and Hannah, spent much of her early childhood with her grandparents. Except for the stirring days in September when the fair was held, the little settlement of about forty persons on Woodbury Hill lived apart from the world beneath them. One day Annie Hawkins' grandmother received a shrivelled heart stuck with pins which her granddaughter robustly advised her to throw on the fire. The neighbours took another view and the solitary-living old woman believed to have sent it was set upon by the men of the Hill. In his parish magazine the vicar reported that at a Unionist meeting in the spring of 1887 'it is hardly necessary to say that in our law-abiding parish the resolution [against Home Rule for Ireland] was carried unanimously'. But Bere like most other Dorset villages at the time was not law-abiding. Gang warfare was usual; the trouble started when young men from one parish invaded another and were resisted so that the groups were soon, according to Mr. William Hardy of Longthorns, 'fighting like dogs'. Well within living memory young men from Winterborne Kingston were stoned out of Bere. Election times, even before the agricultural labourer had the vote, were especially rowdy. Attacks were made on Mr. Bankes and Mr. Sturt at a Dorchester political meeting in 1849 and a man was killed in the scuffling. Lord Palmerston referred to the incident as an example of the irrepressible violence of political feeling in England, when he attempted to justify to the outraged Queen Victoria the assault in London on General Haynau, notorious for his savage suppression of the 1848 risings in Hungary.[1] Elections provided an outlet not so much for passionately held political beliefs as for personal resentments; the inhabitants of Bere, traditionally intransigent, were not likely to let their opportunities slip. In the tumultuous election of April 1880 the Langdown children were shut in the house to keep them out of mischief. Excited by the noise, Annie excaped to see an elderly Liberal supporter dragged face downwards along the gravelly High Street of Bere by his political opponents who were, in Mrs. Hawkins' opinion, 'buttered up with whisky by the Upper Ten' of the parish. The victims of violence were not only the politically committed. During this disturbance Joseph Hewitt, 'a quiet and industrious workman', was looking on when he was knocked down by a horseman supporting the Conservative candidate.[2] George Langdown especially shone during election times. Under the cover of darkness he climbed a high pine tree to tear down the blue flag hoisted by the excise officer. Hannah was more concerned with the serious side of life, the maintenance of her large family and regular attendance at the Congregational chapel where she was a devoted follower of William Barwell, minister 1871-1874. Like most small towns in Dorset, Bere had a strong Nonconformist tradition and

---

[1] *Queen Victoria's Early Letters*, edited by J. Raymond, 1963, p. 175.
[2] *Dorset County Chronicle*, 22 April 1880.

Leaving Home   *The Girls' Own Paper, 23 April 1881*

early in the eighteenth century supported a Baptist minister.[1] By the middle of the following century congregations were attending two Methodist chapels and Baptist and Congregational meeting places. Unfortunately the Congregational school in Butt Lane was closed when Annie was about eight so she was exposed to all the temptations of a Church of England school. Hannah indignantly refused the request of the vicar's wife that Annie, one of the best knitters in the parish, should make her a pair of gloves.

But the 'joy of the elect' was not unalloyed for Annie who started work at thirteen in the manse. She arrived before breakfast and left in the evening after a day of heavy work on light meals. Mothers were reluctant to let their daughters work in houses where only one servant was kept as the most grinding tasks, such as scouring floors and kitchen furniture with sand, often fell on those least able to sustain the toil. Generally only the very young or the old filled such posts since they were precluded by inexperience or physical weakness from obtaining better positions. A desperate need for economy rather than parsimony accounted for the grudging doles of food in the homes of many ministers, whose financial affairs were embarrassingly patent to their congregations. The minister was depen-

[1] John Evans' List of Dissenting Congregations, 1715-29 and Josiah Thompson's State of the Dissenting Interest 1715-73, MSS in John Williams' Library.

dent for his income upon his supporters, prominent among whom were often tradesmen with whom he was expected to deal, and who were in a position to scrutinise the outlay of sums which they had helped to provide.

Worried by the exhaustion of her daughter and harrassed by family cares, Hannah Langdown recalled Annie from service to resume her home tasks. In her struggle to make ends meet Hannah had to rely on her eldest daughter. Annie looked after the younger ones, whose successive arrivals caused her to sigh, 'Oh dear, another baby', and started knitting gloves before she was eleven. The *Family Economist* considered that 'knitting is an employment in which children may easily be interested; the art is simple, the motion of the fingers lively', but with Annie it was a bread-and-butter matter, not one of amusement. Mothers could not afford to spare their daughters when a quick knitter could make one and a half pairs of gloves a day. The rates of pay in the 1880s were 6½d. for a pair knitted with Berlin wool, 5d. for ordinary wool and 5½d. for cotton. The only cheerful colour among the popular dark wools and cotton was maroon Berlin wool, greatly favoured by young knitters.

This longing for brightness and gaiety was especially marked among the children of parents whose lives had been darkened by the terrible struggles of the 1840s. By the last decades of the nineteenth century the battle was over. As the economists had foretold, though they hardly envisaged the suffering involved, supply and demand had found their levels so as 'to remedy the disorders which may casually arise in society'. Out of the throngs of carpenters, tailors and dressmakers only the strongest had survived.

By dint of sticking to their coffin making the Whennels survived as carpenters into the present century; by the excellence of their work the Houses outmatched their many competitors in the tailoring trade. Katherine Lane recalled how her father, John Lane, born in 1833, determined to escape from the family groove of cobbling. He broke his apprenticeship and sailed for Newfoundland. This voyage cooled his enthusiasm for a new life and he returned to carry on successfully the family tradition of shoemaking. From among the numbers of dressmakers in the 1850s, initiative and the ability to drive her apprentices gave Elizabeth Boswell, the woodman's daughter, a place in Kelly's directory. Her brother Isaac struck out for himself in photography, a profession which was finding its feet in the 1870s and booming in the following decades. A photograph album became the hallmark of a rising family as a tea caddy had been in the 1830s. A solid respectability now marked the thriving grocers who were less addicted to their former piratical activities which had caused *Punch* to write, 'Highwaymen are extinct, and indeed where is the fun of risking your life when you can rob as you please simply by opening a shop and using false weights and measures'.[1] The pioneering days of drapers, like the Case family, were over and village businesses had settled back into the humdrum routine of the eighteenth-century mercers. The difference was that whereas the mercers had relied on selling cheap cloths, such as hessian, dowlas and linsey, the chief wares of the late nineteenth-century drapers were knitting wools, tapes and braiding. Some go-ahead men, like George Hibbs, tried to stem the flow of customers to larger towns by stocking bales of good-quality material. It was behind these bales that Hibbs reputedly kept the bottle of whisky with which he sustained Conservative supporters in the election of 1880.

The improved prospects of many Bere inhabitants partly accounts for the search for gaiety in the 1880s. Woodbury Fair was still a great attraction, though the parson of a neighbouring parish considered that it 'would be much better if the whole Fair were suppressed . . . numerous cheap excursion trains now offer more rational outings to more distant points of interest'. [2] But fun is seldom rational, and endeavours to meet the need for it with penny readings, flower shows and evening classes were not altogether successful. The appearance of the village itself was cheered after 1887 when, largely by voluntary contributions, the shop-lined High Street was lit by gas.

Despite the attractions of Bere Annie Langdown longed to escape from the drudgery of child minding and knitting, which allowed her no time for enjoying the old or the new excitements. Her chance came when a Stickley uncle, a butcher in Peckham, wanted help. Equipped with a new dress, made by Elizabeth Boswell, Annie joyfully left for London at the age of seventeen. Hannah Langdown's worst fears were realised; her daughter bought brightly coloured clothes, wore her hair in curls instead of braided plaits, and went to the music hall with her uncle on Monday evenings. As was the case with many girls, Annie returned after a few years to help her ageing and invalid mother; married and settled again in her native parish. Mrs. Hawkins never lost her taste for an active, social life and, once her children were grown up, she opened a small general store which proved a great blessing to the scattered heath dwellings around her home in the south of the parish.

Mrs. Hawkins' life has spanned nearly a century. She has seen the last of society dominated by the horse and the beginning of the space age. With none of her old vigour and commonsense abated, she is

[1] Quoted in *The Family Economist*, 1850, Vol. III, p. 48.
[2] *Proc.*, 1885, Vol. VII, pp. 93-99, O. Pickard Cambridge, Woodbury Hill.

able to dismiss the sending of shrivelled hearts and performances on the television screen as equal manifestations of human weakness in longing to show off before one's fellows.

In looking back over a period when old social groupings and families were swept away we are apt to mourn only the disappearance of classes, the very names of which – peasantry, yeomanry, 'ancient freeholders' – are heavy with historical associations. But the spirit with which the dispossessed ones rose again should not be overlooked; and it should not be forgotten that even the seemingly catastrophic changes of the early nineteenth century brought fresh opportunities. Charles Jesty came to Bere as a surveyor for the new turnpike road to Poole, but he remained to establish a profitable, and still thriving, connection with the parish. Young Felix Miller, a local boy, was in 1841 a house servant who had the luck to marry his mistress, Charity Purchase; and to take over the tenancy of her father's sixty-six acres. His descendants showed an equal ability for catching the main chance when in the 1880s they undertook contracting work with sawing and threshing machines. Steam power also opened a new road to ten of Charles Cobb's twelve sons.

The old village society was not shattered by the onslaught of alien and antagonistic forces. No nearby industrial development disturbed the pattern of rural life; no new lords of the manor disregarded old ties. The same family, watchful of the interests of Bere, remained at Charborough generation after generation. The great walls around the park witness the efforts made to relieve unemployment in the bleak 1840s. The old Bere changed because of man's invincible determination to better his material prospects. That these changes brought great benefits to future generations in no way lightened the darkness into which many of the old gentry, small lifeholders, artisans and tradesmen were cast. It was little comfort for them to feel that the reversal of their fortunes was due not to revolutionary violence but to the inexorable fulfilment of the current economic belief 'that nobody breaks who ought not to break'.

NOTES ON SOURCES USED FOR CHAPTER VI

Verbal Sources
My chief source has been Mrs. Annie Hawkins of Bere Regis. Without the constant help of her wonderful memory and gift for vivid description, no account of Bere in the last decades of the nineteenth century could have been attempted. Mrs. Hawkins also kindly allowed copies to be taken of some of her photographs and of the china oyster seller.

Information about Bere and its neighbourhood was also kindly given by:

F. Cobb (1885-1962), Skippets Farm, Bere.

Mr. S. Cobb, Warren, Bere.

Mr. E. Hodges, lately of Philliols Farm, Bere.

Mr. Hodges kindly allowed me to inspect the eighteenth-century farm buildings. The old farmhouse was destroyed early in this century.

Mr. M. Hopkins, Milborne St. Andrew.

C. Kellaway (1886-1962), West Street, Bere.

Katherine Lane (1879-1961), Bere.

H. Newberry (1880-1963), formerly a blacksmith, of East Holme.

Mr. M. Stickley, Woodbury Hill Farm, Bere.

Mr. and Mrs. J. Strang, Rye Hill, Bere.

Mrs. D. Woolfreys, West Street, Bere.

Accounts of gang fighting between villages were kindly given by:

Mr. W. Hardy, Longthorns, Wool.

Mr. R. Mitchell, Hazelbury Bryan.

Mrs. J. Strang, Rye Hill, Bere.

Written Sources

The parish church of St. John The Baptist, Bere Regis.

By kind permission of the past and present incumbents, Mr. R. Herring and Mr. P. Tranter, the following records were consulted:

Churchwardens' Accounts 1683-1740.

Poor Relief Accounts 1770-1834.

Bere Parish Magazine 1887-1893.

Kindly lent me by Mr. A. Hewitt of Bere.

Catalogue of Bere Regis Fields (undated) inspected by kind permission of the Honourable Martin Fortescue, Morden Estate Office.

Proceedings of Dorset Natural History and Archaeological Society, 1914, Vol. XXXV, pp. 71-75, E. Acland, Dorset Buttony.

Notes and Queries for Somerset and Dorset, 1957, Vol. XXVII, pp. 137-140, Mrs. Jackson's article on Dorset buttons.

Information concerning the Drax family in Yorkshire and the Sawbridges in Kent was kindly sent by Mr. C. K. C. Andrews, County Archivist for North Riding of Yorkshire, and Mr. F. Hull, County Archivist for Kent.

Tadpole Lane, Thornford

CHAPTER VII

Thornford:
The Clay and
Coppice People

The dwindling forests of Dorset between the thirteenth and seventeenth centuries – minor reafforestation in the mid-nineteenth century for sport and for profit – description of Dorset hedgerows and woodlands and their management – opportunities for copse and woodworkers – Thornford and its surrounding countryside – the fluctuating fortunes of the Gould family – their achievements as copse workers, farmers and parochial officials.

'As God has made the back to the burthen so the clay and coppice people make the dress to the stubs and bushes. Under the sole of the shoe is iron; from the sole six inches upwards is a high-low; then comes a leather bam to the knee; then comes a pair of leather breeches; then comes a stout doublet; over this comes a smock-frock; and the wearer sets brush and stubs and thorns and mire at defiance. I have always observed that woodland and forest labourers are best off in the main.'
William Cobbett describing the woodlands of Sussex, 2 January 1822, *Rural Rides.*

THE FORESTS of Dorset were once the playgrounds of monarchs. But, true to the folk-tale tradition, sorrow rather than sport awaited many huntsmen whether royal or common. Thomas de Linde found 'how dangerous it was to be twitching a lion by the eares' when he killed in the Blackmoor Vale a white hart cherished by Henry III. King John, who seldom brought good cheer in his train, favoured hunting in the Gillingham, Cranborne and Bere Regis districts; while King Edward the Martyr chased for the last time deer in the forests round Wareham.

When Thomas de Linde paid heavily for his foolhardy action, the heyday of forest preservation was passing. It was in Norman England, a conquered country, 'that the creation of royal forests, too often at the expense of arable land, was most extensive, and their protection most stringent'.[1] But by the end of the thirteenth century the encroachments of a growing population had started the slow but persistent assault of man on the forests. By seizing the shepherds, swineherds and ploughmen, the Black Death gave a short reprieve to the woodlands but the attacks were only effectively halted in the seventeenth century when nearly all the great trees had been felled. During the Commonwealth Evelyn with his plea for reafforestation was only one of the many visionaries who were seeking to realise, in one form or another, Bunyan's dream of tree-studded meadows where all 'might lie down safely'. In Dorset today only the field names tell of the great struggle of men against trees. *Holts* at South Perrott, *Hackthorn* at Mapperton and *Cockroads* throughout the county recall the woodlands, their felling and the clearings made for netting woodcock.

Although the great chases had dwindled by the eighteenth century, many areas in the north and west of Dorset still presented a wooded appearance. These were the districts which had been forest land in the early Middle Ages and the hard work of reclamation had often been achieved by individual rather than communal effort. As a result enclosures before the seventeenth century were general and the small fields, or *hays*, were surrounded by high, dense hawthorn hedges entwined with bramble and set with oak, elm and maple.[2] Arthur Young might rage about the land wasted and the uncouth appearance of thick hedgerows, 'high, irregular ridges of land . . . often over-run with bushes and wood', but Dorset farmers lived up to Young's contemptuous opinion of them and plodded along their old ways pointing out that well-timbered hedges provided shade and shelter for cattle and that shrouded, or lopped, branches were excellent fuel. Even here they were at fault as advocates of the new husbandry attacked the 'absurd' custom of 'cutting off the heads of growing timber to furnish firewood for the farmer's use'.[3] By the mid-nineteenth century the campaign against straggling hedgerows, was intensified and a characteristically moral note was struck with the cry, 'reform your hedgerows . . . to make way for the young and flourishing trees'.[4]

This reformation of hedgerows was often undertaken by travelling hedgers, or 'strappers'; but hedging and ditching work was eagerly

[1] M. Bloch, *Feudal Society*, 1961, p. 303.
[2] A. Fägersten, *The Place Names of Dorset*, 1933, p. xvii, has pointed out that as a farm or place name *hay* is confined to West Dorset. As a field-name element *hay* appears frequently around Gillingham, Motcombe and Sherborne.
[3] [D. Henry], *The Complete English Farmer*, 1771, p. 16.
[4] *The Family Economist*, 1849, Vol. II, p. 79.

sought by labourers and woodmen as piece-rates were paid. Even within living memory these rates varied greatly. Mr. D. Parsons of Camesworth, Netherbury, remembers that 9s. was paid for hedging and ditching a chain, a full day's work; on the bleak chalk uplands around Sydling St. Nicholas Mr. William Hardy recalls that only 4s. a chain was paid. If these were the rates paid at the turn of this century, the payments fifty years earlier can be put at 3s. to 4s. a chain. Hedgers had to bring their own switching bills and axes and, if they could afford them, gloves which at the end of the nineteenth century cost 10s. Generally men wrapped old socks round their hands, but accidents from slipping bills and axes were not rare,[1] and minor injuries from embedded thorns were frequent. One method of easing out thorns was to eat spoonfuls of black treacle.[2] Clothing was protected by heavy smocks and after 1860 generally by slops or loose jackets made of sacking. Despite Cobbett's admiration for iron soles and stout high-lows nothing could protect the feet of the hedger who often worked ankle-deep in water. In 1848 *The Family Economist* was advising their readers to waterproof their boots by applying a mixture of linseed oil, mutton suet, beeswax and resin; but at the same time the editors were very cautious in hazarding cures for rheumatism, only suggesting that cod liver oil 'sometimes succeeds'. Most woodmen and hedgers reaped in their old age a harvest of 'rheumatisms, pricks and spasms'.

The structure and composition of hedges varied throughout the county. In the west thick growths of hazel sprawled on either side of earth mounds four to six feet high. These Devonshire hedges are often still studded with oak which was kept shrouded, or heavily pruned, and topped. Sparser hawthorn and privet hedges divided the downland fields, many of which were not enclosed until after 1815. These hedges were often thickened by ash which was either allowed to reach maturity or cut after three or four years so that the stem was laid horizontally. Maple and sycamore are scattered widely in Dorset hedgerows but in some areas, notably around Mappowder, maple hedges are as conspicuous by their vivid green leaves in June as by their red foliage in autumn. In East Dorset Stevenson noted that the Canford Heath enclosers, who had to work fast in the face of much opposition including that of the indefatigable Thomas Hyde of Arne, had thrown up banks on which furze was planted. This was only a temporary measure as furze is too straggling

---

[1] Descriptions of prisoners in the Dorchester Jail Records, D.R.O., show that numbers of the men arrested in connection with the 1830 riots had injured or mutilated hands.

[2] Mr. Norris Symonds of Martinstown kindly gave information of this cure which he learned from the late Walter Upwood of the same parish.

to make an effective hedge and, as was apparent in the winter of 1962-63, it dies away after severe cold. Where stone was not available Purbeck farmers had to make shift as best they could with hawthorn unless the lie of the land allowed dikes, or lakes, to mark the field boundaries as at Arne.

Hedgerows played as important a part in hunting as did coverts. Trees, particularly holly, were often planted by gates as a guide to foxhunters. Those who scorned gates found many hedgerow hazards from teasing bullfinches, the young growing hedges, to raspers or high hedges on broad banks. An attempt to jump one of these caused the death of young Lord Guildford in December 1885. His horse fell in trying to leap 'a bank about six feet high, with a ditch on each side and a hedge on the top, . . . recently "plashed" with a double set of binders, the trench between being filled up with the earth taken from the ditches on each side'.[1] This hedge marks the south-west boundary of a Buckland Newton field, which even today is a mournful place. Willows abound and tussocks of coarse grass cover the treacherously uneven ground, waterlogged even in the dry summer of 1964.[2]

When nails and a roll of barbed wire could in a few hours make a secure field boundary, the art of hedging was neglected. The feelings of foxhunters towards the increasing use of wire in the 1890s may be summed up in the words of William Hawkins (1843-1931), owner of Manor Farm, Martinstown, who declared that 'barbed wire should be drawn across the man who invented it'. On this point hedgers agreed with the foxhunters since the heavy toil of their craft was nothing compared with the benefits of piece-rates. In the same way woodmen little heeded the prospect of a crippled old age when they could obtain fuel at their work.

Fuel finding, especially in the early spring, was a daily and harrowing anxiety in most villages of South England. In the north, as James Pigg of *Mr. Jorrocks' Hunt* pointed out, labourers had 'great blazin' fires to come hyem te at night'. Such a blaze seldom cheered Dorset cottagers, many of whom were reduced to trying to burn lumps of chalk as advised by the Dorset Association for the Improvement of Working Classes. In spring, when the winter store was finished children, who were generally the fuel finders, grew desperate. In April 1818 the four Northover children were caught pulling twigs from a Swyre hedgerow; Charles, aged twelve years, went to prison for a month, his sister and two younger brothers were let off with a fortnight. Fourteen-year-old Matilda Lane of Cranborne

[1] H. Symonds, *Runs and Sporting Notes from Dorsetshire*, 1899, p. 105.
[2] I am indebted to Mr. E. Vardy, lately of Knaps Hill Farm, Buckland Newton, for information concerning the place of the accident.

was sentenced in March 1819 to a month's hard labour for destroying underwood.

The wooded appearance of large districts of Dorset was not only due to the straggling, timber-studded hedgerows but also to the second afforestation of the county. This was on a less heroic scale than the first in the early twelfth century; but was equally, and more articulately, resented by the peasantry. According to the poet, William Holloway, the Dorset peasant saw with anguish,

'Yon upland fields, where cheerful peasants earned
Their weekly bread, to proud plantations turn'd.'

The second wave of timber planting started in the mid-eighteenth century when clumps of trees and serpentine waterways were essential to any landowners anxious to establish their claims to sensibility. Although Dorset was noted, according to Stevenson, for its 'profusion of fine seats' the extension of parkland was not marked in the county until the early nineteenth century. A few families like the Pitts at Encombe and the Digbys at Sherborne had set the pace earlier with artificial lakes and effective timber planting, but the great spread of pleasure grounds was not until the 1840s. In 1842 the tithe map shows that the parkland around Minterne House had not yet engulfed small meads such as *Mouse Close, Cowleaze Mead*, and *Froghole Moor*; while two years later the land south of Came House was still meadow. The Framptons at Moreton did not plant their grounds northwards until 1839, by which time the family had acquired a large part of *Moreton Common Field*. 'The prodigious delight in improving and planting' found many outlets at Moreton. In the park a singular effect was achieved by planting two different trees very closely together to give the appearance of a single growth. A hawthorn and chestnut still survive entwined in their uneasy and lop-sided partnership.

Landowners were not only embellishing their immediate surroundings at a time when they thought themselves doomed by the repeal of the Corn Laws, but they were also embarking on the widespread planting of covers for sport. Both fox hunting and shooting greatly increased in popularity in the late 1850s, and landowners preserved their game as earnestly and almost as ruthlessly as the Normans had done. Covers were provided by new plantations or by the extension of existing copses. In the mid-nineteenth century Dorset had some traces of old forest notably in Cranborne Chase and the Blackmoor Vale. Despite their venerable appearance the great trees of the ancient chases were more likely to have come to maturity in the sixteenth century than to have been hung with Hardy's 'druidical mistletoe' in pre-Roman times.

By 1850 the greatest part of Dorset woodland was man-managed copse. Here timber trees, or standards, were grown with underwood which was regularly felled, or coppiced, for poles, rods and in the case of oak, bark for tanning. Just as the economic value of copses was waning because of the reduced tariffs on timber imports their social value for game preservation was waxing. Not only were the old copses retained but they were often extended; laurel, holly, privet and, in East Dorset, rhododendrons were planted for extra cover. Evergreen undergrowth also had the ornamental merit of showing timber trees to great advantage, as in the Carey and old Hethfelton woods near Wareham. The enlarged covers often ate into arable and pasture land. In 1768 the area now covered by King's Court Wood in the parish of Motcombe was all fields; the plantation started in 1839 doubled in size in the succeeding years. Today it is not hard to imagine Motcombe as lying within the boundaries of the royal forest of Gillingham. The rolling landscape is still dominated by oaks growing in hedgerows, in copses and sometimes near the small ponds which dimple the regular fields of the district. Some of these fields were enclosed before the deforestation of 1624 and a few, *Paradise*, *Northayes*, and *Easthayes*, still keep their seventeenth-century names.

In the nineteenth century the oaks at Motcombe started to regain ground they had lost three hundred years earlier, but on the chalkland trees were planted after a far longer absence. Remains of charcoal at Maiden Castle near Dorchester suggest 'that in Neolithic times the Chalk of Dorset was probably clothed with a closed plant community of woodland of the oak-hazel type'.[1] Grazing and cultivation had reduced these woods to open scrub by the time the Roman settlement started, so there was little difficulty in building roads on once wooded chalkland. The road between Yeovil and Dorchester was built across open country that is now dotted with plantations. The names of some of these, such as Great War and Prisoners of War Plantations, indicate that the planting of covers continued well into this century. At Bere Regis, also, the Roman road north of the village had run across open country. The skyline was not broken with covers until the 1840s when Drax aimed at making Bere one of the great hunting districts of East Dorset. These covers included many clumps of gorse, or Fox Pounds, which were fostered at considerable expense to the bewilderment of those old labourers who remembered the struggle in their youth to keep gorse down on the open arable fields. These old men, observing foxes cherished like princes, could also recall their fathers' tales of a fox's head fetching a shilling when churchwardens paid for the extermination of vermin.[2]

[1] W. B. Turrill, *British Plant Life*, 1948, p. 43.
[2] Bere Regis Churchwardens' Accounts, 1732.

Pollen analyses of the peat beds of the East Dorset heathland may show, as they have in other similar areas, that in late Neolithic times alder, oak, elm, ash and lime abounded. But early written records refer to the barren heath with forests restricted to the brown earths which encircle the acid podsols and peats. Around Edmondsham, as at Motcombe, great oaks still hold their own in copse and hedgerow. These are, in the opinion of Mr. Frederick Legg, who was fifty years estate carpenter in Edmondsham, the finest oaks in Dorset.

By the early nineteenth century Stevenson considered that there were only 10,000 acres of woodland in Dorset and that this acreage was 'continually diminishing'; but it was just at this time that trees became fashionable. Landlords not concerned to show their sensibility were interested in the economic arguments encouraging plantations. Hale assured them, 'there is no step the husbandman can take in planting, providing it be done with discretion, that will not yield to his yearly income', and 'it is the peculiar happiness of these plantations that all soils will bear them'. Landowners found that, if not all soils, many areas hitherto neglected could be used for plantations. Willows and osiers were planted in the marshy fields of stream-encircled Fifehead Neville, and Cobbett's 'trashy fir tribe' appeared on the heathland. In Dorset these firs were generally planted as highwood timber, that is, trees not cleared for a crop till they had reached maturity.

Covers for preserving game could also be a profitable investment if copse were planted or extended. Copse provided an opportunity of growing timber on a small scale as well as harvesting the chief coppice crops of hazel and ash. The profits from these crops varied with the age at which the wood was cut. Coppice cut at seven to eight years for hurdles or at fourteen years for dead hedges or railing poles produced yearly about 20s. an acre.[1] Thus copse, which satisfied the sporting and business interests of the landlord, was the most usual type of woodland planted in Dorset. The larger woods such as Honeycomb near Sherborne, Bere Wood and the Middlemarsh and Milton Abbas woods were extended primarily for profit because extensive woods were, as Jorrocks discovered in Pinch-Me-Near Forest, 'werry bad riding' for sportsmen.

Ash and hazel were the most usual coppice trees in Dorset, but the standards varied with the locality. Oak grew best on heavy loams, beech and ash thrived on alkaline soils, while the more tolerant sycamore only demanded depth of soil for its penetrating

---

[1] W. Stevenson, *General View of Agriculture of the County of Dorset*, 1812, pp. 326-327. Mr. Alner of Puddletown, however, considered that Lord Orford's woods fetched, at 10 or 12 years' growth, £8 to £13 an acre.

roots. The standards could be reared from seeds sown either in a nursery or on the site where it was intended they should grow. When sown with coppice or in hedgerows oaks had room to spread their branches and grow 'the tough, curved rib-pieces and crooked knees' needed by the shipwrights.[1] The oak was 'in its service the most universal' as it supplied wheelwrights, cabinet makers, builders and tanners as well as shipbuilders. But the demands of the shipyards were the most pressing in the eighteenth century. When David Garrick assured the excited theatre audience in 1759 that 'England would add something new to this wonderful year' as 'hearts of oak' were her ships, the sentiment was truly British but the shipbuilding timber was mainly imported. Afforestation was under way, encouraged by high timber prices, but it was too late to replace the trees which had been steadily felled, or to regain the land ploughed in preceding centuries.

Cobbett, as vehement in praise as attack, asserted that 'the ash will grow *anywhere*'. Despite this assurance ash highwoods were not common in Dorset; but the trees were widely grown in groves for coppice, as standards with undergrowth and as hedgerow timber. Most of the ash groves, like the one on Black Hill, east of Cerne Abbas, are now neglected; the light bark of the trees and the patches of exposed chalk and flint in the soil give these groves a ghostly appearance. 'A greedy forager', ash with its spreading branches and roots was not well-suited to hedges; nevertheless its vivid green foliage in spring and heavy seed clusters in autumn are one of the most common hedgerow sights on the grey rendsinas of Dorset. If oak was the nation's tree, ash was essentially the farmer's friend. Its wood was used for most of the 'Instruments of Husbandry' which included not only the handles of implements but also plough handles and beams, temporary fencing and the shafts and axles of carts and wagons. As ash was the wood most commonly used on the farm it was lucky that tradition hallowed the practice by claiming that ash handles and axles enabled men to work harder and wheels to turn faster. Ash leaves were considered good for man and beast; they were used as a substitute for tea,[2] and cuttings were 'acceptable to any cattle'. Sacred in Norse legend, ash was believed to have protective powers, but these cannot have been apparent to William Sartin, a mason of Corscombe, who was sentenced in March 1816 to six months' hard labour for topping a maiden ash tree; or, indeed, to the Duke of Monmouth captured crouching under an ash at Horton in East Dorset.

Beech was another obliging tree said by the author of *The Compleat*

[1] J. Nisbet, *The Forester*, 1905, Vol. I, p. 28.
[2] T. F. Almack, *A Village Heritage*, 1961, pp. 63-64.

Body of Husbandry to grow 'almost on rocks', but it thrives best on soils derived from Chalk. Beech was grown for coppice but in Dorset the tree is generally found as a standard with undergrowth or in small highwoods planted for covers or for windbreaks. The wood, which takes a good polish and is not liable to crack, was especially favoured by turners and cabinet makers. In the eighteenth century not only were bedsteads generally of beech, but the leaves were used to stuff mattresses and pillows. *The Family Economist* tried to revive this practice, which had lapsed with the importation of flock and horsehair, on the grounds that beech leaves were unlikely to harbour vermin and gave a 'grateful and wholesome' smell. But by the 1840s that section of the population most in need of sanitary bedding had little chance of gathering beech leaves. As well as being planted in small hillside woods, beech often appears near the remote hilltop barns, like Grove Hill Barn at Martinstown, that are so common on the Dorset chalk downs. In the winter the rattle of dead beech leaves still clinging to the branches and the twittering of sparrows in the hay barns are the only sounds around these lonely buildings.

As an ornament to the countryside oak is often stark, the beech twisted and the ash, with its down-sweeping branches, can be fussy; but the elm, the tree suggesting coffins and disaster in storms, is always pleasing. In spring when light delicate leaves cover the bole, the tree has the shimmering appearance of a fountain. Since the elm favours the medium loams of surface water gleys it often gives height and grace, as at Bagber, to a somewhat featureless landscape. The thriving tree was taken as a sign of soil fertility and, according to Mr. R. F. Miles of Cann, near Shaftesbury, wise land purchasers looked out for 'tall elms and fat cows' to guide their choice.

To encourage the planting of timber and coppice *The Compleat Body of Husbandry* assured its readers that 'here Nature does the whole business'. But Nature is impartial and was as likely to have allowed rats and squirrels to destroy young trees as to foster them herself. It was the ravages of rodents on acorn, beech mast and other timber seeds that encouraged the establishment in the early seventeenth century of man-made plantations for careful raising of young trees.[1] Throughout the seasons the woodmen had to aid Nature at her business. Autumn and spring were the times for planting out seedlings or transplants from nurseries in the areas of wood which had been cleared. Young plants that failed in the first or second year had to be cut back; the healthy had to be encouraged by clearing away the weeds. If the coppice were too thin ash and hazel had to be layered or plashed in autumn. Young shoots were bent and pegged

[1] J. Nisbet, op. cit., Vol. 1, p. 19.

under the soil so as to develop a new root system in the following spring. After seven and twelve years' growth hazel and ash rods respectively could be cut in March. If oak had been coppiced bark stripping followed in April and May when the sap was rising. This stripping was work for women and boys, not for the woodmen who, as Marty South in *The Woodlanders* pointed out, had 'less patience with twigs because their time is worth more'. After the harvesting of oak bark the woods had a brief space of summer quiet when the sun only appeared to the woodman 'in the form of numerous little stars staring through the leaves'. As the last leaves fluttered down timber trees could be felled. Clean felling was essential since 'all boggling at the stump does great mischief' by retarding the growth of healthy shoots.[1] Boggling was primarily due, in Mavor's opinion, to allowing woodmen to take away the chips around felled trees in part-payment for their work.

Coppice with standards not only brought profit to the landlord and provided the 'woodland and forest labourers' with a livelihood, but also gave opportunities to the man who, having saved a few pounds, was anxious to venture on some small enterprise. Few footholds existed to help men on the hard climb from the labouring class to that of the tenant farmer. Until the mid-nineteenth century the chief means by which an agricultural labourer in Dorset could gain independence was by renting a few cows or a small acreage of coppice. The man who rented coppice was responsible for cutting the rods, poles and brushwood. These he sold or had made into spars, sheep cribs and hurdles; the profits were small but a man was launched as his own master.

By renting coppice the Gould family of Thornford were able to achieve the formidable task in the 1880s of lifting themselves back to the tenant-farming class from which they had sunk to labourers earlier in the century. Because the Goulds performed this mighty feat and because their chronicles between the late seventeenth century and the 1930s show how bondage to the soil of one parish could bring fulfilment as well as frustration, their history is both illuminating and absorbing. To understand it some survey is necessary of the parish of Thornford which was the focal point of the family activities, and of the surrounding district.

Thornford lies about two and a half miles south-west of Sherborne, and to the west of the woodland area falling roughly within the triangle Thornford-Holwell-Middlemarsh. This was the heart of timber and coppice growing in Dorset for industry and, as much of the area was covered by the Portman Hunt, was noted for 'hard riding and . . . coverts for stout foxes'.[2] The notable copses in this

[1] Thomas Hale, op. cit., p. 139.   [2] *Country Life*, 18 January 1908, p. IX.

area were Whitfield and Honeycomb to the west, those around
Wootton Glanville in the east and the Middlemarsh woods at the
apex of the triangle. In Norman times this whole district was forest
with small settlements possibly at Folke and Lillington and certainly
at Minterne Magna. The natural forest retreated before the onslaughts of man and beast and the woodlands were still further
tamed in the fifteenth century when landlords started enclosing after
felling 'for the preserving of young spring' of shoots and self-sown
seedlings.[1] So started copse work which was the main industry of
the area until the late nineteenth century. Today many of the
neglected coppices show the struggle which saddened Thomas
Hardy when he sought peace in the woods. The light-demanding
oak and ash battle for survival, while the hardier, shade-tolerating
sycamore, hazel and sweet chestnut strive to hold their own against
entwining ivy, bramble, honeysuckle and, in more open spaces, the
delicate yet crippling bindweed. Part of the parish of Thornford lies
on a fertile raised belt of brown earth derived from Fullers Earth.
To the south this favoured escarpment dips to Hutchins' 'cold
clayey loams' stretching to Chetnole, Leigh and Yetminster. Here
in winter oozing ponds and over-flowing streams seem to set the
whole area afloat; moorhens take possession of the fields as jackdaws
claim a ruin. Willow and hazel abound in this district and the 'plain
and even somewhat gloomy' alders which met the needs of social
extremes by providing wood for clogs and for cigar boxes. At Yetminster in the 1840s willow and hazel were used for rake making.
This was a profitable craft as a wide variety of rakes, including
cornrakes, daisy rakes, drill rakes, and dung drags, were used for
agricultural work. In the North hay rakes were made to last many
seasons, but in the more prodigal South large numbers were made
just to see through a single haymaking season.[2]

Mr. Denis Yarde of Wareham, who grew up in Thornford at the
end of the last century, has described the village as a place 'that took
itself seriously'. At first sight the village is not an attractive one. The
long, straight main street, dominated by the 1887 Jubilee clock,
lacks the interest given by irregular grouping of houses and by trees.
But round the church seventeenth-century houses and cottages display the pleasing buff tinted limestone from local quarries. In one
of these cottages was born David Gould (1876-1965) whose memories throw light not only on the vicissitudes of his own family but

[1] J. Nisbet, op. cit., Vol. I, pp. 15-16. Quotation from the Act for Enclosing
Woods in Forests, Chases and Purlieus, 1482. This act only applied to royal
forests but indicates that coppicing was generally practised.

[2] *Country Life*, 23 November 1961, pp. 1276-8, J. Geraint Jenkins, 'The Waning
Craft of the Rake-Maker'.

also on the daily life of a community which until 1918 seemed forgotten by time.

The Goulds belonged to that class which Melbury in *The Wood-landers* dismissed as 'yeomen, copy holders and such like'. But the annals of this class are the undergrowth of national history; the great events, or standards, take the eye, but coppice as well as timber provides a rich harvest. Neither David Gould's recollections nor the parish records have disentangled all the ramifications of a family which began to play a significant part in Thornford affairs at the end of the seventeenth century. But, if early family connections are not always clear, there is no doubt about the dogged perseverance with which the Goulds sought to build their fortunes on the land. By the middle of the eighteenth century some members of the family were established as small tenants. John Gould paid a church rate of 2d. on a modest holding at Lillington, a parish adjoining Thornford to the south-east. Lillington and its neighbour, Beer Hackett, were early enclosed parishes so that a brisk letting and sub-letting of small holdings were general. It was not until the late eighteenth century that property in this district became concentrated in the hands of a few owners like Lord Digby and Thomas Gollop. This amassing of land by the 'principal proprietors' did not immediately debar the small man from copyholding. In the early nineteenth century when Lord Digby was extending his estates in Thornford, David Gould was still able to add his wife's small copyhold held under Lord Digby to the family tenements. The actual possession of a copyhold or the holding of a 'life' ensuring future tenancy was the most effective matchmaker in the eighteenth-century villages. As well as copyholds small manorial tenants were sometimes able to enclose waste. In this way were set the fortunes of the Moore family who, by not despising bramble-covered patches and by running the first local milk-carriage service to Sherborne, emerged as notable tenant farmers. After 1815 fears that protection might end made landlords anxious either to cultivate every perch of their land or to let it to substantial and efficient tenants. The small man, living from hand to mouth, could make little headway in these go-ahead times. But before the pace quickened David Gould, working with mole-like persistence, had laid field to field and so prepared the way for Richard Gould (1760-1818), the great grandfather of the late David Gould. Richard, like many ambitious men of his time, had little patience with the plodding progress of his forbears.

In the hopeful spring that preceded the glorious summer of 1813, Richard's daughter was christened at Thornford church and he appears in the register as a yeoman. The family had achieved the summit of independence by way of the slippery footholds of small tenancies and copyholds. As well as being the tenant of four separate holdings in Thornford and Lillington, on which land tax amounting to £3 8s. 5d. was paid, Richard Gould owned a small property, Claypits, in the parish of Beer Hackett. Slabs of blue-grey clay still flank the lane leading to the small and secluded farmhouse where brick restorations now conceal the outlines of the original building. Frequent changes of tenancy shown on the land-tax assessments for 1805-15 (that for 1813 is missing) suggest that Richard Gould, like so many other Dorset farmers, was gambling on the prospects of a long war. Only when the fall of Napoleon made it clear that the game, which had enriched many small men as well as increasing the stature of the great, was over did society begin to castigate the evils of 'that seven-headed monster, Speculation'.[1] The panic year of 1816, in which many farmers echoed the despairing cry of Miles Bowker of Charborough: 'the more we do, only the more we loose', saw the fall of the Richard Gould and his relative Charles, who had ventured even further by renting Upper Farm and part of Manor Farm at Lillington. Richard was a casualty of the peace but his domestic circumstances would have made long-term success doubtful even if the war had continued. Not only did Gould lack capital and caution, but, according to his great grandson, he had a gadabout wife who left her husband 'to bide at home' in charge of their eight children.

The Goulds had the heartbreaking task of starting again, of touching their hats as labourers in the parish where they had given orders as masters. They began their struggle at a time when the Government, bewildered by recurring crises, could only leave the victims of depression to sink or swim with the observation that it was 'the natural tendency in the distribution of capital and labour to remedy the disorders which may casually arise in society from such temporary derangements and . . . it often happens that these disorders are prolonged if not aggravated, by too much interference and regulation'.[2] If farmers and landlords could hardly keep their heads above the seas of depression, labourers had an even harder struggle to avoid sinking to pauperism. The buoyancy of character that led the Goulds to speculation in times of prosperity helped them in adversity when they were not paralysed by despairing apathy.

After the crash the Goulds aroused in the district the melancholy

[1] U. Lane, *Hints on Gradual Abolition of Poor Rates*, 1826, Dorset County Museum. The author describing conditions around Shaftesbury considered that speculation was wrecking society which could only be 'new bonded' by compulsory insurance on the part of labourers.

[2] *Report of Select Committee on Agriculture*, 1821, p. 7.

interest attached to families who have known better days, so David (1809-67) one of the sons of Richard Gould[1] was able to marry in 1831 above his expectations as a farm labourer. Judith, his wife, was the daughter of John Vincent, a man of substance who owned a bakehouse. He may have encouraged his daughter to feel she had thrown herself away for after the birth of her son, Charles, in 1836 Judith returned to her father's home to work independently as a nurse. The burden of housekeeping fell on David Gould's daughter, Mary Anne, who not only ran the home but, before she was sixteen, helped maintain it by glove making. At the same age her brother Charles was earning as an agricultural labourer, often working at hedging and ditching around Honeycomb Wood. David Gould, like the labourer in the ballad, was willing to go 'either hedging or ditching, to plough or to reap' so as to keep his family, but all his efforts only brought in 7s. to 8s. a week, which had to be supplemented by his children's earnings. Not only did Mary Anne manage the house and make gloves, a task which only long hours of work could make profitable, but she had the will-power and energy to persevere with her schooling so that she became a teacher herself. All this was achieved at a time when Florence Nightingale wrote 'when night comes women suffer – even physically . . . the accumulation of nervous energy which has had nothing to do all day, makes them feel every night, when they go to bed, as if they were going mad. The vacuity and boredom of this existence are sugared over by false sentiment'.[2] Nothing reveals the chasm between Disraeli's two nations more clearly than the lives of women in the mid-nineteenth century. The few lay awake regretting long and empty hours, the many stumbled to bed dazed with exhaustion from working twelve hours a day. The pace wore out Mary Anne who died at forty-one; but her efforts helped the Goulds to rise again, as she left a small legacy to her brother so that he was able to rent a few acres of coppice in Honeycomb Wood.

After 1854 besides his wage as a labourer, David Gould earned a little extra as parish clerk.[3] The duties of the parish clerk varied with his own inclinations and the wishes of the incumbent who could use his clerk as a secretary, as a curate or as a sporting companion. In general it may be said that the clerk acted as manager

[1] The late David Gould (1876-1965) believed his grandfather, David Gould (1809-67), was the son of Richard Gould (1760-1818) but, although the baptisms of a number of Richard's children are recorded, there is no entry for David.

[2] C. Woodham-Smith, *Florence Nightingale*, 1950, pp. 94-5, quotation from an unpublished novel written 1852.

[3] The sum paid is not known but the Churchwardens' Accounts for the neighbouring parish of Beer Hackett show that in 1827 the clerk received £3 a year.

and producer for the parson. He prepared the church for services, led the congregational responses, read out notices and often kept the registers. The office carried weight not only in the church but also in the parish; by the 'Wessex custom', according to Thomas Hardy, the clerk expected 'to attend all christening, wedding and funeral parties'.

By the mid-nineteenth century the villager yearned for a place in the community; he felt that in the last half century he had been 'lowered . . . in the scale of society'.[1] The offices of parish clerk, of sexton and bell-ringer gave the humble man his one chance of shouldering responsibility outside his own family. Supporters of the Tractarian Movement felt that in the eighteenth century incumbents had forgotten, and minor officials had exceeded, their duties. High Churchmen had scant sympathy with the 'vapouring and fuming' of little men anxious to make their voices heard in parochial matters.[2] Foiled in the Church, these men often turned to the Chapel.

The Goulds had exactly the active and social temperament for the office of clerk and Charles took on his father's position. Both father and son kept their private registers. As the clerk was often a bell-ringer and always the recipient of details of village tragedies, the Gould registers make mournful reading. In 1856 the 'bell tolled one hour' for the last Earl Digby and Henry Hammond was burned to death; in 1861 Susan Barrett died in another of the village fires which happened so regularly yet against which adequate precautions were never taken; four years later Henry Vowell was 'killed by a waggon'. Untimely deaths occurred in most families including the clerk's; two little daughters of Charles Gould (1836-1918) died from scarlet fever in 1875.

In the case of David and Charles Gould the usual story was reversed for it was the son who lacked the opportunities his parent had enjoyed as a boy. Charles early started his working life as an agricultural labourer, but his habit of putting his mind and all his energies on the work in hand marked him out from the other labourers on the Digby estate. He was soon engaged, with his cousin William, almost entirely on hedging and ditching. Though this piece-work was more remunerative than day-work, it was very hard to rise from that class which the French observer, Taine, described in the 1860s as being 'the most wretched and backward of

[1] *The Times*, 12 January 1831. In summing up the causes of the 1830 riots, Mr. Justice Alderson on the Special Commission in Dorchester considered that the agricultural labourer's feeling of social inferiority was an even greater cause of the disturbances than actual poverty.

[2] B. J. Armstrong, *A Norfolk Diary 1850-1888*, 1949, entry for 4 January 1855, the rector of East Dereham withheld their Christmas Box from the bellringers until they conformed to his regulations.

all'. Charles Gould was able to do so because to his own energetic efforts he was able to add to the small legacy left by his equally hard-working sister, Mary Anne. With this money he was able to rent four to five acres of coppice in Honeycomb at about £2 to £4 an acre depending on the quality of the undergrowth; and later small acreages in Green Lane Copse in the parish of North Wootton and in Almshouse Wood running almost to the south bank of the Yeo just east of the Thornford-Sherborne boundary. In Almshouse Wood sycamore brushwood was cut for faggots which blazed up the chimneys of the schools in Sherborne. Brushwood could only be cut after the larger poles had been harvested for hurdle making and the smaller ones for bean sticks. As a child one of David Gould's chief pleasures was helping his father, Charles, bind faggots in Honeycomb Wood. Here the monotony of this dreary winter work could be broken by glimpses of the Portman Hunt and of the great shoots which accounted for pheasants reared at that time, according to 'Stonehenge' [J. M. Walsh], at the cost of 15s. a bird.

Charles Gould could not claim that the hazel had fulfilled for him the fairy-tale wish:

> 'Shake, shake hazel tree
> Gold and silver over me!'

but he could say that copse work, particularly the making of sheep cribs and hurdles from hazel rods, had enabled him to become a tenant farmer.

The rounded, skeleton-like sheep cribs are now generally seen piled at the back of sheds or lying under downland hedges. Hurdles are becoming equally overlooked on farms. Writh, or wattle, hurdles still hold their own in gardens but little use is found for gate hurdles which consist of four horizontal rails morticed into two upright posts six feet apart and kept in place by one central vertical bar and two diagonal ones. Gate hurdles, like writh hurdles, were used for folding sheep; they were of particular use when the ewes had to be confined but the lambs, able to pass under the lowest rail, were to run free.

Even today, hurdle making has hardly changed since Stevenson's time. Eight to ten stakes, about three feet high, were driven into a stand, a slightly curved piece of wood four to six feet long called the flake. In and out of the stakes was woven the 'hedge-work' of whole or split hazel rods which had to be free of any sharp ends which might injure a sheep's fleece. In the mid-eighteenth century when sheep used to 'totally occupy' the Dorset farmer's mind, hurdles were sold at 8s. to 10s. a dozen, but a century later it was difficult to dispose of a dozen at 4s. 6d. to 5s. 6d. Light to handle, hurdles were generally pitched by a boy under the shepherd's direction. Mr.

William Hardy remembers the misery in winter of this fumbling work watched by a shepherd who used his crook first to push over ill set hurdles and then about his shoulders to hasten their repitching. All accounts agree that the shepherd was the autocrat of the farm; but by the end of the nineteenth century his rule was nearing its end. Shepherds found themselves superfluous not only in England but also in Australia where the sheep farmers were unwilling to employ them since 'they always thought they knew better than their master' and preferred untrained men, 'the drifts of English society', who obeyed without arguing.[1] As well as cribs and writh hurdles, Charles Gould sold spars of twisted hazel and willow for holding thatch on rick or house.

True farm gates which Stevenson found 'generally very well made' in the county were the work of carpenters. On large estates such as those belonging to the Monro family at Edmondsham, strong and handsome gates were considered as great an ornament to the property as the timber. Mr. Frederick Legg recalls with pride these eight-barred oak gates, all carefully hung on posts embedded in concrete so as to make easy opening and shutting for the foxhunters.

In Dorset, where there was no outstanding woodworking craft, such as the bowl turning of Berkshire at Bucklebury Common, wood working was mainly in the hands of carpenters and wainwrights. Some villages gained a name for certain products, the rakes of Yetminster and baskets of East Stour were well known, but baskets and rakes were made throughout the county. Similarly, while every parish had its wainwrights some wagon-makers gained a name through a larger district. In the copse-encircled hamlet of Gutch Common, just over the county boundary in Wiltshire, Moses Burden kept fourteen men busy in his wainwright's shop using local oak and elm and, in the 1890s, deal from Poole for wagons used on many North Dorset farms. The woodlands on the brown earths west of Maiden Newton supplied oak and ash for the Galpins of Toller Porcorum whose wagons and coaches were built to stand the steep and rough roads of the central chalk belt of Dorset. From the yards of wagons and coach-makers many fine craftsmen emerged, notably the Parsons of Dewlish. In the mid-nineteenth century the Parsons family, coach-makers at Axminster, thought they were doing well for young Robert by launching him on a clerical career in a London bank. The call of woodworking was too strong for the young man who joined the furniture and cabinet-making firm of Trollope. On the firm's business Robert was sent to Milton Abbas where he married Sidonia Galton of Dewlish, and settled in his bride's parish. Here he established a name for woodcarving which was in demand

[1] *The Family Economist*, 1849, Vol. II, pp. 196-7.

for church restoration in the 1850s and 1860s. Many clergy, influenced by the Oxford Movement, were sweeping away the so-called lumber of previous centuries and adorning their churches with new choir stalls and chancel screens. The parish clerk often found the dignity of his office bundled out with the box-pews and three-tiered pulpits, but village woodcarvers enjoyed a brief period of full employment. Robert Parsons passed on his skill to his son, John (1858-1954) and his grandsons Donald and Leslie. Their wooden workshops at Dewlish are now derelict beside the little, disused chalk cottage which served as an office; but wherever their carvings are found, undying oak leaves keep green the memory of the Parsons family.

Charles Gould made no name for himself as a copse worker outside his own district, but steady application to work he understood and the legacy left him by his sister enabled him to achieve a more hardly won distinction. Just over half a century after the crash of the Gould fortunes he put the family back into the tenant-farming class by renting Spring House. The holding consisted of ten acres at Long Burton, about six miles east of Thornford, and about seventy acres of rough grazing in the neighbouring parish of Holnest. Though nearly all the land had been enclosed in Dorset by the end of the nineteenth century, the consolidation of the enclosures was far from complete. The 1880s were not a propitious decade in which to start farming, but luckily the holding was a dairy farm within reach of Sherborne station. Railways were a lifeline to dairy farmers whose problem became one of getting milk to the station rather than of finding markets. The enterprising Moores, who had risen from cultivators of strips of manorial waste to tenant farmers, came forward with a delivery service. Twice daily in summer and once in winter, the Moore's spring wagons carried the seventeen-gallon churns from Thornford, Beer Hackett and Long Burton to the milk depot at Sherborne.

Charles Gould prospered at Spring House; and young David found employment carrying letters between his new home at Long Burton and the neighbouring parishes of Leweston and Lillington. The boy covered daily distances of four to five miles. Woodmen often complained of their hard, monotonous and lonely work; but if they left the woods they generally wished, as Charles Gould did, to return. In the early 1890s Gould moved to Bembury, a substantial, two-storied rubblestone house in Thornford, and took up copse work again.

After a year or two at Bembury the family rented Lower Farm, an eighteenth-century farmhouse built, David Gould believed, with stones taken from a nearby horse pool. As it was a landmark in a tenth-century charter this pool, now only a damp depression surrounded by five willows, must once have been of considerable depth.

As well as managing the seventy-acre farm Charles Gould, whom age could not tire, continued with some copse work until his death in 1918. With an active father, David found little scope at Lower Farm, so he took employment as a bailiff on an estate at Keynsham near Bristol. His employer, curiously enough, owned Claypits, the holding at Beer Hackett which had belonged to Richard Gould before 1816. David Gould had in 1907 the chance of buying the family property of seventeen acres. Once settled on his own property David Gould married Mabel Eddles, daughter of the dairyman at the neighbouring Lower Farm, Knighton. This beautiful farmhouse was built in the seventeenth century when a thriving community at Knighton found a livelihood in the clay pits which named the Gould farm, and was demolished in 1966.

In 1914 David Gould rejoined his father at Lower Farm, which he took over for the years 1918-1932. These were years of great change but Lower Farm remained part of the Digby estate and David Gould carried on the family tradition of parochial service and social activity. As a bellringer he helped to ring the three bells of the parish church to celebrate the fall of Mafeking; for over twenty years he was a chairman of the Parish Council, and sat on the District Council. He was an enthusiastic supporter and chairman of Thornford Cricket Club which kept up with the times by arranging a match between women playing with bats and men with broomsticks. These matches were popular with village clubs in the late nineteenth century and had the sanction of that arbiter of propriety, *The Girl's Own Paper*. In 1888 a contributor felt that 'no serious objection' could be raised to mixed matches providing 'the girls behave quietly, and only have friends for spectators'.

In his old age David Gould lived in a house built in a field where he and a companion once mowed two and a half acres of barley in eight hours in an attempt to race an oncoming storm. Within walking distance stands the now silent Honeycomb Wood so closely associated with the Gould family. Their history reminds us that, much as a nation needs the commercial drive of the Hydes and the naval fervour of the Roberts family, it also needs the steadfastness of the Goulds who through the generations have served the community as regularly and as unobtrusively as a church clock.

NOTES ON SOURCES USED FOR CHAPTER VII

Verbal Sources
The main source of information for this chapter has been the late David Gould of Thornford, to whose kind patience I am greatly indebted for details concerning his family, copse work and the village of Thornford.

Mr. Denis Yarde, now at Wareham, passed some of his youth at Thornford and gave his picture of the parish and information concerning the Moore family into which his father had married. Mr. E. Wareham, whose family was established in Thornford in the eighteenth century, passed on some of his wide knowledge of local history. Mr. F. L. Wills of Lower Farm, Knighton, gave the history of his farmhouse, which he kindly allowed me to inspect, also information concerning Beer Hackett and, incidentally, put me into touch with David Gould. Colonel J. D. Dalley, lately of Higher Farm, Lillington, also kindly allowed me to inspect his eighteenth-century farmhouse.

Accounts of woodworking were given by:

Mr. Kyrle Burden, formerly a wainwright, of Gutch Common, Semley.

Mr. F. Legg, formerly estate carpenter, of Edmonsham, Wimborne.

Mr. W. Myall, formerly a wheelwright, of East Stour, Gillingham.

Mr. D. Parsons, formerly woodcarver at Dewlish, of Milborn St. Andrew, Blandford.

To Mr. A. Sturdy of Carey, Wareham, I am indebted for general information about forestry and woodworking.

Written Sources

Thornford and District

Dorset Record Office.

Draft Survey of Estates held by lease and copy of the Earl of Digby, 1803.

Thornford Registers.

Baptism, 1677-1813, 1813-1870.

Marriage, 1786-1812, 1813-1836.

Burial, 1677-1812.

Accounts of Overseers of Beer Hackett, 1719-1795, 1796-1836.

Parish Church of St. Michael's, Beer Hackett.

Registers inspected by kind permission of the incumbent, Mr. L. J. Chesterman.

Parish Church of St. Mary Magdalene, Thornford.

Registers inspected by kind permission of the incumbent, Mr. L. J. Chesterman.

Private registers of David and Charles Gould inspected by kind permission of the late David Gould.

Forestry

Thomas Hale, *The Compleat Body of Husbandry*, 1756, deals very fully with forestry. To encourage timber production the ease and speed with which plantations can be established is perhaps overstressed.

J. Nisbet, *The Forester, A Practical Treatise on British Forestry and Arboriculture for Landowners, Land Agents and Foresters*, 1905, 2 Volumes. I have drawn heavily on the book which deals with all branches of forestry in great detail.

Woodworking

W. Rose, *The Village Carpenter*, 1952.

F. Sturt, *The Wheelwright's Shop*, 1st ed. 1923.

Articles by J. Geraint Jenkins as follows:

Country Life 17 October 1957, Broom Maker of the Woodlands.

2 January 1958, Craft of the Village Rake-Maker.

11 September 1958, The Disappearing Gate Hurdle.

12 December 1959, From Withy to Willow Basket.

23 November 1961, The Waning Craft of the Rake-maker.

Folk Life 1963, Vol. 1, Bowl Turners and Spoon Carvers.

I am also indebted to Mr. J. Geraint Jenkins for information sent by letter.

CHAPTER VIII

Gillingham:
The Priest and the
Villager

*Dependence of the early Church on the land –
patronage of land owner and tithes of husband-
men – countryside around Gillingham – strong
hold of Puritanism in seventeenth-century Dorset – the Restoration and settlement of tithe
dispute in Gillingham – John Hume's determination to regain lost tithes – new problems
for the Church in the nineteenth century –
growth of Nonconformity – Church restoration
and reform by Henry Deane, vicar of Gillingham – rise of Shadrach Dunn, seedsman – the
grasp of contemporary needs by Deane and
Dunn.*

'The priest and the villager together understand more
than the priest alone.'

Serbian proverb.

IN TIMES of violent change men seek survival at all costs and only
consider the price when order has been restored. When the Danish
raids increased in frequency and intensity men perforce turned to
the thane and the bishop. These were men of authority capable of
leadership if not always of securing safety. When the raiding Danes
eventually settled and merged with the Saxon population many
found themselves bound to their lord and their church. To the one
they owed obedience, and often service and payments in kind; to
the other, tithes. The subjection of commended men was the more
complete as a partnership between churchman and landowner had
been cemented by their common dependence on the fruits of the

soil. Pressure from above and resentment from below as well as diverging interests of priest and layman often subjected the association to strains and stresses, but breaking point was only reached in the eighteenth century. A common fear of revolution as well as dependence on the land staved off the crisis. The two only parted company at the end of the nineteenth century when the most determined conservative had to admit that anarchy was not around the corner and that the land was no longer England's staple source of wealth. Already by the mid-eighteenth century great national efforts no longer depended on agricultural communities; the ownership of land might add lustre to wealth but did not necessarily confer it. Lip service continued to be paid to the old loyalties in parish and manor, where parson and squire still took the lead; but those in the third estate, whether labourer, yeoman or tenant farmer felt their utility to the community had been restricted to providing labour, rent and tithes. Of these the payment of tithes was most resented.

The parson's predicament in rural parishes was by the eighteenth century patent. The question of tithes could embitter his relations with the squire who often owned part of the tithes and with the farmer who had to pay them. Nor was the labourer detached from the recriminations of his superiors; towards the end of the century many farmers claimed that the burden of tithes prohibited a rise in wages. It was hard for the parson, the focus of all this parish wrangling, to put a foot right. If he battled for his rights he was worldly and avaricious, if he let them go he was shuffling and contemptible. This predicament largely explains why in the early nineteenth century the energies of many clergy and laymen were directed towards the establishment, or the restoration, of the independence and consequently the authority of the parson. The ebb and flow of the incumbent's relations with his parishioners could be charted in the annals of any Dorset parish, but they have an especial interest in Gillingham. The genius of Henry Fielding and of John Constable has encircled the clergy of this parish with unfading light; here also two notable men came to the fore to show the world how much could be achieved by the priest and the villager, even if their aims were as divergent as their careers. Henry Deane, vicar of Gillingham 1832-82, and his contemporary Shadrach Dunn, the founder of the firm of seedsmen, were alike only in their unswerving self-confidence. As this quality, which could mould either a Lord Shaftesbury or a Mr. Podsnap, was characteristic of many mid-Victorians, the lives of Deane and of Dunn illustrate one aspect of an age as well as a chapter of local history. Since the payment of tithes was the link, or the fetter, which most closely bound priest and parishioner until the mid-nineteenth century, some understanding of this obligation, binding on Christians throughout Europe, must be sought.

It is tempting to imagine that early English Christians rendered their tithes freely and joyously; but by the tenth century the payment of tithes had to be legally enforced. The missionaries who originally visited the distant hamlets from the minsters, or mission centres, were gradually replaced by resident priests usually supplied by the most powerful landowner of the district and supported by the contributions, most important of which were the tithes, of the villagers. At the time of Alfred's death 'every church in England had its proprietor, in most cases a magnate or manorial lord, though often a bishop or a monastery and sometimes the King himself'.[1] The interests of the parish priest were, therefore, closely identified with those of the landowner as well as those of the husbandman who was obliged to render from his holding a tenth of the fruits and beasts of the earth, as well as their products, towards the maintenance of the church. So the priest found himself poised between the two worlds of the lord and of the villein.

After the Norman conquest the distance between these two worlds widened immeasurably. The Anglo-Saxon parish priest had little in common with the Norman authorities, whether lay or ecclesiastical, from whom he derived his benefice. Caliban's new masters drove him hard and only in the thirteenth century did the parish priest, generally a vicar acting on behalf of a rector, bishop, abbot or prebendary, gain security of tenure and a fixed share of the parochial income. As tithes were the most considerable part of this income they were the most bitterly contested. Great tithes usually from corn, hay and timber fell to the rector, while small tithes were allotted to the vicar. These were due from cattle, sheep, pigs, poultry, wool, milk, cheese, eggs, hemp, flax, apples, cider and other items dictated by local custom and tillage.[2] Seemingly a cornucopia, small tithes in reality often presented the vicar with the alternatives of incessant prying into sheds, barns and closes, or of penury. The battle was on between vicars and parishioners; their warring cries were sometimes faint but during the fourteenth and eighteenth centuries the tumult of the Lollard sympathisers and of the Radicals shook the walls of the Established Church.

From the fourteenth to the nineteenth centuries the vicars of Gillingham were responsible for the cure of souls at East Stour,

[1] C. J. Godfrey, *The Church in Anglo-Saxon England*, 1962, p. 319.

[2] C. Hill, *Economic Problems of the Church from Archbishop Whitgift to the Long Parliament*, 1956, pp. 78-82.

West Stour, Milton, Motcombe and Bourton. By the early nineteenth century, when the hamlet of Enmore Green was also included,
the parish covered 15,886 acres. To the east this area covers the
heavy, waterlogged gleys derived from Oxford Clay which give way
towards the north of the parish to a fertile brown-earth belt
running from Bourton to Gillingham; westward lie the red-
brown rendsinas of the Corallian upland. These brashy, limestone soils never supported much woodland so were early cultivated.
Field names, *Innox* and *Brambly Furlong* and twisting roadways such
as Wavering Lane and Sandpitts Lane are survivals from the open
arable fields. When these were enclosed, farmhouses like Bleet and
Whistley (originally Westley) were perched on the edge of the
escarpment marking the western boundary of the open fields. These
farmhouses still have the appearance of pioneering outposts, and
indeed farmers have an unceasing struggle to work the hard, flint-
impacted soil where, in dry seasons, a dead animal can lie for weeks
unburied. On the brown earth and gleys east of the limestone upland oak forest flourished until the seventeenth century. These
ancient forests and Gillingham's proximity to the great Saxon
ecclesiastical strongholds of Shaftesbury and Sherborne ensured that
Norman and Plantagenet monarchs would keep a close watch on
the area. William the Conqueror annexed the manor and forest,
both of which remained under the crown until the seventeenth
century, and gave the church to the Abbey of Shaftesbury which,
like all important conventual and monastic establishments, came
under Norman control.

By the thirteenth century even the growing efficiency of royal
administration could not save for the Plantagenets the forests they
loved so well. The gradual clearing of oak forest east of Gillingham
left land of great fertility. Not only were the clay-derived loams
rich in plant nutrients but topography presented few difficulties. No
steep slopes baffled the ploughman and no narrow valleys left the
farmers, as in West Dorset, with the double worry of rushy bottoms
and bracken-covered hillsides. The gently undulating land around
Motcombe, about three miles east of Gillingham, is marked, even
today after a century of successive onslaughts on the hedgerows, by
thick hawthorn and hazel hedgerows studded with oak. Willows
and sometimes oak mark the shallow, bowl-like ponds which dimple
the Motcombe fields. The fluttering of the willow leaves, the reflection in the pond water of scudding clouds, and the rushing flight of
wild duck give the Motcombe fields all the animation and interest
usually associated with more striking scenery. Had thorough drainage been undertaken wheat and oats would have flourished in this
area, but towards the end of the eighteenth century local farmers

preferred well-tended grasslands. Not only were milk, butter, cheese and hay profitable products, but by refusing to plough farmers often avoided the burdensome necessity of paying tithes in kind as many clergy in pastoral areas had accepted a modus, or customary money payment, in lieu of tithes in kind. Rising corn prices and the exhortations of agricultural experts during the Napoleonic Wars had little effect on farmers in long-established dairying districts. Sir John Sinclair was convinced that this conservatism was due to tithes which operated 'in a peculiar manner against the conversion of old grass land into tillage'.[1]

In the sixteenth century individuals chafed against irksome interference by guild, manor court and borough corporation, so the church, most ubiquitous of all organisations, did not escape attack. Criticism of the church as an over-mighty landowning subject encouraged Henry VIII to dissolve the monasteries and to throw into the market not only monastic lands but also 'the right to present to some two-fifths of the benefices in the kingdom'.[2] With this patronage went the right to the great tithes. Until this time the tithe war had generally been a straightforward one for the vicar, who endeavoured to wrest his dues from his rector and his parishioners. Now it became complicated by resentment against not only the avarice but the usurped right of the lay impropriators, or those who had secured former monastic lands and the rights of great tithe and patronage. Under impropriators vicars often found that both a secure tenure and adequate income were lacking, so many intensified their efforts to force parishioners to 'tithe duly and truly'. Many parishioners found, as men often do, a moral justification for withstanding an unpopular levy. Tithes, fees and other offerings should not be presented to an institution from which some considered the Protestant wind had not yet blown away the last cobwebs of Popery.

Puritan demands for the reform of the established church throve in Dorset. Well-to-do citizens of Dorchester, Weymouth, Poole and Bridport had the leisure and the security which enabled them to turn their minds to their further advancement in this world and, by pruning inessentials from their worship and daily life, in the next. These preoccupations seeped inland to the gentry. The Erles of Charborough, the Bonds of Purbeck and the Ashley Coopers of Wimborne St. Giles, all felt the fascination of reforms which might release them at once from the exactions of the church, the state and the devil. In the seventeenth century men turned to Puritanism for numbers of motives which included sincere conviction and a desire

[1] *Communications to the Board of Agriculture*, 1802, Vol. III, p. 6.
[2] C. Hill, op. cit., p. 4.

for self-advancement. It was only in the nineteenth century that Dorset produced a completely disinterested follower of the extreme Protestant ideals: Anthony Ashley Cooper, the seventh Earl of Shaftesbury, showed the world all that was best in Puritanism and only a few of its weaknesses.

Many poorer clergy, and Dorset had her share of underpaid incumbents, were attracted by the new ideas which besides a competent maintenance offered chances of preferment unlikely to fall to obscure parsons under the Episcopalian régime. Bishops had not been lacking who, like Bancroft and Laud, wished to improve the position of the lesser clergy but their efforts were unavailing against the granite determination of the lay impropriators to hold fast to their monastic windfalls. Parishioners sometimes took matters into their own hands. As early as 1584 the burgesses of Dorchester had secured the advowson of depopulated Frome Whitefield and used the proceeds for augmenting the minister's stipend and for charitable purposes.[1] Later the inhabitants of Sherborne made a perpetual settlement of lands upon the vicarage.[2] A few well-disposed gentry made contributions for the better maintenance of the clergy; Sir Francis Ashley granted to Robert Cheke of Dorchester the great tithes of Waterston, near Puddletown, in return for his 'great paines and travaile in expounding of the holie scriptures'.[3] But the 1840 tithe apportionment shows that the great tithes were safely back in the hands of a lay impropriator.

These efforts were but drops in the bucket of clerical poverty. Many incumbents inspired by John White, rector of Holy Trinity, Dorchester 1605-1648, tried to help themselves and secure the salvation of the heathen by investing in overseas trading companies. Of the 120 members of the Dorchester Company for trading with Newfoundland and New England, twenty-one were clergy. It can be argued that 'twenty-one country ministers possessed of little spare cash, would have been unlikely to speculate on a hazardous fishing adventure off the New England coast' and were therefore primarily concerned to provide 'a refuge for Puritans of their own particular way of thinking'.[4] It might also be claimed that the very neediness of the participating clergy was the prime cause for their venturing on overseas speculations. The clerical members of the Dorchester Company included John White who only secured a competent maintenance at the end of his life when Puritans had learnt Anglican tunes and the impropriated parsonages of Seaton and Fordington were purchased to augment the livings of 'preaching

[1] F. Rose-Troup, *John White the Patriarch of Dorchester*, 1930, p. 39.
[2] C. Hill, op. cit., p. 272.   [3] F. Rose-Troup, op. cit., p. 37.
[4] Ibid., Appendix III, pp. 447-8.

ministers', William Tilly, rector of Broadmayne, a tithe-free parish, and William Burgess whose parsonage at Buckland Ripers was worth £40 a year.

On the eve of the Civil War parochial clergy were courted by Royalists and Parliamentarians alike. Both sides were anxious to secure lay impropriations for augmenting the incomes of clergy whose ideas on passive obedience or the constant expounding of the Scriptures were sound. Only Puritan extremists demanded the abolition of tithes. The Quakers found a solution to the problem of tithes by abolishing clergy; but since Anglicans, Presbyterians and Independents wished to keep their ministers, they had to accept tithes until it was possible, in Oliver Cromwell's words, for 'the legislative power [to] settle maintenance another way'. An approach to finding this other way was only made in the early eighteenth century when Queen Anne's Bounty was established to augment the stipends of poor clergy by grants enabling incumbents to purchase land, the rent from which would permanently augment the living.

Some clergy like Edward Davenant, vicar of Gillingham 1625-80, were impervious to financial inducements. A great mathematician, royalist Davenant had little interest in augmenting his income which luckily, since it was at the disposal of his friends, was not inconsiderable. His studies commanded all Davenant's interest and his curates carried out his parochial work. Curates might relieve a vicar of work but not always of anxiety, as in troubled times even these neglected men had expectations of speedy preferment. Davenant's curates had minds of their own. Samuel Forward led the local Clubmen at the end of the Civil War, and Thomas Andrewes went his own way at Motcombe whose inhabitants were determined not to knuckle under to vicar or to manor court. Davenant had to make the best of Andrewes but the royalist scholar can have felt little sympathy for this 'able and orthodoxall devine'[1] especially as he supplanted Davenant for some years during the interregnum. But Davenant, despite the 'infirmityes' which he pleaded in 1650 in extenuation of his pastoral inactivity continued as vicar for twenty years after the Restoration. He lived long enough to see many hopes fade, for Charles II was too worldly and too astute to fulfil the expectations of either the old 'Church and King' men of Davenant's type or of the younger place-seekers like Ashley Cooper.

After 1660 there was no question of the 'legislative power' seeking

---

[1] 1650 Returns to the Commissioners appointed to Enquire into the Value of Livings in Dorsetshire. MS copy written and arranged in 1720 by Henry Rook. D.R.O.

to replace tithes by an alternative method of augmenting clerical stipends. Davenant, wearied by the storms of the 1650s when he temporarily lost his cure, his library and, most important to a scholar, his peace of mind, determined to find his own solution to the constant tithe wranglings with the wayward inhabitants of Motcombe. In 1661 the vicar 'wishing nothing more than to enjoy the remainder of my days in peace and love with my loving parishioners' accepted the arbitration of an old friend, Henry Whitaker. In place of payment of tithes in kind by the farmers of Motcombe, Davenant agreed to a composition of a shilling in the pound rent to be paid quarterly.[1] Like many other vicars the doctor secured peace in his own time at the expense of his successors. This low composition was bound to cause vicarial resentment in the eighteenth century when the confidence of the clergy and agricultural output alike had increased. Agreements on monetary payments, or moduses, in lieu of tithes in kind were often reached locally by the tithe owners and the farmers; to be binding they had to be reasonably satisfactory to the vicar, the usual recipient of small tithes, and to be cemented by 'ancient usage'. The Dorset moduses were considered exceptionally low; compositions quoted by Stevenson ranged from 3s. to 7s. in the pound. Only a wealthy vicar or a peace-at-any-price man could stand on Bowridge Hill and gaze without irritation at the Motcombe red-clover meadows, hay from which could fetch £3 a ton in the district, and at the full-uddered cows each of which would have been worth 15s. to vicars in some parts of the county.

Enterprising parsons anxious to recover their dwindling tithe rights not only had their ecclesiastical superiors encouraging them from the touch-line[2] but they were further incited by lawyers. The country attorney like the parson was gaining in the eighteenth century greater social and professional consequence. Between the two of them tithe cases were blown like autumn leaves into the Exchequer Court. The main points of contention in these cases were lapses in tithe payments, the existence of unduly low moduses and the evasion of payment for agistment, or the letting of keep for another man's cattle.

In Dorset the chase to recover lapsed tithes or to revise unduly low moduses was joined by many familiar figures. Syndercombe, the farming rector of Symondsbury, had a setback when he had to accept a modus of 8d. for a milch cow and 6d. for a heifer, but the Hardy family, lay impropriators of Portesham, fared better when

---

[1] Exchequer Case 16 November 1775, of John Hume against Charles Wright and George Francis. P.R.O. E.126/31. Michaelmas 16.

[2] G. F. A. Best, *Temporal Pillars*, 1964, p. 99.

they secured in lieu of milk tithe 1s. 2d. for every cow pastured on certain lands. The Travers of Loders were the last family to keep out of any current activities and they successfully contested the vicar's rights to hay tithe in some fields. It was possible to play the game of hunt-the-tithe too often. Parson Embris of Thornford had a windfall when in 1735 the Exchequer Court awarded him both the great and small tithes, but when the Digby family became lords of the manor the case was re-opened. The pastorate of George Templer, rector of Thornford 1810-1849, was overshadowed by an unsuccessful battle, lasting seventeen years, to maintain his rights. These included a yearly 5s. placed by farmers on the table tomb of the Ellis family to circumvent the lord of the manor from getting the hay tithe. Disputes over hay and milk tithes arose most frequently as these were the hardest tithes to collect in kind. The feelings of the Hammoon farmers for their rector cannot have been cordial when he secured the right to make his own tithe hay. Any farmer would consider a hailstorm less damaging than the rector's labourers trampling through a meadow to mow their master's tenth.[1] To avoid such friction many tithe owners would put up with low compositions of 3s. an acre for water meadow, and 2s. 6d. for permanent grass and clover ley. What the vicar lost on meadows he did not gain on pastures. The over-grazing of rich grasslands was often due to the tithe relief a farmer secured by letting out keep. The agistment tithe on stock was lower than the tithe a farmer had to pay for his own animals, and it was also easier to avoid. Even when farmers pastured their own stock the vicar's tithe expectations on Lady Day were not always fulfilled. Heavy rains in early spring caused sheep losses and liver-rot was a never distant menace; while the fashionable clover leys increased the incidence of bloat among cattle and sheep. Had Fielding's Parson Trulliber, reputed to have been modelled on John Oliver, curate of Motcombe,[2] entered his pig-sty to find his animals languishing of swine fever instead of displaying them 'all pure and fat, and upwards of 20 score a-piece' the picture would have been as true to life but less pleasing to popular taste.

Since 'almost the whole of the revenues of the eighteenth century establishment came more or less directly from the land',[3] clerical fervour concerning tithe and glebe rights was understandable. Nevertheless even some of his contemporaries felt that John Hume,

---

[1] *Notes and Queries for Somerset and Dorset*, 1894-95, Vol. IV, p. 122, for information concerning Thornford tithe case. H. Wood, MS Index to Exchequer Records, pp. 81-8, summary of Dorset suits. P.R.O.

[2] C. M. Godden, *Henry Fielding*, 1910, pp. 7-8.

[3] G. F. A. Best, op. cit., p. 62.

vicar of Gillingham 1770-1783, went too far in devoting the whole of his pastorate to rounding up tithes. Hume, fortified like many vicars of Gillingham, by episcopal connections and also by the assistance of an able attorney, William Tinney, was determined to break Davenant's agreement with the Motcombe farmers. Since their support of the Puritan Andrewes rather than the royalist Davenant, the Motcombe inhabitants had not grown more amenable to established authority. Village Hampdens from this district, where John Wesley had been welcomed, were constantly presented at the manor court of Gillingham. The hayward of Motcombe refused to impound straying cattle, but his attitude was not unreasonable as William Brickle had broken the pound lock to release his horse. Henry Butt kept an agisted colt on Motcombe Common, while William Leader tried to build a 'cart house' there; and Jane Hardyman sold 'ale and spiritous liquors without lycence'. It is not surprising that in 1792 no constable from Motcombe put in an appearance at the manor Court.[1] In case these activities should smack too much of Jacobinism it should be added that at various times the vicar, the village schoolmaster and the lord of the manor himself were presented at the court.

Hume's predecessor John Perne, vicar between 1744 and 1770, had ruminated over securing a better deal from Motcombe but had been informed by a parishioner with more truth than consideration that as he was 'a man in years' the question were better left to his successor.[2] Hume was the very man to take up the challenge and his tithe book shows how carefully he had prepared the ground.[3] He noted the little gardens tithed at 6d. a year as well as the forty-eight acres of meadow for which he got 1s. 6d. an acre. John Jukes' single house cow was as important to Hume as John Mills' unusually large herd of twenty cows. Jukes was an overseer of the poor in the year 1774 so he got his own back by extracting £1 11s. 4d. from the poor rate for unspecified 'expenses at the Phoenix'. At the same time the Dunns also tried to see how far the poor rates could be stretched. During the years 1774 and 1775 Thomas Dunn secured several times a lump sum of 16s., the largest relief payment made to an individual during these years. At the same time James Dunn of Bourton, probably the father of Shadrach, obtained 5s., his only call

[1] Manor Court Rolls for Gillingham, 1753, 1755, 1766, 1792 and 1798. Some of the forty-four Manor Court Rolls running from the early eighteenth century to the mid-nineteenth were inspected by kind permission of Mr. W. P. Farnfield.

[2] P.R.O. E.126/31.

[3] John Hume's tithe book covers the years 1774-76. For the first year tithe payers were arranged alphabetically. Later he listed haphazardly the arrears due to him for the time that his suit was under consideration. D.R.O.

on the poor rates. Overseers would make more generous payments to tide comparatively well-to-do parishioners over difficult times than they would to those hopelessly sunk in poverty. The overseers were right in their expectations that James would make good, but deceived as to Thomas' prospects since by 1776 he was on the 'establishment' of those receiving regular weekly poor relief.[1]

Parson Hume rode around every acre of his parish and perhaps understood the business of his farming parishioners better than his own. Never can parish have so longed for a non-resident vicar but Hume, though he had let his parsonage and glebe, was seldom absent. Nothing escaped his attention. He knew that the governor of the workhouse was trying to keep his grandson on the House[2] and also which were a farmer's own beasts and which grazing for payment. His calculations for agisted beasts was carefully worked out: for a week's grazing 4s. 8d. was due on three colts, 2s. 6d for three cows and 3s. 6d. for ten sheep. The vicar could be seen gazing over gates and peering into the dusty recesses of barns to discover the hidden sack of apples or the pound bag of clover seed, each tithed at 3d. These constant perambulations and prying into barns, cow-sheds, sheepfolds, pig-sties and even hen-coops brought Hume for the year ending Lady Day 1774 just over a £100. This sum could have been doubled if the Motcombe farmers had not held fast to Davenant's agreement and if the parishioners of Bourton and the Stours had not held back hoping that Hume's teeth would be broken on the Motcombe nut. Their expectations were not fulfilled and one East Stour family, the Metyards, were presented in 1776 with a bill for £85 5s. od. for the five preceding years.

Hume's claim to regain tithes in kind from Motcombe came before the Exchequer Court on 16 November, 1775. The vicar presented Davenant's agreement as being only a temporary composition while on behalf of the tithe payers of Motcombe, the defendants, Charles Wright and George Francis, claimed that the settlement was well established by a century of usage. Furthermore Wright claimed he had not been informed of Hume's intention to revive the payment of Motcombe tithes in kind while Francis, possibly a churchgoer, had grasped the cold fact when a notice appeared on the church door. In the evidence two completely different pictures appear of Francis' fifty-acre holding, once held by John Oliver of Trulliber fame, and of the eighty acres farmed by Charles Wright. To Hume the farms were flowing with milk and

[1] Accounts of the Gillingham Overseers of the Poor, II, 1740-77, Gillingham Museum.
[2] Ibid., Vestry Meeting, 28 May 1775.

honey but to the occupants they might have been cabin plots in Connacht. According to the plaintiff 'divers milch cows from which they respectively had many calves and great quantitys of milk' browsed in the pastures, while 'several sows which had divers large farrows of pigs' wandered around the farmyard with 'great numbers of geese, hens and other poultry'. Wagons creaked under 'great quantitys of hemp and . . . of fruit and garden stuff'. Neither of the defendants gave a glowing account of their farming activities, but Wright's description was particularly sombre. In 1771 and 1772 he kept twenty-five cows for which he cut twenty to thirty tons of hay, but neither sheep nor sows. His one horse was used for his cart and 'other husbandry purposes' while the two chickens he kept in 1772 only produced about twenty-five eggs. However Hume's solicitors, Walter Whitaker and William Tinney, pulled him through so that the small tithes of Motcombe once again had to be paid in kind or a composition more favourable to the vicar accepted; Hume had suggested 4s. a year for every milch cow and 2s. for every acre of grass 'mowed into hay'. 1775 was a good financial year for attorney Tinney as well as the parson for, in addition to his payment for the Exchequer Court case, he got £34 7s. od. from the overseers for 'several tryals at law'. Hume's other solicitor, Walter Whitaker, was by 1783 one of the leading landowners in Stour.[1]

Unlike his attorneys, Hume did not stay on in Gillingham to enjoy his victory, but in 1783 changed with Edward Emily who remained until 1792. Although he was a wealthy man and a pluralist, Emily was as interested in the financial rights of the church as his predecessor had been. Even before his induction to Gillingham Emily had estimated the value of the tithes which was not so high as Hume's victory might have warranted. Hume had hoped for 2s. an acre for mowing grass but, by private agreement, he had compounded with a leading Motcombe farmer for 1s. 6d.[2] while Emily's accounts show that the vicar had been knocked down to 1s. an acre. In the eighteenth century lawyers throve on copyhold and tithe disputes which often proved will-o'-wisps leading the winners to mere paper victories and the losers to ruin. Emily's interest in finance was intellectual rather than avaricious. He was a charitable man and while at Gillingham he busied himself with trying to get back Wyndham's charity, a charge on certain lands at Silton.

The parish of Silton lies north of Gillingham separating the mother church from the chapelry of Bourton. Until the end of the eighteenth century the manor of Silton was in the hands of

[1] Tithe Book of Edward Emily, Gillingham Vicarage.
[2] Tithe Book of John Hume entry for February 1776. D.R.O.

Humphrey Sturt, a man of 'inviolable integrity and a good heart'.[1] A great landowner and a patron of both the arts and agricultural experiment, Sturt well represented the good qualities of the landed gentry of his time. One of his small tenants, James Dunn, also typified the best attributes of his class, energy, determination and, above all, an understanding of men and their needs. This knowledge has enabled the humblest to rise and the lack of it has brought down the most mighty.

Bad seasons in the years 1781-84 sent up corn prices and the prospects of corn merchants. James had started dealing in corn and seeds in a small way and was able to purchase land. Ownership of land was a dangerous speculation for a man without capital yet it was an essential step in the rise of country families. Land tenure enabled the Dunns to expand their seed business and their fellow villagers, the Maggs family, to venture successfully into flax spinning in their home parish and in Bourton.

The eighteenth century had hardly ended when young clergymen help up the activities of their predecessors to ridicule and contumely. The church buildings had been neglected, the churchyards had been used as public thoroughfares, as playing fields and as drying grounds. Owing to its convenient position in the centre of the town, Gillingham churchyard had been used as all three. Where new churches had been built as at Blandford, one of the most pleasing of Dorset churches, their architecture was despised as being worldly and even pagan. The conduct of many of the incumbents was on a par with the condition of their churches. John Fisher, vicar of Gillingham 1819-1832, held these views of the new school of clergy, whose attitude was influenced by the sensitivity of the Romantics and the moral earnestness of the Wesleyans. The strange union of these two forces produced a polarity in outlook which resulted in the Oxford Movement being unable to accept England of the 1840s and also in men of that time not feeling completely at home with Tractarianism. Fisher might have had Hume in mind when he described a fellow clergyman of the old school 'arguing his own case, with powder, white forehead, and a very red face, like a copper vessel newly tinned. He is mixing up, in a tremulous tone, with an eager bloodshed eye, accusations, – apologies, – statements, – reservations, – and appeals, till his voice sounds on my ear as I write like a distant waterfall.'[2]

[1] Sir Lewis Namier, *Personalities and Powers*, 1955, p. 72, quotation from *English Chronicle*, 1780.

[2] C. R. Leslie, *Memoires of the Life of John Constable*, 1911, Everyman ed., pp. 139-140. Letter written by John Fisher to Constable 27 September, 1826, while, as Archdeacon of Berkshire, he was sitting on a commission to settle a dispute between a parson and his parishioners.

However lofty their aspirations, country clergy throughout the nineteenth century were as dependent on income from tithes and glebe as their grandfathers had been. A financial trickle from Queen Anne's Bounty relieved desperate cases of clerical poverty; a few landowners considered the return to the church of impropriated tithes and the Ecclesiastical Commission was gradually enforcing a more efficient husbanding, as well as distribution, of ecclesiastical revenues; but none of these efforts severed the financial ties which bound rural parsons to the land.

John Fisher, nephew of the Bishop of Salisbury, vicar of Osmington and Archdeacon of Berkshire, could afford to write to Constable in a lofty strain from Gillingham: 'They have had one or two smart brushes at the Church in Parliament . . . However, I am indifferent to such attacks. I am at my post, and intend to be found at it, happen what will. The people of this place are given to my charge, and I will discharge the duty, with or without tithes.' But the trouble was that Fisher, just like his scorned precursors, could not be at all his posts at once and much of his work was undertaken by curates. Fisher's reaction on entering 'a dark low underground parlour' of 'a poor curate, living in one of our mud villages on a lonely part of this coast', near Osmington, was of delight at finding on 'the comfortless walls' a print of Stothard's 'Canterbury Pilgrims', not of dismay that his fellow-priest should be living in such conditions.

The new clergy hunted out the failings of their predecessors with particular intensity because they felt that these were largely responsible for the spread of Nonconformity.

During the eighteenth century members of the Society of Friends had been too prosperous and Baptist supporters too humble to arouse much clerical opposition. It was quite otherwise when it became clear that Wesleyan enthusiasm was not a flicker of summer lightning. When the modest little Wesleyan chapels, often hardly distinguishable from dwelling places, appeared the Established Church had to come to terms with the problem of dwindling congregations. Clergy also realised with dismay that defections from their flocks were partly due to Nonconformist zeal in providing education.

In Gillingham the first Wesleyan chapel was a small, unpretentious building far more pleasing than the Gothic-inspired chapel erected forty years later in 1876. Not only was Fisher disturbed by the increasing numbers attending chapel services, he also feared Nonconformist poaching on his own preserves. The Quakers, whose pacifism did not prevent their tilting at the Establishment, were attempting to manage the Gillingham Sunday School, established in 1816, on Lancastrian principles. Reason as well as principle dictated this measure where teachers were lacking to control the sixty or so boys in the school. In this instance, as in many others, Fisher benefited from the glorious commonsense of Constable who advised him to 'be quiet and do all the good' he could. The Quaker community in Gillingham was founded on the rock of the Hannam family. Holding the copyhold of the Town Mills, Stephen Hannam realised the possibilities of silk throwing as well as corn grinding and so handed a thriving concern to his son Josiah who had been well trained for his responsibilities. One of the problems set for the 'leisure hours' in his childhood was: 'I am despatched on a commission from London to Edinburgh, distant by computation, say, 350 miles, and my route is settled as 22 miles a day; you, four days after, are sent after me with fresh orders and are to travel 32 miles a day. Whereabouts on the road shall I be overtaken by you?'[1]

John Fisher turned his back on the materialism of the eighteenth century but his sensitive, studious and beauty-loving temperament made it hard for him to know in which direction to move forward. Henry Deane, his successor at Gillingham Vicarage 1832-82, had no doubts at all. Since the beginning of the eighteenth century the Deanes had followed respectable and prosperous careers in the Church so that Henry Deane not only had all the confidence that such a background can give, he also had private means.

The reason that country pastorates of nineteenth-century clergy 'were so often efficient and attractive'[2] was largely that their fathers and grandfathers – for clerical careers tend to run in families – had kept such a careful watch on their tithes, their glebe and their fees. By the 1840s many country clergy were freed from these mundane cares. Their glebes and parsonages were worth more; the yearly value of the Gillingham benefice was estimated as having risen from £140 in 1650 to £2,000 in 1826.[3] Many incumbents inherited private means and after 1836 parsons secured their tithe rights without unseemly barn-door arguments and inquisitions.

After the dissolution of the monasteries which threw so many advowsons of vicarages and great tithes into lay hands, landowners had a powerful influence on church affairs. By the early nineteenth century men began to weary of the three-cornered tussle between

---

[1] Information concerning the Quaker branch of the Hannam family has been obtained from notes shown me by the late Colonel C. R. Wallis of Charnage, Mere. Josiah and George Hannam's exercise books, dated 1771-74, are in Gillingham Museum. The answer to the problem is 68²/5 miles this side of Edinburgh.

[2] G. F. A. Best, op. cit., p. 406.

[3] E. Boswell, *The Ecclesiastical Divisions of the Diocese of Bristol*, c. 1826, p. 44.

vicars, patrons and farmers. A Hampshire clergyman could write, 'though . . . deriving the chief support for myself, a wife, and eight children, from the revenues of the Church, yet I must candidly acknowledge, that tithes operate as a direct tax on the skill, the capital, and industry of the country; and I believe most of my brethren would rejoice, could any other mode of payment be devised.'[1] The tithe problem commanded the attention of the younger Pitt, the arguments of the Utilitarians and the rhetoric of the Radicals, but violence makes itself heard sooner than words. In November 1830 many clergy received threatening letters and their ricks as well as those of unpopular farmers went up in flames. Sensing the panic among gentry and clergy, bands of labourers came out boldly to threaten farmers, overseers and parsons. The attack on the clergy was due to the personal unpopularity of individuals, to clerical severity on the Bench and to tithes which many farmers cited as a reason for not raising wages. This point was made by the Gillingham farmers when they anxiously assembled on 2 December to agree upon a standard wage rate of 9s. a week providing that tithes and rents were reduced.[2] Some of the clergy were well able to look after themselves. John Tomkyns, rector of Stour Provost 1827-33, agreed to lower his tithes, but when the rectory was surrounded by thirty to forty men during the night of 29 November he shouted, 'I am used to rows, and not afraid of them' and invited the intruders to try to break his head or smash the premises.[3] Tomkyns could have claimed an affinity with Parson Trulliber who 'had in his youth been one of the best boxers and cudgel-players in the county' or with one of Kingsley's muscular Christians.

Fear of revolution, commonsense and public boredom with the whole church-in-danger question enabled Melbourne to pass the Tithe Commutation Act of 1836, though not quite in that 'cool and indifferent' atmosphere which he considered appropriate to religious questions. This act simplified the payment of tithes by making them a yearly rent charge. This charge was estimated by the average value of the tithes for the seven years before 1836 being divided into three equal parts for the puchase of wheat, barley and oats at prices adjusted yearly on the average of those for the seven preceding years. The value of the quantities of grain which could be so purchased gave the yearly tithe rent. The act is an example of early

[1] *Communications to the Board of Agriculture*, 1802, Vol. III, p. 33.
[2] Handbill giving resolutions of a meeting held in Gillingham, 2 December, 1830. Among those present were W. Bell, in the Chair, John Dunn, Samuel Hannam and Thomas and George Matthews. Gillingham Museum.
[3] *The Times*, 14 January 1831. Evidence before Special Commission in Dorchester to try 1830 rioters.

nineteenth-century Whig legislation at its best. The abuses were pruned rather than a principle felled and a way was cleared for future changes which eventually, a hundred years later, ended the tithe rent charge. In 1936 the ties which had, since the establishment of Christianity in this country, bound the church to the land were severed.

Not all the clergy freed from the drudgery of tithe collecting refurbished their parishes with Henry Deane's zeal and efficiency, but the spirit quickened in many Dorset villages. William Palmer of Whitechurch Canonicorum gave regularity to services in a restored church; Henry Austen of Pimperne held evening classes for boys, while Sidney Godolphin Osborne of Durweston brought a new sympathy into the lives of his parishioners. Stern and uncompromising in his determination to show the public the state of the agricultural labourer, 'his personality, so tender and at the same time so strong, made his ministrations to the sick and dying peasantry of Dorset occasions of an almost apostolic inspiration . . . his entrance into a low cottage bedroom dimly illumined by its square window under the thatch, would bring to the infirm, much enduring mind of a troubled labourer, outworn with toil, an honourable serenity'.[1]

Although Henry Deane received a classical education at Winchester he had as keen a sense of the value of money as Josiah Hannam, trained for such an understanding from early childhood. Shadrach Dunn, a contemporary of Deane and of Josiah Hannam the younger, had the same financial acumen without the benefit of any formal education. During the nineteenth century, despite George Gissing's assertion that the world was only glorious for the rich, energy, boundless self-confidence and some degree of luck could take a man whither he willed. Both Henry Deane and Shadrach Dunn reached their destinations but the villager needed luck more than the priest whose course was set fair from the first.

Henry Deane is remembered as the man with a compulsive need to restore or rebuild old churches. Cobbett had refused to believe that the population was increasing as he saw so many empty country churches. Deane and fellow church-building enthusiasts came to terms with the fact that congregations were dwindling while the number of parishioners was increasing. The need was not so much for more seats as for pews from which the clergy could be seen and heard. Also, though this point was not stressed by the

[1] Llewelyn Powys, *Dorset Essays*, 1935, p. 161. Information concerning William Palmer from G. Broom's MS *History of St. Candida and Holy Cross, Whitechurch Canonicorum* (kindly shown me by Mr. C. Knight of Whitechurch) and concerning Henry Austen from evidence before *Poor Law Commissioners on the Employment of Women and Children in Agriculture*, 1843, p. 40.

church builders, people attending church wanted to see their fellow worshippers and be seen by them. Sunday morning was the time when men and their wives could leave their counters, cowsheds and kitchens to show the world by their broadcloth coats and stylish bonnets how the world fared for them. Austerity of doctrine could not quench this desire for display; Margaret Oliphant, the novelist, observed that 'the grim pews of Salem Chapel blushed with bright colours, and contained both dresses and faces on the summer Sundays which the Church itself could scarcely have surpassed'. Deane perhaps recognised that those moving up in the world wanted the fact to be known when he stressed the 'need of additional pews for persons in a class of life above the occupants of the free sittings, but not possessing any of the properties to which the pews are attached'.[1] From his own youth Wesley knew enough of wearisome services, where little could be seen or heard, to insist that the pulpit should be central in his chapels and the pews open. For seeing and hearing he considered the octagon an ideal shape.[2] The octagon also appealed to the ecclesiologists, or those who made a study of church architecture, particularly Gothic, and decoration; and to the agriculturalist William Marshall. As the octagon symbolised regeneration the ecclesiologists thought it an ideal shape for fonts,[3] while Marshall considered 'an octagonal yard is warm and is much more commodious than a square one'.[4] The fashionable shape penetrated to Gillingham where a fine octagonal granary can still be seen at Wyke Farm.

While practical men like Deane stressed the need for more seats as the main reason for rebuilding, the ecclesiologists believed that churches should be restored or rebuilt to allow a proper observance of the rubrics of the English prayer book. Anything that stood in the way of this, whether it were box pews, profane ornaments, sham materials or the parish clerk, whose blundering and officious ways were not always conducive to ritual decorum, was to be swept away. As a friend of Cardinal Newman, Deane was not unsympathetic to Tractarian ideals, but to him the real objection to many of the older churches was that their insufficient lighting and massively pillared aisles engulfed the congregations. Deane's 'singular vigour both in mind and body'[5] found an outlet in visiting, in establishing schools,

[1] Quoted by A. F. H. V. Wagner, *The Church of St. Mary the Virgin, Gillingham*, 1956, p. 18.
[2] G. W. Dolbey, *The Architectural Expression of Methodism*, 1964, p. 67 and p. 101.
[3] B. F. L. Clarke, *Church Builders of the Nineteenth Century*, 1938, p. 89 and p. 91.
[4] W. Marshall, *The Rural Economy of the West of England*, 1796, Vol. 1, p. 318.
[5] *Dorset County Chronicle*, 27 April 1882. Report of sermon by Rev. C. A. Pinhorn, curate of Gillingham.

where he had to train the teachers as well as the pupils, and in church building rather than in the doctrinal disputes of the mid-nineteenth century. He might have been a model for Charlotte Yonge's ideal parson who did not indulge in 'ultra self-neglect' but could be found in a room 'where the fire was brisk, there was a respectable luncheon on the table, and he had even treated himself to *The Guardian*, some new books, and a beautiful photograph of a foreign cathedral. The room was littered with half-unrolled plans.' Deane was seldom without his plans, which were inspired by his own commonsense rather than the accepted ecclesiological pattern of 'the pure, true, noble and catholic style of the fourteenth century'.[1] The pointed arch prevailed in the rebuilt nave of St. Mary's, Gillingham and in the new churches at Motcombe and Milton. In West Stour, however, an east window of the 'corrupt' perpendicular style was allowed to remain, while the original church at East Stour was destroyed to make way for a new cruciform building in the Norman style. The ecclesiologists would have not approved of the rounded arches of this new edifice; nor, in their passionate aversion to sham materials, could they have tolerated the walls which were to have 'three coats of bastard stuccoing and to be drawn and painted in courses and coloured to imitate stone'.[2] Where stone was used for Deane's building it came from local quarries. The pale buff oolitic freestone of St. Mary's was quarried between Marnhull and Todber as was the bluish limestone which gives a bleak appearance to the outer walls of Christchurch, East Stour. With the exception of St. Mary's where the original chancel was left, the interior of Deane's churches fail to please. A harmonious blending of building, decoration and church furniture is lacking so that often a single and extraneous object dominates the whole interior. Attention is held by the magnificent iron stove installed in the 1890s to warm Christchurch, and by the amber-coloured pattern on the staring, white stone pulpit in St. Mary's, Motcombe.

Not only did Deane carry through church restorations and re-building, he helped towards the support of those who ministered in the buildings. Stipends of curates at Motcombe had improved little since the mid-seventeenth century when Thomas Andrewes, 'that constant expounder and preacher,' earned £30 a year for his efforts. John Oliver fared better by putting his energies into farming rather than expounding. It was only in 1838 that Henry Deane secured an annual £50 'to be charged upon the said vicarage of Gillingham free of all charges and deductions to the Rev. Frederick

[1] B. F. N. Clarke, op. cit., p. 79.
[2] George Follet's undated contract for erecting the new church at East Stour. Gillingham vicarage.

James Newall, curate of Motcombe'.[1] Newall's flock had started to stray after Wesley's visit, and by 1870 the Wesleyans in this small village were in a position to erect a handsome stone chapel in a modified Gothic style. Again at Bourton, later to become a separate parish, Deane came to the rescue. By the early nineteenth century the leading inhabitants of Bourton felt the village deserved its own church. The spread of the Napoleonic armies kept Bourton's two flax mills, owned by the Jesse and Maggs families, working full pressure. On a wave of thankfulness for good times and zeal funds were raised in style by the London Opera House singers being engaged to perform *The Messiah*. Enough money was collected by 1813 to build a compact, business-like church but the endowments only produced £30 a year. The peace of 1815 dealt a blow to the linen spinners and to the hopes of the curates of Bourton for an increased stipend, so the village soon found itself with a church but no minister. To remedy this Deane guaranteed a yearly £10 as a charge on Gillingham vicarage, the impropriator of the great tithes promised £20 a year and the Bourton inhabitants, with much less flourish than fourteen years earlier, raised a fund to secure their perpetual curate.

Deane's pastoral record was – even for the mid-nineteenth century – a formidable one: two curacies augmented, churches at Gillingham, Motcombe, Milton, Enmore Green and the Stours restored or rebuilt and schools established in these districts. The natural question arises, from where did all the money come? It came from the land, for country churches were still sustained by the soil as they had been since their establishment. The day-to-day maintenance of churches fell on the occupiers of land, until the church rate was abolished in 1868, and on the occupiers of pews, the rents of which were largely determined by their position and comfort. Embellishment or restoration on the scale planned by Deane depended on donations from individuals and grants from church building societies. The success of fund raising depends on the ability of the organiser, on the participation of a few subscribers ready to encourage others by starting the fund off in handsome style, and on the appeal being launched at a time when the well-to-do have reasonable prospects that their fortunes are unlikely to diminish. Practical, persuasive and energetic, Deane was the ideal fund organiser; moreover, he was lucky in his parishioners. Despite the threat, then the reality, of the repeal of the Corn Laws, the 1830s and 1840s were a propitious time for church building around Gillingham, which was not, in any case, primarily a corn-growing district. To Deane's landowning parishioners Protection was a battle cry round which to rally their ranks

[1] Henry Deane, letter dated 14 September 1838. Gillingham vicarage.

rather than an economic necessity. From the early eighteenth century the Matthews family had slowly consolidated their holdings round the hamlet of Milton, where the Stour turned the wheel of their corn mill and watered their riverside pastures which appear in Constable's painting of Parham Mill. As well as corn millers, the Matthews family were prosperous stock breeders whose Stour meadows provided an early bite for their young cattle which were then often driven to the family's Exmoor farm for the summer months, returning for the winter sales at Gillingham.[1] The Grosvenors were also parishioners of Deane anxious to fulfil their county obligations handsomely. As long as street names exist the Grosvenors will be remembered for their London estates but they were also great property owners in North Dorset, where they left their badge of the wheatsheaf on many farms. Towards the £3,000 needed for the restoration of St. Mary's, Gillingham, the Grosvenors contributed £185 and the Matthews £265;[2] as well, both families were largely responsible for rebuilding the churches at Milton and Motcombe. St. Mary's within convenient reach of Motcombe House, one of the Grosvenor country seats, is now screened by evergreens, but Ss. Simon and Jude by the Stour stands out boldly with its 'pierced spire . . . in rich creamy stone . . . the blue sky looking through'. To gaze at these pierced spires gives a feeling of giddiness but they were one of the joys of church builders in the mid-nineteenth century. After the Grosvenors and the Matthews family came the lesser gentry like the Cards and Bells whose fortunes were from the land though their activities had spread into the professions by the 1830s. Church building societies gave £515 while Deane's own contribution was £550. As the vicar's lavish donations towards building were not confined to the mother church at Gillingham, the source of an income able to bear this heavy expenditure is worth considering. The value of the benefice just before Deane's induction was estimated at £2,000 which was probably an over-estimation. After the Commutation Act the Gillingham tithes were valued at £388 a year but the income from glebe was negligible;[3] also the clergy were 'perhaps the most severely taxed class in the community'.[4] At Deane's death in 1882 the value of the living was put at '£1,313 a year with house . . . Motcombe being as valuable as Gillingham'.[5] Among the mourners

---

[1] *Dorset County Chronicle*, 2 November 1843. Advertisement of sale of stock at Milton Lodge.
[2] A. F. H. V. Wagner, op. cit., p. 21.
[3] 1863 Valuation List for Gillingham. Gillingham Museum.
[4] G. F. A. Best, op. cit., p. 469.
[5] *Dorset County Chronicle*, 20 April 1882. This estimate was given at the end of an account of Deane's funeral.

who followed Deane's coffin through the rain to East Stour or who watched the funeral procession from the side of drawn blinds in Gillingham, probably not a soul remembered John Hume or John Oliver whose efforts, however misdirected, had helped to increase the value of the Motcombe curacy and so had aided Deane in his great work. But the vicar's undertakings could not have been attempted without drawing on his considerable private income. The balance sheet of Deane's estate drawn up a year after his death shows that his income was derived mainly from the land. The Eccliffe estate in the south-west of the parish was valued at £3,000, while his land in East Stour, where he had built a house at Clay Hill for his second wife, was worth £9,000. Outside the land Deane's investments were confined to modest sums in local undertakings such as the Gillingham Gas and Coke Company Ltd. and the Dorset County School and about £2,000 in the London and South Western Railway Company which, after a difficult start in 1856 despite the opening flourish of English, French, Sardinian and Turkish flags, had prospered. Not all the persistence of Shadrach Dunn or the influence of the Grosvenors could stop the line connecting Salisbury with Yeovil, and providing a pipeline for the dairy farmers in North Dorset and Somerset. Not only was Deane's capital in the land but his heart as well. Mr. Harold Butler of Madjeston Farm, Gillingham, relates how his grandfather, George Butler (1835-1903), was leaving St. Mary's after morning service when Deane hastened down the aisle calling, 'George, George, don't forget to look out for a bull for me at the market'. Because of his zeal for church building, for education, and for foreign missions, it is easy to see Deane as one of Kingsley's new vicars who perhaps trusted 'too much in that outward "business" work which they do so heartily', and to overlook the fact that he was also among the last of the incumbents whose stock occupied at least some portion of their thoughts in church if not, as in the case of Parson Richardson's bull at Farleigh Hungerford, the actual church porch.[1]

Baptised in 1799, the year of Deane's birth, Shadrach Dunn not only shared his vicar's interest in harvest weather and market prices, but also his unswerving self-confidence. In 1819 when, according to Thomas Collins Colfox, times were 'looking altogether dreadfully bad' and men seemed 'at their wits' end' Dunn held on to the small Silton tenement he had rented the previous year and continued selling corn and seeds to his neighbours. He was far from his wits' end and realised that if small men lost their heads and farms their fields would go to others, especially to those whose whole dependence was not on the land but on trade and manufacture as well. If har-

[1] P. H. Ditchfield, *The Parish Clerk*, 1915, p. 274.

vests failed the Hannams' mill wheels could continue to turn silk-throwing machinery, and those of the Matthews family to grind corn even if it were imported so that their profits could be turned into the land for a better season.

To politicians the year 1832, when the Reform Bill was passed and when Shadrach Dunn opened his seed business in Gillingham, was pregnant with hope or with disaster; but farmers never recollected 'a more kind season than the year 1832 for crops of all descriptions'.[1] Parliament had been reformed without a revolution, the season was benign and well-to-do farmers felt at ease to indulge in their craze for 'fancy plants'. To talk knowledgeably of the comparative merits of Danzig or of Poland wheat, or of the advantages of broadleaf red clover over white, was one of the hallmarks of progressive farmers in the early nineteenth century. The demand for good seeds was increasing. Small tenant farmers and owners were often content to sow 'the cheapest seeds that can be procured, that is, common clover or rye, or the rubbish of their hay lofts';[2] but more affluent and far-seeing cultivators were willing to spend 8s. or 9s. a bushel for good sainfoin and ryegrass. The gleys to the east of Gillingham and the gritty loams of the Corallian uplands to the west were not promising seed-beds for the most fashionable artificial grasses, sainfoin and lucerne. Rye grass and clover leys provided more humdrum but less hazardous herbage. They also had the safe sanction of custom; Stevenson noted that in clay districts 'red clover is the sort most commonly cultivated'. It was a local strain of this clover, Dorset marlgrass clover named in Dunn's seed catalogue as *Trifolium pratense var Dorsetiensis* that helped to establish Shadrach Dunn's reputation as a seedsman. The undoubted feeding value of the broadleaf red clover lost nothing in Dunn's marketing methods. His temperament was exactly suited to the bustle, the bargaining and the conviviality of the markets at Gillingham, Shaftesbury, Stalbridge, Wincanton and Salisbury. Outwitted competitors and customers who found themselves with more seeds than they had intended to buy said hard things of Shadrach Dunn. Mr. Harold Butler of Madjeston Farm remembers hearing him described as 'the biggest rogue in North Dorset'. But no one could deny that his success was largely due to hard work – he started at 3 a.m. for Salisbury Market and returned at 9 p.m.[3] – or that Dunn thoroughly

[1] *Report of Select Committee on Agriculture*, 1833, p. 54. Evidence of a witness from Wiltshire.

[2] *Communications to the Board of Agriculture*, 1802, Vol. III, pp. 147-153, Arthur Young, 'On the Conversion of Old Pasture into Tillage'.

[3] *The Centenary Edition of the Book of Dunns Farm Seeds*, 1832-1932, p. 2. Notes concerning the Dunn family compiled by Henry Augustus Hammond Dunn (1874-1954).

understood which seeds were likely to suit the soils of his district. Furthermore, broadleaf red clover, equally profitable for fodder, for hay or for improving the soil fertility,[1] was popular in leys which were beginning to take a regular place in crop rotations. Dunn bought his grass seeds from selected farms where the leys, or temporary meadows, were kept comparatively free of weeds. Seeds were sometimes obtained by threshing grasses on cloths, but those picked by hand were most reliable. No task was too wearisome or too time-consuming to be overlooked by the women and children of Dorset in the 1840s and 1850s. Brockington in Wimborne St. Giles was one of the farms specialising in growing Dorset marlgrass, which was harvested by generation after generation of the Friend family. Mr. John Friend still works on the farm where short leys are now sown mainly with ryegrass and fescue rather than the marlgrass which was his father's great pride. Brockington is an eighteenth-century brick farmhouse with a long centre chimney gable like the one at Kington Magna, but the pillared canopies over the north and south entrances are typical of the mid-nineteenth century. Graceful entrance pillars, which also appear at North Bowood and Crepe Farms in West Dorset, were the farmers' bid to give some permanent form to the prosperity they enjoyed in the sunset splendour of the 1850s and 1860s. The pathos of this last gesture is stressed at Brockington where the farmhouse is now empty and becoming derelict.

The pillared canopy also appears at Springfield, the home Shadrach Dunn built to show the world the heights which the Silton smallholder's son had reached. According to Mr. Thomas Hannam, the present owner of Springfield, Dunn made £10,000 from grain dealings in 1848. Because of his wide business connections Dunn had been able to buy grain heavily after the good wheat harvest of 1846 and to sell it profitably two years later when heavy summer rains ruined the hopes both of the farmers and the Chartists. Shadrach, now helped by his son James Hammond, wisely put his profits into land, the investment most likely to withstand the revolutionary onslaughts, which most men believed to be imminent. At the time of his death in 1867 the total rateable value of Shadrach Dunn's landed property was £445. From stone quarries on his own land Dunn built Springfield which stood on the site of a demolished seventeenth-century farmhouse and commanded a pleasing prospect to the south-east of the winding, wooded Stour. Though the new mansion aspired to the designation of a 'seat', Dunn was determined that the grandeur of his home should not eclipse his business interests. Behind the commanding front elevation of Springfield lie

[1] Sir J. Sinclair, *Code of Agriculture*, 1817, pp. 398-401.

lofts for storing seeds and an office from a window of which workmen on the farm and in the granary were paid. Shadrach had little pleasure in his new possession and no time for the landowner's crowning joy, planting the park. The magnificent clumps of elm and chestnut now surrounding Springfield were planted by Charles Hannam (1846-1930), the present owner's father. No sooner was his house finished than Dunn embarked on a struggle that undermined not only his peace of mind but also his fortune. The continuation of the Salisbury-Gillingham line to Yeovil was planned to run through Dunn's newly-acquired property at Bugley. Dunn had not allowed his business dealings to be ousted from his mansion and he should not have allowed them to be overshadowed by pride in his land. The rail connection between Gillingham and Yeovil would have helped him as a seedsman, however much it offended him as a landed proprietor. Perhaps unwise friendships gave him too high an opinion of his new position. Dunn determined to fight the line and was, Mr. Thomas Hannam believes, discreetly backed by the Marquis of Westminster whose concern for progress found an outlet in the development of his London estates not in railway building on the periphery of his Dorset property. Furthermore, Grosvenor had an account tò settle with John Rutter, the Radical bookseller of Shaftesbury, who exerted all the zeal of his principles and temperament towards promoting the railway line. Mr. Hannam's mother, Anne (1848-1939), remembered clearly her childhood passion for walking near the rail-cutting operations. Indeed the navigators were objects of interest to all Gillingham inhabitants and also of envy, as their lordly, independent ways were renowned from the Black Sea to the Atlantic. The long legal battle which Dunn waged with the Salisbury and Yeovil Railway Company was settled in 1863 in the Company's favour. His financial losses forced Dunn to mortgage Springfield and to lose heart in his business which was left more and more to his son James Hammond (1833-1914). On his father's death in 1867 James inherited the property but not the deeds which Shadrach had destroyed in his frantic grief after having had to take out a mortgage. As well as his stores and an office at Springfield, James Dunn had premises in Gillingham. The building still stands, now incorporated into Stickland's garage on the north side of High Street. Its only outstanding feature is the delicate iron railings either side of the front steps. The same pleasing ironwork enlivens the upper windows of Spicketts Farm opposite Milton Church.

James Hammond Dunn was not the man to battle with the world as his father had done, any more than brilliant, retiring Henry Deane (1838-94) could emulate his father's businesslike and purposeful activity. Gentle, modest, kindly James with his high-pitched voice was Jimmy to all the world. Had such a thing been possible in James' youth, a course of study at the South Kensington Museum, which Professor Buckman so ardently advocated in 1882 for the sons of Blandford farmers,[1] would have produced a botanist of note. James Dunn, who introduced the growing of Squarehead Master wheat on rendsinas, had a more profound understanding of plant ecology than his father but lacked the drive to make his knowledge profitable. His preoccupation with plants arose from love and interest and not from a desire to further his business or farming interests. According to Bert Miles, a labourer at Springfield, James' farm management was 'all of a muddle'. Both master and men were constantly distracted by the tricks of James' son, Henry Augustus Hammond (1874-1954). As James Dunn gulped an early breakfast before market Henry scattered tacks inside his father's heavy boots; he enticed Miles into a pig trough and pushed him into the middle of a pond to sink in the mud. James Dunn was incapable of crushing any signs of his child's self-will; his only reaction to his son's saturnalia of practical jokes was to expostulate, 'Oh, Henry, you naughty boy!'

That the seed business as well as the farm failed to prosper was not altogether due to James Dunn's mild and over-conscientious ways. By the 1880s yeoman farmers had their backs against the wall and tenants were becoming over-wrought 'rent-paying machines'. As well as bad seasons and competition from overseas many tenants suffered from leasing land on estates which were too large to be well managed by their owners or their agents. As early as 1870 Professor Buckman declared at Blandford that 'farmers . . . had become scientific men, they would not buy cheap and nasty seed'.[2] But a decade later tenants had to devote their thoughts to paying the rent rather than a careful selection of seeds. When it became clear that the agricultural depression of the 1880s was an escarpment rather than a trough, Springfield had to be sold and eventually passed to the Hannams in 1909. James Dunn moved to Bournemouth but with the determination which often underlies gentle dispositions refused to be parted from his seeds.

By the 1890s Bournemouth had established a reputation for being 'so fascinating and so delightful . . . that people return year after year, and in consequence are gradually forming little coteries that come together once more every winter',[3] but the ripples from these esoteric little groups were far-reaching. The demand for dairy produce was a boon to farmers even so far afield as Frampton;

[1] *Dorset County Chronicle*, 13 April 1882. [2] Ibid., 21 April 1870.
[3] *The Lady's World*, 1887, p. 66.

traders who made profits at Bournemouth were encouraged to open branches in smaller Dorset towns as did the Mundells at Bere Regis; less prosperous dealers were able to hang on till times improved by letting rooms to visitors. James Dunn carried on small dealings from his home and found, as well as gave, encouragement by teaching in Sunday school. Like the Deanes, father and son, Dunn was a painstaking and loving teacher, some of whose pupils later repaid their debt by helping in the seed business. This concern, kept going by the perseverance of James Dunn, was to thrive again through the activity of his son. The energies which he had once put into tormenting the household Henry Augustus Hammond, as he grew older, directed into reviving his father's business. Like his grandfather, Henry had drive, initiative and was lucky in his times. The First World War, like the Second, jerked policy makers and officials into remembering the soil beneath their feet. The plough and the seed drill were busy 1914-18 and Henry Dunn moved his flourishing business to Salisbury where it still remains.

The destinies and temperaments of Henry Deane and Shadrach Dunn, the priest and the villager, were not so diverse as their positions in society. Both men had drive and business-like abilities which were not undermined by any trace of self-doubt, and, above all, both men thoroughly understood the times in which they lived. Henry Deane sincerely wanted all his parishioners to benefit from education and regular services conducted in the type of church he considered most fitting. These aims were shared by all thinking men of the time, though this unanimity was often concealed by bitter wrangling over the kind of teaching and styles of architecture most suitable for the institutions all wished to establish or revive. Deane would have heartily supported the present Bishop of South-wark who declared his unwillingness to pass his days as director of a preservation society. Looking at sketches of the parish churches at Gillingham and East Stour before restoration or rebuilding, the thought crosses our mind that Deane might have dealt more tenderly with the old buildings and that incumbents should hesitate to disparage or obliterate the efforts of their predecessors whether they were directed towards increasing tithes, improving the glebe or erecting churches. Whether piety expresses itself with massive pillars and rounded arches, with the comfortable dignity of neo-classicism or with the exuberance of Butterfield, it deserves consideration and often preservation. If education and the revival of the Christian faith commanded widespread support in the mid-nineteenth century so did the doctrine of self-help which was hardly distinguishable from self-advancement. Henry Deane's forbears had prepared the way for him so, to a lesser extent, had Shadrach

Dunn's by holding on to their Silton tenement when peace sent farmers' hopes crashing. But Shadrach built his own fortune and reputation. He early grasped the need to push his undoubted knowledge of seeds and soils. The enthusiasm for scientific farming made his work easier in the same way that Deane's subscription lists swelled because of a widespread interest in schools and all aspects of church building. Between them the priest and the villager had taken the measure of all contemporary interests and enthusiasms. They realised that a new Gillingham was emerging; the railway station and its imposing hotel, churches, chapels, mills, schools and terraces of houses, the bricks for which were made locally, all told of rising prosperity in the 1860s. Together Deane and Dunn saw their home town setting off on a journey the end of which we can hardly envisage today.

NOTES ON SOURCES USED FOR CHAPTER VIII
Verbal Sources

I am greatly indebted to Miss J. Deane of Bournemouth for information concerning her grandfather the Rev. Henry Deane (1799-1882), vicar of Gillingham, and also her father, the Rev. Henry Deane (1838-94). Miss Deane also had much to communicate concerning the characters and buildings of East Stour, where she grew up in Clay Hill House, built by her grandfather for the second Mrs. Deane. Information about East Stour was also kindly given by Mrs. Ernest Fry who allowed me to inspect her home, the Red House, formerly a Methodist chapel.

A picture of Gillingham and East Stour at the turn of this century was given by Mr. Harold Butler of Madjeston Farm, Gillingham, whose father, George Butler (1859-1941), also lived and farmed in the district. Mr. Thomas Hannam of Springfield has long been associated with the Gillingham district, where his father Charles Hannam (1846-1930) was also prominent; Mr. Thomas Hannam's brother, Stanley Charles (1880-1962), was a director of Dunns Seeds Ltd. Mr. Hannam had much to relate concerning the early history of the Dunns at Springfield, and kindly showed me the house and grounds.

I am indebted to Mr. H. C. Flashman for much information concerning the history of the Methodist churches (now united) in Gillingham and for showing me over the High Street chapel; also, for taking the photograph of Henry Deane's portrait, now in the Gillingham museum. To Mr. Alfred Macey I am grateful for accounts of working conditions among farm labourers at the end of the last century; these conditions were also described by Frank Hill who had lived almost a century at West Bourton where he was born.

I am particularly indebted to Colonel C. R. Wallis (1898-1962) for his ever ready willingness to help all those interested in Gillingham and for allowing me to use the splendid collection of documents which he assembled in the Gillingham Museum. I am also grateful to Mr. W. Slade, the present honorary curator, for much assistance, and especially for the loan of his MS article, 'Gillingham and the Civil War, 1642-60'.

Mr. Farley Rutter kindly gave me an account of his family's activities in Shaftesbury.

Mr. R. Howell of Dunns Farm Seeds Ltd. has given me great help by the loan of papers and by giving me information concerning the Dunn family and their customers. Mr. Howell was acquainted with Henry Augustus Hammond Dunn so remembers his accounts of early difficulties; and also kindly supplied a photograph of H. A. H. Dunn's portrait.

Written Sources
Gillingham and District
General

Lady Theodora Grosvenor, *Motcombe*, 1873, a pleasing study on the lines of M. R. Mitford's *Our Village*.

C. R. Leslie, *Memoires of the Life of John Constable*, 1911, Everyman edition. Leslie only knew Constable for a short time before John Fisher's death, so he has no personal recollections of the vicar of Gillingham, but gives numerous extracts from his letters to Constable.

A. F. H. V. Wagner, *The Church of St. Mary The Virgin, Gillingham*, 1956, short history of the Church (62 pp.) with information concerning Deane's restoration activities.

Gillingham Grammar School, 1958 (64 pp.).

Gillingham Museum

Minute book of Shaftesbury Union, Vol. I, 1688-1739; Vol. II, 1740-77, 1844-94. These accounts also contain Minutes of Vestry Meetings.

Handbills 1830 and 1833 concerning proposals by Gillingham farmers to improve the condition of the agricultural labourers.

Accounts of Ambrose and Charles Howe, farmers of East Stour. These accounts cover the years 1791-1804 and 1843-47.

Valuation Lists for Gillingham 1863-1903.

Map of Gillingham, 1802. The arable and grass fields are distinguished.

Survey of Part of the Manor of Gillingham . . . belonging to Francis Sykes, Esq., taken by James Rice, 1768.

Survey of Palmers Place and Farm, Motcombe, 1818.
These two maps, both giving field names, were shown me by the late Colonel C. R. Wallis at his residence.
Some of the forty-four volumes of the Manor Court Rolls for Gillingham, covering the eighteenth and early part of the nineteenth century, were inspected by kind permission of Mr. W. P. Farnfield, Gillingham.

Gillingham Vicarage MSS
Inspected by kind permission of the Venerable E. L. Seager, Archdeacon of Dorset.
Gillingham Churchwardens' Accounts, 1759-1802.
Tithe Book of Edward Emily, 1782-83.
Annual Reports of the Gillingham Sunday School Society, 1816-20.
Miscellaneous documents and letters concerning Henry Deane (1832-82) also some church-building estimates.

MSS in possession of Miss J. Deane of Bournemouth
Diary of Jane Deane, the first wife of Henry Deane. This covers the years 1839-43 and is interesting in showing how much teaching and social organising fell to the lot of an active vicar's wife.
Sketch Book of Jane Deane.
The Deane family tree drawn up in 1901 by Rev. Richard Grosvenor Bartelot.
Balance Sheet of Estate of Henry Deane, April 1883.
Obituary (cut from newspaper so that name and date were deleted) of Henry Deane (1838-94) ' . . . one of the most remarkable men who have been connected with Oxford within living memory, one of the very few stamped with a distinct touch of genius'.
Letters of condolence to Mrs. Anne Deane, Henry Deane's widow. Mrs. Deane had a wide knowledge of East Stour and helped Miss C. M. Godden with the early chapters of her *Henry Fielding*, 1910.
Various receipts for the Deane estate and documents concerning the admission and institution of Henry Deane to Gillingham.

Public Record Office
E.126/31. Account of John Hume's Exchequer Court Case against Charles Wright and George Francis of Motcombe. Heard in the Michaelmas Term of the sixteenth year of George III.

Dorset Record Office
Silton Registers 1774-1812.

Church History

Tithes

G. F. A. Best, *Temporal Pillars:* Queen Anne's Bounty, The Ecclesiastical Commissioners, and the Church of England, 1964.
C. Hill, *The Economic Problems of the Church from Archbishop Whitgift to the Long Parliament,* 1956.
I have drawn heavily on both these books; on Professor Hill's for a detailed account of tithes in the sixteenth and seventeenth centuries and on Dr. Best's for the events leading to the Tithe Commutation Act, 1836.

Building

B. F. L. Clark, *The Building of the Eighteenth-Century Church,* 1963. A list of eighteenth-century church benefactions in Dorset is given pp. 58-59.
B. F. L. Clarke, *Church Builders of the Nineteenth Century,* 1938. This has been indispensable in providing a background for Henry Deane's restoration and building activities; it also is an extremely entertaining account of fashions in church building.
C. W. Dolbey, *The Architectural Expression of Methodism,* 1963.

CHAPTER IX

Wimborne St. Giles: The Gothic Clods

Lord Ashley's differences with his Dorset constituents – the seventh Earl of Shaftesbury and the problems of land ownership – delegation of authority to land agents – description of Shaftesbury estates in North Dorset – responsibilities of Shaftesbury's agent, Robert Short Waters – Shaftesbury's anxiety for estate improvements and his lack of funds – large scale frauds of Waters involving the whole countryside – the strange behaviour of Westcott – Shaftesbury's discovery of complete chaos in estate accounts – Waters' Chancery suit – his appearance at Central Criminal Court – effects of agricultural depression on the great landowners.

'Those who differ with them [the Anti-Corn Law Leaguers] are not only "griping, selfish, odious monopolists" but they are likewise "gothic clods" and "clay-brained fools" and all this because they prefer the cultivation of their native land, to that of the steppes of Poland or the back woods of America.'

From leader in the *Dorset County Chronicle* for 2 November 1843.

SAVE IN Temperance literature a visit to a public house is seldom the turning point in a man's career. Nevertheless Lord Ashley's speech on 30 November 1843 to the local agricultural society at the Crown, Sturminster Newton showed unmistakably a rift with local opinion. Exception had not been taken to Ashley's advocacy of the Factory Acts which were viewed by the landed gentry as salutary curbs on the growing consequence of manufacturers; but at this meeting squires and farmers felt their member was not only neglecting their interests, but opposing them. His constituents realised that Ashley was not a chip of the old Protectionist block, tenant farmers were offended by his championship of the agricultural labourer, and all considered his exhortation 'to recollect that all wealth, talent, rank and power, are given by God for His own service, not for our luxury, for the benefit of others, not for the pride of ourselves', illtimed when the landed interest had gathered to forget anxiety during a festive and convivial evening. All was set for such an occasion. The large dining hall, still to be seen over the archway into the courtyard of the Crown, now the Swan, was 'tastefully decorated with evergreens and flowers . . . the scene was altogether grand and imposing'. The unusually mild season favoured those riding through the rutted Blackmoor lanes, and the tastes and dispositions of the prominent guests, Lord Grosvenor, Sir Edward Baker, James Farquharson, Harry Farr Yeatman and Anthony Huxtable, farming rector of Sutton Waldron, were well known and congenial to one another. Only the austere president, Lord Ashley, cast a shadow on the proceedings. When he left 'the conviviality of the evening was kept up for more than two hours longer'.[1]

In the early 1840s landowners and tenant farmers were closing their ranks before the threatened repeal of the Corn Laws, a danger which they rightly sensed menaced their way of life rather than their immediate economic prospects. John Hayne might complain that Fordington Field wheat was being ousted from the Dorchester market by Dantzig grain,[2] but what he really feared was that competition would force him to change his leisurely and time-honoured methods of open-field farming. When Fordington Field was enclosed in the 1870s, the tenants of the new farms had to make their way in a bleak, competitive world where farming profits depended on the use of machinery, fertilisers and concentrated feeding stuffs. When the landowners accused Cobden of sponsoring Repeal since, in the words of Mr. Jorrocks, it was 'clearly in his interest (on the grab-all-I-can system) to get the price o' wittles reduced, because then he can get . . . [labour] . . . so much cheaper and pocket the difference', they forgot that they had acted on the same principle when they secured the 1815 Corn Law restricting grain imports. Ashley realised this and felt himself unable to attend 'agricultural

[1] Description of the meeting and reports of the speeches from *Dorset County Chronicle*, 7 December 1843.
[2] *Dorset County Chronicle*, 8 February 1844.

meetings and farmers' clubs, and roar out about Protection, the super human excellence of landlords, the positively divine character of tenants, [to] tickle the ears with fulsome flattery, and rise in popularity as in declamation'.[1] His belief that Repeal would not injure the landowners 'if they do their duty by their estates and the people on them',[2] caused a final rupture between Ashley and his constituents, his father and the tenants on the Shaftesbury estates. Until the death of the sixth Earl of Shaftesbury in 1851 Ashley was not responsible for the well-being of the tenants on the family estates covering about 18,000 acres. He was free to champion the Nestorian Christians persecuted by the Turks, Queen Pomare of Tahiti deposed by the French and the children being worked to death in English factories. The old Earl had had little confidence in his heir's ability as a landed proprietor, or, indeed, in any other capacity. He could only hope that his agent, Robert Short Waters, would see that Ashley's enthusiasm for improvements and his ignorance did not impoverish the estate unduly.

Coming into his inheritance was no gala occasion for the seventh Earl of Shaftesbury who had to face the realities of landownership. The problems almost crushed him, 'What can I do? I am half pauperised, the debts are endless; no money is payable for a whole year, and I am not a young man. Every sixpence I expend – and spend I must on many things – *is borrowed!*' Yet improvements, particularly cottage building, had to be undertaken by a man who had passed his 'life in rating others for allowing rotten houses, and immoral, unhealthy dwellings'.[3] Shaftesbury had neither the ready money for improvements nor the experience to make the estate eventually pay for them. He readily acknowledged his ignorance; 'Parliamentary business and city duties are my calling. How can I, at fifty years of age, learn other things? Land, rent etc., etc., are as Arabic to me'. All the new owner could do was effect the changes he felt to be most pressing; scripture readers were appointed for outlying districts, nine-o'clock closing was enforced nightly at the taproom of Wimborne St. Giles, and the parish church was restored so as to 'look like a church, and cease to wear the appearance of an old ballroom'.[4] After six months Shaftesbury found himself unable to support the upkeep of St. Giles House, the architectural evidence that the Ashley Coopers achieved eminence in the sixteenth century and that their descendants had the means, if not always the taste, to

---

[1] E. Hodder, *The Life and Times of Lord Shaftesbury*, 1886, Vol. II, p. 80. Unless otherwise stated all quotations from Hodder are excerpts from Lord Shaftesbury's diaries and letters.

[2] Ibid., p. 126.   [3] Ibid., p. 280 and 369.

[4] For Lord Shaftesbury's early activities on the estate see E. Hodder, op. cit., Vol. II, pp. 365-370.

BUILDINGS ON GLEYS AND RENDSINAS. **57.** Purns Mill (*above*). Archdeacon Fisher considered part of this building, which replaced the mill painted by Constable, to be '*a huge, misshapen, new, bright brick, modern improved patent monster*'. **58.** Manor Farm, Silton (*below*). Rising prices during the Napoleonic wars enabled the occupiers of this farm to erect an elegant dwelling house to conceal the more down-to-earth eighteenth century outhouses and offices.

GILLINGHAM BUILDINGS. **59.** The old Methodist Chapel, Gillingham (*above*). The growing numbers of modest buildings like this one, built in 1838, caused a land agent to exclaim '*there are too many . . . the labourers are exhausted with bawling, praying and fasting*'. **60.** Octagonal Granary at Wyke Farm (*below*). The octagonal form was esteemed by Methodists, ecclesiologists, and agricultural improvers alike.

GILLINGHAM NOTABLES. **61.** Henry Deane, vicar of Gillingham, 1832-1882 (*left*). **62.** Henry Augustus Dunn, (1874-1954), the grandson of Shadrach Dunn (*c* 1799-1867) (*right*). **62a.** The corner of the sitting room at Jesse's house has hardly changed since the 1860s; dried seaweed is in the case over the clock and a Jesse portrait hangs by the window.

NEW FARMERS. *'For whom yon alter'd mansion rises fair
With stucco'd front and proud, forbidding air.'*

W. Holloway.

63. North Bowood, Netherbury (*above*). Profits from hemp and flax enabled the occupiers to embellish their seventeenth-century farmhouse with a pillared canopy and other refinements. **64.** Springfield House (*below*). The year 1848, disastrous to so many hopes, enabled Shadrach Dunn to realise the profits with which he built Springfield on the site of a seventeenth-century farmhouse.

65. The Old Crown Inn, Sturminster Newton. In the heart of his agricultural constituency, Shaftesbury asked landowners and farmers how labourers 'who have been treated as swine . . . are afterwards to walk as Christians'.

66. Pentridge. The poverty of this district in 1851 shocked Shaftesbury, but times had never been better for William Day who increased his 'apprentice horse-trainers' from eight to twenty-one in the next decade.

67. St. Giles House. Before he was burdened with the responsibility of his inheritance, Ashley longed to be 'under my own vine, and under my own fig tree'.

68. Distant view of St. Giles Church. The church and the parkland were the creation of successive generations of Ashley Coopers.

embellish the family mansion. He returned to London leaving the labourers downcast at prospects of less beer and the tenant farmers bewildered by their landlord's appeals to end payments in kind and to contribute towards school building. Although he sincerely loved the 'dear earth' around St. Giles, Shaftesbury during his long life only visited his estate for short periods on special occasions. In 1856 he agreed to entertain 'a house full of foreigners' to help his father-in-law, Lord Palmerston, 'propitiate the "parlez-vous" and make things go off' after the bitter discussions ending the Crimean War. This Shaftesbury did by taking his visitors to Harvest Home suppers where the Russian and French ambassadors probably felt themselves for the first time in agreement in marvelling at the peculiarities of English country-house entertainment. The day-to-day running of the estate and the carrying out of improvements had to be left to the agent. Before investigating the activities of Robert Short Waters, it is useful to understand some of the harassments which great estates in the nineteenth century imposed on agents and owners alike. Although in many respects the seventh Earl of Shaftesbury was atypical he never cut himself quite adrift from his Ashley Cooper forbears. A quick survey of the position and strength of the landowners in Dorset and of the Ashley Cooper family in particular will help to explain Shaftesbury's dilemma. A man of comparatively moderate means, he was anxious to maintain the land-owning tradition which could enable a contented cottager to say, as happened on the Shaftesbury estate, 'I, and mine, have lived in this cottage, under you and yours, for 250 years,' but he was equally determined that the cottage should be kept in good repair and that its occupier should earn a living wage.

The saying that an Englishman loves a lord had an element of truth. The Norman Conquest brought the tillers of the English soil more under the control of the landowners than was the case else-where in Western Europe; but the lords in their turn found they were more closely bound to the king than was usual in continental feudalism. Both peasant and lord had to make the best of a bad job. The landowner had to check exorbitant demands on his tenants, while the villein felt that, although his legal rights were negligible, his status would be protected by the crown always watchful to curb any extension of baronial powers. An understanding, dictated by the head rather than the heart, grew up between the owner and the cultivator. In the sixteenth century this relationship was strained by rising prices and the increase of enclosures for sheep grazing. A serious clash, like the Peasants' War in Germany, was averted as the most enterprising men of both classes found new outlets, mostly urban, for their energies. Also the Tudors no less than the Norman monarchs favoured the growth of a steady, jog-trotting gentry concerned more with house building and manorial affairs than the maintenance of feudal privileges. When these privileges were openly attacked time had already eroded their foundations. The gibes of Cobbett and of Peacock, who derided the 'game-bagging, poacher-shooting, trespasser-pounding, footpath-stopping, common-enclosing and rack-renting' English squire were repeated with even greater venom by the Anti-Corn Law Leaguers with their onslaughts on the 'gothic clods' who stood in the way of cheap bread and industrial expansion. By the 1880s when the landlords were running into all the difficulties of agricultural depression, they were attacked on all sides. As is usual in popular debates generalisations were favoured and, as early as 1873, Lord Derby sought to counter the 'out-of-doors . . . outcry raised about what was called the monopoly of the land' by a survey of all the landowners of Great Britain. The massive results of this survey were sifted by John Bateman who wisely concentrated on proprietors whose estates exceeded 3,000 acres in extent.[1] These returns show that of the twenty-nine Dorset families holding over 3,000 acres eleven owned over 10,000 acres and could be classed among the landed aristocracy. These great families owned 36 per cent of the whole area of Dorset, excluding waste, so that Dorset took a high place as a county of great seats. 'Rutland was beyond question the most aristocratic county, followed by Staffordshire, Dorset, Cheshire, Nottinghamshire and Northamptonshire, in that order'.[2] The fact that well over half the county was in the hands of large landowners meant that the small owner had given way to the tenant farmer not that farms had necessarily increased in size, though this was advocated by philanthropists and economists alike. The revolution of the last hundred years had been not so much to change the size of Dorset farms (in the 1960s 39.2 per cent of the holdings in the county were under twenty acres)[3] but their ownership.

After the Pitt-Rivers and Wingfield Digby families, the Fox-Strangways and the Ashley Coopers were the largest landowners in Dorset, closely followed by the Drax, Sturt and Weld families. The Ashley Coopers of Wimborne St. Giles had, like many great proprietors in the nineteenth century, shown financial prudence under the Tudors and political circumspection under the early Stuarts and Commonwealth so that they prospered to welcome and thrive under the Restoration. The course was hard but the stakes – property, a

[1] Parliamentary Papers, *Accounts and Papers*, 1874, LXII, Vol. I and J. Bateman, *The Great Landowners of Great Britain and Ireland*, 1883.

[2] F. M. L. Thompson, *Landed Society in the Nineteenth Century*, 1963, p. 33.

[3] *Farmers Weekly*, 19 February 1965, pp. 112-114.

peerage and political power – were high. After he had arrived at the winning post the first Earl of Shaftesbury felt free to follow his own bent, for his championship of religious toleration and of parliamentary rights were not purely political moves. Neither Shaftesbury's political principles nor his ambition commended themselves to Charles II who of all English monarchs was the best able to plumb the motives of place-seekers. Shaftesbury's death in exile did not shake the fortunes of the Ashley Coopers who, like the Russells, were too firmly established to totter just because of an unfortunate tilt with the Crown. Shaftesbury's eldest son, since he was averse to taking any independent action, was exactly the heir to calm royal anxieties concerning over-mighty subjects. Even though his interest was philosophical rather than political, the third earl was not so lucky in maintaining the confidence of kings. A short period as member for Poole did nothing to reconcile him to a life of action; he found it easier to promulgate a system of ethics than to satisfy the clamorous Poole burgesses made exigent by the growing prosperity of trade with Newfoundland. The fourth and fifth earls also kept apart from the rough-and-tumble of eighteenth-century politics and eschewed fashionable revolutionary and romantic enthusiasms for the safer interests of the arts and mineralogy. At the death of the fifth earl the title passed to his brother, Cropley Ashley, who had the practical ability so often developed in younger sons, likely to have to make their own fortunes. Cropley Ashley's heir was considered by many, including his own parents, to be a changeling in the family, but the Ashley Cooper characteristics were strongly marked in him. Despite changing artistic fashions, certain qualities are outstanding in the portraits of the Earls of Shaftesbury. The elegant artificiality of Batoni's fifth Earl and the empire-building stature of the ninth does not conceal that passionate self-will which made the Ashley Coopers more likely to become statesmen than politicians. To this outstanding family characteristic the seventh Earl added a profound veneration for all living creatures. Mr. Reginald Tubbs of Woodlands remembers his father, who was a gardener at St. Giles, telling how the old lord forbade the men to level the ant hills in the park as the ants had as much right there as he had. A man with such intense feelings, one who felt his place to be with the unfortunate in the gutter, was not likely to be a good man of business. His ignorance in money matters, his trustfulness and, above all, his determination to improve at all costs conditions on his estate made him the most likely of men to be deceived. Even had he been more financially alert, Shaftesbury might not have escaped being swindled, for by the mid-nineteenth century companies supplying public services and industrialists were as likely to be cheated as a philanthropic peer.

As their concerns grew in size owners were not able to exert an all-embracing control as they had done a century earlier. More and more had to be left to managers and clerks many of whom were quite as astute as their employers. Benjamin Higgs, 'that model of bookkeepers', defrauded the Central Gas Company of £70,000, while the Elham Valley Railway Company were lucky to detect the peculations of their secretary when he had only disposed of £600 to £700. Able men, however, like Robert Short Waters, who were lucky enough to find benevolent and unwordly employers had a longer run for their money and a better chance of escaping the unpleasant consequences of their frauds.

AGRICULTURAL IMPROVEMENTS.

Land-Steward (to Tenant-Farmer). " WELL, GILES, WHAT ARE YOU GOING TO SOW IN HERE ! "
Farmer. " AIN'T 'ZACTLY MADE UP MY MIND, SIR ; BUT IF WE COULD PUT IN A FEW STEWARDS AND LAND-AGENTS—THEY SEEMS TO THRIVE BEST ON THE LAND NOWADAYS ! "

As their concerns increased in size landowners, like industrialists, had to delegate some of their responsibilities. Great landowners in the sixteenth and seventeenth centuries had employed stewards, but their position was not one of great trust. On the one hand the owner's absolute dependence on profits from his land forced him to keep careful watch over his agent's activities, on the other estate activities, such as the relinquishing and taking up of copyholds, open-field management and the maintenance of footpaths and roads were settled at manorial courts. Over these the steward generally presided, but he had to act in accordance with long-established custom. Enclosures in the eighteenth century added to the complexity of the steward's duties as he was responsible for leasing the newly divided or re-arranged fields and the farms which had been increased in size or created by enclosures. Such arrangements between two individuals, acting without public scrutiny, were subject to all the pressures of bargaining, prejudice, favour and economic fluctuations. Not only was the drowsy manorial watchdog silenced by the mid-nineteenth century, but increasing wealth encouraged urban tastes which kept many landlords away from their estates for long periods. A few great agriculturalists, like Coke of Holkham and Townshend, gave eighteenth-century landlords as a whole an unmerited reputation of being interested in agricultural improvements.

TENANT RIGHT.

Young Squire. "They can't say my Father's an exacting Landlord. All he insists upon is that they should Vote for the Liberals, and Walk a Fox-Hound Puppy!"

In Dorset George Pitt seldom, if ever, visited his manors at Arne and Burton Bradstock; Holland House rather than their seats at Abbotsbury and Melbury was the centre of the Fox-Strangways' interest. In the late eighteenth century the manors of Woodlands and Horton were added to the Ashley Cooper estates, but the owners were little concerned to improve the bleak downland and scrub of their newly purchased lands. More and more was left to the agent, and to his activities rather than his employers' we must look for understanding estate management in the nineteenth century.

Until the last decades of the nineteenth century, when estate management became recognised as a profession, stewards often combined their estate duties with their own farming activities or with legal business. The widespread employment of attorneys as land agents was not surprising when so much estate work was concerned with the complicated processes of letting, taking up and relinquishing copyholds. When manorial usages gradually died out the lawyer attempting to direct the new farming methods became a figure of fun; and it was widely held 'that the employment of attorneys as land-stewards and agents has been one of the chief causes of retardation of agriculture throughout Europe'.[1] But it was the multiplicity of agents and officials, the 'flock of hawks which infest every Hungarian estate',[2] rather than their legal activities that impeded progress on many continental estates. A difference between agents in Great Britain and those on the great estates of the Hapsburg empire was that dishonest agents on the Continent enriched themselves at the expense of the peasantry while the profits of those in this country came mainly from defrauding their employers. The activities of swindling stewards often reached a wide public while the day-to-day usefulness of honest men attracted far less attention. In trying to meet the demands of high-farming, of the growing enthusiasm for fox hunting and shooting, and of the needs for sanitation and cottage building it was impossible to please everyone. Farmers felt too much care was given to game preserving, and the commissioners of 1867 considered that cottage building was impeded by the agent 'who indulges his own crochets to the loss of the employer and the poor'.[3] Without information from land agents, however, the commissioners and the authors of county agricultural surveys before them would have been at a loss to complete their reports. To study the agent of one great estate is to fill in the details of a small corner of a great canvas. It can be objected, furthermore, that neither the activities nor the characters of the seventh Earl of Shaftesbury and his agent, Robert Short Waters, were typical of the ordinary run of landowners and stewards. There is some truth in this objection, but it must be stressed again that even businesslike landlords were not safe from the deceptions of moderately honest men who often readjusted the accounts to obtain money which they intended to repay when their prospects improved. The temptations of Waters were great. He was an able, ambitious man employed by a financially-embarrassed peer whose wide-ranging interests could not

[1] J. C. Loudon, *An Encyclopaedia of Agriculture*, 7th ed. 1871, p. 1123.

[2] *Contrasts in Emerging Societies*, 1965, ed. D. Warriner, pp. 54-55, excerpt from John Paget, *Hungary and Transylvania*, 1829; for similar conditions in the Rumanian principalities, see p. 157.

[3] Second Report of Commission on the Employment of Children, Young Persons and Women in Agriculture 1867, *Reports from Commissioners*, Vol. XIII, 1868-1869, p. 24.

be contained by a mere 18,000 acres mainly in north-east Dorset.[1] For ten years Waters ruled absolutely over this small world. His ascendancy was possible because of the long absences of his employer and of the willingness of well-to-do tenants, artisans and small traders to play into his hands. The tenants felt that no normal estate procedure could be expected from the landlord who had so bewildered them on his first visit; while many humbler men, always haunted by the fear of sinking into the labouring class, shut their eyes to doubtful practices from which they often gained. Furthermore Waters was helped by the terrain of the estates, which sprawled over heath, forest and downland.

From Horton Tower an excellent impression can be gained of the gently rolling and wooded countryside which provides a pleasant oasis between the bleakness of the eastward lying heathlands and the downs to the west. Eastward the Ashley Cooper estates stretched into Verwood where small agricultural profit could be expected from the predominant podsols. These unpromising soils provided little beyond material for hovel building and some opportunities for turf cutting, broom making and work in small pottery and brick works. Even at the end of the nineteenth century Mr. Charles Shuttler of Verwood remembers hearing the parish described as 'the poorest place on earth'. The opening of a branch line in the 1860s only produced a spruce brick hotel, easier journeys for visitors to St. Giles House and declining employment for pedlars of earthenware. West of the river Crane, flowing through the parish of Wimborne St. Giles, the heathlands of Verwood gave way to a wooded and more fertile countryside. On the heavy loams of this area rush flourished in the bottoms and barley on the higher lying land running west of Horton, Woodlands and Chalbury villages. On this ridge stinking iris and dogwood in the hedgerows indicate that brown earths and gleys have been replaced by rendsinas. The Chalk-derived soils predominate in the downlands, or 'steppes' as Shaftes-bury described them, of Gussage All Saints, Monckton up Wimborne and Pentridge parishes which marked the western boundaries of the Dorset estates. There was more to these 'steppes' than wind-swept sheep runs and fields of barley; for on the downs encircling Pentridge William Day and his eight 'apprentice horse-trainers' exercised their horses. However slowly ideas from the outside world penetrated into these remote areas, racing news was always up-to-date and was especially acceptable to Waters who was a horse breeder on a considerable scale.

[1] In 1858 R. S. Waters estimated the acreage of the Ashley Cooper estate at 18,209 acres. The official survey of 1874 gave 15,579 as the total Dorset acreage while according to John Bateman the total estate of the seventh Earl of Shaftesbury covered 21,785 acres of which 17,317 acres were in Dorset.

His known sporting interests did not disqualify Waters from appointment as steward to the sixth Earl of Shaftesbury in 1845. The self-confidence of this young man of twenty-three and the experience gainèd from working with his father, who was agent to a number of estates, offset his youth. Waters' ability, ambition and self-assurance were all typical of the new men who were striving, by any means that came to hand, to lift themselves from the obscurity and drudgery that had been the lot of their forefathers. His ideas of the position and function of a steward were quite different from those held by his predecessor, David Park, who had farmed a small lifehold at Hinton Martell, carried out contract work and gave William Stevenson an unbelievably glowing picture of conditions on the estate. Tenants were unburdened by leases for 'whether they occupy much or little, are never turned out of the farms, for the purpose of laying together; and consequently, though they have no leases, they are as secure in their possessions, if not more so, than such as have'.[1] The truth was, as the seventh earl was to learn to his cost, that the estate was riddled with small lifeholds, the seeming permanence of which induced Park to regard them as freeholds.

Under the old earl Waters acted with circumspection, although he secured French's Farm by forcing its long-established tenants, the Shephards, to move to a farm at Pentridge.[2] Once installed in this farm of 240 acres, Waters built handsome brick stables for his brood mares, kept a comfortable establishment with three maid servants and a groom, and was on good terms with the well-to-do tenant farmers. From the start Waters knew which way the wind blew with the heir who was determined to improve not only the conditions of tenants on his estate but also those of the factory children, the chimney sweeps, the milliners, the lunatics, the Druses of Syria and the Italians oppressed under alien rule. The seventh earl, haunted by the multitude of tasks he had set himself to accomplish and by his guilt at inheriting an estate rife with the abuses he had so long attacked, was only too willing to leave all matters with his steward.

Waters was responsible for collecting rents, for the sale of timber and of bricks and tiles made in the estate brickyard at Sutton, so that about £21,000 passed through his hands annually.[3] As well as col-

[1] W. Stevenson, *General View of the Agriculture of the County of Dorset*, 1812, p. 109. For Park's activities as a lifeholder see Reserved Rents of Hinton Martell and as a contractor, Enclosure Award for Hinton Martell, 1798.

[2] Information concerning French's Farm kindly supplied by Mr. J. Ironmonger who obtained it from the Shephard family still occupying French's Farm.

[3] Lord Shaftesbury's estimate in his answer of 2 March 1865 to Waters' Bill of Complaint filed in Chancery 26 August 1864. Accounts of Waters' activities around Wimborne St. Giles have been taken from the documents in connection with the Chancery suit *Waters* v. *Shaftesbury*. Separate footnote references will not be given for statements taken from the Chancery papers.

lecting rents Waters took upon himself to grant leases. This he did with such aplomb that seven substantial tenants swore that they had never heard of any restrictions on the agent's authority. As a result Shaftesbury was to find himself in the awkward position of stating that 'it has never been my practice to grant leases of any farms on my estate other than leases from year to year', when his steward had let at least five farms on leases for twenty-one years.[1] Waters was also responsible for superintending the improvements which Shaftesbury was determined to carry out despite his financial difficulties. The improvements nearest his heart were cottage building, but in the interests of the estate he also undertook large-scale draining operations and the building of new farms. Shaftesbury had hopes of increasing the value of the high-lying land at the junction of the rendsina and gley soils; and three new farm houses, Knowle Hill, Horton North and Chalbury showed the world that an improving landlord was at work, and Waters how easily such schemes, demanding large quantities of bricks, tiles and some timber, could be turned to his advantage. Knowle Hill Farm, in particular, with its three stories and five gables, proclaims princely expenditure and great enthusiasm. Both funds and zeal were dwindling by the time that Chalbury Farm, the most attractive of the three in its simplicity, was finished in 1858. By this time Shaftesbury was writing desperately and unwisely to his agent, 'I am in some alarm . . . I find myself almost bankrupt . . . what economies can be made at St. Giles? . . . give me as soon as possible an idea'.[2] Waters had plenty of ideas but they did not lie in the direction of economy.

Shaftesbury quite realised that large sums were passing through his agent's hands and that the system whereby rents, amounting to about £10,000 annually, were paid into the Provincial Bank at Blandford, on which Waters was entitled to draw up to £3,000 for estate expenses, was open to abuse. In 1855 the uneasy landowner set up a complicated system of controls. Like many other unbusinesslike people Shaftesbury felt that a system would obviate the necessity for constant vigilance. In place of the single account at Blandford and at Hoare's of Fleet Street he opened three accounts. All estate receipts were to be paid into Shaftesbury's own account at Blandford or at Hoare's, and the agent had 'full and unlimited authority' to draw on the domestic and estate accounts which were

[1] Bill of Complaint filed in Chancery on 6 December 1864 by Edward Lewer and Lord Shaftesbury's reply of 14 February 1865. Details of documents in connection with this case of *Lewer* v. *Shaftesbury* are given in notes at end of Chapter IX.

[2] Extracts from letters quoted by Waters' counsel during the hearing of the *Shaftesbury* v. *Waters* case at Sherborne reported in the *Western Gazette*, 14 April 1865.

fed by Lord Shaftesbury who thus hoped to secure 'a more complete check over the expenditure'. The expediency of some control was obvious as by July 1855 the estate account at Hoare's was not only 'exhausted but overdrawn', sucked dry by the £10,000 which went towards Waters' expenses, mortgage demands and general expenditure.[1] Payments from the domestic account were principally for board wages to servants and for the upkeep of stables and garden. Under this heading Waters got away with £700 in one year for the stables in which there were usually two to three horses and the same number of staff ponies. The head groom kept no accounts for Waters, who only instructed him to find out 'what was a fair average of keep for horses'. On the same easy system the agent claimed £324 12s. 7½d. in 1858 for sending vegetables by rail to the Shaftesbury household in London. This was a high price to pay for cabbages which, although reputedly introduced as a luxury by an Ashley Cooper in the sixteenth century, were growing plentifully in the market gardens of Deptford and Fulham three centuries later. Before the domestic account was closed by the end of 1856, Shaftesbury had opened his drainage account. It is impossible not to have some sympathy with Waters' complaint that 'what created difficulty in my case was the number of accounts I was obliged to keep, such as estate account, private account, domestic and drainage loan account'. The system was certainly complicated, as it was not always clear what items were to be covered by the different accounts, but Waters well knew how to turn the confusion to his own advantage.

To begin with, Waters' system of book-keeping was unusual. In the 1858 account receipts were only partially added up but disbursements were carefully cast up and noted in detail down to expenditure on a scrubbing brush for the school at Gussage All Saints. Furthermore the agent managed to stave off the auditing of such accounts as he had kept until 1859, when his employer insisted that they should be handed to Robert Burnett, a member of Shaftesbury's firm of solicitors, Nicholl, Burnett & Newman. That Burnett never really grappled with the problem with which he was faced is not surprising. He had no means of checking the accounts for 1851-59 and there were long delays before he received the statements for which he was entitled to demand explanations; for example, the 1859 account was only sent in 1862. Appalled at the confusion and too diffident or frightened to draw Shaftesbury's attention to it, Burnett temporized by allowing the account 'errors excepted'. Expenditure on the drainage account, into which Shaftesbury poured £40,000 and from which Waters had unlimited

[1] *Western Gazette*, 14 April 1865.

authority to draw, was never audited at all[1] for the simple reason that the only accounts kept were odd jottings in Waters' personal diaries.

To finance his estate improvements, which included cottage and farm buildings as well as land drainage, Shaftesbury borrowed £5,000 from the Enclosure Commissioners and almost £27,000 from the Land Drainage and Improvement Company. As the estate was to supply labour, drainpipes, bricks, tiles, timber, horses, carts and tools, and the rents of improved farms were to be raised by 6½ per cent, the interest charged on drainage loans, Shaftesbury foresaw 'happy prospects for my drainage efforts',[2] but the activities of Waters and of many of the tenants soon put an end to his hopes. Any increase in rent is hard to swallow especially by farmers never at ease with their landlord who, indeed, thought many of them 'ignorant, selfish and tyrannical', neglecting alike the cultivation of the land and the welfare of their labourers.[3] When Edward Lewer, who rented Horton and Woodlands Farms for his son, refused to pay the increased rent and took his case to Chancery he had support from other tenants on the estate. Lewer was the very man to take the lead. He was a timber merchant and coachbuilder whose drive had secured him a substantial bank balance and an establishment at Merley Hall, Wimborne. The grounds for his complaint were that the new drainage was 'so defective as to be almost useless', and that Waters had granted him a twenty-one year lease which had been subsequently repudiated.

By the time the drainage account was opened in 1856 Waters had made his weight felt among the tenants and had shown traders how profitable his custom could be. Not only did he have unlimited authority to draw on the drainage account but was also responsible for providing the General Land Drainage Company with men and materials. To profit by this golden opportunity, Waters, without Shaftesbury's authorisation, opened accounts at Swindon, Salisbury and Hull for the 'convenience of remitting rents', as the Ashley Cooper property spread into Wiltshire and there was also a small estate at Swine in Yorkshire. Protected by a ring of accounts, from which he was drawing money faster than he paid it in, Waters found that he could make very satisfactory arrangements with the General Land Drainage Company. With the more gentlemanly Enclosure Commissioners, who undertook the first drainage contract, Waters had felt his way cautiously and only claimed £230 for his general services. The surveyors for the General Land Drainage Company

[1] *Western Gazette*, 14 April 1865. Shaftesbury's evidence at the Sherborne hearing.
[2] E. Hodder, op. cit., Vol. II, p. 435.
[3] Ibid., p. 368.

were Denton and Drake. John Bailey Denton was a man of ability and probity and soon dissolved his partnership with Drake, who was a man after Waters' heart. They came to a private arrangement whereby the money which Drake supplied to pay the labourers was collected at Wimborne St. Giles estate office and the payments made were entered by Waters against his expenses. Credit for the sales of brick, tiles, sand, lime and timber from the estate could not be traced in Shaftesbury's accounts, and Drake who might have offered some explanations had died before investigations started. Waters claimed that the estate brickyard at Sutton was too small to supply the large quantities of bricks and tiles needed so he placed most of his orders with Job Snelgrove at Donhead St. Andrew, a village fifteen miles distant. Job was delighted at the rush of orders but found 'that he was repeatedly asked to sign receipts' acknowledging payment for orders which had not been delivered. To make doubly sure Waters then debited these payments to both the estate and the private accounts. As the brickmaker's accounts with the estate were missing after Waters had paid a visit to Snelgrove's widow it was impossible to estimate the magnitude of the deception.

Much of the timber needed by the General Land Drainage Company was imported so that Frederick Lewer, who purchased timber for his father as well as managing his farm, had little share in the blessings of estate improvement. His general dealings with Waters, however, probably did not leave Lewer empty handed as he purchased all the estate timber, the sales of which during the years 1855-65 amounted to £10,000. As Waters kept no detailed accounts of timber sales and the relevant pages were missing from Lewer's files when investigations started, nothing remains to show how the booty was shared. All we can gather from Waters' rambling statements on this issue is an interesting sidelight on mid-Victorian etiquette. Waters declared he was 'intimate with him [Frederick Lewer] from frequently meeting him on business matters but was not on visiting terms with him'. This statement recalls the young man in the 1880s who, asked if he knew a certain family, replied, according to *Punch*, 'Haw – well – a – I go to the House, don'cher know, and dine with 'em occasionally, and all that – but I'm not on *speaking* terms with 'em.'

The elastic drainage account was stretched in all directions. As well as labourers and materials, it covered an extra clerk in the estate office, payments to Waters' blacksmith who made the tools, and horses and carts from the agent's farm, though Waters swore that these were provided at his own expense. The occasional payment of small sums from his own pocket provided Waters with an excuse for recouping himself year after year with sums far in excess

of those he originally expended and eventually for taking Shaftesbury to Chancery as his debtor. Side gains were all very well, but
Waters was wise enough to take no chances so he had himself
appointed agent and surveyor to the Land Drainage Company. In
this way Waters was able to augment his yearly salary of £430 from
Shaftesbury, but neither he nor the Company divulged the terms of
the contract. When the case was heard in Chancery Vice-Chancellor
Stuart decreed that £3,780 belonged to Waters as contractor for the
Land Drainage Company.[1]

The estate improvements cost the landowner £40,000, angered
the tenants, who had to pay increased rents, and enabled Waters to
live regally; but in one respect they fulfilled Shaftesbury's dearest
wish: unemployment in the district was temporarily relieved. The
men were paid and the contractors who supplied the labour were
not unrewarded. One of these, George White of Horton, suffered
from the prevailing complaint of those associated with Waters, loss
of records. Nevertheless White was quite clear that his daily charges
for overseeing had been 4s. 2d. and that 'Mr. Bell [Waters' second
clerk] had asked me to sign blank papers while the works were
going on. I did sign them, I did not know what they were for.' Even
this compliance was not enough as White noticed, when shown the
receipts by Chancery clerks, that some of his signatures had been
forged.

Waters made use of simpletons, of men as dishonest as himself and
sometimes of those in distress. In 1854 William Targett of Old Down
Farm was in difficulties and applied to Waters for remission of his
arrears in rent 'which was the usual custom in such circumstances
on his lordship's property'. Waters directed his clerk, William Westcott, to record the remission, still standing in the 1856 account; but
informed Targett that, as his farm was so cheap, his arrears could
not be overlooked. By degrees the full sum owing was squeezed from
the old man who, as a result of his exertions, had to leave his farm.[2]
Though it was little consolation to the broken farmer, Waters was
finally arrested on the charge of embezzling the sums extorted from
him. Anxious, conscientious William Westcott was neither the man
to watch such a scene unmoved nor one to draw up the accounts
from Waters' draft without a qualm. As early as 1856 he realised
that he was 'committing a crime' in copying 'a messed up account
altogether a muddled up thing'. But what could he do? He was not
a young man and loss of employment would be serious for the large

---

[1] *Dorset County Chronicle*, 16 January 1868, summary of Waters' legal affairs by
his counsel at the Central Criminal Court.
[2] *Western Gazette*, 14 April 1865, evidence of William Targett's son at the
Sherborne hearing.

household he supported at the neighbouring village of Gussage All Saints. But by continuing in the estate office Westcott became more and more involved in Waters' frauds and also provided him with a scapegoat; since, when some of his irregularities were detected, Waters attributed them to Westcott's negligence. Long brooding over his troubles made Westcott's behaviour conspicuous, the last thing Waters wanted. The atmosphere in the estate office was tense; a bottle of hydrofluoric acid stood on the mantelpiece and from time to time Westcott threatened to destroy himself and his family. This probably entertained the young second clerk but he alleged that he was too frightened to remain in the office. Bell's alarm gave Waters an excuse to take action; having failed to persuade Westcott to emigrate, he took advantage of his clerk's guilt-ridden behaviour to obtain his certification as a lunatic. This he did by applying to Shaftesbury who had long been Chairman of the Lunacy Commission. When the case was reported to them the commissioners, on the sole evidence of Waters' letter, 'were of opinion that Westcott was clearly insane, arising from a disordered liver, and requesting that he should be watched as he would assuredly murder himself'.[1] A blank certificate of insanity was sent to Waters who tried in vain to get two Cranborne doctors to sign it. Nevertheless Westcott was dismissed in April 1862 and 'handed over to his friends'. The end of Westcott's story took a turn dearer to Victorian novelists than common in everyday life: right triumphed over wrong. When at last his suspicions of Waters were aroused Shaftesbury interviewed Westcott and found him 'perfectly sane'. The clerk was reinstated at a higher salary, under Waters' successor, Thomas Turnbull, and presumably the bottle of hydrofluoric acid disappeared from the mantelpiece.

While Westcott trudged backwards and forwards between Gussage All Saints and Wimborne St. Giles battling with his conscience, Waters was 'living in an elegantly furnished establishment . . . at the rate of £2,000 a year with an income of £500'.[2] He kept his stables well filled and also his bins with two hundred dozen bottles of wine which, he later explained, were a prudent investment as he had 'the opportunity of buying wine at a very reasonable price in consequence of my father-in-law being a wine and spirit merchant'. The whole district around Wimborne St. Giles knew that Waters was hunting, though he denied having kept his own packs of harriers, betting and drinking; only Shaftesbury, concerned with the sanitary commission and bills to protect chimney sweeps and milliners, retained an 'implicit reliance in Mr. Waters which doubtless caused him not

[1] *Western Gazette*, 14 April 1865, Shaftesbury's evidence at the Sherborne hearing.
[2] Ibid., evidence for the prosecution at the Sherborne hearing.

to look so closely into his accounts as he might otherwise have done'.[1]

Some rumours of his agent's racing interests could not fail to reach Shaftesbury. As early as 1854 he had remonstrated with Waters who quietened his employer by promising 'to discontinue all connection with the turf'. But in November 1861 Palmerston, who was as suspicious of such promises of amendment as he was certain of his son-in-law's 'kindness and generosity of feeling', wrote that rumour still had it that Waters' racing interest was unabated and that he 'was a betting man; all these things if they do not lead a man astray, infuse into his mind habits of restlessness not very suitable to accurate economy'. The Prime Minister then advised that Shaftesbury's solicitors should report 'minutely' on affairs at St. Giles. To take the chill off his warning and advice he sent Lady Shaftesbury £5,000, rightly suspecting that fresh financial complications were looming.[2] Though he still asserted that he 'had not the remotest idea there was anything wrong in the accounts', Shaftesbury asked Robert Burnett, who was auditing them, to report 'anything very glaring'[3]. Burnett hardly knew where to start, but he hinted 'that breeding horses which might afterwards be used for racing purposes was injurious to . . . a land agent'. Waters swore that he then sold his brood mares, adding 'I unfortunately acted on Mr. Burnett's advice and not my father's. My father advised me rather to give up the defendant's agency than to give up so legitimate a business as that of breeding horses upon a farm which I occupied at rack rent, stating it was no business of any landlord in England whether a tenant bred sheep, pigs, cows or horses so long as the rent was paid'. When Burnett at last secured the account for 1859 he found that Waters claimed £1,600 owing to him and also that the estate account was overdrawn by some £4,000. This aroused him to communicate with Shaftesbury, who asked his steward for an explanation. Waters had just the excuse most likely to arouse the sympathy of his employer. He acknowledged mistakes and declared, as Shaftesbury stated in answer to Waters' Chancery bill, that 'owing to the affliction caused by the death of his wife, the accounts of the year 1859 and many of the matters connected with my estates had been left to the management of the plaintiff's clerk, Mr. William Westcott'. The strange thing is that the census returns show that Waters' wife, recorded in 1851, was still alive in 1861. The agent had indeed taken the measure of his employer who wrote to him 'there were indeed some things which might have led to a serious misunder-

[1] *Western Gazette*, 14 April 1865, Shaftesbury's evidence.
[2] E. Hodder, op. cit., Vol. III, pp. 147-149.
[3] *Western Gazette*, 14 April 1865, Shaftesbury's evidence.

standing. All however now appears right and what is wrong must be ascribed to the distress of your mind at that time and the too great confidence you reposed in Westcott'.

Shaftesbury neglected to take seriously the rumours of Waters' erratic behaviour partly because of his unsuspecting nature and partly because, like nearly all great landowners, he was used to overdrafts. After the mid-nineteenth century agricultural improvements brought in 'very meagre rewards' to proprietors,[1] whose estates were already burdened with mortgages, settlements, expenditure on school and cottage building, church restoring and by donations to charity. Incomes which at first sight appear so lordly must be assessed with these expenses in mind. In 1858 Shaftesbury's income from his estates was £17,260, over half of which was ploughed back into the property. As well as his day-to-day estate expenditure – repairs, labour, rates, insurance, legal expenses and improvement schemes – Shaftesbury was paying the salaries of seven school mistresses and one curate, and was supporting the almshouses at St. Giles. But the pleasure of giving was becoming clouded by anxiety about overdrafts the size of which was beginning to alarm even a peer like Shaftesbury with great property and small money sense. By 1862 the drainage account was overdrawn by £5,862 and the estate account by some £4,000; these overdrafts and persistent rumours of Waters' prodigality induced Shaftesbury to request his agent's resignation in July 1863. Waters gave up his post but remained at French's Farm to watch, and if possible control, future developments.

These were hardly reassuring as in August 1864 the timid Burnett was replaced by a public accountant, George Bidwell. This zealous man attacked Waters' book-keeping with the ferocity of a ratting terrier. After 1856 the accounts were neither fully cast up nor balanced, after 1860 no records of receipts existed save odd jottings in diaries, and after 1862 Waters had given up any pretence of book-keeping and no cash books at all had been kept. The complete chaos of the estate accounts for the years 1855-63 gave Waters his chance. Even to produce a statement of errors would take time, so he took the offensive by filing a bill of complaint in Chancery against Shaftesbury. Though reason recoiled from the effrontery of Waters' claims for remuneration as agent of the Land Drainage Company and for repayment of £3,827 expended on drainpipes and of other sums advanced from his pocket, legally he had a case. The bewildering mass of figures with which he and his solicitor, Alexander Hemsley, supported their case could not be easily disputed until Bidwell had made some sense of the estate accounts. The success of

[1] F. M. L. Thompson, op. cit., p. 253.

this red herring across the track of those trying to estimate the extent of his frauds encouraged Waters to follow his first effort with supplemental and amended bills. In his supplemental bill Waters demanded that the rent of French's farm should 'be taken as paid' and, since he had been evicted from the farm, that Shaftesbury should be restrained from selling 'stock, crops and effects of the plaintiff'. He reiterated his claims in the amended bill and endeavoured to stay the legal proceedings arising from his arrest on 27 March 1865 on the charge of embezzling the sums he obtained from Targett. Waters gave a harrowing account of his arrest near Godstone in Surrey. He had been taken to London handcuffed 'by the train in which he was in the habit of travelling' and, on his way to the Quarter Sessions at Sherborne, had passed two nights in cheerless cells. Between his flight from Wimborne St. Giles and his arrest Waters' way of life had been far from austere. The police officer had waited for him at his 'elegantly furnished house' until 11 p.m. when Waters, accompanied by a groom in livery, had driven jauntily up in a tandem.[1]

When the hunting season drew to a close in April 1865 the hearing of the Waters' case at Sherborne, that 'small Melton', provided some interest for disconsolate sportsmen. Waters was far from thinking himself cornered and during the trial was quite at his ease 'giving instructions, and collecting the necessary documents required by his counsel in evidence'. Shaftesbury was not so composed. Before commissions on lunacy, factory conditions and sanitation, his statements were unerringly accurate and lucid, but he was easily floored when cross-examined on the management of his own estate. The prisoner's counsel did not fail to reveal that both Shaftesbury's sons had borrowed money from Waters, or to hint that they did so at their father's instigation. 'God forbid that I should have authorised either of them to do so' exclaimed the unfortunate earl and added, as many a distracted parent has done since, 'this is the way that private family matters are brought out'.[2] It transpired that only small sums had been advanced on the quarterly allowances of the young men, but the disclosure harrowed a father who had 'watched every moment, weighed every expression, considered every thought' of his eldest son.[3] Because of the complexity of the case it was decided that it should be referred to the Assize Court at Dorchester and Waters, released on bail, 'left the court surrounded by friends'. The magistrates' clerk was so exhausted by taking the lengthy depositions that a claim for £10 was made on his behalf. At Dorchester the Grand Jury found true bills for indicting Waters on

[1] *Western Gazette*, 31 March 1865.   [2] Ibid., 14 April 1865.
[3] E. Hodder, op. cit., Vol. I, p. 516.

charges of embezzling, stealing and obtaining on false pretences sums amounting to £14,361, and the case was adjourned to the Central Criminal Court.

Now Waters began to feel the benefits of having enveloped himself in the protecting folds of a Chancery case. The struggle through his 'voluminous' accounts, covering over £390,000, was the very task on which Chancery clerks thrived. Waters' calculations were so complicated that eighty meetings had been held by 1868 to discuss his accounts which filled 'many folio volumes, extended over thirteen years, and . . . 700 objections to items and classes of items had been made by the defendant'.[1] Dickens' description of 'bundles in bags, bundles too large to be got into any bags, immense masses of papers of all shapes and no shapes' in the Jarndyce v Jarndyce case was no exaggeration. Vice-Chancellor Stuart attempted to surmount the bundles of the *Waters* v *Shaftesbury* case and awarded the plaintiff £3,780 as contractor for the Land Drainage Company; but, on appeal by the defendant, his decree was reversed and costs were declared against the plaintiff. Waters immediately declared himself a bankrupt and investigations were in the hands of an assignee who declined to proceed as he would be liable for costs. Criminal proceedings at the Central Criminal Court were delayed while the lawyers fell upon the new complications. It was to Waters' advantage that Chancery investigations should move as slowly as possible though he piteously declared that the strain of waiting was 'such that his health had been much impaired, and he was at times so depressed in spirits that he feared to say what might be the results upon his mind if they were prolonged'. His solicitor struck the same sad note when he described his client 'as a widower with a young child – a daughter' living 'inexpensively and within his means'. The young child was at the time seventeen years of age. But the old Waters was irrepressible and broke out to spoil the picture of a broken man by declaring that he had been offered two 'lucrative situations' abroad.[2] Shaftesbury's solicitors were not guiltless of delays as they insisted on every item in Waters' account being considered separately, while Waters' advisers, knowing well the value of confusion, insisted that the accounts must be taken as a whole. Shaftesbury, harassed by the increase of ritualism and radicalism and the bitterness of the struggle for parliamentary reform

[1] *Dorset County Chronicle*, 23 April 1868, quotation from affidavit of Alexander Hemsley, Waters' solicitor.

[2] *Dorset County Chronicle*, 16 January 1863, summary of proceedings by Waters' counsel before Mr. Justice Shee. For solicitor's description of Waters see deposition of Alexander Hemsley of 28 February 1866.

could only reiterate his old belief that 'these lawyers are harpies'.[1]

As a result of Chancery negotiations Waters' trial, due in November 1866, was delayed until May 1868, when Waters secured a further respite on the pretext of an attack of smallpox. Matters came to a head in the sweltering July of 1868 when *Punch* declared that farmers could only complain 'We shan't hev any nice mouldy hay for the cows this year'. The case came up at the Central Criminal Court on 8 July, and Waters was saved by having been a hunting man. Lord Portman, far-famed master of the Blackmoor Vale Hunt, had suggested to Shaftesbury's advisers a termination of all legal proceedings on both sides, as Waters was a ruined man. No appeal to his heart was ever unheard by Shaftesbury whose youthful prayer, that he might be preserved from the 'hard and worldly commonsense of age', had been answered. Before Chief Justice Bovill was read the agreement, accepted by both parties, in which Waters' accounts were acknowledged to have been 'multifarious, intricate and badly kept' but Shaftesbury agreed to terminate all legal proceedings. Bovill was unable to direct the jury who 'immediately returned a verdict *not guilty* and the defendant was discharged'.[2] Waters was free to take up his lucrative situation abroad and the Lord Chief Justice to pass on to another case of young men aspiring to live above their station. Arthur and Hector Smith, aged fourteen and twelve, were 'addicted to reading trashy publications of the Jack Sheppard class' and they took to stealing. Like Waters, they had their fling when they 'lived at coffee-houses and spent considerable sums of money in buying foils, pistols, and percussion caps, and in going about in cabs'. But they were caught attempting robbery with violence; Arthur was sentenced to seven years penal servitude and Hector to eighteen months' imprisonment, 'not only with a view to punishment but for the purpose of deterring others'. So young men aspiring to high living had the possibilities set fairly before them: they might get away with embezzling thousands or their careers might be rudely checked at the onset. Shaftesbury's comment on the conclusion of an affair in which he certainly lost £14,361, and probably more than double that sum was, 'The Waters affair at an end . . . and well concluded, too, in one aspect, for Mr. W's counsel admitted in open court that "Mr. Waters was deeply grateful to Lord Shaftesbury for what he had done in way of forbearance!"'.' The fruits of this forbearance were debts from which Shaftesbury struggled to free himself until the end of his life. 'My mind returns at every instant to the *modus operandi*. How meet the

[1] E. Hodder, op. cit., Vol. II, p. 453.
[2] *The Times*, 8 July 1868, for account of cases before Chief Justice Bovill at the Central Criminal Court.

demands that must be speedily made?' was the ever-recurring question to which he never found an answer.[1]

When Lord Portman was sustaining Waters and interceding with Shaftesbury's advisers, the effects of industrialisation on agriculture were discussed in *The Times*. The comforting conclusion reached was that 'the large landowners of this country are really the persons, who, after all the ups and downs, after fortunes have been made and lost, finally pocket the stakes. Far safer than the lessees of a German gambling table, they have the odds always a trifle in their favour, and are sure to win. They cannot be broken. Their stake continually rises, and is itself never in peril . . . The position of the British landowner is unexampled in the earth, combining as it does so much that is venerable in tradition, delightful in the opportunities of social enjoyment, dignified in power, and free in possession of our common liberties'. But were Shaftesbury and the other great landowners of Dorset safer than the lessees of a German gambling table?

The year 1868 was a propitious one for surveying British agriculture. England had not proved to be Thomson's 'exhaustless granary for a world', but in the 1860s farmers managed to hold their own with imported wheat, and English barley had few competitors. Transport difficulties and some restricting tariffs kept imported meat and dairy produce from the English market. Nevertheless the horizon was clouded for great proprietors whose estates covered only agricultural land. The Grosvenors could plough the profits from their London rents into their Cheshire and Dorset estates so that the *London Review* noted that the Duke of Westminster was 'lavish in temporal and spiritual care of the poor at Motcombe'. The building of two semi-detached cottages at the cost of £350 to £400 to be rented at £5 a year was well within the means of the Duke, but Shaftesbury who built a pair for £400 to be let, with garden, at £2 10s. to £3 a year truly exclaimed 'philanthropy, combined with a peerage, reduces a man to the lowest point'.[2] He felt that many of the difficulties of estate owners were due to the triumph of the commercial interest over the feudal principle. In believing that the feudal and commercial principles were contradictory, Shaftesbury was wrong since feudalism was as satisfactory an answer to the economic problems of the twelfth century as free trade was to an age of industrial expansion. As Magna Carta protected the interests of the tenants-in-chief, so legislation in the nineteenth century protected the industrialists, who were contributing more to the nation's wealth than the great landowners. As the economic value of their estates declined, landowners stressed the importance of the 'tradi-

[1] E. Hodder, op. cit., Vol. III, p. 237 and p. 245.
[2] Ibid., pp. 453-4.

tions, feelings, habits and affections of many generations'. The truth of their contention is undeniable but it is not one that commends itself readily to any political party.

When he resigned himself to accepting the fact that Waters had lost him sums running into £20,000, Shaftesbury must have wondered whether the odds were a trifle in favour of the landowners; by the late 1870s other great proprietors began to feel similar doubts. The rise of rents which had been steady during the preceding twenty years came to a standstill before starting a downward trend.[1] Bad seasons allowed imported corn to get a firm hold on English markets; not only did the farmers see their old enemy, foreign wheat, triumph but they soon had to struggle against imported meat, cheese and butter, which steam and refrigeration enabled to travel quickly and soundly. Many landowners whose incomes were derived mainly from agricultural estates attempted to augment their incomes by means often more effective in providing headlines than lasting financial profit. Transatlantic heiresses were not in unlimited supply, and industrialists did not always welcome a title, however ancient, on the board. Shaftesbury not only had no sideline assets, but his charitable activities were a constant drain on the estate. Only an exceptionally flourishing property could have supported both Waters and a philanthropic peer. It would have seemed that the Shaftesbury estates in Dorset were particularly vulnerable to agricultural depression since they contained areas of unproductive heath and no industrial undertakings save small-scale brick and pottery works. Yet receipts from the estates suggest that this unpromising property was able to ride the depression surprisingly well. In 1856 Waters' accounts, for what they are worth, show receipts from the Dorset estates to have been £15,975; while the official survey of 1873 gives the annual income as £12,536, a figure which must have been supplied by the accurate and conscientious Turnbull. Yet in 1884, a time when the depression was certainly lifting but hardly perceptibly for most landowners, Turnbull's accounts put receipts at £17,666, of which just over half was put back into the estate.

Though the effects of the depression might be staved off, in the end falling prices rather than mismanagement accounted for the break-up of the great estates. Even in their heyday great proprietors were handicapped in the race for economic survival. Their continued prosperity depended on an agile adjustment of methods and cropping programmes to meet constantly changing demands; but the very extent of their estates made such agility impossible. Landlords might, as Buckman declared, regard their tenants merely as

[1] F. M. Thompson, op. cit., p. 250 and p. 303.

'rent-paying machines', but on great estates tenant farmers often set the agricultural tune. However much they were tied by complicated leases, and those on Lord Digby's estate in the early nineteenth century had twenty-three clauses, farmers managed to follow their own inclinations, or as Arthur Young put it to 'suck the orange, and throw the empty peel in his landlord's face'. In some districts of England landlords were held in thrall by their tenants who insisted on growing corn when conversion to grass and dairy farming would have been more profitable.[1] Well-to-do tenants made their weight felt in estate offices, as Lewer did when he insisted on a rent reduction, which Shaftesbury accepted 'with an expression of regret that an old tenant should drive so hard a bargain'. If substantial tenants with leases took a firm stand, those with lifeholds could afford to snap their fingers at landlords. Lifeholders, with tenements valued at under 20s. a year, were numerous on the Shaftesbury estates. In the early 1840s the twenty-nine lifeholders of Woodlands paid rents amounting to £28 a year; while at Hinton Martell forty lifeholdings produced an annual rent of £15.[2] As lives fell in, holdings were let on short leases or else amalgamated with farms; but waiting for lives to fall in, or for ninety-nine year leases to run out, was slow work. Lifeholders often found building more profitable than farming on their small patches of land. They were responsible for the hovels which so shocked Shaftesbury at Hinton Martell, 'what a domicile for men and Christians I found in that village! Yet, what can I do? and the management of the estate, too, has in great measure passed from me by the grants of these small lifeholds . . . what griping, grasping, avaricious cruelty. These petty proprietors exact a five-fold rent for a thing in five-fold inferior condition! It is always so with these small holders. Everything – even the misery of their fellows – must be turned to profit.'[3] So low had Cobbett's manly, independent lifeholders fallen. The commissioners surveying rural conditions in 1868-69 found the same problems on other estates. They noted that the property of Lord Rivers 'having been long held by life tenants is notorious for its bad cottages'. One of the chief witnesses before the commissioners, Lord Sidney Godolphin Osborne, rector of Durweston, went so far as to wonder whether housing on great estates could be improved 'so long as estates can be tied up for generations, loaded with settlements, and so parchment-hampered that the proprietors are such far more in name than in fact, society at the same time expecting them to live

[1] F. M. L. Thompson, op. cit., p. 255.

[2] Lord Shaftesbury's Reserved Rents 1836-1851. The Woodlands rents include sums paid for encroachments onto the heath.

[3] E. Hodder, op. cit., Vol. II, pp. 367-368.

up to the standard of their supposed proprietorship, it is clear that estate improvement is out of the question. What can be done, when anything is attempted, is chiefly in the direction of making the farms larger to save repairs etc. and get higher class tenants'. The throwing of 'two farms in woone', lamented by William Barnes, often benefited the cottager as much as the landlord.

The living up to the standard expected of great proprietors was, as Osborne suggested, a great drain on the incomes of landowners. This standard was set in the last quarter of the eighteenth century, the golden age of great landlords, of country-house architecture and of landscape planning, and it could only be maintained with difficulty a century later when landowners were far less flourishing. To attain a standard of living recognised by society as desirable is often hard, but to give it up is even harder. It was not easy for great landowners after the mid-nineteenth century to retrench and lower the standards set up by their fathers and grandfathers. The effort was beyond many who, like Sir Walter Elliot in *Persuasion*, considered retrenchment impossible since it entailed 'every comfort of life knocked off! Journeys, London, servants, horses, table – contractions and restrictions everywhere', but some voluntarily made the attempt before being forced to do so by taxation. Shaftesbury sold 'old family pictures' as he considered 'it far better to have a well-inhabited, well cottaged property, people in decency and comfort, than well hung walls which persons seldom see, and almost never admire unless pressed to do so'.[1] The style of living in country houses was magnificent but not comfortable. The indoor staff of twenty-seven kept by the sixth Earl of Shaftesbury was swallowed in the vastness of St. Giles House where the heir could write: 'Here I am in perfect solitude, an immense house, a wide garden, hardly the step of a human being, no sound but that of a distant sheep-bell'. As distant from Lord Ashley as the sheep on the downs was the snug warmth of the servant's hall. Here company was never lacking and, once the housekeeper and butler had retired for their dessert, the fun was uproarious. The ancestral board was not spread or the stables filled for family comfort alone, but because nearly all great landowners had a public position to maintain. Whether they served on the Commission of the Peace or in the Cabinet, landed proprietors were expected to entertain on a lavish scale. The financial burden of their services and entertainments fell on the landowner not on the taxpayer. Satirists, like Thackeray, were not slow to mock the deference paid to the landed aristocracy, nor were reformers backward in drawing comparisons between the squire and the peasant extremely unfavourable to the

[1] E. Hodder, op. cit., Vol. II, p. 452.

former; but few could imagine the tenor of public life without these magnates. Peers who, like Surtee's Lord Scamperdale, shut up the state apartment and lived simply in the plate-room, dining on tripe twice a week, were considered to be cheating their neighbourhood and the nation of entertainment and services which had come to be taken for granted.

As the ownership of a large property almost enforced public activity, estate affairs had to be left to an agent. The agent could cheat his employer or he could ensure the smooth running of the estate, but neither he nor the landowner could make it profitable when seasons were bad or when prices fell. Waters put money into his own pocket that should have gone into his employer's, and his irregularities caused much individual suffering, but he did not lessen the value of the estate. It was under the exemplary Turnbull that the shadow of the depression began to fall across the Shaftesbury estates.

The fall in prices in the last decades of the nineteenth century coincided with the tide of public opinion rising against the great landowners. They were held responsible for the falling value of their land; men saw the broken gates and dilapidated barns and blamed the owners. But the great proprietors no less than the tenants and the labourers were victims of the agricultural depression. When the economic value of great estates declined it was easy to stress the conservatism, arrogance and the over-lavish ways of great land-owners and to forget their public services.

Good deeds and bad are forgotten equally quickly. Few in Wimborne St. Giles remember Waters' strange reign when a bottle of hydrofluoric acid stood on the mantelshelf of the estate office and the agent had involved not only his anguished clerk but the whole district in his frauds. Also passing out of mind are the earl's great services to those whose lives of squalor, disease and poverty were making the English industrial poor a byword of destitution among the countries of Europe. Visitors today to St. Giles House can glance at the bust of the seventh Earl of Shaftesbury with the remark: 'something to do with philanthropy wasn't he?'

Memories of the deformed factory children who 'stood and squat-ted' before Lord Ashley 'in the shapes of the letters of the alphabet', and of his agent's wholesale plundering have passed away like 'the flakes of the burnt books and papers [that] flew out of the chimney over the farm' when Waters departed from Wimborne St. Giles.

NOTES ON SOURCES USED FOR CHAPTER IX

Verbal Sources

As the seventh Earl of Shaftesbury died in 1885, a few people can remember conditions on the estate towards the end of his life. I am very grateful to Mr. J. D. Ironmonger of the Shaftesbury Estate Office for much help in finding families long connected with the estate and also in searching out records. Those who kindly gave me information include:

Mr. J. M. Antell, Knowle Hill Farm, Woodlands.

Mr. W. V. Cutler, Sutton, Wimborne St. Giles.

Mr. Cutler remembers when the Sutton brickworks, closed on the eve of the First World War, were in production. A sulphurous smell from the kilns hung over the district, and in winter the characteristic noise of the yards was the creaking of barrows, loaded with clay, being wheeled along planks. The kilns had to be watched all night, and boys often volunteered for night watching so they could light fires to attract sparrows, which were then easily caught.

Mr. E. Haskell, Charlbury Common, Charlbury, helped in 1899 to pull the carriage of the ninth Earl of Shaftesbury and his bride up the drive to St. Giles House. The firework display on this occasion is remembered by other elderly inhabitants of the district.

Mr. R. Friend, formerly of Brockington, Wimborne St. Giles.

Mr. Friend is the great-grandson of the Robert Friend of Brockington concerning whom Shaftesbury wrote '. . . a blessing to have such a man on the estate: honest to his landlord, good to the labourer, a pious man, a sensible man, a just man!'

Mr. F. Legg, Edmondsham, was for fifty years carpenter on the Munro estate.

Mr. R. Tubbs, Wimborne St. Giles, inhabits one of the seventh earl's improved cottages, built about 1860. According to Mr. Tubbs, Bridgwater hollow bricks were used and this suggests that Waters was throwing his net widely to catch contractors amenable to his policy of getting receipts signed in excess of quantities delivered.

Mrs. Watson (née Froud), Charlbury Common, at the age of nine went with her parents to the funeral of the seventh earl in October 1885; the day was outstandingly bleak and cold.

Mrs. Emily Wooster, Wimborne St. Giles, worked during the 1890s in the still room of St. Giles House when an indoor staff of thirty-two was kept.

Written Sources

The authority most consulted on the life of the seventh earl has been

E. Hodder. *The Life and Work of the Seventh Earl of Shaftesbury*, 1886, 3 Volumes.

This work, described in the *Ladies World*, 1887, as 'perhaps the book of the season', gives a comprehensive picture of the earl's activities as viewed by an author who knew Shaftesbury and was, perhaps, more anxious to stress his religious views than indicate the interesting complexity of his character. This account has been supplemented by:

G. F. A. Best, *Shaftesbury*, 1964.

It is possible to assess the economic and social importance of the great landowners now that the era of their predominance is drawing to a close. Two present-day evaluations are:

G. E. Mingay, *English Landed Society in the Eighteenth Century*, 1963.

F. M. L. Thompson, *English Landed Society in the Nineteenth Century*, 1963.

Although J. Bateman, *The Great Landowners of Great Britain and Ireland*, 4th ed. 1883, set out to correct errors in the official 1873 return, he held strong views on the position of the landed gentry which he gave, in his own words, 'with true Tory barbarity'.

As regards the activities of one family, a good picture of the Bonds of East Dorset is given in L. M. G. Bond, *Tyneham*, 1956. In the 1873 returns the Bonds are shown as holding 4,846 acres.

Reports from Commissioners, Vol. XIII, 1868-9, Second Report of the Commission on the employment of Children, Young Persons and Women in Agriculture, 1867.

As in 1843, Lord Sidney Godolphin Osborne was one of the most prominent witnesses before the 1867 Commission, the findings of which did not please the seventh earl: 'I am grieved by the disingenuous report on the state of this property by the Government Commissioner, the Honourable E. Stanhope. I had hoped, nay, believed, that whenever a Government Commissioner came down he would say at least that we were making progress, that our wages were better than in former years, and our cottage accommodation had vastly improved. Not a syllable. He gives a picture of the county as though it was the same as thirty years ago.' (E. Hodder, op. cit., Vol. III, p. 256.)

Estate Records

I am indebted to Lord Shaftesbury for kind permission to consult:
The Rent Rolls and Accounts for the Shaftesbury Estate for 1856, 1858 and 1884; and also to take photographs.
The Rolls of the Manor of Monckton Up Wimborne 1852-76.
The Reserved Rents (those paid by Lifeholders) of the Shaftesbury estates 1842-51 are in the Dorset Record Office.

Chancery Records

The bundle of documents concerning the *Waters* v *Shaftesbury* Chancery suit, P.R.O., C. 16/242 W. 176, contains:
Bill of Complaint filed 26 August 1864. Robert Short Waters, plaintiff: Rt. Hon. Earl of Shaftesbury, defendant.

Supplemental Bill of Complaint filed 28 September 1864.
Amended Bill of Complaint filed 26 August 1865.
Answer of Lord Shaftesbury filed 2 March 1865.
Answer of Lord Shaftesbury to supplemental Bill of Complaint
filed 10 August 1865.

Depositions and Interrogations
The bundle of documents concerning the *Lewer* v *Shaftesbury* Chancery suit, P.R.O., C. 16/217, L. 134 contains:
   Bill of Complaint filed 6 December 1864. Edward Lewer, plaintiff:
   Rt. Hon. Anthony Ashley Cooper, Earl of Shaftesbury, defendant.
   Answer of Lord Shaftesbury filed 14 February 1865.

Depositions
In quotations from the depositions of both the Waters and Lewer
Chancery suits punctuation has been added and also some spelling
corrections made.

CHAPTER X

Dorchester:
The Sovereign
Seekers

*Nostalgia for arcadian simplicity – impact of
commercial ideas on Dorset in the eighteenth
century – influence of middlemen, millowners
and Methodist preachers – the way prepared
for nineteenth-century contractors, auctioneers
and engineers – their growing importance despite the agricultural depression of the 1880s
and 1890s – Dorchester the headquarters for the
new men – Francis Eddison's steam plough
works – the stock sales of Giles Symonds – new
openings for village craftsmen, contractors and
salesmen – umpirism at Charmouth – the
decline of the village community.*

> They do say that a travellèn chap
> Have a-put in the newspeäper now,
> That the bit o' green ground on the knap
> Should be all a-took in vor the plough.
> He do fancy 'tis easy to show
> That we can be but stunpolls at best
> Vor to leäve a green spot where a flower can grow,
> Or a voot-weary walker mid rest.
> 'Tis hedge-grubbèn, Thomas, an' ledge-grubbèn,
> Never a-done
> While a sov'rèn mwore's to be won.

William Barnes

THE PHRASE 'honest toil' implies that gains from work other than
manual are dishonest. The virtues of a man earning only by the

sweat of his brow were most staunchly upheld by those who did not have to exert themselves in this way. Neither the agricultural labourer nor the peasant before him were at all averse to making money but, as the opportunity so seldom came their way, their sovereign-seeking inclinations remained unnoticed. Acquisitiveness was firmly established, long before the nineteenth century, as the characteristic of the trader, the middleman and the manufacturer. But it was only during the second half of the century that the 'paper-booted' men, the jobbers, contractors, engineers, chemists and auctioneers began to make an impact on rural life that alarmed thinkers like William Barnes, Thomas Hardy and William Morris who all distrusted urban ways. Neither the landlord nor the parson physically tilled the soil, but rents and tithes had for so long been woven into the pattern of country life that they were accepted by the traditionalists without demur. These lovers of old ways only suspected the activities of the new men, Loudon's 'agricultural counsellors, artists, or professors', who profited from the land without cultivating it.[1] These activities were especially resented in Dorset where it was generally held that the desire to make money was an infection carried into an agricultural county by outsiders. Thomas Hardy perpetuated this belief when he created Alec D'Urberville, born Alec Stoke in the industrial north, the arch-outsider and corrupter of village innocence.

Now that nearly a century has passed since Hardy and Barnes took up arms against the new barbarians, it should be possible to estimate dispassionately the nature and extent of their influence. To do this it is necessary to ascertain what headway the commercial spirit had made in Dorset before the arrival of the new men. Even these forerunners, whether newcomers or natives, could not completely free themselves from the fetters of the past any more than they could avoid the obstacles of the present. The shadow of the agricultural depression of the 1880s and 1890s fell over the just and the unjust alike: over the farmers and over the middlemen, contractors and engineers. The careers of these men must be studied against the sombre background of agricultural distress. Farmers on the chalk hills around Dorchester did not escape the depression, indeed they considered themselves particularly hard hit, but as many of their holdings were large, they were willing to take risks by trying new methods and machinery. This readiness to experiment and the nature of the chalkland terrain were encouraging to contractors and engineers, many of whom made Dorchester their centre, bringing both lustre and profit to the county town.

Before the nineteenth century the way had been cleared for the

[1] J. C. Loudon, *An Encyclopaedia of Agriculture*, 7th edn. 1871, p. 1123.

spread of new ideas by middlemen, millowners and Methodist preachers. These men had influenced not only the economy and spiritual life of many country districts, they had also been responsible for changing the appearance of villages. More compact farmhouses, enlarged mills and chapels all told their tale of a new outlook on life.

Since the mid-eighteenth century, butter factors and flax jobbers had accustomed the dairy farmers of the Char valley and the flax growers of Symondsbury to the necessity of brisk calculations of profit and loss. On the whole the services of these men whom Cobbett castigated as 'those locusts, called middlemen, who create nothing, who improve nothing, but who live in idleness' were felt to be worth the percentage of the farmer's profit that they pocketed. Not only the middlemen but also the millowners had familiarised country districts with commercial habits. The clanging bell of Horsehill Mill in the hill-encircled and seemingly remote village of Stoke Abbott summoned the spinners to work, and to those 'habits of system and order', held by many to rank among the greatest benefits of machinery. At Bourton, near Gillingham, regular habits were instilled by the bell at Maggs' spinning mill and the whistle at William Jesse's neighbouring establishment. Both mills, which were flourishing by the end of the eighteenth century, lay at the foot of bleak hills which would have been highly pleasing to the Romantics with their taste for 'surfaces strange and uncouth'; yet in this unlikely spot William Jesse had established a complete industrial unit. The spinning mill formed the nucleus of this unit, which also included a long, louver-ventilated rope-walk, a small blacksmith's shop for machinery repairs and a withy bed where willow could be cut for making reels. Built on a modest scale with local stone, all the buildings, especially Jesse's dwelling house, have great charm. The same pleasing quality appears in many of the stone cottages of Bourton and of other villages where home weaving was customary. Until the 1840s, when the use of power driven looms became general, it was economic for millowners to house their handloom weavers well. The solidly built early nineteenth-century cottages in the main street of Bradpole and around Pymore Mill indicate the value which the manufacture placed on his weaver. Spinners either lived in the village or, in the case of pauper apprentices, in shacks which have disappeared. Bradpole still has the appearance of a village which has known bustling and thriving times. During its heyday in the early nineteenth century work was plentiful for both those working in Pymore Mill and in their cottages. Many hemp spinners still worked in their own homes, probably in more cramped and unwholesome conditions than in the mill; numbers of 'ropers' twisted yarn in their own rope-walks. Flax was woven at home by sailcloth makers who could divide their time between their looms and their plots on the hillsides surrounding the village. Bradpole today gives a good idea of working conditions in that short-lived transition period between cottage industry and large-scale factory production, a time when manufacturers encouraged individual efforts outside their mill walls. By the 1840s this co-operation between factory owner and cottage worker was over. In 1841 a fifth of the inmates of the Union workhouse at Bradpole had, in their better days, been connected with hemp and flax processing. The industrial pace had quickened so that the principal wage-earner of the family had to make a choice between struggling to survive as his own master and earning a regular wage for a twelve-hour day in the mill. Home braiding, netting and winding continued to provide supplementary earnings, mainly for women, until the turn of this century. These extra wages enabled families to survive rather than enjoy economic independence. From the census returns of 1851 and one of William Jesse's wage books of the same year, it is possible to gauge the inadequacy of the payments for home work. The parents of Mary Jukes, Elizabeth Farthing and Elizabeth Carter, all on Jesse's payroll, were receiving relief at home and, therefore lived under the shadow of removal to the Union workhouse at Gillingham, despite their daughters' efforts. At home the old people could huddle over the embers of fast burning furze, but in the workhouse it was decided during the hard winter of 1839 that proper measures should be taken 'to prevent paupers getting their seats too near the stoves'.[1]

Thriving millowners who bought land had a considerable influence on farmhouse building. They had little use for the 'gloomy, preposterous, ruinous' farmhouses and barns built in the seventeenth century.[2] The barns could be dispensed with as men accustomed to calculating the value of time found it profitable to invest in threshing machines, which were the first tentacles of mechanisation to stretch into the remote recesses of the countryside. Before the 1830s steam driven machinery had been mainly confined to mills where the gradual transition from water to steam power had accustomed spinners to the greater demands of steam driven machines. The unheralded appearance in the farmyard of steam-threshing machines aroused the passionate protest of the agricultural labourers in 1830. The same economy drive that prompted the purchase of threshing machines inspired the constant re-arrange-

[1] Minute Book of the Shaftesbury Union, Vol. I, p. 115 and Vol. II, p. 371. Gillingham Museum.
[2] *Communications to the Board of Agriculture*, 1804, Vol. I, p. 2.

ment of cowstalls in rectangles, circles and octagons, in an effort to secure feeding, milking and storage in a minimum of time and of space. Glimmerings of time and motion studies are suggested by the design for pigsties adjoining the kitchen to facilitate throwing 'dishwater, offals etc.' into the trough.[1] Farmhouses as well as outhouses had a new look which is well exemplified by Purcombe Farm in the extreme north-west of Symondsbury parish. This farm

·1839·   ·1879·

FARMERS COULD LIVE THEN.   FARMERS CAN'T LIVE NOW.

Value of Produce :—Oats, 17s. 6d. per qr. ; Barley, 23s. 6d. per qr. ; Wheat, 13s. 6d. per bag ; Cheese, 42s. 6d. per cwt.   Value of Produce :—Oats, 26s. per qr. ; Barley, 45s. per qr. ; Wheat, 24s. per bag ; Cheese, 80s. per cwt.'

was purchased at the end of the eighteenth century by the rope maker, Joseph Gundry who, like Mr. Gradgrind in *Hard Times*, liked a 'calculated, cast up, balanced, and proved house'. Complaints that commercial values were ruining the countryside were loud in the last decades of the nineteenth century; but already in 1825 Constable lamented, on hearing of the destruction of Purns Mill, Gillingham, by fire, that 'there will soon be an end to the picturesque in the Kingdom'.

By the end of the eighteenth century signs of a brisker and more commercial approach to agricultural problems were not lacking, nor were indications of a more independent attitude towards the long recognised heads of the village hierarchy. The authority of the squire was undermined rather than flouted by poaching, but chapel

[1] *Communications to the Board of Agriculture*, 1804. Vol. I, p. 49.

THE FORERUNNERS OF THE DARK SATANIC MILLS. **69.** Horse Hill Mill. In secluded Stoke Abbott there was little need for the small, high windows favoured by many millowners anxious for protection against spies and machine smashers. **70.** Jesse's Mill, Bourton. A late eighteenth-century industrial unit. Flanking the dwelling house are the spinning mill and the blacksmith's shop for the repair of machinery.

NONCONFORMIST CHAPELS. **71.** Fifehead Magdalen (*above*). The Baptist chapel, built 1863, in this purely agricultural parish was almost hidden in the wooded outskirts of the village. **72.** Stoke Abbott (*below*). The numbers of weavers and spinners in the parish gave the Methodists confidence and funds to erect their chapel in the main village street.

THE ENGINES AND THEIR DRIVERS. **73.** The Cobb family at Bere Regis, *c* 1906 (*above*). A gathering for the funeral of Charles. All the sons in the group save two were, or later became, steam-engine drivers. **74.** (*below*). Eddison's Steam Plough works at Fordington, 1885.

Giles Symonds, 1835-1904.
'*With ready wit and humour broad*
He pleased the peasant, squire and lord.'
From an auctioneer's epitaph in a
Lincolnshire churchyard.

75. (*above*). Engagement photograph 1874. **76.** Poundbury Sheep Fair,
c 1900 (*below*). Giles Symonds pointing in the centre.

THE AGRICULTURAL INTEREST.

Landlord (to Tenant who had given up Farming at the end of his Lease, to await better times). "WELL, JACKSON, HOW DO YOU LIKE LIVING ON YOUR CAPITAL?"

Farmer. "NOT TOO WELL, MY LORD; BUT I FIND IT CHEAPER THAN LETTING YOU LIVE ON IT!"

building was an open affront to the parson. In villages, like Stoke Abbott, Burton Bradstock and Charmouth, where spinners, weavers and rope makers were numerous enough to provide both a respectable congregation and funds, Nonconformist chapels were boldly built in the shadow of the Established Church. In parishes 'uncontaminated by the enticement of manufactures' sites for chapels were often only available on the outskirts of villages, so that these buildings often gained from their surroundings a grace that was sometimes lacking in their architecture. The most attractive of the many isolated chapels of Dorset is the small stone Baptist chapel almost hidden by great beech and chestnut trees in the parish of Fifehead Magdalen.

Three main waves of chapel building swept Dorset. Already in the early eighteenth century congregations of flax spinners and weavers were listening to the Word in cottages and barns;[1] but most Dorset chapels in the vicinity of spinning mills were built in the early nineteenth century. Many of these, like the Wesleyan chapel at Loders and the Unitarian one at Bridport, are pleasing and elegant build-

HIGH WEST STREET.
DORCHESTER

ings, the simplicity of which reflects the advantages of limited funds. The second period of activity was in the 1860s and 1870s when congregations and funds were increasing, and unfortunately many of the worshippers wanted to show, as at Gillingham and Sherborne, that Nonconformity could well afford to rival the Church of England with a Gothic splash. By the eve of the First World War the great influence of Nonconformity was waning and only a few small and hut-like chapels were erected. Just as much as the middlemen,

[1] John Evans and Josiah Thompson, Lists of Dissenting Clergy, 1715-1775, MSS in John Williams' Library, show that in the early eighteenth century there were preachers at Bridport, Beaminster, Charmouth and Netherbury.

the spinning mills and the threshing machines, the increasing numbers of Nonconformist chapels were portents of changes in rural society. The congregations in the chapels differed from those in the churches in that few did not aspire to, and often achieve, a marked improvement in their material condition; all had the chance of obtaining positions of responsibility in their chapel hierarchy, and many were stimulated by 'the bustling and exciting nature of Methodism'.[1] Better living conditions, more responsibility and intellectual stimulus were the great needs of the more intelligent Dorset villagers in the early nineteenth century. By this time the vitality, shown often in violence and cruelty, and the sense of social cohesion which had marked life in eighteenth-century villages was disappearing. The loss of the close-knit village community would not have been serious, had the expanding towns which attracted villagers been able to foster similar feelings of unity and animation. Though Dickens exaggerated when he wrote that in Coketown 'everything was fact between the lying-in hospital and the cemetery', it is true that large towns had little room for the stories, the jokes, the feuds and the grievances that had given village life its zest. These shared experiences of everyday life enabled village communities of the eighteenth century to give national events a parochial importance which made them of personal interest to every inhabitant. Frequently pealing bells kept the village in touch with the world. They announced that the king had returned safely from his travels, that a princess had married, that victories had been won, and even that creditable attempts had been made, such as Vernon's unavailing attack on Cartagena.[2] Bonfires and fireworks blazed on Sydling hills after Camperdown; while seven wagons with Spanish prize rumbled from Exeter to London, the first wagon carrying the 'Spanish colours prostrate under an English flag'.[3] Such displays brought flax jobbers, weavers, spinners, labourers, farmers and millowners a satisfaction that they were not to feel again. The real tragedy after 1815 was not so much that the peace impoverished many of these men, but that it offered them little part to play in their village community and so lessened their feeling of participation in national events.

In the mid-nineteenth century the plight of the Dorset labourer, benighted and destitute in the midst of agricultural prosperity, made headlines in *The Times* and the *Illustrated London News*. At a time when the population of many Dorset parishes, particularly

[1] *Osborne's Guide to the Grand Junction*, 1838, p. 157.
[2] Bere Regis Parish Accounts, 1739. 1s. was paid for ringing the bells after a rumour that Cartagena had been taken.
[3] *Western Flying Post*, 23 October 1797 and 2 December 1799.

those on chalk downland, reached a nadir of poverty, apathy and lack of opportunity bound villagers to the soil more closely than ever before. Their shackles were only loosed by agricultural depression and the railways. The one finally ended any hopes of increasing demands for labour on the farms, and the other opened the way to opportunities further afield.

When agriculture throughout the country suffered in the late 1870s from the cumulative effects of bad seasons and foreign competition it was small consolation to Dorset farmers to learn that 'if the decadence of agriculture has not been altogether arrested here, it has not . . . proceeded on its downward course so rapidly as in some other parts of England'.[1] It seemed bad enough: landowners dropped about 33 per cent of their rentals, the incomes of tenant farmers fell even more drastically, while the wages of agricultural labourers could fall no lower and remained at 10s. to 12s. a week. The one advantage possessed by the labourer, untrammelled by the responsibilities of an estate or the cares of a farm, was freedom to move. The surprising thing was that farms were cultivated and that contractors and middlemen could flourish during this prolonged agricultural black-out. To those looking back over the decades a depression appears unrelievedly black but, to those who lived under the leaden skies, rifts in the clouds let through a few glimmers of sunshine. The fall in grain prices was undoubted; at Sherborne market wheat sold at 76s. a quarter in 1855 and at 34s. in 1885, and the fall in barley prices, though less drastic, was equally marked. But even arable farmers had their moments of hopefulness. The parish agricultural returns show that there were slight local rallies even in wheat and barley growing as, at Maiden Newton in 1888 and Puddletown in 1887. Stockbreeders were not completely downcast; the numbers of cattle, horses and pigs increased for the whole county between the years 1881 and 1893. But the pride of Dorset farming, the vast flocks of sheep which amazed Defoe and irritated Arthur Young, were vanishing like morning clouds from the hilltops. In Bincombe the numbers of sheep were halved in one year [2] (1884-85); less dramatic reductions occurred in all chalkland parishes. Many farmers struggled on through the ups and downs; a few were declared bankrupt, while others quietly slipped out of farming having made arrangements for their creditors to get 4s. to 10s. in the £. Sheep rearing and corn growing undoubtedly declined and

---

[1] *Reports from Commissioners*, 1895, XVII. Report from R. Henry Rew on the County of Dorset, p. 9. Unless otherwise stated, accounts of the depression in Dorset have all be taken from this report.

[2] In this instance disease rather than policy reduced the flocks, which increased in subsequent years.

this fact had widespread publicity as all accounts of chalkland depression reached Dorchester. Rumours of bankruptcies and failures spread through the markets, grievances were aired at the Dorchester Farmers' Club and one of the great chalkland farmers, George Wood Homer of Athelhampton, had the ear of the assistant commissioner reporting in 1894 on agricultural distress in Dorset.

Until awakened by the railway promoters Dorchester was the sleeping beauty among the county towns of England. The Roman splendours of Durnovaria were followed by no outstanding Christian achievements in the way of cathedral or abbey building so, without the renown of an outstanding fair, Dorchester had little claim to national attention. In the eighteenth and early nineteenth centuries travellers paid their respects to the Roman antiquities, glanced at the tree-lined walks of the town though these were, in Stukeley's opinion, 'incommodious by harbouring flies', and showed real interest in the breweries which produced 'the finest malt liquors of the kingdom; so delicately clear and well tested that the best judges . . . look upon [them] to be little inferior to common wine, and better than the sophisticated, which is usually sold'.[1] Despite its antiquities, assize courts and breweries, Dorchester in 1830 could only boast of 'three streets and one or two lanes'.[2] The county town could then hardly hold its own with Cerne Abbas; was eclipsed by bustling, rope-making Bridport, and never had the royal patronage that established Weymouth as a fashionable resort. The opening of the Southampton to Dorchester railway in 1847 secured a rail connection with London which in turn brought new enterprises, entertainments and hopes to the town, the very structure of which was changing. Medieval Dorchester began to leap its walls when the Fordington open fields were enclosed in the early 1870s, so that land became available for building.[3] The population of over-crowded and cholera-ridden Fordington almost doubled itself between 1871 and 1901 as the village on the town doorstep spread into the Great Field, where the 2,000 lawns, or strips, had for centuries barred the expansion of Dorchester southwards. Enclosure not only benefited the tenement dwellers of Fordington, but also the Pope brothers, whose new and massive Dorchester Brewery gave a new look to an old industry, and the developers who built the estates for families seeking to change their quarters above shop and business for

[1] *Description of Dorchester*, 1716, pp. 554-5. Dorset County Museum.
[2] Communication of 5 December 1830, to the Home Office from Captain Frederick Hovenden in charge of defence measures during the 1830 risings. P.R.O. HO. 140/127.
[3] I am indebted for this line of thought to Mr. D. W. Lloyd who deals fully with town development in his *Victorian Dorchester*, written for the meeting of the Victorian Society in Dorset, 24-26 September 1965.

'desirable residences' outside the old town. These were the people who by 1870 began to feel all the excitement of stimulating contacts with the world. Joseph Fison of Ipswich, 'manufacturer of sulphuric acid and chemical manures', was searching for agents; the Christy minstrels, especially 'the vigorous drummer – a young darkie with carroty hair', delighted audiences at the Town Hall. The minstrels were closely followed by the Tyrolese singers, and by Kaptain Kole's Komic Koncert at which 'a sausage maker [was] in attendance to receive all children in arms!' At this time England was too small to hold her legion of entertainers. As the Prussians marched into the heart of France, Mr. Strang's company from the Alhambra, rightly named *excentriques anglaises*, was performing in Paris. The 'eccentric English' were not the only Britons to realise that a continental war need not darken their prospects. A member of the Dorchester Farmers' Club wondered if England might expect to be 'called upon for an increased amount of produce at better and more remunerative prices'.

Early in the morning of 10 August 1870, the inhabitants of Dorchester had a free entertainment. Shattering roars caused dogs to bark and householders to draw their curtains. Two sets of double-cylinder twelve horse-power engines were driving slowly through Dorchester on their way to Henry Mayo's farm at Cokers Frome where Francis Eddison carried out his first contract for steam ploughing in Dorset.

In establishing his Steam Ploughing Works at Dorchester, Eddison launched a bold attack on the chalk downlands where it seemed that sheep and barrows would protect forever the short turf on the surrounding hills. The true magnificence of this austere countryside appears in September when the long ridges and rounded coombes, stretched under pale autumn skies, have the timeless serenity only to be found in chalk country. It was not to preserve these beauties that many local farmers criticised Eddison's decision to establish his works and plough-hiring service at Dorchester, by now the un-rivalled centre of the chalk spine of Dorset. The great variety of soils on Chalk renders cultivation difficult. On the hill summits the shallow topsoil makes it impossible not to bring lumps of solid chalk to the surface. The further hazard of coming against rock was well known to all ploughmen in central Dorset. The crews of steam-plough sets, however, did not take kindly to advice from local labourers. On one occasion when the plough was being drawn across a field on Dickley Hill, between Cerne Abbas and Sydling, Mr. William Hardy of Longthorns remembers how the plough reared like a bucking horse when the shares hit an outcrop of rock and the steersman had to jump for his life. The light, well-drained grey rendsinas of the lower slopes need the very treading which steam ploughing avoided. To secure a firm topsoil thousands of sheep, penned in folds which were shifted day by day, moved slowly across the arable fields. As well as treading the soil sheep provided the manure needed by rendsinas which often lack organic matter. In dry weather these soils are so powdery that it is impossible to lift them on a soil-ampling auger. When steam-plough sets were at work clouds of dust smothered the steersman who had to toil in goggles with a handkerchief tied over his mouth. The rich alluvial soils frequently found in valley bottoms produced meadows which no farmer would dream of allowing a plough to approach. All these drawbacks were offset by one great advantage for steam-plough contractors: farms on Chalk-derived soils were often over 500 acres, and so larger than elsewhere in the county. Steam ploughing and cultivation to be effective needs a wide area of operation, preferably a field of over twenty acres. Not only did the sweep of the hills favour fields of this size, but the straggling hawthorn hedgerows, which sometimes enclosed smaller fields on the lower slopes, could easily be grubbed up. The clearing was often done by steam cultivation, or scarifying. The gorse, which appears on pockets of clay with flint overlying the Chalk, had long provided the labourer and the baker with fuel and the farmer with an excuse for not ploughing his downland. With steam cultivation gorse covered areas were quickly cleared; but many felt that help in clearing gorse from the hillsides and couch from the fallows had come too late; after 1875 there were few incentives to reclamation and clean farming.

If the choice of his headquarters was mistaken, the timing of Eddison's venture was right. In August 1870 the Emperors of Russia and Austria and the farmers of England still had hopes of a long war between France and Prussia. Also the ground had been well prepared for Eddison by the representative of John Fowler and Co., Thomas Richardson, who had spoken with apostolic fervour to the Dorchester Farmers' Club in January.[1] All were to share in the benefits of steam cultivation which would give 'a warm, dry, mellow and improved soil . . . the true acme, the real charm and test of good farming'; labourers, striving to keep pace with the machines, would learn 'habits of system and order in all their operations'. In short, steam ploughing was 'a glorious triumph of human genius

[1] *Dorset County Chronicle*, 20 January 1870. Report of talk to the Dorchester Farmers' Club on steam cultivation by Thomas Richardson, representative of John Fowler and Co. of Leeds. During his talk Richardson alluded to a letter in *The Times* in which Bailey Denton enthusiastically supported steam cultivation. This was the surveyor concerned with the drainage of the Shaftesbury estates, see p. 212 *supra*. A discussion followed the talk in which the objections to steam ploughing on chalk were raised.

over soulless matter, and one which . . . will . . . have a tendency to increase our wealth as a nation, as well as add strength, glory and honour to our British Constitution by elevating the conditions of all classes in society'; a revolutionary machine, indeed. But Dorchester farmers were earth-bound enough to feel misgivings about the price they would have to pay for the benefits of more efficient farming. The tireless lecturer informed them their success in the future would depend on their having 'the intelligence of a mechanic, the business habits of a merchant, the mathematical talent of an accountant, and a shrewdness and perceptive genius of a banker'. Never before had the point been so clearly made in Dorset that farming was a business and not only a way of life. Some glimmerings of this fact had appeared during the agitation over the repeal of the Corn Laws but, for a quarter of a century after 1846, fair seasons and reasonable prices had lulled farmers into forgetting, as Richardson now reminded them, how close the foreigners were to treading on their heels.

Trying to hire steam-plough sets to chalk-belt farmers, who felt the world had nothing to teach them about the management of sheep and corn, was no easy undertaking. Today when the public in this country have both purchasing power and a well whetted appetite for goods of all sorts, it is hard to realise how hard salesmen had to work a century ago. In the country resistance to the use of mechanical inventions was particularly strong, and could only be overcome by the salesman's complete mastery of the machines he offered the public. The farmers' determination to maintain their old ways had already broken John Galpin who tried to hire steam ploughs in the Dorchester area before Eddison's arrival. Where they agreed to steam cultivation at all, the farmers were unwilling to pay more than 3s. to 4s. an acre, a rate which was uneconomic for the contractor. So John Galpin soon retired since 'he could not please everybody, and was glad to be relieved of the chance of offending everybody'.[1]

Francis Eddison (1841-88) was bewitched by steam and drew even farmers on chalk downland under its spell by his tact and energy. These qualities he inherited from his father, Edwin Eddison (1803-67), who helped to get the unaccommodating Thomas Babington Macaulay returned for Leeds in 1831. Eddison became Town Clerk of Leeds, so Francis and his five brothers grew up at the heart of civic affairs at a time when the excitement, mystery and vast possibilities of steam power still hung over the city. Steam was the Pegasus which John Fowler determined to harness to the plough at his Hunslett Works near Leeds; four of the Eddison boys were

[1] *Dorset County Chronicle*, 20 January 1870.

infected by his enthusiasm. Two of them, Walter and Francis, established undertakings from which machines took the names of Cowley and Dorchester around the world.

Eddison established his Steam Plough Works at Fordington where it remained until recently, and lived, until ill-health forced him to move into Dorchester, at Martinstown. Here he was surrounded by notable chalk-belt farmers, William and Henry Hawkins, John Homer and Henry Duke. Before Eddison's arrival, Henry Duke had already, 'with more pluck than prudence' according to his neigh-bours,[1] invested in a steam-plough set, while the great ploughing activities of Henry Hawkins of Clandon were only halted by the earthworks of Maiden Castle. Arthur Hawkins (1876-1966) re-membered Eddison as a frequent and pleasant visitor to his father, William Hawkins (1843-1931) of Manor Farm. But these were visits for pleasure not business as Hawkins hated all innovations, refusing even to accept the new Summer Time so that his labourers had to return home for their mid-day meal at 3 p.m.

It soon became clear that though steam cultivation might add lustre to the British constitution, the expenditure on a steam-plough set was more than most farmers could afford. The work had to be done by contractors, and Eddison was the first man to operate on a county-wide scale, and to maintain machine shops for repairs. In 1885 the Dorchester Steam Plough Works, with its twelve sets of steam ploughs to be maintained and repaired, presented 'a busy and animating scene such as one could hardly realise being enacted in a quiet country town'. The reporter added, with more enthusiasm than accuracy, that the 'importation of "foreign" labour [was] unnecessary'.[2] But a large number of the men, who presented such 'an unusual appearance of respectability and intelligence' when they assembled at a works' dinner, were from the Midlands and Eddison's native Leeds. Even at the turn of the century Percy Balson (1878-1966), employed at Eddison's for fifty years, remembers that 'the wonderful men in charge [were] mostly north countrymen'. A few local men, like Balson himself, the Manleys and the Kings attained positions of responsibility, but 'foreigners' remained the backbone of the works. Men in the repair shops worked a twelve-hour day; they, and the whole neighbourhood, were aroused by a hooter at 5.45 a.m. Thomas Hardy tried to have this hooter silenced but by the 1890s Eddison's had switched to the hire of road-making equipment so that financial stability enabled them to disregard the whims of poets. In the field daylight determined the working hours of the ploughing crews, and also of the unfortunate carters who had to carry the large quantities of coal and water needed by the engines.

(1) *Dorset County Chronicle*, 20 January 1870.   (2) Ibid., 9 February 1885.

Mr. William Hardy remembers struggling to harness his horses at dawn while the cries of 'water, water!' echoed round the hilltops north of Grimstone. For the work of hauling to the steam-plough sets a carter earned a shilling a day, a not inconsiderable addition to his weekly wage of 12s.; but most carters would have agreed with the Martinstown farmer who declared he would only be interested in steam ploughing if a coal mine lay at one end of the field and the sea at the other.

Carters hauling for the plough crews felt that steam cultivation increased both the strains and drudgery of their work. Many employers shared this dislike and did not make use of a contractor's services without qualms. They felt that these specialists were in danger of becoming the key men of society; and that a disruptive influence was exercised by their foremen and mechanics who un-settled villagers with their breezy prodigality in public houses and tales of eventful journeys to distant lands. These fears were not unfounded for the sons of agricultural labourers longed for a way out of the 'slavish work' that lay before them.[1] They looked enviously at the steam ploughmen whose mechanical knowledge and earnings, rising to 30s. a week in a good season, entitled them to bawl their orders to the carters. Enterprising boys had a chance of getting into 'this species of village aristocracy',[2] since the crew of each steam-plough set generally included a foreman, two engine drivers, a steersman guiding the plough as it was drawn backwards and forwards between the two engines, and a cook. The last-named was generally a boy-of-all-work who, if he could watch what was going on in the intervals of cooking, running errands and cleaning the sleeping vans, had the opportunity of becoming an engine driver.

Eddison declared in 1885 that with his workmen at his back he 'would even dare to face Khartoum',[3] but the situation on his door-step was equally challenging. The agricultural depression dealt steam cultivation a knock-out blow. Eddison saved his works by switching to road-rollers. In 1886 the first road roller, from Aveling and Porter, steamed into the yard of the Dorchester Steam Plough Works. This was Eddison's last and most profitable venture. A year after he died the newly established Dorset County Council took over

[1] This description of agricultural work was given by the wife of a Blandford labourer, who added that boys 'like to be good scholars, because it helps them get away'. Commission on the Employment of Children, Young Persons and Women in Agriculture, *Reports from Commissioners*, 1868-9, Vol. XIII, p. 15.

[2] H. Bonnett, *The Saga of the Steam Plough*, 1965, p. 45. Quoted from a lecture in 1867.

[3] *Dorset County Chronicle*, 9 February 1885.

road maintenance and the equipment was waiting for them in Eddison's yard.

Steam-plough sets were a seven days' wonder, but steam-traction engines came to stay, and to give smaller contractors their chance. The story of the Cobbs of Bere Regis might be repeated in many Dorset parishes. Samuel Cobb was a man of endurance who held on to his thirty acres on Woodbury Hill through the hard 1840s. His son, Charles, profited by this tenacity and was able to invest in horses for haulage work. A profitable contract for hauling water to Bovington Camp – a modest collection of tents at the turn of this century – enabled Charles to replace his horses by a steam-traction engine. Labour was no problem to Cobb who had seventeen children, twelve of whom were boys. All save two of his sons were engine drivers, working for their father, Eddison's or other contractors. Once employed this family of travelling drivers seldom assembled save on special occasions like the funeral of young Charles, who died in Cornwall while working for Eddison's. All men in a small community faced the same problem when they made money quickly, that of living up to the expectations of their friends and relations whose reaction to success was the anticipation of constant celebrations. Charles Cobb enjoyed company and gaiety, and could find both in the public houses of Bere Regis by putting his hand in his pocket. Often contractors booked their orders but failed to keep their accounts; they earned sovereigns but neglected to save them. The First World War kept many a tottering contractor on his feet, but the crash came after 1918. Ruin overtook Charles Cobb who liked to treat his friends at the Drax Arms, and de Mattos, Eddison's successor at Dorchester, who used regularly to present the driver of the Waterloo to Dorchester train with a sovereign.

When Francis Eddison died in 1888 the gay, confident Dorchester of 1870 had disappeared. In country towns the agricultural depression took its toll of casualties no less than in the villages. The popular *Raphel's Book of Fate* guaranteeing to 'tell the fate of anyone' was hardly necessary. The most respectable tradesmen and farmers faced bankruptcy. In Dorchester the shutters went up on shop after shop, as many owners had not the resources to tide them over even temporary difficulties. When Henry Bascombe fell ill, his drapery business failed. With more capital behind them Genge, Dixon and Jameson struggled through the hard times, though their advertisements in January 1888 were hardly encouraging: 'owing to the continued depression in the home and foreign markets they have secured many of the following parcels desperately cheap!' The contents of the parcels included blankets at 2s. 11½d. each; forty years earlier the trustees of the Beauchamp Bequest at Mappowder had paid 4s. 9d. apiece for blankets distributed to paupers. Sales of agricultural machinery, which in the 1860s and 1870s had seemed certain to increase, either dwindled or remained stationery. Farmers could not be tempted even by salesmen like Scutt of Moreton who offered machinery for men 'wanting the maximum of work with the minimum of labour'.

By ordering a road roller in 1886 Eddison had foreseen the needs of the future; others who were quick enough to do the same managed to ride the depression. The greatest of these needs was for education in all its forms. Parents were seeking schools for their girls as well as their boys, and young people wanted acquirements which had played no part in the bread-and-butter calculations of their parents. Young Lupin Pooter in *The Diary of a Nobody* spoke for his generation when he told his plodding, cautious father, 'Look here, Guv., excuse me saying so, but you're a bit out of date. It does not pay nowadays, fiddling about over small things. I don't mean anything personal, Guv'nor. My boss says if I take his tip, and stick to big things, I can make big money . . . It is not speculation, it's a dead cert'. For young people seeking the 'big things' Westbrook's drapery stores advertised 'the Parisian art of *Dress Cutting* taught by a certified teacher in a few easy lessons'; and Herr Greiner of Wimborne, to whom 'distance was no object', offered lessons in German and Italian. The bewildered little daughters of substantial farmers were packed off to school to pick up those accomplishments which, with the farmers' more lavish ways of living, were considered by many to be the root of agricultural distress. Not only did farming fathers have to pay extra for music lessons but they lost the services of their daughters who were unlikely to leave the piano for the churn. At South Grove Cottage, Dorchester, Alice Symonds got 'board and tuition in the English language, geography, history, writing and arithmetic with various kinds of useful and ornamental needlework' for twenty guineas a year.[1] At this rate school mistresses could not have been placed among Barnes' money-grubbers; these small gains were often the only means of survival for women who could earn their living in no other way. Seaside education was particularly in demand, and Bournemouth was ready for the challenge. Regular visits by the Marquis of Westminster, the patronage of royalty, in the person of the Nawab Nazim of Bengal, a pier and a sanatorium all entitled Bournemouth to offer a season, and to serious consideration by parents who wanted a mild climate and a genial social atmosphere for their children.

As well as education, the ability to sell goods to a pennywise

[1] Old school bill dated 28 June 1870, kindly shown me by Mr. N. J. Symonds of Martinstown.

public was a great aid to advancement at the end of the nineteenth century. More sophisticated salesmanship became general in the markets. The stock figure of the simple son sent to market with a pig was replaced by the auctioneer. Professional auctioneers took the place of gifted amateurs, like Thomas Candy of Stoke Wake whose now legendary skill in estimating stock weights and values enabled him to rise from an agricultural labourer to a substantial dairyman.[1] The once rigidly controlled prices and procedure in markets were undermined in the sixteenth century, and jettisoned in the early nineteenth by those respectable revolutionaries, the utilitarians. The farmer found himself with freedom to sell as he pleased at a time when prices, after fluctuating for some decades, settled to steady downward trend. Business continued in the Dorchester Corn Exchange but it was mostly in the hands of factors, men like dapper Homer Scutt, whose outlook was commercial rather than agricultural. Business was brisker in the Cattle Market established in 1859. In times of uncertainty and price fluctuations stock changed hands quickly, so the clouds of the 1880s parted for the great triumvirate of Dorset auctioneers, Thomas Ensor, Henry Duke and Giles Symonds.

Giles Symonds' namesake and grandfather founded the fortunes of the family at Pilsdon. He died in 1819 worth £3,500 and in his will cancelled substantial debts owed him by his sons-in-law, Thomas Slade and John Roper. Of his six sons only two, a sailmaker and a tanner, did not till the soil, but many of his army of grandchildren spread their wings to leave the county and break with the family tradition of farming and milling. Three particularly deserve to be remembered with gratitude in Dorset: John Symonds Udal (1848-1925), Henry Symonds (1817-95) and Giles Symonds (1835-1904). The first two preserved for us ways of living among the villagers and gentry that are now acquiring an antiquarian interest. John Symonds Udal, having doubtless observed some strange goings-on as Chief Justice of the Leeward Islands, turned his attention to Dorset customs and beliefs, and published in 1922 his monumental *Dorsetshire Folk-Lore*. Genial, breezy Henry Symonds of Gorwell and Milborne St. Andrew described, hedge by hedge and field by field, hunting runs during the first half of the nineteenth century. This ardent sportsman remembered his wedding day chiefly because he lent a horse to his new brother-in-law who had to hunt in 'white cord trowsers'.[2] Giles Symonds, working

---

[1] I am indebted to Dr. S. F. Jackson, lately rector of Mappowder and Plush, for drawing my attention to Thomas Candy, and to Mr. F. N. Kent for allowing me to see the Stoke Wake Registers.

[2] H. Symonds, *Runs and Sporting Notes from Dorsetshire*, 1899, p. 38.

with his nephew, John Sampson, made his name as a Dorset auctioneer. A country auctioneer must have a full knowledge of all branches of agriculture and the confidence of farmers. Giles Symonds, the son of a farmer and a successful stockbreeder himself, had both. His first stock sales were at Cerne Abbas, a centre that was out-distanced in the 1880s by its rival, Maiden Newton. Here Symonds and Henry Duke battled to control the moribund market revived by rail communications. The farmers and tradesmen of the district decided that 'Mr. Symonds deserved their support, and they should all pull together to make the market prosperous'.[1] All Maiden Newton inhabitants had every reason to pull together; a flourishing market benefited the whole neighbourhood, and particularly the innkeepers, who were often ruined when the old coaching routes fell into disuse. The brisk trade brought by well-attended markets dwindled during the depression, when the assistant commissioner noted that the market ordinary was 'everywhere . . . shorn of its ancient glory'. The Hodges family of Maiden Newton triumphed over adversity. In the cheerless 1830s Henry Hodges, who had been a carpenter on the Weld estate, built the Gothic battlements of the Castle Inn as an act of faith in the future and of devotion to the work he had loved at Lulworth Castle. Hodge's faith was justified; his son, George, flourished for sixty years beneath the inn's elegant turret. When the lavish farmers' ordinaries were no longer patronised on market days, George Hodges catered for fishermen as the Frome, 'one of the best dry-fly trout streams of the West',[2] flowed at his doorstep.

Though he was active in outlying markets it was in Dorchester that Symonds could most easily be found by his clients, 'noblemen, gentlemen and others', anxious to purchase stock or agricultural seeds, to have valuations for probate and legacy duties, or to sell their furniture. To his regular stock sales in Dorchester the transport of cattle was facilitated by a 'conveyance for loading and unloading', and of humans by cheap market tickets issued by the Great Western Railway.[3]

Symonds, Ensor and Duke all had the complete confidence of the farmers and landowners, but their profession was a tempting one for men aiming at a quick turnover and a short life in the business. A member of the irrepressible Waters family showed all the family bluster and glibness when he assured clients at Salisbury that he was only disposing of 'a carefully selected cellar of wines' because the

[1] *Dorset County Chronicle*, 20 January 1888.
[2] *Country Life*, 7 December 1907, p. CIV.
[3] *Dorset County Chronicle*, 10 May 1888 and 12 January 1888.

executors of the late owner considered it 'inadvisable to maintain them for his young family'.[1]

It was fitting that one so apt for genial and friendly intercourse with his fellows should die suddenly on Christmas Eve 1904. Not one of the great gathering at the funeral in Sydling church would have disagreed that 'the name of Giles Symonds was a synonym for integrity and honour'.[2]

The activities of auctioneers and valuers were increasing in importance at the end of the nineteenth century, so that men of moderate means sometimes hesitated to call upon the services of the potentates of the sale ring and sale room. Umpirism, which was Edward Vince's contribution to 'moving with the times', met the needs of the less affluent man. The idea of unofficial, neighbourly arbitration in disputes over buying and selling was no innovation. Sixteenth-century disputants often reached the decision to 'let neighbours make an end of it'.[3] The offices of a good neighbour as arbitrator remained in demand throughout the eighteenth and early nineteenth centuries. As legal precedents hardly kept pace with industrial development, disputes between manufacturers were often referred to an unofficial arbitration.

Edward Vince (1848-1917) came from a Norfolk farming family and to him, as to Eddison, Dorset had all the exciting possibilities of unknown territory. He chose wisely in settling at Charmouth, as shopkeepers in a moderately comfortable community with a regular influx of summer visitors fared better in the 1880s and 1890s than those in market towns, like Dorchester, who depended on the agricultural interest for their support. During the last decades of the nineteenth century the public expected a great deal from their shopkeepers in the way of attention, service and a variety of goods. When he arrived in Charmouth in 1888 Edward Archer Vince, already well experienced in business, was determined to show just how far a shopkeeper could go in meeting the needs of his customers. In his store they could purchase all their personal and household needs, insure their lives and property, and also send their telegrams and buy their stamps. Furthermore, customers could be certain of fair dealing as goods and services were offered by a man who typified all that was best in the Nonconformist Liberal of the day. In undertaking 'umpirism' Edward Vince bridged the gap between friendly arbitration by a neighbour and the professional services of a valuer. The advantages of Vince's scheme were that his charges, 1 per cent

[1] *Dorset County Chronicle*, 13 January 1870.
[2] *Bridport News*, 30 December 1904.
[3] Quoted by M. Campbell, *The English Yeoman in the Tudor and Early Stuart Age*, 1960, p. 384.

to $1\frac{1}{2}$ per cent of the value of the goods in question, were low; and that the details of his estimates were made known to vendor and purchaser. While he undertook valuations of stock and agricultural machinery, Vince specialised in arbitrating between purchasers and vendors in the retailing trades. The scheme was launched in a shower of recommendations from Vince's wholesalers: 'Your mode of valuation is an absolute check against error or fraudulent trans-action . . . no better system extant . . . the system only needs to be known to be adopted . . . few men, if any, more suited for the position of stock valuer in the provision and grocery trades . . . a very upright and shrewd man of business'. But the real cornerstone of Vince's success as an umpire was his respected standing in Charmouth and the neighbouring countryside. During his ten years' stay in Dorset Vince certainly made money, but he also left an example of fair-dealing and integrity which has not been forgotten in Char-mouth.

Cross-fertilisation of communities was one of the most important social developments of the late nineteenth century. Many of the strangers who came to Dorset enriched themselves and the com-munity as well. Not least among the services of these immigrants was that they often made Dorset men bestir themselves. Once stirred many left the villages and often the county. As the large corn and sheep farms were hardest hit by the depression, Dorchester became a stepping stone to the outer world. By 1881 a decline in the population was already noticeable in most of the villages within an eight-mile radius of Dorchester. The departure of the enterprising rather than the entry of strangers was the real cause of the slow disintegration of village life that saddened Barnes and Hardy. Just as the capitalist clothier had profited by village unemployment in the sixteenth century to foster cottage weaving, so three centuries later contractors and agents of business concerns took advantage of a similar situation to find labour. The arrival of these money makers from outside fanned rather than created desires for financial gain. They were the result not the cause of the break-up of the village community.

Young people were ready to accept the enticements of the out-siders. In the 1870s village children were awaking after a long night of apathy and undernourishment. In the earlier decades of the century their spirits and limbs had been cramped by drudgery, rusty black clothes, ill-fitting boots and the weight of minor ail-ments that were never quite cured. A more lively education and varied diet, white pinafores and Sunday School outings helped to encourage boys and girls to live more hopefully. In nearly every village stories of successful sorties by fellow-villagers emboldened

MOVING WITH THE TIMES IN CHARMOUTH. **77.** The main street in Charmouth (*above*). Mortimer's general stores, later taken over by E. A. Vince, with young Ashton outside in a straw hat and apron. **78.** E. A. Vince, 1848-1917 (*left*). '*Great gains are to be made . . . by going out of the common road.*' **79.** E. A. Vince of Charmouth moves with the times with a horseless carriage and umpirism (*right*).

80. The Charmouth May Queen and her attendants, 1899. White dresses, jaunty hats and outings helped to give confidence to village children. Frankie Coles made his way on to the reporting staff of the *Daily Telegraph*.

young people to take the opportunities, offered by recruiting agents, of plunging into the outer world. Young John Rogers, a mason in Martinstown, signed on with the building contractor, John Booth, and found himself building a church in Constantinople. New scenes did not always change the ancient trend of the countryman's ambition to hold land. On his return Rogers tried unsuccessfully to make farming pay; and the sole monument in Martinstown to the man under whom one more turret rose beside the Bosphorus is the small brick shed he built for his horse and cart. George Ashton of Charmouth travelled even further afield, and his adventures support the verisimilitude of some of Samuel Smiles' success stories. The son of a Charmouth agricultural labourer, George was lucky enough to be taken on as errand boy by Vince's predecessor, George Mortimer, and also to obtain evening help with his education. In his spare moments the boy taught himself the morse code and improved his handwriting, so that he was promoted to a clerk and eventually to postmaster at Taunton. Here he might have been content to rest had not an impetuous and romantic marriage sent him across the Atlantic. A position of responsibility with the South American Cable Company led to Ashton's settling in Equador where he amassed a fortune before his untimely death. It was not necessary to go so far afield as Equador to make a fortune; but few opportunities came to those who stayed at home in the village. The need to bestir themselves had long been realised by girls who had been leaving home for domestic service since the eighteenth century. The reanimation in village life in the 1880s inspired more ambitious aspirations, the chief of which was dressmaking. Westbrook's might promise to teach 'the Parisian art of *Dress Cutting* . . . in a few easy lessons'; but for dressmaking apprentices the course was long and hard, particularly in well-known establishments, like the one run by the Misses Nunn and Harlow in Dorchester. Here thirteen-year old Hannah Louisa Hardy (now Mrs. Balson) started work at the turn of this century. After two years' work without pay as an apprentice, she was offered 2s. 6d. a week as a sleeve improver. Backed by a determined mother Hannah stood out for, and secured, 3s. The sleeve, bodice and skirt improvers assisted the hands who felt that their earlier struggles were well repaid by the 10s. to 12s. they earned weekly. Until the First World War cut the trimmings from life, women's clothing seemed overloaded; but it must be remembered that the yards of braids and ruching were lifelines to girls striving to better themselves as improvers and hands in workshops throughout the country.

From the experiences of her own family, Hannah Hardy early learned something of the efforts needed to secure success. Her father had taught himself to read by following in his Bible the Scripture readings in chapel; while her uncle, William Hardy, had launched himself as a successful baker in Croydon. Hardy worked for his uncle in Corfe Castle until, in a fit of irritation, the uncle accused his nephew of being lazy. William retorted that if he were lazy he would go, and left the bakery immediately. In the 1830s subordinates had to accept reproofs in silence; in the 1870s they could enjoy the luxury of taking umbrage. William Hardy threw all his efforts into obtaining a small baker's shop in Croydon. Unfortunately his first customer came merely to return empty ginger beer bottles and the new proprietor was quite unable to produce the few pence due back on the bottles. But when William Hardy died he left over £35,000. A new moral was being drawn from the tale of the heedless apprentice and one which did not lack a large and attentive audience.

The manor, the Church, agricultural and friendly societies and village schools had done their work. The villager was ready and eager to become, for better or for worse, a townsman. By the time that machines in fields, barns and dairies could lessen the toil of men, few were left to savour the triumph of feeling themselves masters where formerly their lives had been bound to the soil.

NOTES ON SOURCES FOR CHAPTER X

Verbal Sources

Dorchester and Martinstown

For information concerning steam cultivation and conditions in Dorchester and Martinstown at the turn of this century I am greatly indebted to the following people:

Percy Balson (1878-1966), Dorchester, foreman, employed Eddison's 1900 to 1950, and Mrs. H. L. Balson.

Mr. Sidney Cobb, Bere Regis, formerly a steam-engine driver.

Mr. Bert Churchill, Martinstown, formerly a carter and the grandson of John Rogers, builder, and Mrs. Rose Churchill.

Mr. William Hardy, Longthorns, Wool, formerly a carter at Sydling St. Nicholas and Cerne Abbas. Mr. and Mrs. Hardy have not only an unrivalled knowledge of life in villages on the chalk belt at the turn of this century, but also the power to recreate a past age by description and anecdote.

Arthur Hawkins (1876-1966) and Charles Hawkins (1874-1964), Martinstown, the sons of William Hawkins (1843-1931) of Manor Farm, Martinstown.

Mr. and Mrs. N. J. Symonds, Martinstown. Mr. Symonds is the son of Giles Symonds (1835-1904) and has very kindly let me have access to some family papers and to use photographs. A family history has been privately printed:

H. Symonds, *A Memoir of the Family of Symonds in Somerset and Dorset*, 1933.

Mrs. H. White, formerly of East Lulworth, but born in Dorchester.

Maiden Newton

Mr. H. Hodges, now of Wool, kindly gave me information concerning the activities of his grandfather and father at the Castle Inn.

Charmouth and Bridport

For much kind help I am indebted to:

Mr. T. A. Munden, Bridport, for information concerning the Bridport Unitarian Chapel, built in 1794. Mr. Munden's family has been established in Bridport since the eighteenth century and had close connections with Newfoundland, where four Munden brothers were active in sealing.

Mr. R. W. J. Pavey, Charmouth, who has allowed me to use his great store of memories, notes and photographs.

Written Sources

Steam Cultivation

H. Bonnett, *The Saga of the Steam Plough*, 1965.

This has been supplemented by accounts taken from the *Dorset County Chronicle*. The *Dorset Evening Echo*, 7 October 1965, carried an account of 'Eddison's gripping story'.

I am very grateful to Mr. D. H. Fox of the Eddison Plant Ltd., who was kind enough to supply me with photographs and written information from:

Percy Balson, Dorchester.

Mr. L. James, formerly of Eddison's.

The Rev. R. C. Stebbing, Tacolneston Rectory, Norwich.

Mr. John M. R. Eddison, engineering consultant of Newtown, Connecticut, U.S.A., kindly sent information concerning his grandfather, Francis Eddison; and family history was also kindly supplied by Mr. Robert Eddison, London.

Dorchester and Surrounding Villages

Royal Commission on Agricultural Depression. *Report from Commissioners*, 1895, XVII.

The Parish Summaries of Agricultural Returns for Dorset, 1866-1917. P.R.O.

Some information concerning Dorchester in the late nineteenth and early twentieth centuries has been obtained from family papers and photographs. Dr. Elias William Kerr of Cerne Abbas and Dorchester, was Mayor of Dorchester, 1903-04.

Charmouth

Mr. F. H. Vince, now of Watford, very kindly supplied me with information concerning his father, E. A. Vince (1848-1917), and has allowed me to use family photographs.

APPENDIX A

SUMMARY OF CHANGES IN COPYHOLD OWNERSHIP
AT ARNE AND SLEPE 1750-1815

Based on information contained in manor court rolls; land-tax assessments for Hasilor hundred; abstract of titles and leases of Lord Rivers and 1778-88 survey.

Area	Copyholders in 1750	Acreage of Holding			Copyholders after 1750
		A	R	P	
Arne	Thomas Cockram	50	1	18	1788 Thomas Hyde 1794 John Davis 1795-97[1] James Talbot
	Lewis Cockram	5	0	3	1801 John Barker
	Robert Cleeves	84	1	16	1753 Thomas Hyde 1794 John Davis 1795-97 James Talbot
	Hatch	16	3	16	Before 1772[2] Thomas Hyde 1802 John Barker
	Whitelake	13	3	8	Before 1772 Thomas Hyde
	William Chisman	103	0	7	c. 1750 John Jacob 1795-97 Thomas Abbott 1807 John Barker
	William Somner	62	2	17	1802 John Barker
	Thomas Langley	2	3	20	after 1772 Miss Somner 1801 John Barker
	Alice Mercer	65	1	34	1762 James Talbot
Slepe	Christopher Baker	26	3	0	1795-97 George White 1802 John Barker
	Joseph Baker	52	0	27	1750 Part taken by Richard Talbot whose holding had increased by 1778 to 65a. 1r. 34p.
	Thomas Baker	41	1	9	1845 S. Dugdale[3]
	George Loop	53	3	28	1782 Thomas Hyde 1802 John Barker
	Martha Turner	27	3	12	1789 Elizabeth Harris 1802 John Barker

[1] Land-tax assessments for Hasilor hundred are missing for the years 1795-97 so exact date of the transfer is unknown.

[2] 1772 is the date of survey of Arne Tenants in *Notes and Queries for Somerset and Dorset*, 1915, Vol. XIV, p. 181.

[3] This holding long remained in the hands of the Bakers as from 1801 the land was occupied by the clay-mining Pikes of Wareham. They were tenants too profitable to be disturbed by the Bakers or the landowner.

APPENDIX B

Land holdings in Whitechurch Canonicorum based on the Tithe Apportionment 1844.

HOLDINGS OF 1-10 ACRES

Name	Tenure	Occupation	A	R	P
S. Backaller	T	Ag. Lab.	5	0	3
W. Baker	O	n.s.	7	0	30
I. Bevis	T	Hemp Dresser	2	2	1
J. Bowditch	T	Ag. Lab.	6	2	10
R. Bowditch	T	Ag. Lab.	2	3	5
W. Bowditch	T	Weaver	3	1	7
J. Bullen	O	Owner of 387 acres at Whitechurch	9	3	9
R. Button	O	n.a.	3	1	4
J. Chedd	O	Carpenter	1	2	36
J. Colleypriest	T	Ag. Lab.	3	3	27
J. Copp, Jun.	O	n.a.	9	3	36
J. Cox	T	n.a.	1	1	20
J. Cosens	T	Ag. Lab.	7	0	36
R. Denning	O	Yeoman (Symondsbury)	4	1	30
R. Durrant	T	n.s.	1	2	19
Robert Eveliegh		Mason			
Susan Eveliegh	O	n.a.	1	3	28
W. Eveliegh		n.a.			
Mary Farrant	T	n.s.	1	0	18
Richard Fooks	O (2)	Publican	6	1	21
Robert Fooks	O	Ag. Lab.	1	3	21
J. Gerrard, Jun.	T	Farmer	1	0	38
Margaret Gould	O	Miller	5	2	13
S. Greening	O	Ag. Lab.	3	2	4
G. Guppy	T	Ag. Lab.	1	0	28
J. Hallet	T	Ag. Lab.	1	0	16
W. Hallet	O	Independent	2	3	15
J. Hargreaves	T	Minister	1	2	34
R. Harris	T	n.a.	6	2	18
Agnes Holman	O	Widow	2	1	6
J. Jefford	T	Ag. Lab.	3	0	15
R. Miller	T	Ag. Lab.	1	3	39
T. Miller	O	Independent	5	1	6
S. Mills	T	n.a.	8	1	27
S. Norman	T	Ag. Lab.	3	2	6
Jacob Orchard	O	Farmer	4	0	6

Land holdings in Whitechurch Canonicorum based on the Tithe
Apportionment 1844.

HOLDINGS OF 1-10 ACRES (*continued*)

Name	Tenure	Occupation	A	R	P
John Orchard ⎫ Joseph Orchard ⎭	O	n.s. n.s.	1	3	4
W. Orchard	O	n.s.	1	0	37
B. Powell	⎧ O ⎩ T	Butcher	⎧ 2 ⎩ 5	1 3	32 4
D. Powell	O	Manufacturer	6	0	16
P. Powell	T	Beer retailer	4	0	3
S. Powell	T	Carpenter	3	0	21
T. Powell	T	Ag. Lab.	7	1	8
J. Power	T	Carpenter	9	0	15
H. Quick	O (2)	Ag. Lab.	2	2	2
J. Richmond	T	n.s.	3	0	19
G. Rockett	O	Flax comber	3	0	7
S. Sladen	T	Farmer (Chideock)	1	2	23
W. Snell	T	n.s.	1	0	24
E. Spencer	T	Ag. Lab.	4	1	28
E. Staple (or Stape)	O	Mason	1	0	38
D. Stone	O	Ag. Lab.	1	3	30
C. Turner	T	Publican	1	3	12
G. Turner	T	Ag. Lab.	1	2	1
J. Turner	T	Farmer (Wootton)	9	2	36
J. Wakeford	T	Ag. Lab.	1	2	15
T. Wakely	O	Ag. Lab.	1	1	10
W. Wakely	O	Ag. Lab.	1	3	17
J. Walbourne	O	Ag. Lab.	8	1	11
J. Wheaton	T	Butcher	2	1	5
Whitechurch Wardens	O	–	1	2	8
J. Withey	T	Twine manufacturer	3	3	14
W. Young	⎧ O ⎩ T	Porter	⎧ 3 ⎩ 1	0 0	16 4

Land holdings in Whitechurch Canonicorum based on the Tithe
Apportionment 1844 (*continued*).

HOLDINGS OF 10-30 ACRES

Name	Tenure	Occupation	A	R	P
J. Bradford	T	n.a.	22	1	33
James Bridle	{ O	Farmer	{ 2	1	14
	T		17	1	15
John Bridle, Sen.	O	Ag. Lab.	23	0	5
R. Broom	{ O	Farmer	{ 2	1	14
	T (4)		16	0	29
J. Chick	O	n.a.	19	0	20
J. Collier	{ O	Farmer	{ 9	2	31
	T		3	0	35
J. Copp, Sen.	O	Farmer	11	0	6
H. Glyde	T	n.a.	13	1	10
J. Hoare	T	Farmer (Marshwood)	21	2	7
James Hoskins	{ O	Farmer	{ 2	3	36
	T		13	2	26
Mary Hunt, Jun.	O	Independent	10	3	15
G. Miller	T	Farmer (Wootton)	12	3	20
G. Mills	{ O	Mason	{ 9	1	29
	T		3	1	10
J. Morse	O	Owner of 742 acres in Whitechurch	10	2	20
R. Pitfield	T	Mason	11	3	4
R. Pook	{ O	Farmer	{ 4	0	11
	T		16	3	3
R. Roper	O (2)	Farmer	28	1	14
J. Record	T	Dairyman	17	3	26
James Rendell	T	n.a.	22	1	26
W. Salter	T	n.a.	17	2	28
Elizabeth Stoodley	T	Widow (Marshwood)	16	3	3
J. Taylor	O	Schoolmaster	13	0	3
S. Warren	T	Farmer (Marshwood)	21	0	37
C. White	O	n.a.	12	2	38
E. Wilson	O	Vicar of Whitechurch	27	2	18

Land holdings of Whitechurch Canonicorum based on the Tithe Apportionment 1844.

HOLDINGS OF 30-50 ACRES

Name	Tenure	Occupation	A	R	P
J. Bennet	T	Farmer	30	0	5
T. Dare	O	Farmer	35	1	2
S. Eveliegh	O	Farmer	46	0	28
C. Genge	T	Farmer	44	1	12
J. Gerrard, Sen.	T	Farmer	31	3	1
A. Orchard	T	Farmer	45	0	30
R. Rendell	T (2)	Publican	36	1	1
A. Tucker	{ O T	Rector (Wootton)	{ 21 23	1 0	36 38
R. Tucker	O	Farmer	40	1	4

HOLDINGS OF 50-100 ACRES

Name	Tenure	Occupation	A	R	P
J. Baker	T (2)	Farmer	53	0	37
S. Bartlett	T (2)	Farmer	56	2	27
R. Bridle	T	Farmer	88	0	32
R. Collypriest	T	Farmer	79	1	14
J. Copp	T	Farmer	63	2	1
A. Elliot	T	Yeoman (Symondsbury)	60	2	7
J. Gillingham	T (2)	Farmer (Marshwood)	73	3	29
John Hoskins	O	Farmer	50	0	28
R. James	{ O T	Farmer	{ 28 29	3 3	4 35
J. Lugg	T (3)	Farmer	61	1	8
J. Membry	{ O T (3)	Farmer	{ 8 35	1 2	39 9
R. Mills	{ O T (3)	Farmer	{ 26 43	2 2	30 39
T. and J. Paul	T	n.a.	72	2	21
Sarah Roper, Jun.	{ O T	Widow	{ 21 36	3 1	24 22
J. Swaffield	T	Farmer (Wootton)	86	0	23
R. Tucker	{ O T	Farmer	{ 40 37	1 1	4 29
J. Turner	T (3)	Farmer	65	0	10
M. Wakely	O	Farmer	54	3	28

Land holdings in Whitechurch Canonicorum based on the Tithe
Apportionment 1844.

HOLDINGS OF OVER 100 ACRES

Name	Tenure	Occupation	A	R	P
R. Barrett	T	Farmer	158	0	3
Lord Bridport	O	Owner of 901 acres in Whitechurch	248	0	8
S. Bowditch	T	Farmer	182	2	10
T. Bridle	T (2)	Farmer	115	0	15
S. Durrant	T (2)	Farmer	105	3	5
C. Fry	T	n.s.	212	3	25
W. Genge	T	Farmer	108	1	37
G. Glyde	T	Yeoman	303	2	10
R. Glyde	T	Farmer	222	2	36
J. Green	T (4)	Farmer	142	3	15
R. Greening	T (5)	Farmer	131	3	35
J. Harris	T (2)	Farmer	113	2	18
D. Legg	T (2)	Farmer	168	3	6
J. Manley	T (2)	Yeoman	154	2	35
U. Powell	T	Farmer	202	1	26
Job Rendell	T (6)	Farmer	168	3	32
W. Snell	T	Farmer	117	2	3
R. Taylor	T	Yeoman (Symondsbury)	105	0	4
W. Taylor	T (2)	Farmer	190	3	35
T. Turner	T (2)	Farmer	221	3	13
G. Udal	T	n.a.	195	0	32
W. Zeally	T	Farmer	147	2	8

NOTES ON TABLES OF LAND HOLDINGS IN
WHITECHURCH CANONICORUM 1844

Land tenure

The acreages and tenure, indicated by O for owner and T for
tenant, have been obtained from the tithe apportionment for
Whitechurch Canonicorum, 1844. Reference has also been made to
the 1851 census returns in which are shown the acreages farmed by
some of the occupiers appearing in the tithe apportionment.

Only the actual occupiers, owners or tenants, of the holdings are
shown; so that John Bullen, one of the chief landowners in Whitechurch, appears as occupying under 10 acres. If the holding
occupied was not a consolidated unit, the number of separate
tenements is shown in brackets beside the form of tenure.

Holdings of under one acre have not been taken into account.

Occupations

The occupations of occupiers of land have been taken from the 1841 and 1851 census returns for Whitechurch Canonicorum and its neighbouring parishes. Occupiers holding land in Whitechurch Canonicorum, but living outside the parish, have been indicated, wherever possible, by their home parish being shown in brackets beside their occupation.

The nomenclature of the census returns for occupations has been followed. Where a name appears in the returns without an indication of occupation, the phrase 'not shown' (n.s.) is entered; 'not available' (n.a.) indicates that the landholder has not been traced in the returns consulted. Agricultural Labourer has been abbreviated to Ag. Lab.

Two men in Whitechurch Canonicorum and the neighbouring parishes sometimes had the same Christian and surnames. In these cases the most likely of the two, from the point of view of their occupation and habitation, has been chosen. In this connection it should be noted that two Job Rendells were farming in Whitechurch in 1841, but not in 1851; so that probably the six tenements shown for Job Rendell in 1844 were held by two men, but it has been impossible to separate the holdings.

FLAX AND HEMP PRODUCTION IN LODERS

(in stones)

Name of Grower	Place of abode in 1794	1793 Land Tax Assessment			1789		1791		1792		1794	
		£	s.	d.	Hemp	Flax	Hemp	Flax	Hemp	Flax	Hemp	Flax
Elizabeth Adams	Loders	—	—	—	34	—	—	—	—	—	—	—
H. Adams	,,	3	13	4	170	—	43	—	—	—	—	—
J. Axe	,,	—	—	—	—	94	179	288	84	390	67	30
Martha Axe	,,	—	—	—	145	—	26	—	—	—	—	—
J. Bagg	,,	—	—	—	75	—	115	—	—	—	—	—
J. Barrett	,,	—	—	—	—	—	135	—	—	—	97	—
H. Barrett	,,	—	—	—	31	—	—	—	150	—	41	—
Agnes Biddlecombe	,,	2	6	8	33	—	25	—	28	—	—	—
W. Bishop	,,	—	—	—	—	324	50	—	42	—	—	355
E. Brown	,,	—	—	—	90	—	—	—	—	—	—	—
J. Brown	,,	—	—	—	73	—	37	—	21	—	—	—
R. Brown	,,	—	—	—	—	—	34	—	38	—	—	—
Sarah Brown	,,	—	—	—	—	—	36	—	—	—	—	—
S. Brown	Litton Cheney	—	—	—	46	—	—	—	22	—	—	—
H. Burbidge	Loders	—	—	—	—	—	—	—	33	—	—	—
P. Burridge	,,	—	—	—	58	—	34	—	44	—	—	—
T. Chick	,,	5	12	0	—	—	—	128	13	153	—	—
E. Cole	Shipton Gorge	—	—	—	92	—	208	389	24	—	—	—
R. Cravett	Loders	—	—	—	—	—	—	—	14	—	—	—
Sarah Cross	,,	—	—	—	—	—	—	—	27	—	—	—
J. Edwards	,,	—	—	—	—	—	216	—	—	—	—	—
C. Fookes	,,	—	—	—	—	1165	—	557	—	657	—	—
Anne Fuzzard	,,	1	8	0	—	—	130	—	66	—	49	—
Mary Gale	,,	—	—	—	—	—	34	—	38	—	39	—
Matthew Gale	,,	—	—	—	155	—	34	—	—	—	—	—

Name	Place	£	s	d								
J. Greening	”				31							
Martha Gurridge	”										12	
E. Hansford	”				50							
F. Hansford	”						22		163			
H. Hansford	”				32	28	53		38	380		
James Hansford	Powerstock								77	147		
Job Hansford	Loders				63							
Joseph Hansford	”	11	1									
R. Hansford	”								25			
R. Hayward	”			4	48						22	
W. Hayward	”											
J. Honeyborne	”				65		128		52			
R. Honeyborne	”	1	6	8	69		108		36		94	
Mary Langford	”				34				90			
J. Marsh	”					108		22	52			
W. Marsh	”	8	8	0	156		238	64	155	202	122	104
H. Munden	”				87		66		32		28	
S. Munden	”				71		78		71		60	
S. Pitcher	Netherbury									248		
G. Samways	Loders				68	52	95		72		35	
M. Shipton	”								51		26	
J. Snook	Shipton Gorge	6	8	8					75			
H. Stibey	Loders						83	58	50		50	
J. Symes	”	2	4	0			25					
S. Symes	”				58	39						
Elizabeth Travers	”						37					
G. Travers	”	5	5	4	52							
J. Travers	”				96		123	65	93	155		
F. Trevett	”				71							172
G. Udal	”	5	4	0	183							
W. Vallens	”								24		56	
J. Wallbridge	”								22			
Mary Waldron	”				81		34		52		25	
W. Warren	”				147		268	23	87			
Sarah Way	Askerswell								19			

FLAX AND HEMP P

Name of Grower	Place of abode in 1794	1793 Land Assessmer		
		£	s.	d
E. Baker	Symondsbury	10	19	2
E. Barnes	Bradpole	–		
R. Barnes	,,	–		
J. Bradford	,,	–		
W. Brown	Chideock	–		
J. Butcher	Symondsbury	–		
C. Chick	Bradpole	2	13	4
R. Cosens	,,	–		
B. Cox	Symondsbury	–		
Anne Curland	,,	–		
J. Davie	Bridport	2	2	0
J. Follett	Whitechurch Canonicorum	–		
R. Fookes	Symondsbury	1	3	10
B. Frome	Bradpole	–		
H. Gifford	Bridport	8	12	10
J. Hayward	,,	–		
J. Henry	Chideock	–		
R. Hodder	Whitechurch Canonicorum	–		
R. Hussey	Symondsbury	6	0	4
T. Hussey	,,	7	0	0
W. Hussey	,,	5	4	0
W. Miller	Symondsbury	–		
T. Oxenbury	Bradpole	–		
W. Perham	Symondsbury	13	9	7
J. Pitfield (Sen & Jun)	,,	57	19	8
J. Roper	Chideock	–		
J. Sprake	Symondsbury		8	0
J. Stevens	Bradpole	2	14	6
D. Stone	,,	3	14	0
R. Symonds	Bradpole	–		
J. Taylor	Chideock	–		
J. Tucker	Marshwood	–		
Gaius Udal	Chideock	–		
George Udal	Symondsbury	–		
R. Wakeley	,,	–		
S. Warren	Chideock	1	14	0
P. Whettam	Symondsbury	–		
J. Welch	Bridport	–		

	1789	1791		1792		1794	
np	Flax	Hemp	Flax	Hemp	Flax	Hemp	Flax
	128	64	69	18	102	–	–
	–	–	–	53	–	–	–
	24	–	–	–	–	–	–
	319	–	–	–	–	–	–
	–	–	113	–	202	–	–
	–	–	81	–	–	–	–
	432	–	–	–	171	–	–
	–	–	–	–	114	–	–
	102	–	–	–	–	–	–
	–	–	–	–	27	–	–
	–	–	–	–	97	–	–
	–	–	–	–	618	–	–
	466	–	546	–	581	–	515
	–	–	–	–	506	–	–
	–	–	–	–	43	–	–
	–	–	–	52	–	–	–
	–	–	–	–	–	–	285
	–	–	–	–	176	–	–
	263	–	–	–	–	–	–
	61	–	–	–	157	–	20
	129	–	344	–	279	–	51
	–	–	–	–	274	–	180
	313	195	–	–	–	–	–
	–	–	–	–	189	–	136
	–	–	–	–	–	–	98
	–	–	–	–	104	–	–
	–	17	–	–	–	–	–
	48	29	33	41	94	–	–
	47	–	–	–	–	–	–
	402	51	562	–	435	–	–
	–	–	–	–	494	–	249
	–	–	–	–	275	–	–
	–	–	208	–	–	–	68
	–	–	–	–	53	–	–
	–	–	167	–	322	–	207
	355	–	–	–	–	–	–
	460	–	326	–	312	–	302
	–	–	–	32	–	–	–

NOTES ON APPENDICES C AND D

Loders and Symondsbury have been chosen for investigation as they were respectively the leading hemp and flax producing parishes in Dorset. Estimates for production have been taken from the county records of payments of hemp and flax bounties; these are only available in the Dorset Record Office for the years 1789, 1791, 1792 and 1794.

The 1789 and 1791 records give, against the number of stones of hemp and flax produced, only the name of the grower and his place of abode, not the location where the crops were raised in the grower's home parish. In the returns for the years 1792 and 1794, which show the place where the crops were grown, one grower sometimes claimed bounty for crops grown in several parishes. If the greater part of the estimated production has been given under Loders or Symondsbury, the total production has been included under these parishes, even though a small proportion of the crop had been grown elsewhere.

Occasionally the returns for the years 1789 and 1791 include payments for crops grown in 1788 and 1790; these production figures have been included under the years 1789 and 1791.

Land-tax assessments have been used for the year 1793 as this is the only year during the period 1789-94 for which complete and legible returns are available for both parishes. The land-tax payments have only been included to indicate how widespread was the custom of sub-letting and to suggest, in the case of the owner or tenant grower, the scale of his farming operations. The land-tax assessment returns give the names of the owner who, according to Claridge was responsible for paying the tax, and of the tenant, where the land was not worked by the owner. In the appendices concerning hemp and flax production land-tax payments are shown if the grower owned and occupied the land for which tax was paid or if he were a tenant presumably working the land. For example, Elizabeth Adams owned land worth 8s. but as it was leased (possibly only temporarily) to Robert Hansford, the payment is shown against Hansford's name together with £6 4s. od. he paid for his own land and £4 9s. 4d. paid for the land he rented. John Marsh leased his land, on which 16s. was paid, to Benjamin Fuzzard who owned and occupied property assessed at 12s. Benjamin Fuzzard did not claim bounty for flax or hemp growing so £1 8s. od. is shown against Anne Fuzzard on the supposition she was his wife or a near relative. Similarly the £1 6s. 8d. paid for land owned and occupied by William Langford has been shown for Mary Langford.

APPENDIX E

Prisoners appearing before the Special Commission at Dorchester, 10-12 January 1831. Compiled from calendar and register of prisoners in Dorset County Jail.

BLACKMOOR VALE

Home Parish	Name	Age	Sentence
Buckland Newton	Angle Lock[1] George Sansome[2]	26 –	HL 6 months A
Hazelbury Bryan	John Smart	22	HL 1 year
Mappowder	Charles Coombs John Durrant William Durrant Thomas Horlock[1] George Jackson George Legg John Legg Edward Marsh James New Thomas Samways John Symonds	24 58 23 27 44 35 22 27 34 24 48	T HL 1 year HL 3 months HL 6 months HL 3 months HL 6 months T Bill ignored T A A
Pulham	Jacob Mitchell John Mitchell Silas Mitchell Joseph Sheppard Samuel Sillwood Henry Spicer	23 21 27 40 20 21	TKP + £50 „ „ T TKP + £50 T
Stalbridge	James Harris	32	TKP + £50
Stoke Wake	Abraham House James House Charles Symes Adam Thorne James Thorne	22 24 20 21 30	T HL 1 year T T T

[1] Appear in register and not in calendar.

[2] Appears in calendar and not in register.

265

Prisoners appearing before the Special Commission at Dorchester, 10-12 January 1831.

NORTHERN VALES

Home Parish	Name	Age	Sentence
East Stour	James Davidge	24	HL 1 year
	James Stacey	28	TKP + £50
	Thomas Vowells	22	HL 1 year
	Robert Weller	46	HL 4 months
Henstridge	George Bugby	19	TKP + £50
	James Hobbs	18	,,
	John Sansome	16	,,
Shaftesbury	George Elkins	18	HL 6 months
	George Elkins	24	T
	Harry Elkins	34	T
	Charles Foot	27	TKP + £50
	William Moore	18	HL 18 months
Stour Provost	John Ayles	25	TKP + £50
	John Dore	32	,,
	David Hatcher	37	,,
	Stephen Hatcher	28	T
	Robert Pike	21	TKP + £50

POOLE BASIN

Winfrith Newburgh	Hezekiah Grant	15	TKP + £50
	William Somers	22	,,
	John Toms	16	,,

Abbreviations

A – Acquitted

HL – Hard Labour

T – Transported for seven years

TKP + £50 – Entered into recognisance of £50 to keep the peace for two years

Prisoners appearing before the Special Commission at Dorchester, 10-12 January 1831.

CHALK UPLANDS

Home Parish	Name	Age	Sentence
Cranborne	John Read	24	HL 1 year
Edmondsham	Joseph Pope	51	T
Fordingbridge (Wilts)	James Wilkins	22	HL 1 year
Handley	William Anstey	39	A
Martin (Wilts)	William Stokes	26	HL 1 year
Pentridge	James Thick Robert Zillwood (or Sillwood)	50 23	A HL 6 months
Tollard Royal	James Rymond	29	HL 2 years
Shroton or Iwerne Courtney	William Newell	18	HL 3 months

APPENDIX F

Tenant holdings in the manor of Bere Regis in the mid-eighteenth century. Based on Isaac Taylor's map, estimated date 1773-76.

HOLDINGS UNDER 10 ACRES

Name	Closes			Open Arable			Open Meadow			Total		
	A	R	P	A	R	P	A	R	P	A	R	P
Barnes	0	1	28	–	–	–	–	–	–	0	1	28
Burgess	1	2	38	3	3	22	–	–	–	5	2	20
Guy	3	2	02	5	3	08	–	–	–	9	1	10
Kitcat	0	1	26	6	0	06	–	–	–	6	1	32
Rawles	1	3	12	2	0	10	–	–	–	3	3	22
Satchell	4	3	16	6	0	28	–	–	–	11	0	04
Shave	2	3	33(1)	–	–	–	–	–	–	2	3	33
Stockley	2	0	12	0	3	02	–	–	–	2	3	14
Welch	0	2	15	5	2	22	0	1	05	6	2	02
Yarney	0	0	16	0	1	35	0	2	33	1	1	04
										50	1	09

(1) *Elders Mead* attached to mill.

Note

In some cases holdings are shown in the name of two or more members of the same family. As Taylor does not always give initials, family holdings have been entered together.

Tenant holdings in the manor of Bere Regis in the mid-eighteenth century. Based on Isaac Taylor's map, estimated date 1773-76.

HOLDINGS 10-30 ACRES

Name	Closes			Open Arable			Open Meadow			Total		
	A	R	P	A	R	P	A	R	P	A	R	P
Arney	3	1	29	22	2	37	–	–	–	26	0	26
Battrick	4	3	01	22	1	38	1	1	18	28	2	17
Bellas	6	3	22	9	3	15	–	–	–	16	2	37
Clench	5	3	24	9	0	32	–	–	–	15	0	16
Coke	9	0	21	12	2	28	–	–	–	21	3	09
Felton	9	1	34	13	3	19	0	2	15	23	3	28
Gould	5	3	07	16	0	18	0	3	08	22	2	33
Hewett	10	3	01	8	2	03	–	–	–	19	1	04
Langdown	2	3	32	10	2	35	0	2	31	14	1	18
Manuel	23	0	32	0	3	26	1	2	27	25	3	05
Poor	3	1	02	11	1	12	–	–	–	14	2	14
Sarjeant	1	2	30	21	1	36	–	–	–	23	0	26
Telly	16	2	10	11	2	10	1	3	00	29	3	20
Toms	13	0	09	7	3	31	–	–	–	21	0	00
Whennel	7	1	27	9	3	28	–	–	–	17	1	15
Young	13	2	23	12	2	15	0	0	24	26	1	22
										346	3	10

Tenant holdings in the manor of Bere Regis in the mid-eighteenth century. Based on Isaac Taylor's map, estimated date 1773-76.

HOLDINGS 30-60 ACRES

Name	Closes			Open Arable			Open Meadow			Total		
	A	R	P	A	R	P	A	R	P	A	R	P
Ash	20	0	13	42	0	22	2	2	35	64	3	30
Brown	27	3	00	5	1	11	4	1	24	37	1	35
Chip	24	1	24	27	3	14	1	0	19	53	1	17
Fry	29	1	34	20	1	06	1	0	29	50	3	29
Gallop	11	1	35	24	1	38	0	0	32	36	0	25
Little	19	3	16	26	3	14	0	3	28	47	2	18
Martin	14	1	02	18	0	04	1	1	27	33	2	33
Perham	11	0	26	26	3	16	1	1	26	39	1	28
Seymour	34	3	02	3	0	33	–	–	–	37	3	35
Smith	17	2	11	25	2	32	1	1	17	44	2	20
										446	0	30

Tenant holdings in the manor of Bere Regis in the mid-eighteenth century. Based on Isaac Taylor's map, estimated date 1773-76.

HOLDINGS OVER 60 ACRES

Name	Closes			Open Arable			Open Meadow			Total		
	A	R	P	A	R	P	A	R	P	A	R	P
Clark	22	0	10	43	0	16	1	2	06	66	2	32
Compton	58	0	28	89	2	19	3	2	13	151	1	20
Ekins	125	0	17[1]	–	–	–	0	2	34	125	3	11
Homer	55	2	28	60	1	14	4	1	0	120	1	02
Mate	244	3	08[2]	55	3	09	1	0	31	301	3	08
Pleydell	96	3	32[3]	–	–	–	–	–	–	96	3	32
Spear	69	3	06	5	2	07	1	2	36	77	0	09
Williams	97	0	14[4]	7	1	17	0	3	27	105	1	18
Woolfrey	37	0	04	39	3	06	2	1	23	79	0	33
Charity Trustees	56	0	04	4	1	33	8	3	8	69	1	05
										1193	3	10

[1] Philliols Farm

[2] Court Farm

[3] Doddings Farm

[4] Stockley Farm

INDEX OF PERSONS

INDEX OF PLACE NAMES

INDEX OF SUBJECTS